Court Culture and the Origins of a Royalist Tradition in Early Stuart England

R. Malcolm Smuts

UNIVERSITY OF PENNSYLVANIA PRESS

PHILADELPHIA · 1987 *upp*

D0209913

Printed in the United States of America.

Library of Congress Cataloging-in-Publication Data

Smuts, R. Malcolm (Robert Malcolm)
    Court culture and the origins of a royalist
tradition in early Stuart England.

    Bibliography: p.
    Includes index.
    1. Great Britain—History—Early Stuarts,
1603–1649.   2. Great Britain—Court and courtiers.
3. Great Britain—Civilization—17th century.
4. London (England)—Intellectual life—
17th century.   5. Stuart, House of.   6. Art patronage—
Great Britain—History—17th century.   I. Title.
DA390.S68   1987   941.06′1   86-27243
ISBN 0-8122-8039-3 (alk. paper)

Designed by Adrianne Onderdonk Dudden

Court Culture and
the Origins of a
Royalist Tradition in
Early Stuart England

To MaryBeth

CONTENTS

PART TWO

THE FORMATION OF A NEW COURT CULTURE

LIST OF ILLUSTRATIONS

ACKNOWLEDGMENTS

In preparing this book, I have incurred more debts than I can properly acknowledge. The foremost are to Lawrence Stone, who supervised the thesis from which it grew and who has since read and commented on two subsequent drafts. His suggestions, criticisms, and encouragement have been invaluable. Anthony Grafton, Earl Miner, and T. K. Rabb also helped with the original thesis. At a later stage I benefited from several long conversations about literary matters with Philip Finkelpearl, who also provided valuable comments on early drafts of Chapters 3 and 4 and saved me from a number of errors. Others who read part or all of the manuscript and provided useful suggestions include Mordechai Feingold, Myron Gutman, John Headley, John Pocock, Kevin Sharpe, and my colleagues at the University of Massachusetts at Boston, Frank Broderick, Tom Brown, Tim McCarthy, and Renée Watkins. My parents have been unstinting of their time in reading successive drafts and providing detailed criticism from the perspective of educated lay readers. My sister, Barbara, provided encouragement and moral support.

I would also like to thank the staff of the Worcester College Library, Oxford University, for allowing me to examine the books of Inigo Jones and the Duke of Northumberland and for granting me access to the papers of John Scawen relating to Covent Garden.

Among other scholars who have studied court culture, my greatest debts are to Stephen Orgel and Roy Strong. Their pioneering work appeared just as I began work on this book and has provided constant stimulation. I have sometimes disagreed with their conclusions, but it is abundantly clear how much I owe to their labors.

Above all, I would like to thank my children, Robert and Felicia, and my wife, MaryBeth. I dedicate the book to my wife in gratitude for her patience and understanding during the long and sometimes frustrating period when it was being researched and written.

I INTRODUCTION

This book is a study of culture and its relationship to politics within the English royal court during the half-century before the outbreak of the Civil War in 1642. The importance of this period in the history of royal government has always been obvious, even though scholars continue to differ profoundly over its interpretation. Changes during the same span of time in the taste and outlook of the royal entourage are much less well known, yet in their own way they are almost as striking. During these years, the court became more firmly anchored in London, more distinct from provincial landed society in its outlook, and more sympathetic to the Baroque cultures of Europe. The Crown's great servants stopped keeping military retinues, participating in tournaments, and building prodigy houses on their country estates and began to attend the theater and amass large collections of European art. In virtually every area of cultural life, a revolution in taste occurred. Anyone who compares a major work of Elizabethan court architecture to a building by Inigo Jones, a madrigal of the 1590s to a song by Henry Lawes, or a portrait by Gower to one by Van Dyck will begin to appreciate the scale of the transformation. Caroline styles often have much closer affinities to the styles of the eighteenth or early nineteenth centuries than to work completed barely a generation earlier. And these stylistic changes were symptomatic of a much more fundamental reorientation of attitudes, values, patterns of conspicuous consumption, and modes of thought and feeling.

These developments had an especially profound influence upon Charles I (r. 1625–1649) and his generation of courtiers, who grew up as they took place. Charles was the first English king to have known from adolescence the work of Jonson, Donne, and Shakespeare, and the first to have any meaningful appreciation for Renaissance and Baroque art. He was also the first English monarch since the Middle Ages to have spent some time in a great European court, the first since Mary Tudor (r. 1553–1558) to have married into one of the major Catholic dynasties of the continent, and the first, also since Mary, to welcome a papal envoy to his court. He was surrounded by men who had spent years in Spain, France, or Italy, where they had learned to appreciate the court cultures of Madrid, Paris, Florence, and Rome.

The outlook of Charles and his entourage was therefore shaped by a culture fundamentally different from that of the late Elizabethan and early Jacobean courts, and of provincial England even in the 1630s. The cosmopolitan trends affecting the royal entourage had a much more limited and uneven impact on most of the nation.[1] Early modern courts always stood more or less apart from the nations they ruled, as centers of cosmopolitanism and cultural innovation. But this was especially true of England on the eve of the Civil War.

The subject of early Stuart court culture thus has considerable significance, both in its own right and for its relevance to an understanding of the ruling group whose power collapsed in the 1640s. Yet the topic is one that historians have never adequately explored.[2] Moreover, most of the work they have devoted to it has been anchored in ideas and debates of political historiography, so that cultural evidence has been selectively examined and sometimes distorted to buttress arguments about the origins of the Civil War.

Not many years ago, that war was usually seen as the result of a crisis in relations between the state and society, caused by the court's extravagance, isolation, and absolutism.[3] The conflict between "the court" and "the country" was viewed as essentially political and religious, but several scholars also saw it as a contest between separate cultures. As the court grew more cosmopolitan and opulent, they argued, it antagonized an essentially xenophobic and puritan nation, so that political tensions were reinforced by moral and aesthetic differences. In Lawrence Stone's words:

> The Country . . . stood for an experience of the world confined to the shires of England, as opposed to the sophistication bred of the grand Tour

through France and Italy; for the maintenance of open hospitality for all, as opposed to the offering of luxurious private dinner parties in the City; for a highly conservative taste in Jacobean architecture, as opposed to the new-fangled classicism of Inigo Jones; for a highly conservative taste in painting, as opposed to the courtly continental innovations of Van Dyck. . . . By the early seventeenth century England was experiencing all the tensions created by the emergence within a single society of two distinct cultures, cultures that were reflected in ideals, religion, art, literature, the theater, dress, deportment and way of life.[4]

This interpretation had the considerable merit of providing a framework for attempts to synthesize political and cultural history during a period of immense importance for both. It drew attention to the cultural dimensions of early Stuart politics, while stimulating case studies which attempted to explore the relevance of the court-country dichotomy to an understanding of art and literature.[5] Unfortunately it also encouraged some misleading oversimplifications which seriously impede understanding of cultural developments.[6]

The most serious of these oversimplifications is a tendency to reduce the diversity and complexity of the period into a simple bipolar model. It is one thing to underline the broad differences in taste and outlook that separated Charles I from most of his subjects, and quite another thing to argue for the existence of "two distinct cultures" which reinforced an ideological cleavage that would soon lead to civil war. A fully unified "country" culture never existed in early Stuart England. There were instead any number of provincial subcultures, each shaped by the peculiar historical, social, and economic background of a particular locality.[7]

At first glance the court appears to be more compact and cohesive than the country, but on closer inspection it also becomes a problematical concept. Under the strictest definition the court consisted of the monarchs' immediate entourage and those institutions of the royal household responsible for their personal and ceremonial needs.[8] But in an age when all power and government patronage ultimately flowed from the king, a much larger social network always formed around this relatively compact group. In the narrowest sense the court did not include place-seekers like the young John Donne, diplomats like Sir Henry Wotton, ecclesiastical magnates like Archbishop Laud, or statesmen like the Earl of Salisbury. Yet all these figures spent much of their adult life in the court's shadow seeking royal favor, and all had a greater impact on court culture than did most privy chamber servants. Many other English peers and gentlemen normally lived away from the court but still paid it occasional visits and maintained relations with a court patron. The fact that the royal family usually spent most of the year in the western suburbs of London, which already attracted an appreciable number of landed visitors, encouraged these casual contacts. Whitehall was increasingly the hub of an amorphous metropolitan upper-class society, which at one time or another included most peers and a significant minority of the greater gentry.[9]

The court was therefore an institution with a distinct nucleus but a vaguely defined periphery.[10] Its relatively open and fluid structure had a decisive importance in cultural affairs. It meant that the court easily absorbed new styles and ideas developing in London or among aristocrats with no formal connection to the royal household, just as country peers and gentry sometimes learned to appreciate court fashions during visits to London.[11] Charles I's culture certainly differed substantially from that of most provincial squires, but this does not mean that country landowners never shared his tastes. Nor were cultural preferences an infallible guide to an individual's social and political orientation. Van Dyck painted a number of future parliamentarians, including the Earl of Warwick, who engineered the mutiny that put the navy in Parliament's hands, and at least two court poets later supported Parliament's cause.[12] In culture, as in everything else, relations between court and country were far more complex than some historians have implied.

This does not mean that cultural developments were irrelevant to politics, only that the relationship between the two needs far more careful analysis than it has often received. Instead of making sweeping generalizations about two antagonistic cultures, we need to examine how particular tastes and values affected attitudes to specific issues.

The study of court culture has also been distorted by the distaste of many modern scholars for the Stuarts and their entourage. The royal court is still often portrayed as a "decadent" and "parasitic" society, living in an atmosphere of "unreality," cut off from all meaningful contact with the nation.[13] Its culture is therefore assumed to be the product of a hothouse environment, a form of flattering propaganda or a frivolous amusement of the ruling coterie.[14] Contemporaries did sometimes criticize the court as corrupt and extravagant, and there is much in its culture that today seems stilted and artificial. But the claim that these facts reflect the decadence of an old regime tottering on the brink of a revolutionary cataclysm rests on large assumptions which are rarely subjected to much critical scrutiny. The court was far less isolated than is often supposed, and we will see that its culture was often deeply moralistic and politically ambivalent.

Even when pejorative labels and simplified dichotomies are avoided, there remain dangers in interpreting court culture as part of a larger story of conflict between the Stuarts and a rising opposition. Cultural works certainly conveyed political ideas and sometimes referred to issues causing friction between the Crown and Parliament.[15] If treated carefully, they can illuminate political attitudes, but the habit of reading masques, poems, and paintings as "documents in the running debate that was moving the nation toward civil war" can seriously mislead.[16] To begin with, there is no real evidence that the Stuarts ever used culture systematically as public propaganda. In fact, it is remarkable how infrequently they employed cultural works to project a flattering image of the king to audiences beyond the court itself.[17] With few exceptions, court theatricals, royal portraits, and panegyrics were created for a restricted society with access to the king's palaces. They would have been singularly ineffective vehicles for arguments aimed at a broad public.

Even if we grant that many cultural works did have a polemical or controversial purpose, we still need to explore carefully the issues they were intended to address. Recent work has cast serious doubt on the traditional interpretation of early Stuart politics as a continuous struggle between Stuart absolutism and parliamentary constitutionalism.[18] Yet scholars still often treat court culture as the expression of an embattled absolutist philosophy, without paying adequate attention either to the ambiguities and complexities of contemporary politics or to the difficult problem of explaining in detail how political events affected cultural trends.

After all these reservations have been made, however, the fact remains that much court culture had an undeniable political meaning, while many political issues had a cultural dimension. To take one example, the differences between the Caroline church and its Puritan critics were undeniably cultural as well as theological in nature.[19] Moreover, from the onset of the Civil War, contemporaries employed cultural images and symbols. The stereotypes of Roundheads and Cavaliers, puritan philistines, and royalist aesthetes are simplistic distortions, but those distortions are rooted in contemporary usage and tell us much about the passions that tore the nation apart. In many ways the Civil

War did become a struggle between rival cultures whose roots are discernible in the prewar period.[20] If the old concept of a steadily mounting court-country opposition culminating in the revolution of the 1640s does not adequately explain how these cultural differences arose and influenced political attitudes, then we need to formulate an alternative interpretation.

The present work attempts to do no more than help point the way toward this goal through a systematic examination of the cultural environment of Charles I and his generation of courtiers. My chief purpose is twofold: first, to furnish a general cultural history of the early Stuart court by synthesizing materials found in specialized studies and filling in gaps that still exist in our knowledge of the subject; second, to relate that history to a specific range of political and religious attitudes which seem most relevant to it. I have also attempted to show how the prewar culture of the court provided materials used to construct a partisan royalist tradition in the 1640s and after.[21] Provincial cultures and reactions to the court have been deliberately excluded, however, except when they are directly relevant to our central concerns. Politics is treated as a secondary theme, subordinated to the major focus on cultural history.[22]

Even within these limits, I have had to make decisions about what to include and what to leave out with which some readers may disagree. It will perhaps be useful to indicate briefly the reasoning behind these choices.

I have found little to suggest that cultural trends were directly influenced, except in limited ways, by constitutional controversies. Works produced at court often did express a belief in the divinity of kingship, and some elaborated fairly complex ideas about the nature of the royal office. But the concept of the divine right of kings was not in itself controversial, and the status of the monarch was never a subject for systematic debate until after 1642. Except for a few glancing illusions to things like the ship money tax, cultural works did not engage directly in the secular political controversies raised by Parliament, in either the 1620s or the 1640s. There is no good reason to assume that those controversies provide the most meaningful context within which to examine even the political significance of most cultural works.[23]

Court culture was profoundly shaped, however, by arguments over the issue of England's proper role in the religious and military conflicts between Protestant Europe and Catholic Europe. The court was always divided over this question, and both Elizabeth and Charles were some-times forced to pursue foreign policies that ran counter to their deepest aspirations.[24] For a number of complex reasons, however, England be-came a chief protagonist in the wars of the late sixteenth century, whereas after 1603 the kingdom remained at peace, except for a brief and disastrous interlude in the late 1620s. This shift in policy was clearly reflected—indeed, somewhat exaggerated—by changes in the imagery of royal cults and more generally in the cultural tone of the court.

Part One of this volume shows how the pressures of international religious conflicts shaped the cultural traditions used to glorify English monarchs from the late sixteenth century down to the end of Charles I's continental wars in 1630. It is not intended to be an independent survey of either the politics of these years or the cults of successive monarchs. Its central purpose is to explain how the temperamental paci-fism of James I (r. 1603–1625) and the military and political blunders of Charles's early years led to a decisive break with the religious and patriotic traditions that had grown up around Elizabeth (r. 1558–1603).

Part Two turns away from an analysis of royal cults and the political context in which they evolved, to a broader consideration of cultural changes in and around the court. It is important to recognize that most of those changes were not directed by the Crown. The early Stuarts never developed a well-organized program of cultural patronage or an official cultural philosophy, such as the court academies of the Valois, the Bourbons, and the Medicis tried to promulgate on the continent. Charles I and several members of his entourage certainly had pro-nounced tastes, especially in the fine arts, which led them to spend thousands of pounds promoting styles of which they approved. But even in the 1630s the Crown usually dispensed its patronage haphaz-ardly and opportunistically.

This means that we cannot trace the continuous development of a unified tradition. Instead, we will need to examine a number of loosely related cultural trends, not only within the court but in London and on the continent, which coalesced into a reasonably cohesive culture only in the 1620s and 1630s. Two of these were particularly important. The first was the development of greater London into a cosmopolitan capital city boasting an extraordinarily vital literary and intellectual culture. The interaction between the court and the great metropolis at its door-step was critically important in several respects. It transformed the court's ambience while immeasurably enriching its cultural and intellectual life. Yet it also helped fuel a powerful reaction against courtly and urban manners that ironically had a profound influence on the court itself. As paradoxical as it may sound, Stuart court culture was at once an outgrowth of the trend toward a more urbanized and cosmopolitan aristocratic society and an expression of a deep mistrust of the transformations this trend was bringing about. The failure of historians to appreciate this ambiguity has long obscured the nature of the court's social outlook and the true significance of much anticourt rhetoric.

The second major development was the reestablishment of friendly relations between England and Spain, Italy, and Flanders, after the peace of 1604, and the subsequent influence of these societies and of Bourbon France on the English court. England had never been totally isolated from the continent, but during the long wars of Elizabeth's reign contact with areas dominated by Spain and the papacy was limited. This changed under the Stuarts, with the result that foreign aristocratic cultures began to influence significantly English court habits and tastes, especially with respect to art, architecture, and music. For Charles himself, this influence was undoubtedly magnified by his trip in 1623 to Madrid, where at an impressionable age he saw the greatest royal art collection in all Europe. The desire to emulate and perhaps even surpass the Spanish court stimulated his patronage and colored his outlook down to the Civil War.

Part Three of this volume explores how the court's sophisticated and cosmopolitan culture shaped the political assumptions and habits of the royal circle during the 1630s. Chapter 8 deals with the influence of classical and Baroque religious attitudes on both the court and the king. Charles firmly believed in the need for the Church of England to maintain its independence from the papacy, but he also had far more liking for the beauty of the Mass than for the austere worship of the Reformed tradition. A ruler who counted Peter Paul Rubens, Anthony Van Dyck, and Inigo Jones among his friends, and who received gifts of art from the Vatican, naturally felt little sympathy for puritan scruples about idolatry. The court always harbored a variety of religious opinions, ranging from moderate puritanism to Roman Catholicism. By the 1630s, however, the atmosphere in the court was far more conducive to Catholic modes of thought than to puritan modes of thought. This must have been obvious to anyone who spent much time in London, and it helps explain both the ascendancy of Laud and the deep suspicions of the court's religious allegiances, which helped precipitate the Civil War.

Chapter 10 explores the secular cult that grew up around Charles and his queen during the 1630s, celebrating the pacific policies the king had been forced to adopt by the fiascoes of the 1620s. Roy Strong, Stephen Orgel, and others have already published important essays on this subject. I have tried to avoid duplicating their efforts, while advancing an analysis differing from theirs in important respects. Orgel and Strong emphasize the masques' use of "Neo-platonic" imagery to elevate the king above political conflict as a terrestrial image of God. This interpretation is broadly congruent with the arguments of several intellectual historians who treat Stuart absolutist thought as a doctrine rooted in Platonic cosmology. I will argue that while neither approach is entirely wrong, both present an incomplete and misleading view.[25] They make the political outlook of the court appear more abstract and otherworldly than it really was, obscuring the court's awareness of political instability and historical change. By redressing this imbalance it will be possible to deepen understanding of the political outlook of the regime on the eve of the crisis that destroyed it.

NOTES

1. There was some contact between the court and the provinces, especially among the upper strata of landed society, but there is no doubt that a gap existed, even if some people managed to bridge it. See below, pp. 7–8, and Chapters 3 and 4 for specific examples and discussion.

2. Almost all the important work on the subject has been done by scholars outside the discipline of history whose methods and concerns are different from those of professional historians. This is not meant to minimize the considerable contribution several of these scholars have made, which I have acknowledged, in notes throughout this book. See esp. Stephen Orgel and Roy Strong, *Inigo Jones: The Theater of the Stuart Court*, 2 vols. (London: Sotheby Parke Bernet; Berkeley and Los Angeles: University of California Press, 1973); Stephen Orgel, *The Illusion of Power* (Berkeley and Los Angeles: University of California Press, 1975); Roy Strong, *Charles I on Horseback* (New York: Viking, 1972); Christopher Brown, *Van Dyck* (London: Phaidon, 1982; Ithaca, N.Y.: Cornell University Press, 1983); and the first attempt at a general synthesis, Graham Parry, *The Golden Age Restored* (Manchester: Manchester University Press, 1981). Although this work and Parry's cover many of the same topics, the approach of this book is fundamentally different. Parry's work provides more description of masques, pageants, and other cultural forms. Mine tries to deal more systematically and at greater length with the interaction of cultural history with social, political, intellectual, and administrative history.

3. First developed in the 1950s by H. R. Trevor-Roper, this view was later systematically expanded by Perez Zagorin and Lawrence Stone into an overarching interpretation of the early Stuart period. See esp. Hugh Trevor-Roper, "The General Crisis of the Seventeenth Century," in Trevor Aston, *Crisis in Europe, 1550–1660* (London: Routledge, 1965); Perez Zagorin, *The Court and the Country* (New York: Atheneum, 1971); Lawrence Stone, *Causes of the English Revolution* (London: Routledge; New York: Harper & Row, 1972), esp. pp. 91–117.

4. Stone, *Causes of the English Revolution*, p. 106. See also P. W. Thomas, "Two Cultures: Court and Country Under Charles I," in *The Origins of the English Civil War*, ed. Conrad Russell (London: Macmillan, 1973), pp. 168–193; and "Charles I of England: The Tragedy of Absolutism," in *The Courts of Europe*, ed. A. G. Dickens (London: Thames and Hudson, 1977), pp. 191–211.

5. See esp. Christopher Hill, *Milton and the English Revolution* (Harmondsworth: Penguin, 1977); and Margot Heinemann, *Puritanism and Theater* (Cambridge: Cambridge University Press, 1980).

6. The court-country interpretation has been heavily criticized by political historians in recent years (see below, note 18), but this onslaught has rarely touched on cultural issues. The argument developed here is essentially independent of "revisionist" historiography, although there are some important points of contact.

7. For a recent discussion, see David Underdown, *Revel, Riot, and Rebellion: Popular Politics and Culture in England, 1603–1660* (Oxford: Oxford University Press, 1985).

8. See Charles Carlton, *Charles I: The Personal Monarch* (London: Routledge, 1983), p. 123.

9. See below, Chapter 3, for a discussion.

10. For purposes of this study the term "court" will include individuals with active social connections to the royal entourage even if they did not enjoy a household post. It will exclude provincial dependents of prominent courtiers (such as Buckingham's agents in the counties), unless they also spent considerable time attending the court itself. The definition is therefore broader than Carlton's (above, note 8) but considerably narrower than Zagorin's (*The Court and the Country*, p. 41). Institutions like the Inns of Court and the more fashionable of London's theaters are treated as lying outside the court but as having considerable influence upon it. This approach is the only one that makes sense of cultural events. Carlton's definition is useful in some political contexts, but it would have the effect of excluding from the court many of those who most deeply influenced its ideas and tastes. Zagorin's definition, on the other hand, would include men who had never seen a court masque or a Van Dyck portrait.

11. And in some cases also during visits to the country houses of prominent courtiers, though one suspects this was a less important mode of transmission. The court at Whitehall probably had far more visitors than all the *major* country seats of court aristocrats, and some forms of court culture, like the masques and the buildings of Inigo Jones, were almost exclusively confined to the capital.

12. Thomas May and Edmund Waller.

13. All these terms have been used in recent works, most notably by P. W. Thomas. The bias is even clearer in some older accounts, e.g., Alfred Harbage, *Shakespeare and the Rival Tradition* (New York: Macmillan, 1952).

14. See Zagorin, *The Court and the Country*, p. 71: "The Court's atmosphere emphasized its isolation. Its higher circles breathed an artificial air. Its theatricals with their precious, sentimental love themes were the amusement of a coterie."

15. A good Jacobean example is analyzed by D. J. Gordon in "*Hymenai*: Ben Jonson's Masque of Union," in *The Renaissance Imagination*, ed. Stephen Orgel (Berkeley and

Los Angeles: University of California Press, 1980), pp. 157–184, which may be compared to the accounts of the parliamentary debates over the unions of England and Scotland in Wallace Notestein, *The House of Commons, 1604–1610* (New Haven: Yale University Press, 1971).

16. Orgel and Strong, *Inigo Jones*, vol. 1, p. 63.

17. On this point, see David Bergeron, *English Civic Pageantry* (Columbia: University of South Carolina Press, 1971), esp. chaps. 2 and 3; and R. M. Smuts, "The Political Failure of Stuart Cultural Patronage," in *Patronage in the Renaissance*, ed. Guy Lytle and Stephen Orgel (Princeton: Princeton University Press, 1981), pp. 165–187.

18. See esp. Conrad Russell, *Parliaments and English Politics, 1621–1629* (Oxford: Oxford University Press, 1979), esp. pp. 1–79; J. S. Morrill, *The Revolt of the Provinces* (Cambridge: Cambridge University Press, 1976); and the essays in *Faction and Parliament*, ed. Kevin Sharpe (Oxford: Oxford University Press, 1979).

19. Below, and Chapter 8.

20. It would be difficult to disagree with Anthony Fletcher's comment (*The Outbreak of the English Civil War* [London: E. Arnold, 1981], p. 407): "No one who knows the Puritan world of lectures, fasts and exercises and who has also raised their eyes to Rubens' apotheosis of Stuart monarchy on the ceiling of Inigo Jones's Banqueting House in Whitehall can possibly doubt that there was a clash of cultures in the 1630s."

21. Below, Chapter 10. It is not being argued that court poets and artists were already preparing to fight the Civil War as an embryonic royalist party in the 1630s. The point is that, once the war broke out, many earlier traditions took on a partisan significance, which they sometimes retained until long after the Restoration. Students of political ideas and political imagery during the last six decades of the seventeenth century could profitably pay more attention to the main subject of this book.

22. Since we are dealing with court culture, the political sections are normally court-centered. I have attempted, however, to provide enough background in Chapter 2 to give readers unfamiliar with the period sufficient information to place the materials being discussed within a meaningful context. Students of early Stuart political history may want to skim this material.

23. This is not to say that court masques, poems, and portraits have nothing to do with the issues that arose in Parliament, only that the relationship is usually indirect. The danger lies in assuming that court poets and artists normally had the king's quarrels with Parliament in mind when they were creating works for the Crown. Occasionally this may have been the case, but even from a strictly political point of view the court had many concerns other than Parliament, notably the situation in Europe and the policy debates taking place within the court itself.

24. Ironically Elizabeth was forced into a war against Spain when she would have preferred peace, whereas Charles was forced to make peace in 1629 after failing to wage a successful war. Thus Elizabeth, who detested wars of religion, became a symbol of crusading Protestant heroism, whereas Charles, who would have liked nothing better than to lead a victorious war against Spain, was linked to a pro-Hapsburg policy.

25. See esp. W. H. Greenleaf, *Order, Empiricism, and Politics* (London: Oxford University Press for the University of Hull, 1964).

Part One

The Cults of Monarchy
and
The Wars of Religion

2 THE STUARTS AND THE ELIZABETHAN LEGEND

THE ELIZABETHAN CULT

In 1603 the Stuarts inherited a throne that had stood for a generation as a bulwark against the ambitions of Spain and the Counter-Reformation. England's international leadership of the Protestant cause was, to be sure, due largely to circumstances beyond her ruler's control. Elizabeth did her best to keep out of the religious wars sweeping across the continent, knowing how ruinously expensive they were and how dangerous to all constituted authority. Given the chance, she would gladly have compromised with moderate Catholics on most doctrinal issues, disciplined puritans, and maintained cordial relations with the great European powers. But events forced her to ally herself with Protestants more radical than she and to become progressively involved in continental wars until she was the chief European defender of the Reformation.

The Elizabethan royal cult reflected this heroic role far more than it did the queen's cautious and conservative temperament. Drawing upon courtly, popular, and Protestant traditions, the English constructed an image of their ruler as a champion both of secular liberties and of pure religion. She became the chief symbol of a cultural tradition embodying the aspirations, the religious values, and the patriotism that grew out of the lengthy victorious struggle against domestic and foreign enemies.[1]

So long as the religious wars lasted, this image provided invaluable support to royal authority. The moment tensions began to lessen, however, it proved in some ways a liability. Wartime propaganda acquired a life of its own, bedeviling efforts to make peace. Elizabeth died before having to rule a kingdom no longer united by a clear external threat, but this only made matters worse for her successors. Around her memory grew a legend of a uniquely glorious reign, when England held at bay Europe's greatest power. James I had to rule against the backdrop of a tradition inimical to his own pacific ideals and his desire for friendship with Spain.

Many of the political difficulties he and his son faced derived from their inability to surmount this problem. In the early seventeenth century the Crown could draw upon substantial reserves of loyalty, which not even the events of Charles's reign entirely exhausted. But devotion to the throne was conditioned by strong prejudices about how an English monarch ought to behave, largely defined by Elizabeth's golden legend. In cultivating the Habsburgs and bickering with Parliament, the Stuarts seemed to depart from this tradition, undermining the heritage of their own royal office.

THE DECENTRALIZATION OF PATRONAGE

We need to begin by asking how the Elizabethan legend attained such immense symbolic importance. Part of the explanation lies in the military crisis itself, which gave every patriotic Protestant Englishman compelling reasons to rally behind the throne. But equally important was the skill of the queen and her entourage at encouraging devotion from men beyond the orbit of the royal household. Elizabeth's cult owed much of its vitality to the fact that it was never entirely the product of a narrow, courtly milieu. Paradoxically, the queen inspired a rich and multifaceted tradition glorifying her rule because she did not create an elaborate court culture financed and controlled from the center.

In this she was at odds with the dominant trend of her own times. The sixteenth century was a golden age of royal patronage across Europe.[2] A generation earlier, Elizabeth's own father had erected a string of opulent palaces as he patronized Holbein and put together the most distinguished musical establishment in Christendom. By contrast, Elizabeth built no palaces and recruited no foreign artists or musicians of the first rank. She did patronize the miniaturist Hilliard, along with a number of important composers, but by and large her reign marks a low point in the history of English royal patronage, between the pinnacles of Henry VIII and the early Stuarts.[3]

This did not mean that the royal court ceased to lend crucial support to English high culture, for the monarchy's great servants largely filled the vacuum created by the decline in Crown patronage. Burghley and Leicester appear to have been the most generous and systematic patrons, although lesser figures, like Sir Philip Sidney and Sir Walter Raleigh, also created their own affinities of writers and poets.[4] The Elizabethan cult developed primarily through the efforts of these courtiers and their clients to win the queen's favor by devising ever more ingenious forms of adulation. The intense competition for place and favor thereby contributed to the creation of cultural propaganda.[5]

That propaganda would have had a very limited impact had it remained confined within a narrow courtly circle. Consequently Elizabeth took every convenient opportunity to carry the pageantry of her court before popular audiences. She moved the annual feast day of the Order of the Garter from Windsor Castle to London and encouraged the Garter knights to attend with mounted retinues that paraded down the streets. The queen's routine movements through the capital took place in great splendor, with huge processions of courtiers, guards, and delegations from the city's livery companies in attendance. But the greatest pageants occurred during the summer months, when Elizabeth took her retinue on progresses through the home counties.[6] Up to six hundred strong, with heralds in the lead and lumbering baggage carts bringing up the rear, the court would set off over provincial roads to show Gloriana to her people.

Whenever Elizabeth passed through a town on progress, she was honored by an oration, and sometimes a civic pageant. When she settled for the night at the house of some unfortunate lord, complete with her massive train, she expected to be elaborately complimented and entertained. Borough corporations and country landowners thus found themselves pressed into the work of glorifying their royal mistress, and a few rose to the challenge with remarkable energy. When the Earl of Hertford heard she was moving toward one of his small country residences in 1591, he hired 280 workmen to erect a small village to house the court and construct the setting for a pageant.[7] They dug a pond in the shape of a crescent moon of Diana, goddess of chastity. In it stood an island fortress and a ship, to symbolize England and her navy, and a huge snail made of trimmed hedges, to represent the queen's enemies. When Elizabeth arrived, water deities came out of this enchanted pool to pay homage in song and verse to the mistress of the seas. Then the ship and fortress attacked the snail with blazing cannon, blowing it up in a profusion of fireworks. The entertainment dragged on through three days of drizzle as both court and country folk watched. Finally Elizabeth departed, to the doleful laments of the water gods, whose mistress was deserting them, in the direction of her next host.

Even after the queen settled for the winter in Whitehall, she continued to bask in praise bestowed by men beyond her court. Clergy who owed their promotion to court patronage preached in support of the regime. Scholars and poets wrote verse and prose in her service. Musicians composed loyal ballads, and acting companies staged patriotic plays.

This approach to cultural patronage and court pageantry not only gave rise to a royal cult far more opulent than anything the royal household could have financed, it also fostered a level of spontaneous activity that more rigorous controls would probably have stifled. The cult of monarchy took shape through something resembling a ceremonial dialogue between court and country, as the royal household and various individuals and communities joined in adoring the queen, responding to each other's cues, and weaving new variants around the stock symbols of the reign.

THEMES OF THE ELIZABETHAN CULT

As one might expect, the cult that emerged under these conditions embodied an enormous variety of cultural traditions. A biblical Judith, pagan goddess, and chivalric heroine rolled into one, Elizabeth appealed to her subjects in many cultural languages, which spoke to different audiences on different levels. Court wits enjoyed elaborating conventional motifs of royal propaganda with esoteric symbolism. For them the royal cult included the fashionable lore of Hermeticism, Petrarchanism, and classical mythology. Yet it also embodied habits of thought as old and popular as the morality play.

Among the most prominent themes of Elizabeth's cult was a concept of the queen as empress of the seas and guardian of the liberties of foreign peoples. As Frances Yates has shown, this imperial imagery was rooted in an international tradition ultimately deriving from the cult of Augustus Caesar, (r. 31 B.C. – 14 A.D.) and more immediately from the dynastic propaganda of Emperor Charles V (r. 1519–1556) and other European rulers. In particular, Elizabethan panegyrists echoed those of the Habsburgs, the Valois, and the Medici in claiming that their monarch would soon establish a universal empire in which the peace and justice of the mythical Golden Age would return to the earth.[8]

Before long, however, imperial imagery became intertwined with peculiarly English aspirations arising from the realm's struggle with Spain in the 1570s and 1580s. In 1585 the Dutch provinces offered to name Elizabeth as their sovereign, thereby creating the prospect of a North Sea empire with the world's greatest navy. This might have allowed England to seize control of the New World silver which supported Spain's armies, and perhaps ultimately to invade the heartland of Catholicism. The queen hesitated to undertake such visionary schemes, but members of her entourage, including Leicester and, after his death, Essex, were ready to experiment with a Dutch alliance and aggressive maritime policy. Poets and propagandists sympathetic to these leaders gloried in dreams of English imperial conquests. Spenser hinted at them in the *Faerie Queen:*

> Then shall a royal Virgin reign, which shall
> Stretch her white rod over the Belgicke shore,
> And the great Castle [Castile?] smite so sore with all,
> That it shall make him shake, and shortly learn to fall.[9]

Michael Drayton, more pointedly, prayed that Elizabeth's "empire" might "stretch her arms from East to West / And Albion on the Appennines advance her conquering crest."[10] The dream survived into the 1650s, haunting Cromwell's Protectorate.

Elizabethan imperialism thus came to center on the oceans. This suited those at court and among the peerage who had invested in piracy. The privateering fleet played somewhat the same role in Elizabeth's reign that raids on France had played in the late Middle Ages, allowing a few well-born adventurers to search for glory and profit. The glamour of sea warfare was ultimately broadcast far beyond the elite, however. Hakluyt's huge collection of documents concerning the exploits of the sea dogs appeared in the 1580s. Over the next two decades, epics, ballads, and other popular works celebrated the achievements of England's sailors:

> How that their lofty minds could not be bounded
> Within the cancels, that the world do bound;
> How that the deepest seas they searched and sounded,
> Making the foremost seas our praise resound:
> > And nations which not fame herself had seen;
> > To carol England's fame, and fame's fair Queen.[11]

The whole population was thus encouraged to share vicariously in the romance of marine warfare.

In glorifying England's mariners, Hakluyt adapted chivalric concepts of knight errantry to suit the exploits of privateers. By doing so, he participated in a revival of medieval styles and themes that left a profound imprint on late Elizabethan culture. Around the mid 1570s the English elite largely turned its back on Italianate and classical forms which had gained ground steadily since the early Tudor period.[12] The classical architecture exemplified by Somerset House (1547–1552) and Longleat (completed 1572) gave way before a fascination with towers, courtyards, and expanses of glass inspired by late medieval native architecture. Hilliard and his school created a brightly colored two-dimensional style of portraiture, at its best in miniatures, deriving from medieval illuminators.[13] From the late 1580s the public theaters started popularizing stories of medieval kings, while the Accession Day jousts brought the influence of neo-medievalism into court pageantry.

Today Elizabethan medievalism seems to be tinged with an air of make-believe, especially in contrast to the humanist thought of the previous generation. But neo-medieval culture suited the needs of a wartime period.[14] Despite the hostility of humanists, tournaments and chivalric romances were popular throughout Europe, partly because they expressed so well the swashbuckling instincts of noblemen who still saw themselves primarily as warriors. Around 1580 Sidney commented, "Truly I have known men who even with the reading of *Amadis de Gaul* have found their hearts moved to the exercise of courtesy, liberality and, especially, courage."[15]

From the Crown's point of view, such bellicose sentiments were far from an unmixed blessing. Elizabeth constantly lived with the nightmare that the English nobility would divide, as its French counterpart had, into Protestant and Catholic factions whose quarrels regularly erupted in civil war. The court's chivalric literature and pageantry therefore stressed the overriding importance of loyalty to the queen's person, in an effort to channel potentially dangerous aspirations into acceptable channels. Despite her fears of rebellion, Elizabeth would not afford to dispense with her nobility's military services, since she lacked a professional army and the resources to bear the full burden of the realm's defense on the seas. This fact may help account for the ultimate failure of such mid-Tudor critics of chivalry as the queen's tutor, Roger Ascham, to carry the day.[16]

Conveniently, English chivalry had long helped to justify the Crown's wars.[17] Heroic kings—the legendary Arthur, Edward III, and Henry V—were national symbols of courtesy and prowess, and the Order of the Garter was an exclusive society of knighthood under the monarch's leadership. Whenever England went to war in the late fifteenth and sixteenth centuries, accounts of the exploits of legendary royal conquerors circulated with official encouragement.[18] Shakespeare's *Henry V* and Spenser's *Faerie Queen* continued a tradition of propaganda already more than a century old.

Interwoven with this secular cult was a set of religious concepts which turned the queen into a divinely chosen leader of God's people. Even before Foxe's famous martyrology appeared, Protestant ballads hailed Elizabeth as a modern counterpart to the biblical Judith and Deborah.[19] But *The Acts and Monuments of the Christian Religion* did more than any other work to establish Elizabeth as a godly queen in the public mind.[20] This massive narrative, placed in all English churches by order of the Crown, treated her as a modern Constantine who had rescued Christ's elect from persecution and would now protect them from the forces of Antichrist.

Foxe's volumes held a twofold significance as political propaganda. They converted the Marian persecution into a national legend, remembered in grisly detail long after the mid-Tudor generation died out. But even more important, they reinforced a tradition, already established in the writings of earlier English Protestants like John Bale, of interpreting contemporary history as part the great eschatological struggle between the forces of Christ and Antichrist. Mary Stuart (r. 1542–1587), the rebels of 1569, and the St. Bartholomew's Day Massacre of

1572 soon took their place within the constantly unfolding story of conflict between the chosen people and Satan's minions moving toward its apocalyptic climax. The defeat of the Armada—by the hand of God controlling winds and waves, according to the English—added a crowning touch to the legend.

In the late sixteenth century the Crown had much to gain from such attitudes. Yet there remained a latent danger that the ideas and images through which Protestants expressed their devotion might be used to criticize royal policies that did not seem militant enough. This already began to happen in the middle of Elizabeth's reign, as parliamentary orators like Peter Wentworth adopted the role of Hebraic prophets, chiding their queen for her reluctance to purify the church and cut off the Scottish Jezebel.[21] In the next reign the concept of England as a modern Israel became a weapon in the arsenal of men seeking a more aggressively Protestant foreign policy than James pursued.

THE AMBIGUOUS LEGACY OF ELIZABETH

In ways like this, Elizabeth's golden legend ultimately helped perpetuate concepts of political leadership that the Stuarts and their entourage either would not or could not fulfill. The seeds of this development were already planted in the sixteenth century. For all its short-term success, Elizabethan government was limited by a lack of the financial, bureaucratic, and military resources needed to wage war effectively in Europe. In peacetime this liability was not too damaging, but as the wars of religion and the Spanish threat grew more serious, and as the eagerness of some Englishmen to enter the fray grew more intense, the Crown found itself caught in a dilemma. If it failed to act vigorously against the catholic enemy, it became vulnerable to charges of weakness and vacillation. Yet the moment it went to war, it had to raise unprecedented sums of money and impose unaccustomed burdens on local magistrates, in ways that could strain the traditional partnership between the monarch and the county elites. Not until the late 1620s did this lesson become fully apparent, but even in the last dozen or so years of Elizabeth's reign ominous signs of stress began to appear.

To her credit, Elizabeth realized that, whatever puritans and swashbuckling courtiers might argue, the nation would never finance a full-scale war. She therefore did her best to limit international commitments. Even the essentially defensive war of the 1590s, however, dangerously overstrained the government's resources. By continental standards, England suffered very little: taxes remained lower than in most of Europe, and the common people never faced the depredations of ill-disciplined armies. Nonetheless, the Crown had to raise much greater sums than the English were accustomed to paying. Unfortunately the 1590s brought some of the worst harvests of the century, while several towns suffered from a trade depression. A population in the midst of an economic crisis therefore faced extraordinary fiscal demands from the government, always an explosive combination of circumstances in early modern Europe. The queen's agents met with some local resistance and widespread sullen resentment as they went about their work.[22]

The Earl of Essex and his faction regarded the queen's policies as not ambitious enough. Essex resolutely opposed the efforts of Elizabeth and Burghley to make peace, while posing as a conquering hero frustrated by the incompetence and jealousy of rivals who mismanged the war. Elizabeth found herself blamed both for the high level of war taxes and for the military restraint that kept those taxes from rising higher still.

By the late 1590s the queen's popularity had worn thin. The financial strains of war and Elizabeth's parsimony led to a drying up of royal rewards and a resulting outcry from disappointed courtiers, while her flirtations with her subjects lost their charm, now that she had aged into a shrewish spinster of nearly seventy. Rancorous battles for control of the court, culminating in Essex's rebellion and execution, further discredited her rule. Only her death in 1603 halted the erosion of support. The bitter memories of these last years eventually receded as the queen became associated with the glorious period of the late 1580s and early 1590s: with the careers of Sidney, Drake, Raleigh, and Essex and with the Armada, the sack of Cadiz, and the pursuit of Spain's treasure on the high seas. These triumphs provided an implicit contrast with the far less heroic reign of James I.

THE JACOBEAN PEACE AND ITS RAMIFICATIONS

James's accession in 1603 and conclusion of peace with Spain a year later rendered the Elizabethan cult largely obsolete. Many Elizabethan traditions were not readily transferable to a male successor, who could hardly pose as a royal virgin and chivalric mistress of the realm's courtiers, soldiers, and sailors. More important, James showed no inclination to engage in foreign wars on behalf of European Protestants. Court artists and poets had to adapt to these changes, creating a royal cult suited to the pacific aspirations and temperament of their new sovereign.

THE CULT OF PEACE

Negotiations to end the Anglo-Spanish war had already begun under Elizabeth and probably would have reached fruition had she lived. Religious warfare receded throughout Europe in the early seventeenth century, as Henry IV (r. 1589–1610) imposed his tolerant rule upon France and the war in the Netherlands drew toward stalemate. The crisis of the 1580s, when European hegemony seemed within Philip II's grasp, had given way to a prolonged and inconclusive struggle that none of the protagonists could afford. Within England, Essex's rebellion destroyed the most effective militant court faction, while the rise of the pro-Spanish Howard earls of Northampton and Suffolk strengthened the advocates of peace.[23] Developments both at home and abroad had thus created conditions favoring détente with Spain.

James's commitment to peace went far beyond these concerns, however. His experiences in Scotland, perhaps the most turbulent kingdom in Europe, had taught him to detest violence and had given him an almost mystical belief in the duty of kings to alleviate conflict.[24] Upon reaching the English throne, he sought to implement this ideal on an international plane by attempting to mediate between Protestant and Catholic Europe, in hopes of bringing nearer the day when religious divisions might be peacefully resolved.

The king's pacific ideals naturally influenced those who produced pageants, masques, and panegyrics in his honor. From his triumphant entry into London in 1603 to the masques of the 1620s, poets and artists praised him as a monarch:

> Whose strong and potent virtues have defaced
> Stern Mars' statues and upon them placed
> His and the world's blessed blessing.[25]

Elizabethan themes were adjusted to conform to this emphasis. Medieval warrior-kings and references to England's maritime power virtually disappeared from court masques and poems, except for those written for James's warlike son Henry. King Arthur was converted from a symbol of chivalric prowess into one of British unity.[26] The imperial theme was now associated almost exclusively with the internal peace and prosperity of the British Isles and the dynastic union of England and Scotland, rather than with dreams of overseas dominions.[27]

The same shift of emphasis affected religious themes, although here the transition was less complete. On one level the tradition embodied in Foxe's *Book of Martyrs* continued to flourish throughout the Jacobean period, especially after the failure of the Gunpowder Plot gave rise to a new national holiday, commemorating the latest deliverance from the strategems of Antichrist.[28] James's theological interests and writings also fitted in well with the concept of godly monarchy. The parallel between England and ancient Israel took on more peaceful connotations. If Elizabeth had posed as the successor to heroines who rescued the Jews from oppression, James preferred comparison with law-giving kings.[29] Panegyrists associated his efforts to restore St. Paul's Cathedral with Solomon's rebuilding of the Temple in Jerusalem, but they did not often allude to Israel's battles with Egypt or Babylon.

OPPOSITION TO THE PEACE

The Jacobean peace probably served the nation's best interests and undoubtedly saved the Crown from insolvency, but James's pacific and pro-Spanish policies nonetheless provoked considerable discontent. Especially in London and a few other coastal towns, commercial rivalries kept hatred of Spain alive. The privateering by both sides that had developed during the war proved impossible to stop after 1604. Those who profited or hoped to profit from plundering Spanish shipping formed a relatively small but vocal interest group, while the raids of the notorious Dunkirk pirates from the Spanish Netherlands posed a constant danger to the seagoing community.[30] As English merchants began trading on a large scale in the Americas and East Indies, they sometimes ran afoul of Spanish authorities.[31] There was thus no shortage of materials on which inherited prejudices might feed. One observer reported in the early 1610s, "Upon Sunday last there were diverse merchants and merchants' wives at Court [who] made grievous complaint to the King, the one of their servants, the other of their husbands, imprisoned and put to the galleys in Spain. . . . The Nation generally wishes this peace broken, but *Jacobus Pacificus* I believe will scarce incline to that side."[32] The economic downturn of the late 1610s and early 1620s also helped revive memories of profitable Elizabethan piracy and fed the myth that England never prospered so well as when at war with Spain.[33]

By no means all discontent with the court's policies stemmed from such motives. Many informed Englishmen, including several diplomats and courtiers, believed with some reason that the Spanish Crown still dreamed of a European empire. They saw the Jacobean peace as a momentary respite while Spain recovered her strength and attempted to divide Protestant Europe.[34] Even if an immediate war was not warranted, military preparedness and alliances with foreign Protestants appeared to be essential. The king's pro-Spanish orientation seemed to jeopardize the realm's security.

The thinly veiled Catholicism of several influential courtiers aroused more insidious fears. In 1612 Lewis Bayly, a former chaplain to Prince Henry, preached in the church of St. Martin's-in-the-Fields, whose parishioners included a number of privy councillors: "Religion lays a bleeding; and no marvel . . . when diverse Councillors hear mass in the morning, and then go to a Court Sermon and so to the Council, and then tell their wives what passes, and they carry it to their Jesuits and Confessors."[35]

These suspicions were sometimes further exacerbated by the influence of Tacitus and other classical and Renaissance historians who fostered a sinister view of court politics. According to Sir Simonds D'Ewes, at the news of Prince Henry's death most people recalled Tacitus's account of the poisoning of Prince Germanicus.[36] They also remembered the recent assassination of Henry IV of France by "the jesuited Ravillac" and wondered darkly if the prince had not been murdered by Catholic enemies. The anecdote illustrates how ancient tales of courtly intrigue and murder could fuse with modern phobias to create a climate of acute mistrust. This mode of thought had an incalculable but probably significant effect in undermining confidence in the government.[37] We must keep this in mind if we are to understand the fears aroused by the Spanish Match, the rise of Arminianism, and Buckingham's career.[38]

FAILURE TO ESTABLISH A NATIONAL CULT

James might have alleviated anxieties caused by his foreign policy and the presence of suspected Catholics on his council if he had done a better job of displaying the qualities of a heroic king concerned about his people's welfare. Unfortunately he rarely participated in tournaments and showed little interest in military affairs. Worse, he did not like to appear before cheering crowds and sometimes treated them with open contempt. James's Scottish experience had done little to prepare him to fulfill the sort of public role that Elizabeth had defined. There was no elaborate cult of royalty north of the Tweed, and there was no tradition of great progresses and royal entries. The instability of the northern kingdom had also given him a visceral dislike of unruly crowds and a deep mistrust of anything that savored of "popularity," which he tended to associate with seditious Presbyterians.[39] The throngs of apprentices and laborers that surrounded his coach whenever it appeared in London's streets, shouting their greetings in his ears, struck him as highly indecorous and perhaps a bit frightening.[40]

It was therefore difficult for him to act like a king who valued the devotion of his humbler subjects. D'Ewes thought it worthy of remark that during the procession that opened the 1621 Parliament James spoke graciously to people along his route: "Contrary to his former and hasty passionate custom, which often in his sudden distemper would bid a p—— or a plague on such as flocked to see him."[41] Some fourteen years earlier the Venetian ambassador had remarked:

> He does not caress the people nor make them that good cheer that the late Queen did, whereby she won their loves; for the English adore their sovereigns, and if the King passed through the streets a hundred times a day the people would still run to see him; they like their King to show pleasure at their devotion, as the late Queen knew well how to do; but this King manifests no taste for them but rather contempt and dislike. The result is he is despised and almost hated.[42]

In few other respects was the contrast with the old queen more striking or more damaging to James's popularity.

The frequent coarseness of James's court further undermined his prestige. There is no need to repeat here the squalid details of the Overbury scandal or to summarize Harington's account of the raucous entertainment given the king of Denmark on his visit in 1616, when men and women vomited from drink in the royal presence.[43] Even apart from these spectacular lapses, however, courtiers sometimes behaved in very undignified ways. The chaplain of the Venetian ambassador recorded the following scene at a banquet following a masque in 1617:

[James] glanced around the table and departed and at once like so many harpies the company fell upon their prey. . . . The meal was served in bowls or plates of glass; the first assault threw the tables to the ground and the crash of glass platters reminded me exactly of the windows breaking in a great midsummer storm. . . . At two hours after midnight . . . half disgusted . . . we returned home.[44]

A seventeenth-century commonplace held that kings are set on a public stage, where their every vice attracts attention, and another held that men inevitably judge a ruler by the quality of his entourage. On both counts James failed to maintain minimal standards of decorum.

Perhaps even more damaging was the court's growing expense and perceived corruption. Recent work has shown that James's financial difficulties were not entirely of his own making. Inflation, Elizabethan debts and sales of Crown lands, the antiquated structure of royal finances, and the reluctance of local gentry to assess themselves and their neighbors at realistic rates in the subsidy books all contributed to government's financial woes.[45] But James's bad management and generosity to courtiers undoubtedly exacerbated the problem and encouraged distrust of the royal entourage. Even before 1603, resentment was building against the venality and extravagance of courtiers, who were blamed for the Crown's financial difficulties and the growth of taxes and other burdens. As expenditures increased in virtually all household departments and the money disbursed in court pensions approached £50,000 a year, mistrust inevitably grew. The fact that many of the chief beneficiaries were Scottish favorites or English courtiers suspected of Catholic sympathies only made matters worse.[46]

These shortcomings do not mean that James was a bad king in any absolute sense. He had a number of political talents, as Jenny Wormald and others have recently argued,[47] but the ability to project a majestic and dignified image and to inspire reverence for himself and his entourage was not among them. Although the traditional portrait of a slovenly, homosexual king presiding over a debauched court is grossly exaggerated and one-sided, it does contain a significant core of truth. The lapses of decorum within the court, the presence there of unpopular Scottish and homosexual favorites, the mounting costs of the royal household, and James's own surliness in public all tarnished the monarchy's prestige, inhibiting spontaneous public support. There are no Jacobean parallels to the *Faerie Queen*, the *Book of Martyrs*, or the profusion of loyal ballads produced in the 1580s and 1590s. In an age when Englishmen were writing and gossiping about politics more than ever before, their ruler had ceased to be an effective symbol of national aspirations. The continuing vitality of the Elizabethan cult in the early Stuart period stemmed in large part from this circumstance.

ELIZABETHAN SURVIVALS AND REVIVALS

Throughout the early Stuart period, the English continued their adulation of the dead queen.[48] Foxe's *Book of Martyrs* was reprinted for the seventh and eighth times under James and Charles. Thomas Heywood wrote a play about her reign which enjoyed two revivals and seven printings before the Civil War. Orators in the House of Commons, from Sir Edward Coke to Oliver Cromwell, praised her memory. In London thirty-two parish churches erected memorials extolling her in jog-trot verse:

> Chaste Patroness of true Religion,
> In Court a Saint, in Field an Amazon
> Glorious in life, deplored in death,
> Such was unparallel'd ELIZABETH.[49]

Even her accession day remained a public holiday. Gradually this adulation took on a political significance, as Elizabeth's name was associated with austerity, military preparedness, and Protestant alliances, in contrast to the perceived extravagance and pro-Spanish policies of James I.

For some time the hopes of those seeking a return to Elizabethan policies crystallized around James's heir, Prince Henry. This precocious adolescent attracted a following of young noblemen, clergymen, poets, and courtiers united by the desire to change both the tone and the policies of the court. Henry criticized his father's extravagance and turned his own household into a model of decorum. He took an interest in the navy, befriended Sir Walter Raleigh, one of the last of Elizabeth's sea adventurers, and discussed strategy for a future war against Spain.[50] He rapidly gained a reputation as a champion of Protestant and national interests. Michael Drayton, who enjoyed the prince's patronage, hinted broadly of future military glories in a poem commemorating Henry V's victory at Agincourt:

O, When shall English men
With such acts fill a pen,
Or England breed again
Such a King Harry?[51]

Another admirer proclaimed, "The eyes, the hopes of all the Protestant world be fixed upon your Highness, all expecting your gracious faithfulness, and readiness in the extirpation of that man of sin [the Pope]."[52]

The militaristic tone of the prince's court was further underlined by several magnificent tournaments. *Prince Henry's Barriers*, a masque created by Inigo Jones and Ben Jonson for one of them, illustrates how the prince's court exploited historical traditions to make oblique comments on contemporary affairs.[53] The spectacle opened with a scene of the Fallen House of Chivalry (see Plate 1, Chapter 4), a symbol of the glories of England's past and the indolence of the present:

Those obelisks and columns broke down
That struck the stars, and raised the British crown
To be a constellation; shields and swords
Cobwebbed and rusty; not a helm affords
A spark of luster, which were wont to give
Light to the world, and make the nation live.[54]

King Arthur and the Lady of the Lake appeared, sang of the glories of England's former kings, and predicted that the prince would soon follow their example:

Harry the fifth, to whom in face you Henry are
So like, as Fate would have you so in worth
Illustrious Prince! The virtue ne'er came forth
But Fame flew greater for him than she did
For other mortals; Fate herself did bid
To save his life. . . .
War knew not how to give 'im enough to do.[55]

The masque thus suggested that the proper place of an English prince is at the head of the kingdom's warriors. Yet elsewhere Jonson added several qualifying notes, and the masque's closing lines warned Henry to temper his valor with wisdom and follow his father's example.[56] The ambivalence of this entertainment illustrates the difficulty of sustaining a bellicose, neo-chivalric culture in the court of a pacific king.

Like Elizabeth, Henry knew how to carry such spectacles before the
public. The continuator of Stow's *Annals* described the festivities ac-
companying his creation as Prince of Wales:

> In the afternoon in the tiltyard there were diverse earls, barons and others
> being in rich and glorious armor, and having costly caparisons, wondrously
> curiously embroidered with pearls, gold and silver. The like rich habile-
> ments for horses were never seen before. [They] presented their several in-
> genious devices and trophies before the King and Prince, and then ran at
> tilt, where there was a world of people to behold them. . . . That night
> there were other naval triumphs, and pastimes upon the water, over against
> the Court with ships of war, and galleys fighting, one against another, and
> against a great castle, builded upon the water. After the battle then for an
> hour's space there were many strange and variable fireworks in the castle
> and all the ships. . . . the Thames in a manner being covered with boats
> and barges full of people, besides the shore on both sides were surcharged
> with people.[57]

These events may have been so successful as to arouse James's envy.
The Venetian ambassador reported that at the conclusion of the festivities Henry was not allowed to enter London on horseback. "The
reason is the question of expense or, as some say, because they did not
desire to exalt him too high."[58] Once again a militant anti-Spanish policy had become associated with a more open and popular style of leadership than James chose to practice.

After Henry's premature death in 1612, his sister Elizabeth, who
married the Calvinist Elector Palatine in 1613, became a second focal
point for patriotic aspirations.[59] In the end, however, those seeking a
more aggressive king could only pin their hopes on Charles, a sickly
adolescent whose political views remained unknown.

THE POLITICS OF RELIGIOUS WAR

So long as Europe remained at peace, the issue of England's proper response to religious conflict across the Channel was not extremely
urgent. However, the outbreak of the Thirty Years' War in 1618 and
the crushing defeat of James's son-in-law, the Elector Palatine, in 1620
greatly increased pressure to lend military assistance to continental
Protestants. The king chose instead to attempt to restore the Palatine's

position through diplomacy.[60] Two years before, he had proposed that Prince Charles marry a daughter of the Spanish royal family. Negotiations for this match now intensified, with the English hoping to use it as leverage to persuade Spain to restore the conquered Palatinate. The Spanish court was itself divided over the desirability of the match but wished to keep James preoccupied with it, and managed to prolong negotiations for more than four years.[61]

Charles had meanwhile persuaded himself that he was in love with the Spanish infanta. In 1623 he and the royal favorite, Buckingham, traveled incognito to Madrid to cut through the diplomatic tangle and woo her in person. This voyage caused a sensation both at home and abroad, since it rendered Charles a potential hostage of the Spanish Crown and encouraged rumors that he would soon convert to Catholicism.[62] Even within the court, men protested vigorously against the proposed match. The government imprisoned one of Charles's own chaplains for preaching against it. Lancelot Andrewes, dean of the Chapel Royal, strenuously objected to the Spanish terms in an unpublished poem:

> . . . a Church must at St. James be built
> Besides the Cross at Cheap must be new guilt
> Besides, a toleration must be wrought,
> The Sea of Rome about this Island brought
> All these Besides would make a man beside
> Himself to be detained so far a Bride.[63]

The public reaction, especially in and near London, was even more vociferous. Evelyn, who was four years old at the time, still recalled the furor caused by Charles's trip to Madrid when he wrote his diary some forty years later.[64] To forestall a campaign from the pulpit, the Crown had to issue a proclamation against references to the subject in sermons. More difficult to stop were pamphleteers, in particular one Thomas Scott, who went into exile in the Netherlands and there produced twenty-one tracts on the subject, which he had smuggled back into England.[65]

The agitation against the Spanish match might well repay a systematic investigation, employing the methods Rudé and Brewer have developed in analyzing movements of popular protest and political propaganda in the eighteenth century.[66] The opponents of James's policies could not deploy anything like the network of journalists, printers, and political clubs which served the Wilkesite movement in the 1760s, but there already existed channels for the dissemination of printed propaganda and perhaps organized means for arousing demonstrations. Like the Wilkesites, the anti-Spanish propagandists simplified issues into a few vivid formulas which even the unsophisticated could understand. Their pamphlets belong to the formative period of political journalism in England, when national affairs had just begun to encroach upon the awareness of people outside the traditional political elite.[67]

From our point of view, the significant point about the writings and sermons concerning the Spanish match is the extent to which they employed Elizabethan traditions to discredit Jacobean policies. Most of the anti-Spanish writers took as their starting point the eschatological view of history popularized by Foxe. Spain belonged to the kingdom of the Antichrist and so was driven by an insatiable blood lust against God's people.[68] Since she had proven no match for English naval power a generation before, Spain now employed more devious methods of conquest. Instead of attacking England directly, her agents worked to build a secret party at the English court and a fifth column of Catholics in the countryside.[69]

The architect of this conspiracy, Scott alleged, was Spain's ambassador, Gondomar, a man "culled and picked out from a million . . . to [better] understand our State . . . than any of our natives."[70] By bribing James's ministers, he prevented the rigorous enforcement of laws against English Catholics, enabling them to proselytize and conspire in relative freedom. He persuaded James to keep the realm at peace as the navy decayed and the military virtues of the population were sapped by "stage plays, masques, revels and carousing."[71] Simultaneously he sowed dissension between the king and Parliament to prevent James from hearing the complaints and counsels of his subjects. By giving England a Spanish queen, he now hoped to open the way to the kingdom's complete subversion. Within a few years of her arrival, Catholics "should work so far into the body of the State, by buying offices and the like, whether by sea or land . . . in Church or State (all being exposed to sale) that with the help of the Jesuits they would undermine them with mere wit . . . and leave the King but a few subjects whose faiths he might rely upon."[72] James thus appeared as the hapless victim of a corrupted court and a Machiavellian ambassador. The vague fears of court papists that had existed in some quarters for at least a decade acquired more definite shape.

As a foil for this depressing image, Scott took every opportunity to recall the glorious reign of Elizabeth. He attributed one of his pamphlets to the ghost of the Earl of Essex and another to that of Sir Walter Raleigh, who had been executed in 1618 at Gondomar's insistence after attacking a Spanish base in South America. In *Vox Coeli* (1623) he recorded a conversation in the "Star Chamber" of heaven between Henry VIII, Edward VI, Mary, Elizabeth, and Prince Henry, conferring like so many Homeric gods over England's fate. Elizabeth bewailed the decay of her navy:

> O my Ships my Ships: God knows they were still dear to me because necessary to England. Where is my Drake, my Cumberland, my Forbusher . . . My Raleigh? Alas they want me, and King James and England want them; for when they lived and I reigned our Valor could stop the Progression of Spain; Yea my Ships domineered in his seas and Ports. . . . [73]

All lamented James's inaction except Mary, who gloated over Spain's success. These pamphlets already foreshadow the dark fears that erupted in Parliament in 1628–1629 and again in 1641 that the nation's failure to live up to her Elizabethan past was due to a sinister conspiracy at almost the highest levels of English government.

We cannot know how many Englishmen shared these views, but there is evidence of widespread alarm in the early 1620s over court conspiracies and Spanish plots. It may or may not be true, as one anonymous pamphlet claimed, that people in taverns all over London were gossiping about the corruption of English courtiers by Spanish money and wishing that "Queen Elizabeth were alive again, who . . . would never have suffered the enemies of her religion to have unbalanced all Christendom."[74] But London crowds certainly reviled and even attacked Gondomar and other Spaniards, and in May 1623 D'Ewes recorded in his diary, "Daily more and more libels were dispersed, in which did plainly appear the misery of a discontented and almost daring people."[75] In a few provincial elections, distrustful voters denied seats to men associated with the court or with recusants.[76] In 1621 John Chamberlain reported, "God knows how it comes to pass, but sure men's hearts begin to sink, and [they] fear that religion is in hard case as well at home as abroad." Two years later he observed that "many of our churchmen are hardly held in, and their tongues itch to be talking" about the Spanish match.[77] Some thirty years later Lucy Hutchinson, the wife of one of Cromwell's generals, recalled attacks on the match in words evoking the charged religious atmosphere of the period:

> . . . The ministers warned the people of the approaching judgements. . . . God in his mercy sent his prophets into all corners of the land, to preach repentance and cry out against the ingratitude of England . . . and by these a few everywhere were converted and established in the faith . . . but at court they were hated, disgraced and reviled, and in scorn had the name Puritan fixed upon them.[78]

A rhetoric that had once unified the nation behind the throne was now used to castigate the court.

All this suggests that the tensions which erupted at the end of the 1620s had a longer and more complex gestation than some historians have argued.[79] The accusations hurled at Buckingham, Weston, and other ministers of Charles I were not simply a response to short-term events. They were also rooted in stereotypes of court conspiracy and "Jesuitical" intrigue which dated from Elizabethan times and grew steadily stronger as Spanish influence at Whitehall increased under James I. Until Charles's reign, distrust of the court had not yet poisoned the atmosphere sufficiently to precipitate a rupture between the Crown and Parliament. As Russell has shown, the leaders of the Commons in the 1621 session were anxious to avoid confrontations with the king.[80] Yet this does not necessarily indicate that men trusted the court. It is likely that politically sophisticated members of Parliament wished at all costs to avoid offending James precisely because they feared playing into the hands of Gondomar and his allies on the Council, by provoking a quarrel like that which had terminated the 1614 session in circumstances that strengthened the pro-Spanish faction at Whitehall.[81] Their willingness to remain silent over domestic grievances which had figured prominently in earlier sessions may indicate how alarmed some of them were over the drift of royal foreign policy.

It is in any case clear that the European war and the proposed Spanish match sharpened divisions over religion and foreign policy that had existed throughout James's reign.[82] If the political nation was not yet ideologically divided, a fissure had appeared within its ranks that foreboded more serious problems to come if the match was not abandoned.

It is crucial to realize, however, that this fissure did not divide the court from the country, but rather split both internally. Nothing like a majority of the political nation was actively opposed to the Crown's policy. Although the Spanish match was almost universally unpopular, the intensity of the feelings it aroused varied enormously from district to district. As Scott himself admitted, in most places fear of papists and courtiers had not yet effectively undercut traditional patterns of deference: "The Country-people . . . will every one stand by the great Man, their Lord or Neighbor or Master, without regard of his Honesty, Wisdom or Religion."[83] At the same time, the court was itself divided over the match, so that those seeking a breach with Madrid could look for allies on the Privy Council itself. If Gondomar's conspiracy existed, the best chance for defeating it was through a realignment within Whitehall, which might free the king from corrupt influence and lead to a resumption of Elizabethan policies.

In the last two years of James's reign, such a realignment seemed to occur. A few months in Madrid convinced Charles and Buckingham that Spain would never agree to a marriage alliance on acceptable terms.[84] They returned home nursing a sense of wounded honor, determined to seek revenge, and began pushing the tired old king toward war. The public responded enthusiastically. London had not had a significant occasion for rejoicing since the marriage of Princess Elizabeth some ten years earlier, and as the prince arrived without his Spanish bride it staged a tumultuous welcome. "I have not heard of more demonstrations of public joy than were here." wrote John Chamberlain:

> . . . such spreading of tables in the streets with all manner of provisions, setting out whole loggerheads of wine and butts of sack, but especially such numbers of bonfires . . . the people were so mad with excess of joy that if they met with any cart laden with wood they would take out the horses and set cart and all on fire.[85]

Buckingham enjoyed an ephemeral popularity among anti-Spanish activists. "Who doth not look upon him as an oak or cedar, sound at the heart," wrote Scott. "He hath shown himself more faithful to God, to the King, Prince and his Country, than . . . our . . . fears could . . . suffer us to imagine."[86]

Encouraged by this response, the prince and duke attempted to enlist the aid of the Parliament of 1624 against the court's remaining Hispanophiles and James's lingering resistance to war. They encouraged the impeachment of the antiwar treasurer, Lionel Cranfield, and argued for an unprecedented grant of six subsidies and six-fifteenths, or about £900,000.[87] The Commons ultimately passed half this amount, far too little to support a land war in Europe but enough to allow Charles to claim that Parliament had become a partner in the war effort.[88]

In August 1624, Thomas Middleton's A Game of Chess, a satire of Spanish policy, opened in London. No one has ever explained how it got past the Crown's censor, Henry Herbert, although the fact that he belonged to Pembroke's anti-Spanish court faction is suggestive. Powerful figures, perhaps including Charles himself, probably encouraged the play. In any case, it ran for an unprecedented nine days before packed houses containing, in Chamberlain's words, "all sorts of people, old and young, rich and poor, masters and servants, papists and puritans . . . churchmen and statesmen," before the Spanish ambassador finally got it closed down.[89]

James's death in March 1625 removed the last significant obstacle to war. Charles barred Catholics from his father's funeral and made them feel unwelcome at court, while stepping up enforcement of the recusancy laws. Troops paraded in London through the summer, privateers received letters of marque, and in the fall the first enemy prize ships arrived in London. "They have been received with great expressions of joy and firing of cannon," the Tuscan ambassador reported. "It is boasted that the days of Queen Elizabeth are revived."[90] Thus the king set out to assert his leadership of those who had been clamoring for war. The mixture of xenophobia, anti-Catholic prejudice, and youthful high spirits that had inspired the mobbing of Gondomar's coach a short time before could now find a more acceptable outlet.

Despite these auspicious beginnings, the war policy was a major political gamble because it required unprecedented levels of extraordinary taxation.[91] Charles had staked his honor and the security of his kingdom on active and continuing parliamentary support. The failure of that support precipitated a major constitutional crisis, which eventually undercut the war effort and set the stage for the experiment in prerogative government.

Several things account for this disastrous turn of events. Part of the blame lay with the failure of the government's ambitious military and diplomatic strategy. Charles and Buckingham attempted to place themselves at the head of an international coalition by forming an alliance with France and promising to subsidize the king of Denmark to invade Germany, while simultaneously raising an English army to recover the Palatinate and a naval force to attack the Spanish coast.[92] Within little over a year, every one of these projects had foundered. A planned Anglo-French invasion of Germany never materialized, partly because the two governments could not agree on its goals and partly because the French refused to commit themselves openly to it.[93] Englishmen conscripted for this ill-fated expedition died of disease by the thousands without reaching the theater of war. The naval assault on the Spanish coast failed to accomplish anything, the Danes were routed in November 1626, and Richelieu eventually decided to crush a Protestant rebellion at home instead of fighting Spain.

These humiliations increased parliamentary distrust of the government's competence and integrity, while also alienating some war supporters from Buckingham, who was blamed for all that had gone wrong.[94] The duke's near monopoly of Charles's favor, his engrossing of offices, and his extravagant lifestyle gave further impetus to these developments. The court had traditionally distributed offices and influence widely among competing factions, thereby widening its base of support. But Charles had allowed Buckingham a virtual monopoly of influence, thereby isolating him as a natural scapegoat when royal policies failed. By 1626, opponents of the war were making common cause with those who favored it but thought it was being mismanaged, in order to destroy the duke.

An additional complication was the king's marriage to Henrietta Maria, sister of Louis XIII. In diplomatic terms it made some sense, but a nation that had just celebrated its deliverance from a Spanish papist queen was not enthusiastic about receiving a French one. In a private agreement annexed to the marriage treaty, Charles had to promise the French to relax persecution of English Catholics, a pledge he honored sporadically as he responded by turns to pressures from Paris and the House of Commons. Diplomatic considerations were therefore working at cross purposes with the king's domestic strategy of appealing to the xenophobia and religious prejudices of his people. The fact that Buckingham's mother and father-in-law were both recusants made him especially vulnerable to suspicions that he secretly favored papists.

After 1626 the Crown's support for anti-Calvinist "Arminian" clergy like Richard Montagu and John Cosin, who were regarded by a few parliamentary leaders as secret papists, added another bone of contention.[95] The people most antagonized by Arminianism were those whose religious outlook should have made them sympathetic to the war. The main responsibility for the court's policy lay with Charles, but Buckingham and a few outspoken clergy received the blame.

Even without these obstacles, the Commons probably would not have approved the enormous taxes needed for England to become a major participant in the Thirty Years' War. Lingering suspicion of the court's motives, local resistance to the demands of the central government, and simple reluctance to pay for a distant war formed virtually insurmountable obstacles. It is undoubtedly significant that, unlike most members of Parliament, neither Charles nor Buckingham had any direct experience with local government. The anti-Spanish demonstrations they witnessed in London, and the special pleading of a few privy councillors eager for military conflict, apparently gave them an unrealistic view of the nation's willingness to sacrifice for the war effort.

When events showed how wrong this optimism was, the Crown vacillated between two policies, each advocated by a different group within the Privy Council.[96] The first of these consisted of a renewed attempt to mobilize public support by invoking the threat of foreign invasion and appealing to patriotism and anti-Spanish sentiment. By doing so, the government hoped either to render Parliament more tractable or to prepare the ground for a nonparliamentary levy. As relations with the Commons deteriorated in 1626, Charles prepared a speech warning the House that if it failed to grant him supply he would appeal to its constituents:

> If there be by this delay [in passing subsidies] a disbanding of friends and allies, a general distraction in most parts of Christendom, a disrespect of this Nation among all neighboring princes . . . I will acquit myself of it, and lay it upon you. To God, and the people whom you [re]present . . . you shall answer to all you force me to . . . and for all my loving people . . . I am confident they never loved any king better than myself.[97]

It is not clear whether the speech itself was ever delivered, but it reflects ideas that were under serious consideration. Shortly after the end of the session, the Privy Council considered a plan to assemble the freeholders of each county to hear an official justification of the king's demand for money. These ad hoc meetings were then to deliberate and vote on whether to grant the taxes Parliament had refused. The Council wisely abandoned this scheme, which would undoubtedly have resulted in another defeat, but the fact that it was even entertained suggests how desperately some councillors coveted public support.[98]

It is within the context of this policy that we should place the campaign of preaching the government initiated in 1626. Laud's chaplain, Peter Heylin, recalled later:

> When [Queen Elizabeth] had any business to bring about among the people, she used to tune the pulpits . . . to have some preachers in and about Lon-

don, and other great Auditories in the Kingdom, ready at command to cry up her design. . . . Which course was now [1626] thought fit to be followed. . . . [99]

The notorious sermons by Robert Sibthorpe and Roger Manwaring, which elevated the royal prerogative above all earthly constraints, belonged to this campaign, but so did others justifying the king's measures in different terms. William Hampton, protégé of the Earl of Nottingham, mounted the outdoor pulpit of Paul's Cross in London to deliver a "Proclamation of War from the Lord of Hosts." He recited the usual litany of atrocities committed by Spain and drew the familiar parallels between the present wars and the ancient conflict of Israel and Babylon. He used these themes, however, to chastise the English people for refusing adequate aid to their ruler: "We have a most gracious King . . . who is more careful and desirous of our safety . . . than we ourselves: his wants are great, his expenses greater. . . . O let us not discourage him by our backwardness." [101] The sermon ended with a warning that if the nation refused to supply the king it might suffer the fate of the Jews during the Babylonian captivity. The sort of Foxeian rhetoric previously used by opponents of the Spanish match was here employed to support nonparliamentary taxation.

The failure of these pleas to achieve the desired effect strengthened the advocates of the second policy, of supporting the war through arbitrary taxation. The disastrous events of 1626 and 1627 tipped the balance in favor of this approach. As Richelieu prepared to reduce the Huguenot city of La Rochelle, Buckingham embarked with an English army to aid the Protestant stronghold. According to the Tuscan ambassador, he hoped to win over the "puritan faction" with a dramatic victory. Instead he suffered the most humiliating defeat of the war. Meanwhile, in Germany, the king of Denmark, who had still not received his English subsidy, was completely routed. [102] At home, Charles presided over an almost bankrupt government, its troops ready to mutiny for lack of pay, facing threatened invasions from either or both of the continent's greatest powers. In desperation and anger, he invoked the ill-defined emergency powers of the Crown to billet troops upon English towns, levy a forced loan, and imprison gentlemen who refused to pay it.

These actions provoked profound suspicion and bitter resentment. In November 1627, London celebrated the Accession Day of Elizabeth with the usual ringing of bells and lighting of bonfires and then ignored the king's birthday less than a week later. After his defeat on the Isle of Rhé, nasty squibs began to circulate about Buckingham:

> But is the Duke come safely home again
> Triumphing o'er his conquer'd countrymen,
> As if such valiant leaders' mournful slaughter
> Were but the subject of a coward's laughter
>
> . . . .
>
> Stay, stay at Court and now at Tennis play,
> Measure French galliards, or go kill a grey.
> Venus's pavilions do become thee best
> Periwigs with helmets use not to be pressed.[103]

A picture displayed at Bartholomew Fair showed him leading an elderly naked woman and sported the caption "All you that will follow me I will take you to the naked Isle of Rhé."[104]

In 1628 Charles summoned a new Parliament, hoping to repair the damage inflicted during the previous year. The members assembled bearing complaints from all over England about violations of the law by officials acting on royal commands. After lengthy discussions, the Commons passed the Petition of Right, a document intended to vindicate the legal principles which Charles's actions had endangered.[105] So long as there seemed some hope that Charles might accept its interpretation of the law, the Commons refrained from direct attacks on Buckingham. However, the king's first, equivocal response to the petition unleashed a flood of denunciations of the duke, who was blamed for all the catastrophes of the previous three years. He was accused of endangering the military security of the realm while at the same time jeopardizing its religion and subverting its liberties. Sir John Eliot dubbed the troops being prepared for a new expedition to France "praetorian guards." Others complained that Buckingham was surrounded by "papists and atheists." Ironically Charles's wars against both the major Catholic powers of the continent ended up magnifying suspicion that his court was controlled by secret papists and bribed tools of Spain.

Tempers cooled after the king reluctantly assented to the Petition of Right, but the fears voiced during the session remained just below the surface. In 1628 Buckingham was murdered while preparing a new expedition to aid La Rochelle. The people, one courtier complained, received the news with joy, and a few daring men toasted the assassin in public taverns.[106] Charles had to inter his favorite in the middle of the night for fear of a public demonstration. The next year Charles summoned another session of Parliament, hoping that Buckingham's removal had paved the way to a reconciliation. He was again disappointed: the Commons launched a vigorous attack on Arminian clergy at court, who were accused of being Jesuit agents. Meanwhile, puritan clergy began sounding warnings even more ominous than those heard at the time of the Spanish match. In April 1629 Archbishop Abbot complained that certain "preachers do little less than seditiously divulge that religion itself doth totter and the purity of the gospel is in great hazard."[107] In 1630, when the queen gave birth to the future Charles II, reports came in of "puritans" who refused to join in on the official celebrations, saying God had already provided for the succession in the line of Elizabeth and the Elector Palatine.[108]

In these circumstances, any realistic hope of reconciliation between Crown and Parliament vanished. Without Parliament, in turn, the war effort was impossible to sustain indefinitely. By 1630, peace was concluded with both France and Spain, and eleven years of government without Parliament had begun.

The return to a neo-Elizabethan policy thus had the paradoxical outcome of producing a rupture between king and Parliament and decreasing the likelihood that England would again seek to oppose the Habsburgs by force of arms. Even after 1630 an anti-Spanish faction remained at court, but it never decisively altered Charles's policies.[109] Arminianism in the church, peace with Catholic Europe, and non-parliamentary government at home became the hallmarks of the reign. More clearly even than in James's lifetime, the tradition embodied by the *Book of Martyrs,* the exploits of Drake, Raleigh, and Essex, and the legendary harmony between Elizabeth and her parliaments stood in sharp contrast to the conduct of the royal court and the cultural imagery it used to glorify the king.

NOTES

1. For discussions of the cult of Elizabeth, see esp. Francis Yates, *Astrea* (London: Routledge, 1975), pp. 29–120; and Roy Strong, *The Cult of Elizabeth* (London: Thames and Hudson, 1977).

2. Roy Strong, *Splendor at Court* (Boston: Houghton Mifflin, 1973); Frances Yates, *French Academies of the Sixteenth Century* (London: Warburg Institute, 1947).

3. For a brief discussion, see Roy Strong, *The English Icon* (London: Routledge; New Haven: Yale University Press, 1969), p. 1. Even Hilliard was not granted a regular salary until very late in the reign, unlike earlier court miniaturists (Roy Strong, *The English Renaissance Miniature* [New York and London: Thames and Hudson, 1983], p. 69).

4. The most extensive study is Eleanor Rosenberg, *Leicester: Patron of Letters* (New York: Columbia University Press, 1955). The immense subject of Elizabethan cultural patronage still awaits its historian.

5. For a stimulating discussion of the effects of courtly habits on the development of English poetry, see Daniel Javitch, *Poetry and Courtliness in Renaissance England* (Princeton: Princeton University Press, 1978).

6. See esp. Lawrence Stone, *The Crisis of the Aristocracy* (Oxford: Oxford University Press, 1965), pp. 451–454.

7. John Nichols, *Progresses of Queen Elizabeth* (London, 1823), vol. 3, pp. 100–121.

8. Yates, *Astrea*, pp. 1–28, 88–111; John Headley, "Habsburg Empire and Ghibellinism," *Medieval and Renaissance Studies* 7 (1978): 93–127. Douglas Brooks-Davies, *The Mercurian Monarch* (Manchester: Manchester University Press, 1984), chap. 1, provides a detailed account of this and related themes in Spenser's *Faerie Queen*.

9. *Spenser: Poetical Works*, ed. J. C. Smith and E. de Selincourt (London: Oxford University Press, 1912), p. 158.

10. Nichols, *Progresses of Elizabeth*, vol. 3, p. 65.

11. The lines are from a poem by Sir Charles Fitzgeffrey entitled "Sir Francis Drake: His Honorable Lifes Commendation and His Tragicall Deathes Lamentation," quoted in Elkin K. Wilson, *England's Eliza* (Cambridge, Mass.: Harvard University Press, 1939), p. 294.

12. See esp. Strong, *English Icon*, pp. 13–20; Mark Girouard, *Robert Smythson and the Architecture of the Elizabethan Era*, 2d ed. (New Haven and London: Yale University Press, 1983), pp. 81, 97–101, 107–108, 162; and Gordon Kipling, *The Triumph of Honour* (Leiden: Leiden University Press for the Sir Thomas Browne Institute, 1977).

13. Strong, *English Renaissance Miniature*, chaps. 1–4, traces the line of descent. Kipling, *Triumph of Honour*, explores the importation of Flemish illuminators by the court of Henry VII, who established the techniques of miniature-painting in England.

14. For a discussion, see Yates, *Astrea*, pp. 88–111.

15. *Selected Poetry and Prose*, ed. David Kalstone (New York: Signet, 1970), p. 237.

16. For discussions, see Stone, *Crisis of the Aristocracy*, pp. 205, 206; and, on changing aristocratic concepts of honor, Mervyn James, *English Politics and the Concept of Honour, 1485–1642* (Past and Present Supplement, no. 3, Oxford: Oxford University Press, 1978).

17. Arthur Ferguson, *The Indian Summer of English Chivalry* (Durham, N.C.: Duke University Press, 1960), chap. 5.

18. Ibid., pp. 159–162.

19. Wilson, *England's Eliza*, p. 6.

20. The fullest treatment is William Haller, *The Elect Nation: The Meaning and Relevance of Foxe's Book of Martyrs*, (New York: Harper and Row, 1963). However, this needs to be corrected in light of Katherine Firth, *The Apocalyptic Tradition in Reformation Britain* (Cambridge: Cambridge University Press, 1979), pp. 106–109 to which the following paragraph is indebted. See also Peter Lake, "The Significance of the Elizabethan Identification of the Pope as Antichrist," *Journal of Ecclesiastical History* 31 (1980); Paul Christiansen, *Reformers in Babylon* (Toronto: University of Toronto Press, 1978); and, for a discussion more favorable to Haller's interpretation, Christopher Hill, "The First Century of the Church of England," in *Collected Essays, Volume Two: Religion and Politics in*

Seventeenth Century England (Hassocks: Harvester; Amherst: University of Massachusetts Press, 1986), esp. p. 29. This view of England was often associated with a belief in the imminence of the Apocalypse.

21. J. E. Neale, *Elizabeth I and Her Parliaments: 1559–1581* (London: Cape, 1958), p. 318. Neale probably exaggerated the importance of such confrontations, but they certainly occurred.

22. For studies of these developments in two localities, see Hassell Smith, *County and Court: Government and Politics in Norfolk, 1558–1603* (Oxford: Oxford University Press, 1974); and Peter Clark, *English Provincial Society from the Reformation to the Revolution: Politics and Society in Kent, 1500–1640* (Hassocks: Harvester, 1977), pp. 224–228, R. B. Wernham, *After the Armada* (Oxford: Oxford University Press, 1984), pp. 470–474, documents Parliament's reluctance to grant the high taxes that the government demanded in 1593.

23. For the rise of the Howards, see Linda Levy Peck, *Northampton: Patronage and Policy at the Court of James I* (London: Allen and Unwin, 1982), pp. 15–21.

24. See, e.g., his comments on the union of England and Scotland, in which the religious dimension of his commitment to peace and strong royal government comes through very clearly (*The Political Works of James I*, ed. Charles McIlwain [Cambridge, Mass.: Harvard University Press, 1965, repr. of 1918 edition], pp. 271–73). For an interesting and important discussion of the impact of James's Scottish career on his conduct of England, see Jenny Wormald, "James VI and I," *History* 68 (1983): 187–209.

25. John Nichols, *Progresses of James I* (London, 1828), vol. 1, p. 393. For a discussion, see Graham Parry, *The Golden Age Restored* (Manchester: Manchester University Press, 1981), chap. 1.

26. Roberta Brinkley, *Arthurian Legend in the Seventeenth Century* (New York: Octagon, 1967), pp. 9–10.

27. D. J. Gordon, "*Hymenai:* Ben Jonson's Masque of Union," (Berkeley and Los Angeles: University of California Press, 1980).

28. Haller, *Elect Nation*, chap. 7, esp. pp. 234–235.

29. This imagery was rooted in a Scottish tradition which James himself had helped formulate. See Arthur H. Williamson, *Scottish National Consciousness in the Age of James VI* (Edinburgh: J. Donald, 1979), chap. 2.

30. The antiquarian and chronicler John Stow blamed the discontent of "pretended gallants, young citizens, apprentices, yeomen and servingmen" who hoped to profit from privateering for London's cool reception of the peace treaty (*Annals* [London, 1631], p. 845). For a discussion of the mixture of religious and economic motives behind the "imperial" ambitions of a powerful group of Essex landowners led by the Rich earls of Warwick, see William Hunt, *The Puritan Moment* (Cambridge, Mass.: Harvard University Press, 1983), esp. pp. 161–66.

31. Spain controlled Portugal and her Eastern empire in this period, although she did not succeed in keeping the Dutch and English out of Asia. The real rivals of the English East Indian merchants were the Dutch, whose local agents murdered several Englishmen in the Amboyna massacre of 1618. But Dutch competition did not arouse the same kind of xenophobia in the popular mind as Spanish rivalry did.

32. Sir Henry Neville, quoted in Nichols, *Progresses of James I*, vol. 2, p. 50.

33. For an example of this attitude, see CSPVen., vol. 15, p. 245.

34. See e.g., Archbishop Abbot's comments in a letter to Sir Dudley Carleton at the start of the Thirty Years' War (SP, 14/109/157; July 29, 1619): "We of the religion look on when the King of Spain useth all means to strengthen his party, by seeming to seek peace through our ambassador, but sending 500 thousand crowns, as he did 400

thousand crowns not long before, to maintain the war. I am glad that the states [the Dutch] think upon some forces to be sent into Germany. We have received summons also but there is no moving here." Although the outbreak of war in Germany added to the urgency of Abbot's remarks, similar fears of the consequences of English inaction had been growing for some years before the outbreak of hostilities. It should, however, be noted that these are the sentiments of a privy councillor; pressures for a more Protestant foreign policy came from within the government as well as from external sources.

35. Chamberlain, *The Letters of John Chamberlain*, ed. N.C. McClure (Philadelphia: American Philosophical Society, 1939) vol. 1, p. 392. The preacher, a former chaplain to James's recently deceased oldest son, Henry, cited the prince's authority for this statement. His choice of St. Martin's-in-the-Field may indicate a desire to reach a *court* audience, which may have included some of the secret Catholics about whom he was complaining. For discussions of popular fears of papist conspiracies, see Carol Z. Wiener, "The Beleaguered Isle: A Study of Elizabethan and Early Jacobean Anti-Catholicism," *Past and Present* 51 (1971): 27–62; Robert Clifton, "The Popular Fear of Catholics During the English Revolution," *Past and Present* 52 (1971): 23–55; and "Fear of Popery," in *The Origins of the English Civil War*, ed. Conrad Russell (London: Macmillan, 1973), pp. 144–67. There is a need for investigation of similar anxieties among the educated and politically active. For a good example of the sort of mentality involved, see the account of Sidney's fears of the likely outcome of a marriage between Elizabeth and the French Duc d'Alençon contained in Fulke Greville's *Life of Sidney* (1870 ed.; *The Works in Verse and Prose Complete of Fulke Greville*, vol. 4, ed. Alexander Grossart [New York: AMS Press, 1966], pp. 53–64). Greville compiled this work in the reign of James I.

36. *The Autobiography of Sir Simonds d'Ewes* (London, 1845), vol. 1, p. 49.

37. See Chapter 4, below, for a more extensive discussion of the topic of distrust of courtiers.

38. See below, pp. 32–42.

39. See his comment to the 1621 Parliament: "But who shall hasten after grievances and desire to make himself popular, he hath the spirit of Satan" (J. R. Tanner, *Constitutional Documents of the Reign of James I* [Cambridge: Cambridge University Press, 1966], p. 266).

40. Nichols, *Progresses of James I*, vol. 1, p. 413.

41. *Autobiography*, vol. 2, p. 170.

42. Nicolo Molin, June 1607, in CSPVen. vol. 10, p. 513. English observers also noted James's ungracious behavior before crowds. See e.g., Nichols, *Progresses of James I*, vol. 1, pp. 188, 413; and SP, 14/2/26.

43. *Nugae Antiquae* (London, 1804), vol. 1, pp. 348–354.

44. The original Italian text of this letter and an English translation are printed in Stephen Orgel and Roy Strong, *Inigo Jones: The Theater of the Stuart Court*, 2 vols. (London: Sotheby Parke Bernet; Berkeley and Los Angeles: University of California Press, 1973), vol. 1, p. 284.

45. For a discussion, see Conrad Russell, "Parliament and the King's Finances," in *Origins of the English Civil War*, pp. 91–116.

46. Robert Ashton, "Deficit Finance in the Reign of James I," *Ec. H. R.* 10 (1957): 15–24.

47. For radically contrasting views of James I, see Wormald, "James VI and I," pp. 190–192; and D. H. Willson, *James VI and I* (London: Cape, 1956). No responsible historian today would endorse Willson's portrait without qualification. However, a careful reading of his notes will show that the traditional deprecating portrait of James is not *entirely* the product of biased and apocryphal sources. There is a fair amount of contempo-

rary evidence, some of it cited in the last two paragraphs, which shows that projecting an image of majesty was never James's strong suit. What is needed is a portrait that recognizes James's shrewdness and the genuine idealism and vision behind some of his policies without ignoring his failings. In particular, the king's skill as a behind-the-scenes intriguer and negotiator should not be allowed to obscure his shortcomings as a public figure, which even Wormald appears to acknowledge.

48. For a general discussion, see Haller, *Elect Nation*, chap. 7.

49. John Stow, *Survey of London* (1633), p. 823.

50. Roy Strong, *Henry Prince of Wales and England's Lost Renaissance* (London: Thames and Hudson, 1986) reached me too late to be taken into account in the text. See also Sir Charles Cornwallis, *A Discourse of the Most Illustrious Prince Henry* (London, 1641), pp. 11, 13; Frances Yates, *The Rosicrucian Enlightenment* (London: Routledge, 1972), chap. 1; Parry, *Golden Age Restored*, chap. 3.

51. *Poems of Michael Drayton*, ed. John Buxton (Cambridge, Mass.: Harvard University Press, 1950), vol. 2, p. 530.

52. Daniel Price, quoted in E. K. Wilson, *Prince Henry and English Literature* (Ithaca, N.Y.: Cornell University Press, 1946), pp. 91–92.

53. For two discussions, see Roy Strong, "Inigo Jones and the Revival of Chivalry," *Apollo* 86 (1967): 102–107; and Norman Council, "Ben Jonson, Inigo Jones, and the Transformation of Tudor Chivalry," *English Literary History* 47 (1980): 259–275. Council seems to give insufficient attention to the possibility that some of the ambivalence of the masque may reflect Jonson's ticklish position in having to please both the warlike Henry and the pacific James. However, his analysis is fundamental for any detailed consideration of *Prince Henry's Barriers*.

54. *Ben Jonson: The Complete Masques*, ed. Stephen Orgel (New Haven and London: Yale University Press, 1969), p. 143.

55. Ibid., p. 153.

56. Ibid., pp. 157–58.

57. Stow, *Annals* (1631 ed.), p. 992.

58. CSPVen., vol. 11, p. 507.

59. Yates, *Rosicrucian Enlightenment*, pp. 28–42.

60. The only diplomatic strategy with any hope of success was somehow to induce the king of Spain to break with his Austrian cousins and restore the Palatinate to Frederick. James did send a few English troops to Germany, and he was prepared to pressure the Habsburgs with veiled threats of war, but he insisted on keeping his diplomatic channels to Madrid open.

61. For a recent detailed account, see Roger Lockyer, *Buckingham* (London: Longman, 1981), chap. 5. The match was formally concluded when Charles capitulated to virtually all the Spanish demands in 1623, but by that time he was no longer bargaining in good faith.

62. A typical European response was that of the French diplomat the Comte de Tillieres, who commented that the journey "seemed better undertaken to give a plot to a romance than to represent the conduct of a sage prince" (Tanneguy Leveneur, Comte de Tillieres, *Memoirs inedits . . . sur la cour de Charles I* [Paris, 1862], p. 51). *The Diary of Sir Simonds D'Ewes* records the horrified reactions of one student at the Inns of Court.

63. BL, Harl. MSS 4955, fol. 70.

64. *Diary*, ed. F. S. de Beer (Oxford: Oxford University Press, 1959), vol. 1, p. 5.

65. Marvin Breslow, *A Mirror of England* (Cambridge, Mass.: Harvard University Press, 1970), chap. 3; P. G. Lake, "Constitutional Consensus and Puritan Opposition in the 1620s: Thomas Scott and the Spanish Match," *Historical Journal* 25 (1982): 805–826.

66. George Rudé, *The Crowd in History* (New York: Oxford University Press, 1964); and *Wilkes and Liberty* (Oxford: Oxford University Press, 1962); John Brewer, *Party Ideology and Popular Politics at the Accession of George III* (Cambridge: Cambridge University Press, 1976).

67. Derek Hirst, *Representative of the People?* (Cambridge: Cambridge University Press, 1975).

68. "Doth not the rage and cruelty executed upon the Germans and Bohemians . . . by long experience tell us what . . . enemies we have to deal with?" Scottish clergyman Alexander Leighton asked in *Speculum Belli Sacri* (1624), p. 182: "Namely the brats of the bloody whore. The ripping up of women . . . the bathing in the blood of inoffensive children . . . cast but your eyes upon the Spanish provision of '88 and you may see how like the base bramble Abimileth they were determined to burn the inhabitants . . . as if they would have made the torments of the English a terror to all nations." Although in many respects Leighton was not representative even of English radical opinion, these legends of Spanish cruelty were commonplace.

69. Greville's *Life of Sidney* once again anticipates these fears. In describing the Elizabethan alliance of Spain and the papacy, Greville writes: "This conjunction was not like the ancient undertakers, who made open war by proclamation; but craftily—from the infusion of Rome—[they did attempt] to enter first by invisible traffic of souls; filling people's minds with apparitions of holiness, specious rites, saints, miracles, institutions of new orders. . . . And when by these shadows they had once gotten possession of the weak, discouraged the strong, divided and doubtful . . . then to follow on with the Spanish, less spiritual, but more forcible engines, viz. practice, confederacy, faction, money . . . war" (*Works*, vol. 4, pp. 45–46). In Scott's pamphlets the Spanish have adopted the methods of subversion Greville attributes to Rome, although they have still not renounced the possibility of one day attacking England directly. It is again clear that the anxieties aroused in some minds by the Spanish match were rooted in older fears. There is probably a good book to be written on the fear of Catholic plots and Spanish and French subversion in England, from the 1570s down to the reign of James II, tracing the various forms taken by the concept of an international conspiracy against England and the role of that concept in shaping domestic political rhetoric. Caroline Hibbard, *Charles I and the Popish Plot*, (Durham: University of North Carolina Press, 1983) deals admirably with the topic on the eve of the Civil War, but does not attempt to trace it back very far into the preceding period.

70. Thomas Scott, *Vox Regis*, (1624) p. 9.

71. Thomas Scott, *Vox Coeli*, (1624) p. 53.

72. Thomas Scott, *Vox Populi*, (1620) p. 12. Cf. D'Ewes's comment (in *Autobiography*, vol. 1, pp. 182–183): "All men knew the Jesuits to be the sworn instruments of the Spanish King, and would easily bring to pass, by poison or otherwise, the abortive ends of our King and Prince, after he should once have two or three children by the Spanish lady, who then, overliving them, would be sure to train up her offspring in the Romish religion."

73. Scott, *Vox Coeli*, p. 54.

74. *Tom Tell Troth* (1622?), p. 2. The pamphlet is undated but internal evidence clearly indicates it was written in the early 1620s.

75. *Diary*, p. 135.

76. BL, Harl. MSS 389, fols. 48v and 61; Hirst, *Representative of the People?* pp. 140ff. Hirst does point out that it was uncommon for the court to become an issue before 1640, but his evidence shows that in at least a few cases candidates were discredited by suspicions concerning their religious and political affiliations. This does not prove that voters suspected the sort of conspiracy outlined in *Vox Populi*, but it does sug-

gest heightened suspicion of both courtiers and Catholics. See also Peter Clark, "Urban Opposition to the Early Stuarts," *Historical Journal* 21 (1978): 1–26.

77. *Chamberlain Letters* vol. 2, p. 382.

78. *Memoirs of Colonel John Hutchinson*, ed. J. Hutchinson, 4th ed. (London, 1822), vol. 1, p. 119.

79. See Conrad Russell, *Parliaments and English Politics, 1621–1629* (Oxford: Oxford University Press, 1979), chap. 7; and Fletcher, *The Outbreak of the Civil War*, (London, E. Arnold, 1981) pp. xxi ff., for the view that the fear of a court conspiracy which dominated the 1629 debates was the product of short-term circumstances.

80. Russell, *Parliaments and English Politics*, chap. 2, and "The Foreign Policy Debate in the Parliament of 1621," *Historical Journal* 20 (1977): 289–309.

81. See Robert Muir, *The Addled Parliament* (London: Oxford University Press, 1958), esp. chap. 10. The Earl of Southampton, an anti-Spanish privy councillor, was worried in 1624 that indiscreet members of the Commons might alienate the king and thus inadvertently help to improve Anglo-Spanish relations (Robert E. Ruigh, *The Parliament of 1624* [Cambridge, Mass.: Harvard University Press, 1971], p. 43).

82. For a recent discussion, see Kenneth Fincham and Peter Lake, "The Ecclesiastical Policy of James I," *Journal of British Studies* 24 (1985): 198–202.

83. Scott, *Vox Populi*, p. 14. This was Scott the pamphleteer, not his namesake, the radical politician from Canterbury.

84. The fullest account is still Samuel R. Gardiner, *Prince Charles and the Spanish Match*, vol. 2 (London, 1869). This should now be supplemented by Lockyer, *Buckingham*, chaps. 5 and 6.

85. *Chamberlain Letters*, vol. 2, p. 515.

86. Thomas Scott, *Vox Dei* (1623), pp. 58–59.

87. The subsidy and the fifteenth were the two traditional parliamentary taxes collected from the shires and boroughs according to schedules of payment drawn up, respectively, in the fourteenth and early sixteenth centuries. Since the amount of each was theoretically fixed (the actual yield was slowly declining), whereas prices had more than tripled in the previous century, it was necessary to grant more than one of each to provide the Crown with a sufficient sum. However, there was strong resistance to this procedure, which made it very difficult for the Crown to obtain substantial grants form Parliament.

88. Even though the Commons did everything possible to avoid committing itself to a war in Germany. The best discussion is Ruigh, *Parliament of 1624*.

89. Chamberlain Letters, August 21, 1624, vol. 2, p. 578. For a recent discussion, see Margot Heinemann, *Puritanism and Theatre* (Cambridge: Cambridge University Press, 1980), chap. 10.

90. Dispatch of November 26, 1625, in *Eleventh Report of the Royal Commission on Historical Manuscripts* (London, 1887), Appendix 4, part 1, p. 37.

91. The cost of the war was about £1,000,000 a year, nearly double the annual revenues of a government that had rarely balanced its budget in peacetime. Much of the money would in any case have to be covered by loans since, as the Council realized, there was no chance that Parliament would grant this much. In the short run the government managed to raise the necessary sums primarily on its own credit, through such expedients as pawning the crown jewels to foreign bankers. In the long run, however, sufficient loans would not be forthcoming unless the government showed an ability to increase its revenues sufficiently to secure its credit. Parliamentary subsidies were important not only in themselves but also as evidence that the Crown enjoyed the political support necessary to meet its obligations. Foreign governments too based their calculations partly on Parliament's behavior, for much the same reasons. Thus, the longer the war lasted the more important Parliament became.

92. They devised this strategy partly to placate James, who refused to consider a general war against Spain without the support of continental allies, including Catholic France. By the time James died, the alliance was in place, although the war had not yet begun. It is also likely that Charles and Buckingham believed, with considerable justification, that only a general European alliance could defeat the Habsburg block. For an illuminating discussion, see Thomas Cogswell, "Foreign Policy and Parliament: The Case of La Rochell, 1625–1626," *English Historical Review* 99 (1984): 241–267.

93. Samuel Rawson Gardiner, *A History of England under the Duke of Buckingham and Charles I, (London, 1875)* vol. 1, chap. 4. It is by no means self-evident that these efforts were doomed from the outset. Lack of cooperation from the French and the Dutch, and an unpredictable outbreak of infectious disease, crippled Mansfield's army. The Cadiz expedition made a successful landing and might have taken the city if the attack had been pressed more vigorously. Thus, with better luck and better generalship in the field, the English might have won a major victory, and this in turn would presumably have made it easier to gain supply from Parliament at home. On the other hand, there is no doubt that Charles and Buckingham gave a number of hostages to fortune in 1625. Given the uncertainties of seventeenth-century warfare and the inexperience of the English in launching major expeditions, the military failures are not particularly surprising. A more prudent king, like James I, would presumably have hedged his bets more carefully.

94. Again, this was true within the Council as well as within Parliament. The Earl of Pembroke on the Privy Council and (from 1626) Sir John Eliot in the Commons are the most prominent examples of men who supported the war but detested Buckingham. In their different ways, both contributed to the attempt to impeach him in 1626.

95. The Arminians (named after the Dutch theologian Jacobus Arminius) denied the Calvinist doctrine of double predestination and generally favored a more ornate liturgy. See below, Chapter 8, for a discussion and references.

96. On this point, see the important thesis of Richard Cust, "The Forced Loan and English Politics, 1626–1628" (University of London, 1984; also London: Oxford University Press, 1987).

97. SP, 16/27/99.

98. Cust, "Forced Loan," draws a firm distinction between the supporters of this plan, whom he regards as moderates, and the hard-liners, including both Charles and Buckingham, whom he sees as being already committed to more authoritarian measures. While there was undoubtedly some division on the Council, this strikes me as an exaggeration. It should be remembered that Charles and Buckingham began the war by trying to enlist public and parliamentary support and turned to arbitrary measures only when they believed Parliament had betrayed them. There seems to be no reason to suppose that Charles would not have welcomed a renewed partnership with Parliament or the political nation on acceptable terms. The problem was how to achieve those terms and, if they proved unattainable, how to support the war anyway.

99. Peter Heylin, *Cyprianus Anglicus: The History of the Life and Death of William Laud* (London, 1671), p. 153. For additional evidence that this campaign took place, see the comments in John Rous's *Diary from 1625 to 1642* (London, 1856), pp 6 and 8, and the instructions to Abbot on sermons to be delivered during a public fast in SP, 16/31/18.

100. William Hampton, *A Proclamation of Warre from the Lord of Hosts* (London, 1627).

101. Ibid., p. 35.

102. It was this defeat that precipitated the decision to levy the Forced Loan.

103. Rous, *Diary*, p. 22.

104. Ibid., p. 31.

105. Specifically, it declared that Englishmen could not be taxed without their con-

sent in Parliament, that troops could not be billeted upon them (except in the case of innkeepers, who had to be paid), that imprisoned individuals could not be denied bail, and that no one could be compelled to serve the king overseas.

106. Gardiner, *England Under Buckingham and Charles I* (London, 1875), vol. 2, p. 341.

107. SP 16/140/37.

108. Quentin Bone, *Henrietta Maria: Queen of the Cavaliers* (Urbana: University of Illinois Press, 1972), p. 73; Heylin, *Cyprianus Anglicus,* p. 198.

109. R. M. Smuts, "The Puritan Followers of Henrietta Maria in the 1630s," *English Historical Review* 93 (1978): 26–45.

Part Two

The Formation
of a
New Court Culture

3 THE COURT AND LONDON AS A CULTURAL ENVIRONMENT

To this point we have concentrated on forms of art, literature, and pageantry that reflected reactions to the Crown's religious and foreign policies. Yet the cultural changes occurring within the court between the 1590s and the 1630s cannot be understood simply as a response to politics. Before pursuing our analysis into the period of Charles's personal rule, we need to examine the complex transformation in the taste and outlook of the royal entourage that occurred during the preceding generation. The first step will be to reconstruct the environment in which that transformation took place.

THE COURT AND THE CAPITAL

To do this we need to determine which of the court's environments most concerns us, for in the early seventeenth century the court rarely spent the entire year in one place. Each spring, as the weather turned fair and provincial roads became passable, the royal family normally took a shrunken retinue on a progress through the home counties. For several months a settled court life virtually ceased to exist as the monarchs traveled and hunted around the countryside and most courtiers dispersed to their country estates. Only as the climate turned cold and damp did the full court reassemble in and around the Tudor palaces of

Whitehall, St. James, and Denmark House, just to the west of London.[1] In an age when most gentlemen still lived year-round in the country, courtiers had already become an amphibious aristocracy, continually migrating back and forth between the capital and their rural estates.

Until the seventeenth century the court's culture was formed in the provinces as often as in London and its environs. Most of the best Elizabethan court poets, including Sidney, Greville, and Raleigh, came from landed families and wrote verse that usually was not particularly indebted to London models. The most impressive court architecture consisted of rural prodigy houses erected by provincial craftsmen. Several of the most influential court theatricals were devised for performance during a progress, by local poets and gentlemen. Londoners like Hilliard and Lily, and London institutions like the theaters, also shaped court taste, especially toward the end of Elizabeth's reign, but urban influences were never dominant.

Under James I the situation changed. Court culture was still sometimes displayed in the country, but it was now usually created in or near the capital, or at least by men who normally resided there. The king's artists had their studios in London. Ben Jonson and most other Jacobean court poets were born and bred in the capital, as was Inigo Jones, most of whose buildings were erected in urban or suburban settings.[2] The progress entertainment became less important than the court masque, which normally occurred in the Whitehall Banqueting House.[3] More important, the new styles and tastes which most influenced the court tended to originate in London or in foreign cities. The theaters, the Inns of Court, and the examples of the Venetian aristocracy and the courts of Paris and Madrid mattered far more than any new developments in the English provinces. We will therefore concentrate on Whitehall and its surroundings, not because this was the only environment courtiers knew, but because it is where new cultural developments generally took place.

The increasingly urban tone of court culture reflected the capital's emergence in this period as a national center of landed society. Until very late in Elizabeth's reign, the court had been the only significant attraction for peers and gentry in the London area. In the Jacobean period the city's western suburbs emerged as a largely independent focal point of upper-class life. Simply by strolling a few yards outside Whitehall, courtiers found themselves in a sophisticated metropolis, full of amenities for men of their social status.

No firm social or geographic boundaries ever separated the court from other fashionable milieus in the capital, since court society was never contained within a single building or confined to a narrow coterie. Unlike Louis XIV, the early Stuarts never tried to force their attendants and ministers to take up residence within a royal palace. Every great courtier maintained his own household near Whitehall, each a miniature court in its own right which functioned as the nerve center for its owner's affinity. Within their London houses, the court nobility feasted and entertained clients, colleagues, foreign ambassadors, and the royal family itself.[4] The cost of supporting these opulent establishments often came close to bankrupting men who were among the kingdom's richest. "The first thing to be noted," Rubens commented in 1629 about the English court, "is that all the leading nobles live on a sumptuous scale and spend money lavishly, so that the majority of them are hopelessly in debt."[5] Much of the splendor of the court, and a fair proportion of expense of staffing the central government, was always borne by a few great courtiers, who tried to recoup their outlays from the licit and illicit profits of office.

The oldest and most important cluster of courtiers' and noblemen's palaces lay just to the north and east of Whitehall, along the Strand.[6] In the 1620s, the Queen, the Duke of Buckingham, the Earls of Arundel, Bedford, Salisbury, Dorset, Pembroke, and Essex, Lord Treasurer Weston, and Sir Francis Cottington all had residences in this district.[7] Others built in London itself or, more frequently, in one of the villages to its north and west. Thus Lionel Cranfield bought a mansion in Chelsea, the Earls of Northumberland maintained Sion House near Richmond, the Earl of Holland lived in Kensington, and Sir John Coke lived in Tottenham.

Mixed in among the palaces of the great were the town houses and lodgings of more ordinary courtiers. Among court artists and architects active in the 1620s and 1630s, for example, Inigo Jones, Orazio Gentileschi, Balthazsar Gerbier, and Daniel Mytens lived on or very near Strand, and Van Dyck resided in the city parish of Blackfriars, while the sculptor Le Sueur settled near Smithfield. Other royal servants found accommodations near the Inns of Court, along the city's western boundary, or to the southwest, in the streets and courtyards adjacent to

Westminster Palace and the Abbey. Court society was thus dispersed over a wide area and oriented around a number of greater and lesser centers.[8]

That society was also open to infiltration by peers and gentry with no formal connection to the king's household or government. In the Stuart capital, place-seekers always substantially outnumbered placement. Service under the Crown had long provided the chief opportunities for propertyless younger sons, peers with lands encumbered by debts, and restless spirits not content with the life of a country land-owner.[9] In every generation the Crown elevated a few such men into the ranks of the nobility, rescued others from acute financial difficulties, and appreciably augmented the incomes of several hundred landed families. The ambitious and impecunious therefore flocked to London in hopes of making their fortunes.

The main base of operations for young men embarking on this quest was the Inns of Court, conveniently located barely a mile from West-minster, where at any given time several hundred gentlemen were en-rolled.[10] Most had no higher ambition than to take the bar or return to their counties with a smattering of legal knowledge, but a substantial minority tried to use the Inns as stepping-stones to a court career, as John Donne did in the 1590s. They studied history and political theory, purchased fashionable clothes, and imitated the polished manners of court society. The more fortunate eventually won the patronage of a royal minister or favorite, but the patron normally expected years of service before seeking to gain a significant post for his protégé. Except for the select few with influential relatives, entry into the court almost always required a long and expensive apprenticeship, spent cultivating the favor of the great and haunting the antechambers of Whitehall, with no guarantee of ultimate success.

Quite apart from these marginal courtiers, a growing number of landed men made their way to London each winter to participate in what people already called "the season." They came to press lawsuits in Westminster, to visit Whitehall or simply to spend time in England's only large city. At the end of the sixteenth century, London had emerged as a fashionable gathering spot for country peers and wealthy gentlemen. Until then, virtually all great English landlords without a court office lived year-round in the country, unless a lawsuit or other business compelled them to visit the capital. And when they did come they normally left their families behind. Among most of the parish gentry, these habits did not change until well after the Civil War, but by the early seventeenth century many peers and a significant minority of the greater gentry were closing up their country houses at the first sign of cold weather and wintering in the capital. Some permanently reduced their household expenditures and the scale of their hospitality to have more money to spend in the city.[11] In all, Stone has estimated that by the 1630s, two-thirds of the peerage and several hundred gentry owned or leased London residences.[12] If we add those who lodged with relatives, at the Inns of Court, or in temporary accommodations, it seems likely that well over a thousand landed men visited the capital each year.

One measure of this trend is the dramatic increase during the early seventeenth century in the supply of luxury housing available in the London area. For the first time the city spread substantially beyond its Roman boundaries, as wealthy residents and entrepreneurs built in the region between London and Westminster.[13] In James's reign most of the growth occurred on vacant land along the Strand or in Westminster proper, although Drury Lane and St. Martin's Lane were constructed to the north as fashionable new streets.[14] The real boom began in 1629, when the Earl of Bedford obtained a license to develop Covent Garden, the pasture and orchard adjacent to his Strand palace. By 1639, a baronet, six ladies, and seventy-six gentry resided here, and more upper-class accommodations were under construction a few yards away in Lincoln's Inn Fields.[15] At the outbreak of the Civil War, the built-up area extended nearly half a mile north of the river to High Holborn and as far west as Soho. By that date the total population of the western suburbs, including Westminster, probably exceeded 40,000, making it the largest urban community in the realm aside from the City itself.[16] London's West End had sprouted up in little over a decade.

Enterprising Londoners quickly exploited the economic opportunities created by the migration of gentry to the capital. In 1620 an observer recorded the names of thirty-one inns and taverns between Scotland Yard and the far end of the Strand. A West End hotel industry had already emerged.[17] The food and beverage trades also prospered. In the 1620s the single ward of Farringdon Without, just to the east of the Inns of Court, boasted four inns, four vintners, over twenty victuallers and five professional cooks.[18] In 1619 the Venetian ambassador Busoni was especially impressed with the capital's pastry shops, its fruit and vegetable markets, and its unlimited supply of tobacconists, some of whom provided rooms where gentlemen might relax and gossip over a pipe, much as the coffeehouses would do a generation later.[19]

The capital's commerce and manufacturing were equally stimulated. In the sixteenth century, Protestant exiles from the Netherlands and France had helped establish several new luxury industries in London which now prospered under the stimulus of an expanding market. Products that had been rare luxuries in the 1580s—including silk stockings, elaborate lace collars, Venetian glasses, watches, and coaches—became relatively common by the early seventeenth century. England's expanding overseas trade supplied a growing variety of imported luxuries, notably large quantities of sugar, spices, citrus fruits, silks, wine, and tobacco. Specialized shops sold everything from imitation flowers fashioned of animal horn to trained falcons.[20] This range of luxuries and amenities may have attracted as many landed families as the court itself. For the gentry, at least, London was already the home of a consumer society boasting a quantity and variety of goods which earlier generations could not have imagined.

Between them, the court and London had thus given rise to a fashionable urban society larger and more complex than either could have supported alone. Without the presence of Whitehall and its satellite palaces, that society might never have developed, yet once established it grew rapidly and matured in ways that the Crown could never entirely control. It was not only the court and its bureaucracy that, in Trevor Roper's words, "sucked up the wealth of the whole country and poured it down on the city of [its] residence."[21] A large number of independent peers and gentlemen contributed at least as much to the capital's good fortune. At the height of the season the majority of those hanging around the king's palaces and other gathering spots of London, spending their money on city luxuries, were courtiers only in a very tenuous sense.

PATRONS AND AUDIENCES

The influx of country landowners into the capital was of immense importance to the court's cultural life. Until it occurred in the late Elizabethan period, court culture was almost entirely the product of royal and aristocratic patronage and consequently reflected the values and lifestyle of a small group of prominent men and women. In the seventeenth century this was never entirely the case. Great court patrons still sometimes decisively influenced cultural trends, especially in music and the fine arts,[22] yet the presence in London of a large and wealthy leisured elite, willing to purchase books, paintings, and theater admissions, added a vital element of diversity. Courtiers freely took advantage of London's cultural amenities, while poets and artists employed by the Crown earned additional income in the capital. Ben Jonson wrote for the stage and for patrons unconnected with the court years after he became James's unofficial laureate, while Van Dyck accepted commissions from scores of country peers and gentlemen who visited his studio while vacationing in London.[23] Without these supplementary earnings, most court poets and artists could not have supported themselves adequately.

Early Stuart court culture thus developed under the dual stimulus provided by a few very wealthy and prominent court patrons and a much wider pool of less wealthy but sometimes equally sophisticated cultural consumers. We need to pay attention to both sources of support to understand the final product.

THE PATRONAGE OF THE GREAT HOUSEHOLDS

Throughout the Tudor and early Stuart period, cultural patronage formed an essential element in the conspicuous consumption of great courtiers. Every major court household spent some money on music, art, and literature, and a few were cultural centers capable of rivaling Whitehall itself. The third Earl of Pembroke and his Herbert relatives patronized a number of poets and playwrights, including Jonson, Shakespeare, Daniel, and Donne. The Earl of Salisbury pensioned Nicholas Lanier, who later supervised the modernization of Charles's orchestras, and Inigo Jones, who probably helped design Hatfield House.[24] Ten years later Buckingham retained his own architect, supported a ducal orchestra, pensioned the Florentine artist Orazio Gentileschi, retained Robert Herrick as his chaplain, and produced his own masques. He may also have spent more remodeling York House than Charles did on the projects of Inigo Jones.[25]

Only the really great operated on this scale, but even lesser courtiers were often significant patrons. In the 1630s, Endymion Porter gathered a circle of poets around himself, to which Herrick paid a stilted tribute:

When to thy porch I come and (ravished) see
The state of poets then attending thee
Those bards and I all in a chorus sing,
We are thy prophets Porter; Thou our King,[26]

Davenant was the most successful of several poets who owed their entry into royal service chiefly to Porter's recommendation. Other important patrons included Sir Kenelm Digby, who benefited Van Dyck and Ben Jonson, and Sir Francis Cottington, who commissioned works from le Sueur and other court artists.

To put this patronage in perspective, we need to recognize that by the standards of Stuart court society most of it cost relatively little. Exceptions must be made for the prodigy houses and larger town mansions, which consumed thousands or tens of thousands of pounds, and for some of the greatest art collections amassed after 1615. If we leave these aside, however, it is clear that culture was one of the cheaper forms of conspicuous consumption in which courtiers engaged. The pensions of poets, musicians, and all but the best artists usually ranged between £20 and £60 per annum, while £10 made a handsome present even to a poet of Jonson's stature. Van Dyck's portraits sold for between £30 and £50, less than some courtiers spent for a suit of clothes. A masterpiece by Titian or Leonardo might bring a few hundred pounds. These sums were not small, but they appear almost insignificant compared with the thousands of pounds great courtiers spent annually on jewels, clothing, gambling, and lavish banquets. In this period a courtier's wardrobe might cost more to maintain than an orchestra, and a single evening of entertaining in the grand style or a few hours at cards more than a room full of art treasures and the gratitude of a dozen poets.[27]

To poets, artists, and musicians, royal and aristocratic patronage was of immense importance. It not only provided income but also conferred prestige, protection, and access to the ruling elite. One of Jonson's epigrams, "To My Muse, the Lady Digby," vividly expresses how fully he and other poets coveted these benefits:

Go, Muse, in and salute him [Sir Kenelm Digby]. Say he be
    Busy, or frown at first; when he see thee,
He will clear up his forehead: think thou bring'st
    Good Omen to him, in the note thou sing'st.
For he doth love my Verses, and will look
    Upon them (next to Spenser's noble book)

And praise them too. O! what a fame't will be?
   What reputation to my lines and me,
When he shall read them at the Treasurer's board?
   The knowing Weston, and that learned Lord
Allows them? Then what copies shall be had,
   What transcripts begg'd? how cry'd up, and how glad,
Wilt thou be, Muse, when this shall them befall!
   Being sent to one, they will be read of all. [28]

This kind of private circulation among court patrons and connoisseurs was both more gratifying and potentially more lucrative than success with the general reading public. [29] Jonson's position as author of most court masques elevated him to the pinnacle of his profession. Jones's work for the Crown raised him from the status of a master builder to that of a gentleman architect. And along with the professionals, Whitehall attracted a number of amateur poets, including John Donne, who wrote verse in their spare time as they pursued political careers. [30] The court therefore had little trouble retaining an impressive amount of talent at relatively modest cost.

It is important to realize that in this period patronage rarely entailed a relationship of complete dependence. "Court" poets and artists normally lived and worked on their own, away from the residences of their patrons. Their social and intellectual horizons extended beyond the court itself, to encompass the sophisticated and dynamic metropolis at Whitehall's doorstep.

THE CONTRIBUTIONS OF LONDON

Among the many attractions luring peers and gentry to London were a variety of cultural amenities that no provincial town could rival. Although lacking a university, the city was a center for many different forms of intellectual inquiry. Within its boundaries one could study subjects ranging from human anatomy to various ancient and modern languages, including, according to one proud citizen, "Greek and Latin. . . Hebrew, Caldean, Syriac . . . Arabic . . . Italian, Spanish, French, Dutch . . . [and] Polish." [31] The capital was also the chief home of the renaissance of the common law taking place in the 1590s and the early seventeenth century and of the closely related discipline of antiquarian research. Until 1614 the Society of Antiquaries gathered periodically in Westminster. When its meetings ceased, men interested in antiquities still gathered informally in the homes of Robert Cotton and John Selden, both of whom had amassed large private collections of books and manuscripts, which they placed at the disposal of scholars, lawyers, statesmen, and theologians.[32]

In addition, the capital boasted more preaching clergymen, expounding a wider variety of opinions, than any European city except possibly Amsterdam. Its puritan lecturers and radical congregations were notorious among conservatives, but it was also the home of Lancelot Andrewes, John Donne, Archbishop Laud, and other "high church" divines, while in the embassies of France, Spain, and Venice an Englishman could witness the Mass and perhaps talk to a Catholic missionary.[33] In an age that treated the sermon both as a major literary form and as a demanding intellectual exercise, this abundance of clergy represented a tremendous cultural resource.

Even more impressive were the achievements in the fields of poetry and drama. Throughout the last decades of the sixteenth century, the capital boasted a number of amateur poets who wrote verse in their spare time as they pursued careers in the law, the church, or the service of the Crown. Some, like Fulke Greville and Raleigh, belonged to the court. Increasingly after about 1590, however, the most gifted tended to come from the Inns of Court, which had developed a surprisingly mature literary subculture. Campion, Donne, Marston, Ford, and Beaumont were all at one time or another enrolled in one of these legal academies.[34] It was here, more than at the royal court, that new fashions in poetry and new intellectual trends most often developed.[35]

By the end of the sixteenth century, London also supported a number of professional men of letters. A few of these, like Thomas Nashe and Michael Drayton, survived largely on royalties from their publications. A much more significant source of income, however, was the stage.

James Burbage built the first London theater in 1576, to provide a permanent home for a company of players that had previously wandered from town to town, performing in inns and courtyards. Others soon imitated his venture, so that by the late 1590s London boasted several repertory companies, each performing as often as six days a week throughout the year, except during Lent and in times of plague.[36] The actors required a steady supply of new plays, for which they paid up to £10 each in the sixteenth century, and as much as £20 by the 1610s. At this rate a man who turned out two dramas a year could earn a respectable income. Shakespeare, who wrote, acted, and invested in a leading company, retired as a gentleman.

The acting companies quickly attracted an upper-class clientele, as the government of London found to its chagrin when its constables raided a theater in 1600 and turned up "not only . . . gentlemen and servingmen, but lawyers, clerks, country men that have law cases, the Queen's men [courtiers], knights and, as it was credibly reported, one earl."[37] In the late 1580s a group of entrepreneurs, including playwright John Lyly, tried to profit from this fashionable audience by converting a boys' choir into an acting company, opening an indoor theater, and staging plays designed to please people of courtly taste. The experiment eventually failed, but at the turn of the century two new boys' companies commenced operations at theaters near the Inns of Court. They charged several times the admission price of the more public theaters across the river in Southwark and could therefore hope to turn a profit from comparatively small, select audiences.[38]

After some initial difficulties these private theaters, as they were called, began to prosper. In 1608 the descendant of Burbage's company, to which Shakespeare belonged, bought the indoor Blackfriars Theater to increase its wealthy clientele. The boys' companies soon folded as their success attracted competition from more accomplished, adult actors. In 1618 a Venetian observer remarked upon the elegance of London playgoers: "There are theatrical performances throughout the year in various parts of the city, and these are always frequented by many people devoted to pleasure who, for the most part, dress grandly and colorfully, so that they appear . . . more than princes."[39] Under Charles, the Crown had to take steps to alleviate the jams of aristocratic coaches clogging the entire Blackfriars district whenever a new play opened.[40]

Although the private companies enjoyed the protection of the Crown and regularly performed at court, most of their income came from other sources. They probably drew their largest clientele from the Inns of Court, but they also attracted gentry visiting the city, merchants and professional men, and even a few shopkeepers and artisans aping the habits of the elite. The indoor theaters prospered because play-going had become as much a part of the London scene as fashionable clothes and political gossip. The dramatists who wrote for them had to please a well-to-do but large and heterogeneous public with assertive tastes.[41]

Nondramatic verse remained partly sheltered from this intense public scrutiny, since poems often continued to circulate only in manuscript. Yet in this sphere too the emergence of a relatively large upper-class reading public in London proved to be of decisive importance. Even when they were not published until years after their composition, as in the case of most of Donne's works, poems were often widely copied and imitated by students at the Inns of Court, courtiers, dramatists, and self-proclaimed wits. A literary and intellectual community had grown up, broader and more open than the circles that had gathered in the 1570s and 1580s around patrons like the Countess of Pembroke and Sir Philip Sidney.

From that community the court recruited most of its poets and writers, so that by the early seventeenth century the best court literature was usually produced either by professionals, like Jonson and Chapman, or by marginal courtiers, like Donne. As a result court verse rapidly incorporated the stylistic innovations pioneered at the Inns of Court and in the theaters, just as the work of Inns of Court poets and professional dramatists was frequently shaped by the desire to attract court patronage. These conditions fostered a continuous cross-fertilization between courtly and urban forms, which goes far to account for the vitality of Jacobean culture. Jonson's masques, with their vigorous comic interludes and fluent dialogue, could only have been written by a man who had served an apprenticeship in the theaters. Conversely, the theater companies could not have survived without the protection of the Crown and, in some cases, the business created by the large consumer society which the court helped to create.

THE COURT, THE CITY, AND THE PROVINCES

The early Stuart court is still frequently depicted as a narrow and isolated society increasingly out-of-touch with the rest of England. It should by now be evident that this picture is profoundly misleading. In seventeenth-century England a radical division between court, city, and country was impossible, if only because all three constantly met and interpenetrated in London's western suburbs. Far from being isolated, Whitehall was a magnet for hundreds of ambitious and curious landowners and thousands of tradesmen and entrepreneurs eager to profit from the nation's biggest consumer market. Every winter its corridors filled with the king's uninvited guests. By the 1630s, Whitehall was slowly being engulfed by the capital's fashionable West End. In many respects it was the least isolated environment in the British Isles, the only truly national and international center of landed society in an age when most activities took place on a local level.

The culture developing within this environment was a highly eclectic one in which urban and courtly, native and foreign elements freely combined. The court elite had no scruples about patronizing talented men of plebian background, like Inigo Jones and Ben Jonson, or adapting a public tradition, like that of the theater, to its own purposes. In the Jacobean period it also failed to define any clear stylistic preferences. Individual patrons had pronounced tastes, but collectively the court patronized a surprisingly wide range of styles, as diverse as those of Larkin and Mytens, Audley End and the Banqueting House, or the epics of Michael Drayton and the odes of Ben Jonson. Thus Jacobean court culture was neither very cohesive nor sharply differentiated from that of the most sophisticated and cosmopolitan segments of the landed elite.

This does not mean that on some level we cannot draw a valid contrast between the court's culture and the cultures of provincial England. The point is simply that it will be a contrast like that between the ends of a continuum rather than between two radically separate categories. Despite all the contacts that existed between courtiers and some provincial landowners, the court and its neighborhood formed a unique environment within the British Isles. As a center of wealth, power, and conspicuous consumption, Whitehall had no rivals, just as London had none as a market for luxury goods and sophisticated cultural amenities. Equally important, nowhere else could a well-educated gentleman enjoy the company of as many of his social and intellectual equals. The capital offered a kind of variety and stimulation available nowhere else. One contemporary cataloged its attractions: "witty, learned, noble and pleasant discourses all day . . . variety of wits . . . delicate wines and rare fruits, with excellent music and admirable voices, masques, and plays, dancing and riding, diversity of games . . . poems, histories and strange inventions of wit . . . rich apparel, precious jewels . . . royal buildings and rare architecture."[42] Many of these things were unavailable in the countryside; others could be procured only with difficulty. Thus the very openness and diversity of court society contributed to its distinctive ambience.

As the court grew more firmly rooted in London, the bonds tying it to provincial landed society slowly weakened. Elizabeth's court functioned as the greatest member of a federation of great households whose influence crisscrossed the realm in a dense network of personal bonds. The queen's massive progresses and the retinues of provincial gentry maintained by her servants bridged the gap between the court and the elites of at least the southern counties. The prodigy houses, the Accession Day jousts, and the poetry of Sidney and Spenser were all products of an aristocratic society oriented around great, peripatetic households which ruled over a kingdom that remained agrarian and half-medieval in character.[43]

A generation after Elizabeth's death, much of this system still survived, for example, in the affinities that court aristocrats like the Earls of Pembroke and Newcastle still maintained among the gentry of their native counties. Nevertheless, as royal progresses declined in size, absentee estate-management developed and the coach facilitated travel, courtiers found themselves under less pressure to establish bases of influence outside the capital. Slowly but surely, most began to spend less money constructing prodigy houses, dispensing lavish hospitality, and retaining indentured followers in the provinces, and more on the luxuries of city life. It is symptomatic of changing attitudes that Audley End, completed in 1616, was the last major country palace erected by a courtier until after the Restoration. Already in the early 1620s, Cranfield made do with a relatively modest country seat purchased secondhand, investing instead in a surburban residence in Chelsea.[44] Buckingham lavished most of his architectural patronage on the Strand palace of York House. Anthony Fletcher has shown how, in Stuart Sussex, several leading families slowly lost their predominance within the local gentry community because the court distracted them from the county's affairs.[45]

To some extent these developments were offset by the growing impact of the court and capital on country districts. The sale of London products in provincial towns, the dissemination of London news, and the eyewitness accounts of gentry returning from London vacations all helped to spread urban and courtly manners deep into the provinces. It would be a mistake, however, to exaggerate the importance of such contacts in overcoming the cultural distance separating Whitehall from most country manor houses. Even in the eighteenth century, when the capital's influence was far greater than in the early Stuart period, many

English gentry remained stubbornly loyal to a rustic lifestyle and deeply suspicious of the court and the city.[46] In the early seventeenth century, hostility was probably less pervasive than ignorance and indifference. A few score Caroline provincial gentry patronized Van Dyck; several hundred may have regularly visited the capital and assimilated its manners.[47] Yet the vast majority still had little direct experience of urban life, and to all appearances little appreciation for the court's cultural innovations.[48] The styles of Inigo Jones and Van Dyck, for example, were not widely imitated in the provinces even in the 1630s. Much inevitably depended on the taste and intellectual energy of individual gentry, so that broad generalizations need to be treated with caution. None of the county studies published to date, however, has made out a case for the widespread dissemination of courtly and urban styles among more than a tiny minority of the landed elite. Most of the parish gentry, especially, appear to have remained immersed in the affairs of their neighborhoods and their estates. They must often have regarded the court as a distant and exotic place.

To speak of a simple dichotomy between court and country is therefore to oversimplify a more subtle and complex process of cultural differentiation. Central to that process was the emergence of a new, metropolitan pattern of upper-class life within a predominantly agricultural society whose elite had never previously shown much attraction to cities. That pattern began to emerge in the Tudor period and continued to develop until long after the Restoration. It affected a minority of England's greater country landowners as well as courtiers. But it was at court, between the last years of Elizabeth and the reign of Charles I, that it evolved most rapidly. The Stuart court's love of the theater, its cosmopolitan outlook, and its fascination for Italian and Spanish aristocratic cultures need to be seen against this backdrop. These tastes were symptomatic of a slow but fundamental change in the nature of court society, as it became more firmly anchored in a great European capital.

NOTES

1. The last is the name normally given in this period to Somerset House, the great Strand palace of Lord Protector Somerset, which was erected in the 1540s. It was assigned to both Anne of Denmark (hence the new name) and Henrietta Maria while the king alternated between the other two (except when St. James was occupied by Henry or

Charles as Prince of Wales). There is no full-scale modern study on the court as an institution. Much can be gleaned, however, from Gerald Aylmer, *The King's Servants* (London: Routledge, 1961), and, on the ceremonial side of court life, from Per Palme, *The Triumph of Peace* (Stockholm: Almquist and Wiksell, 1956). See also G. R. Elton, "Tudor Government: The Points of Contact, The Court," in *Transactions of the Royal Historical Society:* 26 (1976): 211–228; and Lawrence Stone, *The Crisis of the Aristocracy* (Oxford: Oxford University Press, 1965), chap. 7.

2. Below, pp. 61–64. Donne and Davenant, to name but the most obvious additional examples, were born and raised in or near London, and although Donne lived much of his life in the country, his style was formed at the Inns of Court. It is significant that none of the major court poets of the Jacobean period came from an established country family, as Wyatt, Sidney, and Greville had in the previous century. (Lord Herbert of Cherbury was not really a court poet, since he was rarely in residence near Whitehall and never was an intimate of the king.) In the Caroline period we again meet with gentlemen poets at court, such as Thomas Carew and Sir John Suckling, but they worked within a tradition set by Jonson, Donne, and other Jacobeans based in London.

3. And even those first performed in the country, like *The Gypsies Metamorphosed,* were often composed by Jonson or some other London poet. The point is not simply that the masques took place at Whitehall; it is that the court was no longer absorbing theatrical forms and images created by provincial amateurs. For example, there is no Jacobean counterpart to Sir Henry Lee's invention of the Accession Day joust.

4. There are many examples of courtiers entertaining the monarchs. See, e.g., Chamberlain's report to Carleton on November 21, 1623 *Letters of John Chamberlain,* ed. N. E. McClure, Philadelphia, *American Philosophical Society,* 1939 (Chamberlain, vol. 2, p. 527): "The great feast [was] held at York House on Tuesday night. The King, Prince and Spanish ambassadors were all present. . . . I hear . . . of superabundant plenty when twelve pheasants were piled in a dish." In 1628 the duke's architect, Balthazar Gerbier, entertained the king and queen at an estimated cost of £1,000 (*The Court and Times of Charles I,* ed. Thomas Birch [London, 1849], vol. 1, p. 321).

5. *Letters of Peter Paul Rubens,* ed. Ruth Magurn (Cambridge, Mass.: Harvard University Press, 1955), p. 314.

6. Stone, *Crisis of the Aristocracy,* p. 395.

7. The names of the more affluent residents of the Strand and adjacent areas can be most conveniently found among the overseers' accounts for the parishes of St. Martin's-in-the-Fields, St. Clement Danes, and St. Mary le Strand in the Westminster Public Library (F330–367, B19–24, and G2). No fewer than 31 peers (including several ladies and one duchess) are listed as paying rates at some date between 1629 and 1633 in the parish of St. Martin's-in-the-Fields alone. Most of these would have lived within fifty yards of the Strand.

8. For Jones and Mytens, see the overseers' accounts of St. Martin's-in-the-Fields; for le Sueur, see Henry Peacham, *The Complete Gentleman* (London, 1634), p. 108; for Gentileschi, see below, Chapter 6. Leases to courtiers of Westminster tenements owned by the dean and chapter of St. Peter's are preserved in the Westminster Abbey Muniments Room (e.g., 18113–18116, 18120–18123).

9. See esp. Wallace MacCaffrey, "Place and Patronage in Elizabethan Politics," in *Elizabethan Government and Society,* ed. S. T. Bindoff et al. (London: University of London, Athlone Press, 1961), pp. 99–108.

10. For a general treatment, see William Prest, *The Inns of Court, 1590–1640* (London: Longman, 1972). The opening chapters of Philip Finkelpearl, *John Marston of the*

Middle Temple (Cambridge, Mass.: Harvard University Press, 1969), are valuable on the cultural ambience of the Inns of Court.

11. The best accounts are Stone, *Crisis of the Aristocracy*, pp. 384–398; and F. J. Fisher, "The Development of London as a Center of Conspicuous Consumption in the Sixteenth and Seventeenth Centuries," *Transactions of the Royal Historical Society*, 4th series, vol. 30 (1948): 37–50.

12. Stone, *Crisis of the Aristocracy*, p. 397. There is at present no reliable modern survey, although one could probably be compiled from surviving parish and other records, notably the returns of peers and gentry lodging in the suburbs in the Bodleian Library (Oxford) Bankes MSS. Until one is compiled, estimates of the number of gentry lodging in the capital must be treated with caution.

13. The almost simultaneous development of the eastern suburbs does not concern us, as these did not attract courtiers or gentry. There were a few landed residents of the somewhat smaller northern suburbs, such as Clerkenwell, which in 1637 housed the Earls of Exeter and Newcastle (SP, 16/357/92). The westward expansion of London is vividly revealed by a comparison of Braun and Hogenberg's topographical map of 1572 and Hollar's of ca. 1660, both reprinted in F. J. Fisher, *A Collection of Early Maps of London, 1553–1667* (Lympne Castle, Kent: Harry Margary in association with the Guildhall Library of London, 1981). For printed discussions, see N. G. Brett-James, *The Growth of Stuart London* (London: Allen and Unwin, 1935); and Lawrence Stone, "The Residential Development of the West End of London in the Seventeenth Century," in *After the Reformation: Essays in Honor of J. H. Hexter*, ed. Barbara C. Malament (Philadelphia: University of Pennsylvania Press, 1980), pp. 167–212. Both are concerned primarily with the latter half of the century but are useful on the pre-war period. This richly documented topic is still far from being exhausted.

14. There was also sporadic development elsewhere, notably along High Holborn and to the north toward Bloomsbury, which already had a few residents by 1623 (as is proven by the assessor's list for rebuilding St. Giles'-in-the-Fields Church in that year preserved in the Camden Borough Library).

15. Alnwick Castle MSS, YIII/2/4 envelope 10; SP, 16/402/75.

16. The state of construction around 1650 is richly documented in the surveys compiled by Parliament of land confiscated from the Crown, which was the ground landlord for most of the western suburbs. See PRO E317 Middlesex (various) and BL, Add. MSS 22060. A 1635 survey of Covent Garden, the one large area of which the Crown was not ground landlord, is preserved in the Greater London Record Office, E/BER/CG/E4/1. There is no good study of population trends specifically in this area, although Roger Finlay, *Population and Metropolis* (Cambridge and New York: Cambridge University Press, 1981), provides a useful perspective. The parish register of St. Margaret's Westminster shows 400–500 baptisms a year in the 1630s. St. Martin's-in-the-Fields registered about 350–400 baptisms annually in the same period. If we assume a birth rate between 30 and 35 per 1000 this indicates a population of roughly 12,000–15,000 for St. Margaret's parish and 10,000–12,000 for St. Martin's. Adding St. Clement Danes, St. Mary le Strand, and St. Giles'-in-the-Fields would almost certainly bring the total up to or above 40,000. This is, of course, intended as no more than a very rough figure, which needs to be refined by more rigorous demographic analysis.

17. BL, Harl. MSS 6850, fols. 31–32.

18. Guildhall MSS 30181. The cooks ran catering establishments.

19. CSPVen. vol. 15, pp. 101, 102.

20. Ibid., pp. 102, 257. See the 1633 edition of John Stow's *Annals* (e.g., 1631 ed.

pp. 869, 1039–1041) for an interesting contemporary discussion of the development of the manufacturing and retailing of luxury consumer goods in the capital, ca. 1560–1620. For a recent scholarly analysis, see Joan Thirsk, *Economic Policy and Projects: The Development of a Consumer Society in Early Modern England* (Oxford: Oxford University Press, 1978).

21. Hugh Trevor-Roper, "The General Crisis of the Seventeenth Century," in Trevor Aston, *Crisis in Europe, 1550–1660* (London: Routledge, 1965), p. 75.

22. Below, Chapter 5.

23. The only major figure whose services appear to have been virtually monopolized by the Crown was Inigo Jones, in the 1620s and 1630s.

24. Lawrence Stone, *Family and Fortune* (Oxford: Oxford University Press, 1973) pp. 79–81.

25. Below, Chapter 5.

26. *Poems of Robert Herrick,* ed. L. C. Martin (Oxford: Oxford University Press, 1965), p. 324.

27. Thus the £1,500 a year Buckingham spent on his wardrobe was nearly as much as the £1,900 pounds Charles I spent on the royal orchestra (see above, and below, Chapter 5).

28. *Works of Ben Jonson,* ed. C. H. Herford and Percy and Evelyn Simpson, 11 vols. (Oxford: Oxford University Press, 1925–1953), vol. 8, pp. 262–263 (hereafter cited as H & S).

29. Patricia Thompson, "The Stigma of Print: A Note on the Social Bases of Tudor Poetry," *Essays in Criticism* 1 (1951): 139–164.

30. For an interesting case study, see Arthur F. Marotti, "John Donne and Patronage," in *Patronage in the Renaissance,* ed. Guy Lytle and Stephen Orgel (Princeton: Princeton University Press, 1981), pp. 207–234.

31. George Buc, "The Third University of England," appended to Stowe, *Annals* (1631).

32. On the antiquarians, see esp. F. J. Levy, *Tudor Historical Thought* (San Marino: Huntington Library, 1967), chap. 4; and Kevin Sharpe, *Sir Robert Cotton* (Oxford: Oxford University Press, 1979).

33. Doing so was illegal, but it happened anyway.

34. Finkelpearl, *Marston,* chap. 2.

35. Although they often spread quickly to Whitehall. Most of Donne's *Songs and Sonnets* and some of his satires, e.g., were written at the Inns of Court, but soon began to circulate in manuscript among his courtier friends. Since the Inns were a training ground for future courtiers, it makes sense that court styles often developed there, and it is sometimes difficult to draw a firm boundary between court poets and Inns of Court poets.

36. Alfred Harbage, "Copper into Gold" in *English Renaissance Drama,* ed. B. Henning et al. (Carbondale, Ill.: University of Southern Illinois Press, 1976), pp. 1–14, is a concise summary.

37. Quoted in Andrew Gurr, *The Shakespearean Stage* (Cambridge: Cambridge University Press, 1970) p. 141.

38. Ibid., p. 142. The classic discussion of this topic is Alfred Harbage, *Shakespeare and the Rival Tradition* (London: Macmillan, 1952), Harbage's account of the early theatrical audience needs to be qualified by Ann Jennalie Cook, *The Privileged Playgoers of Shakespeare's London* (Princeton: Princeton University Press, 1981). The "popular" nature of Elizabethan audiences appears to have been greatly exaggerated by Harbage, although I did not find all of Cook's arguments entirely convincing. The distinction Cook draws between a narrow, privileged gentry elite and an unprivileged majority too busy

working and surviving to attend the theater is not sufficiently subtle for London, with its prosperous shopkeepers, small merchants and tradesmen, and artisans from gentry families. Until we have more and better studies of the social history of the capital, the issue will be difficult to resolve. See, however, the trenchant criticism of Cook's conclusions in Martin Butler, *Theatre and Crisis, 1632–1642* (Cambridge: Cambridge University Press, 1984), Appendix 2. Also useful is W. A. Armstrong, "The Audience of the Elizabethan Private Theaters," *Review of English Studies,* n.s. 10 (1959): 234–249. It is abundantly clear from recent research that the relatively wealthy and "privileged" play-going population must have numbered in the thousands and may have exceeded ten thousand. Harbage's description of the indoor houses as "coterie theaters" is very misleading. Nevertheless, the distinction between the two types of theaters remains legitimate and important, provided it is not exaggerated.

39. Dispatch of Orazio Busoni of January 24, 1618, printed in Stephen Orgel and Roy Strong, *Inigo Jones: The Theater of the Stuart Court,* 2 vols. (London: Sotheby Parke Bernet; Berkeley and Los Angeles: University of California Press, 1973), vol. 1, p. 281.

40. SP 16/205/32.

41. As the playwrights often complained. See, e.g., Davenant's prologue to *The Platonic Lovers* (*Dramatic Works* [London, 1872], vol. 18, pp. 12, 13):

. . . you are grown excessive proud
For ten times more of wit than was allowed
Your silly ancestors in twenty year
Y'expect should be given you here.

.   .   .   .
They would expect a jig or target fight,
A furious tale of Troy, which they ne'er thought
Was weakly written, so 'twere strongly sought

.   .   .   .
And such had you been too . . . had not
The poets taught you how t'unweave the plot
And track the winding scenes, taught you to admit
What was true sense, not what did sound like wit
Thus they have armed you 'gainst themselves to fight.

Since writing this paragraph, I came across the much longer and very valuable account in Butler, *Theatre and Crisis,* chap. 6, which reaches similar conclusions about the theater audience. However, Butler persists in distinguishing the heterogeneous theatrical audiences, which he associates with the "parliamentary classes" (p. 100) from "the hothouse atmosphere of the court" (p. 129). His own analysis tends to show how grossly oversimplified this dichotomy is. The court, even more than the Long Parliament, drew its members from precisely the same groups that attended the theater; in this context, at least, the distinction between court and parliamentary gentry is highly artificial.

42. Nicholas Breton, *The Court and the Country* (London, 1618), reprinted in *Inedited Tracts* (Roxburghe Library, 1868), p. 178.

43. As foreigners often noted, e.g., a Venetian ambassador in 1607: "The nobles, as in France and Germany, reside almost entirely in the country" (CSPVen. vol. 10, p. 503). The resort of the gentry to London was blamed, by James I among others, on foreign influences: "As we imitate the French fashion, in fashion of clothes . . . so have we got up the Italian fashion, in living miserably in our houses and dwelling in the city: but let us in God's name leave these idle foreign toys, and keep the old fashion of England: for it was wont to be the honor and reputation of the English nobility to live in the country" (*The Political Works of James I,* ed. James McIlwain [Cambridge, Mass.: Harvard University Press, 1918], p. 343).

44. Stone, *Crisis of the Aristocracy*, pp. 552, 553; Menna Prestwich, *Cranfield: Politics and Patronage Under the Stuarts*, (Oxford: Oxford University Press, 1966) pp. 266, 381–84.

45. Anthony Fletcher, *A County Community in Peace and War: Sussex, 1600–1660* (London: Longman, 1975), pp. 22–25.

46. Isaac Kramnick, *Bollingbroke and His Circle: The Politics of Nostalgia in the Age of Walpole* (Cambridge, Mass.: Harvard University Press, 1968), esp. chaps. 2, 3, and 8.

47. For a good example, see Fletcher's discussion of Sir Thomas Pelham's addiction to the metropolis in *County Community: Sussex*, pp. 43–44. It should be noted, however, that Pelham had married into the family of Sir Henry Vane the elder, one of Charles's secretaries of state.

48. See Sir John Summerson, *Architecture in Britain* (Harmondsworth: Penguin, 1953), chap. 10; and Roy Strong and Oliver Millar, *The Age of Charles I* (London: Tate Gallery, 1972), p. 89. Allen Everitt has argued that "probably three out of four" of the gentry never visited London ("The County Community," in *The English Revolution, 1600–1660*, ed. E. W. Ives [New York: Barnes and Noble, 1968], p. 49). And of course by no means all visitors would have assimilated much court culture. Butler, *Theatre and Crisis*, pp. 294–299, has some sensible things to say on this topic.

4 CLASSICAL CULTURE AND MORAL REFORM

THE IMAGE OF THE COURT

The distinctive ambience of the royal court and the society orbiting around it did not escape the notice of contemporaries. The contrast between courtly sophistication and simple country manners was already a commonplace in our period. Some observers praised the elegance and refinement of life in the capital, compared with what Donne once called "the barbarousness and insipid dullness of the country."[1] Thus Suckling bragged about Caroline London:

> There you shall find the wit and wine,
> Flowing alike and both divine,
> Dishes with names not known in books,
> And less amongst the college cooks,
> With sauce so subtle that you need
> Not wait till hunger bids you feed,
> The sweat of noble Jonson's brain,
> And gentle Shakespeare's easier strain,
>
> . . . .
> Then think what company's designed
> To meet you here, men so refin'd,
> Their very common talk at board,
> Makes wise, or made a young count-lord.[2]

More often, however, the countryside was associated with virtue and happiness while the court was denounced as a "market of noise and novelties," characterized by servility, hypocrisy, ambition, and extravagance:

> The Court is fraught with bribery, with hate,
> With envy, lust, ambition, and debate;
> With fawnings, with fantastic imitation,
> With shameful sloth, and base dissimulation.[3]

Such criticism has provided a rich mine for scholars intent on discovering ideological origins for the "English Revolution." It has often been taken as evidence of "cultural and moral alienation," paralleling the "growing political alienation of the 'court' from the 'country.'"[4] Poets and playwrights who satirized the court, like Michael Drayton and Thomas Middleton, have figured in recent monographs as representatives of an oppositionist country literary tradition, whereas court literature has been stigmatized as decadent and obsequious.[5] The contrast between "court" and "country" manners thus appears to become one aspect of a prerevolutionary crisis.

The moment we examine the evidence carefully, however, this outwardly plausible interpretation runs into difficulties. To begin with, contemporaries did not always associate the court with ardent royalism and the country with opposition. On the contrary, they sometimes regarded the courtier as a seditious malcontent, and the rural squire as a man who instinctively reverenced his king. "Let me tell you," the country spokesmen in Nicholas Breton's tract, *The Court and the Country*, exclaims, "though we see not our Sovereign every day, yet we pray for him every hour; and holding ourselves unworthy of his presence, are glad when we may get a sight of his Majesty."[6]

Further, attacks on court vices were by no means the monopoly of puritans, country squires, "bourgeois" playwrights, and others who might have formed an embryonic opposition. They also occur repeatedly in drama written for the private theaters, in verse by aspiring courtiers like Donne and court poets like Jonson, in the prose works of royal servants such as Sir Henry Wotton and the Earl of Strafford, and even in a few court masques.[7] Far from being the hallmark of a "country" movement, complaints against the court and the city were a prominent motif in court culture itself. They bear witness not to alienated provincial opposition but to the ambivalence felt by men caught up in the scramble for place and power at Whitehall.

This statement will appear paradoxical only if we insist on seeing the conflict of court and country as one separating two antagonistic groups, instead of recognizing that it was frequently fought out within the minds of individuals.[8] Most courtiers came from landed families, and many retained strong ties with their native counties. The contrast between courtly and provincial lifestyles was one they appreciated from personal experience. Moreover, the growing size and complexity of the court and upper-class London was not the result of deliberate government policy. On the contrary, few people objected more strenuously to the influx of gentry into London than James I and Charles I. The notion that courtiers, from the king on down, should sometimes have criticized their own milieu while extolling the allegedly simpler and more virtuous habits of the country is therefore less remarkable than it might at first seem. Such criticism is of prime importance, however, if we are to understand the court's cultural outlook.

SOCIAL AND ECONOMIC COMPLAINTS

Perhaps the most common charge leveled against the court and the city was the claim that they undermined the traditions of a paternalistic landed society. As gentry flocked to London and plunged headlong into its expensive pleasures, they abandoned the duties of keeping hospitality, dispensing charity, and maintaining order in their home shires. The provinces thus found themselves stripped of their natural leaders, while the poor were deprived of work and the kingdom's economy was dislocated by the flow of wealth to the capital. One observer argued:

> As for retailers . . . and handicraftsmen, it is no marvel if they abandon Country Towns and resort to London: for not only the Court, which nowadays is much greater and more gallant than it was in former times . . . is for the most part either abiding in London, or near unto it . . . but also . . . the Gentlemen of all shires do fly, and flock to the City, the younger sort of them to see and show vanity, and the elder to save the cost . . . of hospitality and housekeeping.[9]

With the benefit of hindsight we can see the growth of the court and London as a vital stimulus to economic growth which encouraged the expansion of England's overseas commerce and the creation of a more highly integrated domestic market. Contemporaries generally took a much less optimistic view.[10] The capital's consumer society offended moral prejudices against vanity and luxury, while also raising fears about rural unemployment and the loss of bullion to pay for imports.[11]

These anxieties were reinforced by cyclical concepts of history inherited from classical and Renaissance sources, which suggested that excessive prosperity will tend to corrupt a society and bring about its downfall. Stuart intellectuals therefore frequently regarded luxury and ostentation as ominous signs that England had passed her zenith and was slowly succumbing to the diseases peculiar to mature societies. "The excess of feasts and apparel are the notes of a sick state," wrote Ben Jonson, in a society notorious for both.[12] The fear became more pointed when contemporary vices seemed to resemble those associated by classical sources with the corruption of the dying republic or the decadent empire of Nero, Tiberius, and Caligula. The diatribes against Roman vices Jonson paraphrased in *Catiline*, for example, had a very topical flavor:

> Her [Rome's] women wear
> The spoils of nations in an ear
> Changed for the treasure of a shell;
> And in their loose attires, do swell
> More light than sails, when all winds play:
> Yet, are the men more loose than they!
> . . . .
> Hence comes that wild, and vast expense
> That hath enforced Rome's virtue thence
> Which simple poverty first made:
> And now, ambition doth invade
> Her state, with eating avarice,
> Riot and every other vice.
> Decrees are bought and laws are sold
> Honors and offices for gold. . . . [13]

With its gargantuan banquets, sex scandals, public sales of titles, and venal officers, the Jacobean court provided parallels to every one of these abuses, as Jonson's spectators would have recognized.

THE CORROSIVE EFFECTS OF AMBITION AND POWER

Along with the temptations of London's consumer society, a courtier had to contend with pressures generated by intense competition for places and promotion. At all costs he had to please, even if this meant disguising his feelings, bending his principles, and molding his personality to suit others.[14] "The rising unto place is laborious," wrote Bacon, "and it is sometimes base; and by indignities men come to dignities."[15] Such subservience took a heavy emotional toll on the proud, ambitious individuals the court attracted. Even the most successful had to live with what John Chamberlain called "the court fever of hope and fear that continuously torments those that depend upon great men and their promises."[16] Many frittered away their best years in a round of false hopes and endless frustrations, such as Spenser characterized in "Mother Hubbard's Tales":[17]

> To lose good days that might be better spent;
> To waste long nights in pensive discontent;
> To speed today, to be put back tomorrow;
> To feed on hope, to pine on fear and sorrow;
> To have thy prince's grace, yet want her peers;
> To have thy asking, yet wait many years;
> To fret thy soul with crosses and with cares;
> To eat thy heart with comfortless despairs;
> To fawn, to crouch, to wait, to ride, to run,
> To spend, to give, to want, to be undone.[17]

The favor of the great was notoriously unreliable. "For Noblemen in general it is dangerous to be familiar with them," Thomas Wentworth's father advised him, "for their thoughts are bestowed upon their own weighty causes and their estates and their actions are governed by policy. Again albeit they be most courtly in words, yet they could be contented that rich gentlemen were less able to live without depending on them."[18] The warning was doubly appropriate if the nobleman was also a royal favorite struggling to maintain his position. Joining the court often meant becoming a pawn in a ruthless political game, played by men with too much at stake to feel bound by ordinary rules of morality. As Sir Henry Wotton put it, the court was a "place of . . . servility in the getting, and . . . uncertainty in the holding of fortunes," where a sudden shift of the political winds could destroy years of assiduous effort.[19]

Contemporaries admitted frankly that in such an environment no man who remained completely honest, sincere, and upright was likely to prosper. To survive, one needed to deceive and manipulate. One anonymous discourse argued, "The courtier knoweth the secrets of Court, judgeth them not, but useth them for his particular advantage. He is a great dissembler, for he that knoweth not how to put on that vizard is not fit to live in the courts of princes."[20] Hypocrisy, double-dealing, and guile were widely regarded as inherent vices of the courtier's trade. Thus Francis Beaumont once wrote, in a verse epistle "from the country" to his friend Ben Jonson:

> . . . we want subtlety to do
> The City tricks, lie, hate and flatter too:
> Here are none that can bare a fained show,
> Strike when you wink, and then lament the blow.[21]

The clear implication was that since Jonson lived at court he must expect to encounter all these things.

From the 1590s through the 1620s, the atmosphere of intrigue and uncertainty was further magnified by the spectacular rise and fall of a series of royal favorites, whose meteoric careers added a constant element of instability to court politics. Scores of able and ambitious men found their hopes for advancement depending on such things as the homosexual preferences of James I and the realignments and vendettas that followed the destruction of Essex or Somerset.[22] The world of sycophants, flatterers, spies, and conspirators portrayed in plays like Jonson's *Sejanus* and Chapman's *Bussy d'Ambois* reflected a side of Jacobean life that most courtiers knew intimately.

Discontent was also exacerbated by the fact that from the 1590s the number of men seeking court posts began to outstrip significantly the supply of patronage.[23] As early as the 1590s, Thomas Nashe described a frustrated individual "complaining as though our commonwealth was but a mockery of government and our magistrates but fools, who wronged him in not looking into his deserts, not employing him in state matters."[24] Men like him became ever more common as James's reign progressed.

The training given to courtiers reinforced their tendency to grumble and gossip about their superiors. An aspiring place-seeker had to know how to gather news and analyze political intrigues, whether as an ambassador reporting on the inner workings of a foreign court or as a domestic "intelligencer," supplying a patron with news. The period from about 1590 to 1630 saw an enormous expansion in the volume of news circulating about court affairs, despite James's efforts to prevent people from talking about "mysteries of state." Some news was recorded for provincial lords and squires, but the capital always remained the chief center of political gossip. Contemporary satires and letters are full of accounts of the self-proclaimed experts who haunted the fashionable spots of the capital, talking endlessly of court affairs:

> He, like a privileg'd spy whom nothing can
> Discredit, libels now 'gainst each great man.
> He names a price for every office paid;
> He says our wars thrive ill because delay'd
> That offices are entail'd, and that there are
> Perpetuities of them lasting as far
> As the Last Day, that great officers
> Do with pirates share, and Dunkirkers,[25]

So Donne described one of them in the last years of Queen Elizabeth. The type became even more common in the next two reigns.

THE FASHION FOR SATIRE

Luxury, ostentation, and cutthroat competition had always plagued the royal court and ever since the Middle Ages had given rise to outraged complaints.[26] Neither the abuses we have been examining nor the attacks on them were entirely new in the late sixteenth and early seventeenth centuries. There is no doubt, however, that literature criticizing the court became both more common and frequently more incisive in the decades around 1600.[27]

This trend was largely inspired by such classical writers as Juvenal, Martial, Horace, and Tacitus, who provided models for new forms of naturalistic satire and "analytic" history among the generation coming of age in the 1590s.[28] The vogue for Tacitean histories began in the universities in the 1580s and spread rapidly among the young followers of the Earl of Essex and other intellectuals about the court. Neo-classical satires first appeared in the early 1590s, written mainly by young men associated with the Inns of Court like Donne, Jonson, and John Marston.[29] Both genres were characterized by efforts at greater realism and insightfulness and by a pervasive cynicism concerning the behavior of the rich and powerful. Both were often seen as vehicles for cryptic references to living individuals, including prominent members of the court.

The Crown quickly took alarm at this fashion and tried to restrain it. When three volumes of printed satires appeared in 1597 the government ordered all copies of them burned by the public hangman and prohibited future publication of satiric works. Three years later the antiquarian John Haywarde was imprisoned because the Privy Council believed that his history of the reign of Henry IV made veiled comparisons between the queen and the tyrant Richard II. But the taste for naturalistic descriptions of vice and political intrigue proved impossible to suppress. The theaters soon responded with a string of satiric comedies and realistic political histories, in which contemporaries insisted on finding allusions to contemporary events.[30] "The players do not forbear to present upon their stage the whole course of the present time," a loyal courtier complained early in James's reign, "not sparing either Church or King, with such freedom that any would be afraid to hear them."[31] The Crown imprisoned Ben Jonson in 1597 for writing an allegedly seditious play, and both Jonson and Chapman in 1605 for co-authoring a comedy which satirized James and his Scottish favorites. A few years later the king threatened to close down acting companies that continued to satirize his favorites. Thereafter poets and playwrights usually became more discreet, but satires of court vices and tragedies pivoting around tyrants continued to grace the stage until the closing of the theaters in 1642.

It is important to place this literature within a contemporary frame of reference. In the seventeenth century, royal power and aristocratic privilege had not yet come under the kind of systematic attacks that developed during the Enlightenment and the democratic revolutions of the eighteenth century. The modern habit of blaming moral decadence on reactionary institutions and unjust social systems had not developed, and the belief that human life may be improved by political revolution was not widespread. Most contemporaries believed that since mankind was inherently sinful, all societies were prone to corruption. As William Camden put it:

> In one age there will be more adulterers, in another time there will be excessive riot in banqueting. . . . In another age cruelty and fury of civil war will flash out; and sometimes carousing and drunkenness will be counted a bravery. So vices do ruffle among themselves, and usurp one upon another. As for us we may say of ourselves: we are evil, there have been evils, and evil there will be. There will always be tyrants, murderers, thieves, adulterers, extortioners, church robbers, traitors, and other of the same rabblement.[32]

To cure vice was impossible; one could only hope to understand it well enough to erect some defenses.

In light of these assumptions we cannot automatically assume, as some scholars have done, that plays about corrupt courts and evil rulers were perceived as indictments of the reigning monarch or the prevailing political system. The Crown certainly did not act as if this was the case. The plays that got into trouble with the king's censor were almost invariably accused of making seditious references to particular policies, to prominent members of the court, or to the Scots around James I, rather than more generalized comments about arbitrary government.[33] Provided they avoided specific targets, plays about tyranny normally passed the censor without difficulty and were sometimes performed at court, with the monarchs in the audience. Beaumont and Fletcher's *The Maid's Tragedy,* to mention but one example, provides such a bleak portrait of a depraved ruler that in the 1660s the Crown refused to allow it on the stage for fear it might encourage antiroyalist sentiment. Yet before the Civil War it was not only licensed for public performance but also played at Whitehall for Charles I.

This does not mean that Jacobean and Caroline plays were devoid of serious political content, only that we cannot assume that dramas depicting arbitrary rulers and depraved courts were *necessarily* subversive in intent. No one in the period denied that kings sometimes rule badly and that courts are frequently corrupt. Such commonplaces did not by themselves detract from the ruler's prestige. What mattered was whether the evils depicted on the stage were perceived as being similar to contemporary events, and this inevitably depended on the predispositions of the audience as much as on the content of a play. Jonson's *Gypsies Metamorphosed,* for example, can be interpreted as a harmless entertainment or as a scathing indictment of the court's corruption, depending on how literally one takes the masque's transformation of Buckingham into the leader of a band of begging, thieving gypsies.[34] Here the problem of interpretation is relatively straightforward. In most plays it is far more difficult, since actual courtiers would not appear among the cast and any references to contemporary events would have to be indirect enough to get past the censor. With enough ingenuity it is often possible to construe early Stuart plays as containing political allusions. But whether contemporaries would have perceived the same allusions is almost always impossible to establish.[35]

Moreover, criticism and satire are not necessarily expressions of opposition. They can be offered in a loyal spirit, to counteract flattery and to encourage reform. According to a Renaissance commonplace, one of the courtier's highest duties was to warn the prince against conduct that might harm his position through discreetly veiled criticism.[36] Hence covert allusions and satiric complaint might be regarded as perfectly legitimate tools of a court poet. This was certainly the view of Ben Jonson, who was both the Jacobean court's unofficial laureate and the playwright most often accused of writing seditious works. These facts do not betray an inconsistency within Jonson or a violent oscillation in his political views, for neither he nor his contemporaries saw the England as divided between royalists and parliamentarians, supporters and oponents of James I.[37] So long as the political landscape was not polarized into two clearly marked camps, men could remain within the court and yet speak out boldly against its faults without feeling disloyal.

THE DECLINE OF ELIZABETHAN CONCEPTS OF COURT VIRTUE

It was one thing to castigate court vices, but it was quite another to prescribe a remedy for them. Some hoped to effect a cure for the evils of the time by reviving the neo-chivalric and religious values associated with Elizabeth's war against Spain. This is what Prince Henry, and in a somewhat different way the pamphleteer Thomas Scott, stood for.[38] So long as the realm remained at peace, however, these aspirations could find no constructive outlet. Some courtiers continued to view themselves as warriors, but they could make war only by enlisting in a foreign army, a dilemma well illustrated by the autobiography of Lord Herbert of Cherbury, who absorbed the neo-chivalric ideals of the 1590s in his youth and spent much of his adult life seeking to fulfill them as a soldier of fortune on the continent.[39] Those who refused to live abroad could demonstrate their sense of honor and their prowess only by fighting duels. Yet in doing so they risked both the strong displeasure of James and the denunciations of preachers and moralists. Swashbuckling behavior was slowly becoming dissociated from any larger, patriotic or religious cause, except in the dreams of people like Prince Henry and Thomas Scott.

Perhaps largely for this reason, neo-medieval culture lost its appeal at court shortly after the prince's death, even among those who favored war with Spain. The decline of the tournament, which disappeared altogether by about 1630, reflects this change. Pembroke and Arundel, who jousted with Henry in the early 1610s, soon turned to other interests, notably the collecting of Renaissance art. In the early 1620s Jonson dismissed contemptuously the whole tradition:

> Of errant Knighthood, with the Dames, and Dwarfs,
> The charmed boats, and the enchanted wharfs
> The Tristrams, Lancelots, Turpins and Peers,
> All the mad Rolands, and sweet Oliveers.[40]

Courtiers who still saw themselves as warriors increasingly emulated the aristocratic soldiers of France, Spain, and Italy, rather than the heroic figures of England's past, as the Elizabethan knight evolved into the Stuart cavalier.

The more sober Protestant and humanist virtues exemplified by Elizabethan statesmen like Burghley and Walsingham proved better suited to the atmosphere of the Stuart court, but these also came under stress. The third Earl of Pembroke and diplomats such as Sir Thomas Roe and Henry Wotton still saw themselves as learned statesmen dedicated to the international Protestant cause. Bacon developed his ambitious schemes for improving the common law; Salisbury, Northampton, and Cranfield all struggled valiantly against the waste and venality that threatened to cripple royal administration. But in the end all significant reforms failed, and many of the reformers found themselves tainted by corruption. Salisbury and Northampton were rightly accused of enriching themselves with public funds, Bacon was impeached for bribery, and Cranfield was impeached for peculation.[41] Even for men who escaped scandal, the venality of the regime, the lax attitude of the king, and the intractable financial problems of the Crown proved insurmountable obstacles.

Starting in the 1590s the prestige attached to court service was therefore slowly eroded from two different directions. People were becoming more aware of the court's extravagance and corruption and more ready to criticize its abuses. But simultaneously the system of ideals that Elizabeth's entourage had pieced together from Castiglione, the romances of chivalry, and the literature of humanism began to break down.[42] These developments had a profoundly demoralizing effect. Men came to Whitehall seeking not only wealth and power but also honor. Some, like the earl of Arundel, wanted an opportunity to perform acts of statesmanship befitting a great aristocrat. Others, such as Sir Henry Wotton and John Donne, sought recognition for extraordinary training and talents. Many simply wanted a post that would provide them with a gentleman's income. Even more than most landed men, however, courtiers coveted the good opinion of others. As Elizabethan ideals decayed, they faced the implicit challenge of defining a new pattern of aristocratic virtue that was congruent with the peaceful climate of the Stuart period and the growing sophistication of life in the capital. These conditions go far to explain the growing influence of cultural traditions descending from Roman antiquity, which were uniquely suited to the needs of Stuart court society.

EARLY STUART CLASSICISM

Since the days when Erasmus visited England and formed his friendship with Thomas More, the outlook of the English court had been affected by the study and imitation of classical civilization. In the course of the reign of James I, however, particular strains of Latin thought and culture, deriving from the late republican and early imperial periods, began to play an unprecedented role in shaping English court culture. The poetry of Jonson and his Caroline successors, the architecture of Inigo Jones, and the collections of ancient statues amassed by the Earl of Arundel and other courtiers all reflect this trend.

The imitation of Latin antiquity affected not only aesthetic taste but also moral and intellectual attitudes. The political ideology of the empire, the ethical ideas of Latin poets and philosophers, and whatever people could discover about the habits of the roman aristocracy all left their mark. In the early 1630s Shakerley Marmion poked fun at men who claimed to govern their entire lives by antiquarian research:

> . . . I have searched
> The dust of antiquity to find out
> The rare inventions I am versed in,
> My several garbs and postures of the body
> My rules for banqueting and entertainment:
> And for the titillation of my laughter
> Buffoons and parasites, for I must tell you
> I still affect a learned luxury.[43]

These lines reduce the ideal of classical imitation to absurdity, but they also hint at the ambitious purposes that underlay the movement.

BEN JONSON AND THE IMITATION OF ANCIENT LITERATURE

No one exemplified the determination to use classical culture to guide a reformation of court life better than the Crown's unofficial laureate, Ben Jonson. Yet no seventeeth-century poet has suffered more from misunderstandings created by the classicist label. In the seventeenth century, Jonson's devotion to ancient literature considerably enhanced his prestige. In modern times it has too frequently been taken as the hallmark of a formal and derivative style, admirable for its elegance and craftsmanship but lacking the spontaneity and emotional resonance of great poetry. However, this view rests on a fundamental misconstruction of the meaning of classical imitation, both for Jonson himself and for the humanist tradition in which he stood. [44]

Within that tradition the true imitator of antiquity was not a man who simply borrowed from ancient texts and followed classical rules of composition. He was, in Jonson's own words, a writer who converts "the substance . . . of another poet to his own use . . . not as a creature that swallows what it takes in crude, raw or undigested; but that feeds with an appetite and hath a stomach to concoct, divide and turn all into nourishment." [45] As the digestive metaphor suggests, the emphasis always lay on the act of assimilation and transformation, through which an author adapted classical elements to meet his own requirements. Jonson's work fully embodied these precepts. He borrowed widely from Greek and Latin sources, but freely altered, rearranged, and recombined to produce new and sometimes unexpected effects. He wanted his audience to recognize his borrowings and to relish how he manipulated them. His quotations from the classics are not just ornaments, but contribute to the play of wit and intelligence which distinguishes his best work. [46]

This sort of poetry demands an acute and educated audience, as Jonson never tired of reiterating. His muse, he bragged in the prologue to *Cynthia's Revels*:

Shuns the print of any beaten path;
And proves new ways to come to learned ears:
Pied ignorance she neither loves, nor fears.
Nor hunts she after popular applause,
Or foamy praise that drops from common jaws.
The garland that she wears their hands must twine,
Who can both censure, understand, define
What merit is: then cast those piercing rays,

> Round about as a crown, instead of honored bays,
> About his poesie . . . [47]

The references to twining, censuring, defining, and piercing evoke the kind of vigorous response Jonson hoped to elicit. Good verse draws understanding readers into the process of handling and refashioning literary materials, uniting poet and audience in a shared intellectual labor.[48] By doing so it creates an invisible community of learning and intelligence that preserves the cultural heritage of the past against the ignorance and stupidity which threatens to engulf it.[49]

Jonson expressed this ideal not only through his verse but also in the role he fashioned for himself as London's foremost literary celebrity. As his reputation and his standing at court grew, younger poets and patrons sought his friendship. By the 1620s he had gathered several of these into a "Tribe of Ben," which met periodically at a London tavern to exchange their work and discuss literature and scholarship.[50] Jonson sat enthroned in a special chair, topped by a bust of his favorite poet, Horace, to preside over gatherings which included Thomas Carew, Robert Herrick, Sir Kenelm Digby, and probably the Earl of Newcastle. Jonson's impact upon the court stemmed not only from his work but also from his direct personal influence over leading patrons and poets of the younger generation.

This strong sense of community was, in turn, bound up with Jonson's conviction that literature should not only entertain but also instruct and reform. A good poem or drama never exists in a vacuum, as a self-contained literary artifact. It must somehow challenge its readers to view themselves and their society with a more acute ethical vision. This does not mean that all literature is overtly didactic, for wit, laughter, and aesthetic pleasure all have a proper place within the good life. Jonson had a strong sense of fun, evident in the masques, in the comedies, and in poems like "An Execration upon Vulcan," with its playful treatment of classical mythology.[51] Yet in one form or another the urge to instruct and criticize was rarely entirely absent from his work.

Somewhere behind this view lay the classical belief that the first poets were priests, kings, and lawgivers whose verse called savage people together and taught them to revere the values that make social life possible.[52] Jonson's roots lay in a classical and humanist rhetorical tradition which treated eloquent language as an "instrument of society," capable of molding behavior and shaping customs and institutions.

This conviction comes through repeatedly both in *Discoveries* and in
the poems, as in a verse epistle to Selden:

> [You have] watch'd men, manners too,
> Heard what times past have said, seen what ours do:
> Which grace shall I make love to first? your skill,
> Or faith in things? or is't your wealth and will
> To instruct and teach? or your unwearied pain
> Of gathering? Bounty in pouring out again.
> What fables have you vexed! What truth redeemed!
> Antiquities search'd! Opinions dis-esteem'd!
> Impostures branded! And authorities urg'd!
> What blots and errors, have you watch'd and purg'd
> Records, and authors of! how rectified
> Times, manners, customs. . . . [53]

The lines describe an extremely aggressive form of scholarship—a
process of judging, correcting, reworking, and applying inherited materials—which is equally important for the jurist, the poet, and the historian.[54] Each in his own way studies the past to illuminate the present
and to furnish himself with weapons against injustice, ignorance, and
corruption.

To fulfill this ideal requires not only study but also close observation
of one's own times. The man who imitates only what he finds in books
will inevitably fall short of his models, both because slavish emulation
never results in great writing and because the best ancient poets were
imitators of nature as well as of texts. The satirists Jonson most often
emulated—Horace, Martial, and Juvenal—employed a conversational,
"plain style" to present lifelike portraits of Roman social life. As Jonson
once put it, they created a "direct and analytic sum / Of all worth and
first effects of arts . . . [a] poesie . . . rammed with life."[55] To reproduce
this effect, an author needed to treat them "as guides, not comman-
ders," teaching him to use his own eyes and wit to examine and portray
human behavior.

Jonson's commitment to the concept of imitation therefore led directly to what is sometimes misleadingly called his "realism": his keen
eye for detail and flair for mimicry and satire. He was notorious in his
own age as an examiner and reporter of other men's behavior. "Alas,
sir, Horace," a character exclaims in *The Poetaster*, in an allusion to
Jonson himself, "he is a mere sponge; nothing but humors, and observation, he goes up and down sucking from every society, and when he

comes home, squeezes himself dry again."[56] But this piece of self-satire is as oversimplified as the view that Jonson made poems by stitching together phrases culled from other authors. His "discoveries made upon men and manners," no less than those he absorbed through reading, formed part of a stock of raw materials which he refined and reworked in the service of higher aesthetic and intellectual goals.

ETHICAL CONCEPTS

Jonson's approach to ancient moral philosophy developed organically out of these ideals.[57] He treated classical ethical concepts not as abstract and static ideas but as principles informing his vision of his own society and his convictions about how men ought to live within it.

Deeply embedded within Jonson's system of values lay the Socratic dictum that virtue depends on knowledge, both of the world and of oneself. Vice, on the other hand, stems from an underlying debility or deformity of the mind, which makes it the slave of irrational fears and desires. Among these are sensual passions, "spiritual Rebels [that] raise sedition against the understanding" by arousing turbulent desires and jealousies.[58] Ultimately more dangerous, however, are the snares created by the mind itself. The soul "is a perpetual Agent, prompt and subtle; but often flexible and erring; entangling herself like a Silkworm," so that those unaccustomed to self-scrutiny and self-criticism will inevitably become trapped in a bondage of their own making.[59]

This affliction affects not only individuals but also societies which create artificial wants and needs:

> What petty things they are we wonder at! like children that esteem every trifle. . . . They are pleased with cockshells, whistles, hobby horses and such like: we with Statues, marble pillars, pictures, guilded roofs, when underneath is lath and lyme. . . . yet we take pleasure in the lie, and are glad we can cozen ourselves.[60]

As society grows more complex the obsession with useless and deceptive ornaments tends to increase, progressively infecting all aspects of public and private life. A nation suffering from this sickness will not only squander its wealth in useless ostentation, but also prove defenseless against charlatans who learn to manipulate its appetites and delusions. The belief we encountered earlier, that the opulence of Jacobean

London signaled the beginnings a cycle of moral and political decay, thus rested on solid intellectual foundations.

Yet however much he disapproved of fraud and artifice, Jonson remained fascinated by them. "Statues, marble pillars, pictures and guilded roofs" may be lies, but they also require imagination and dexterity.[61] In fact, the act of creating them bears more than a superficial resemblance to the work of a poet and playwright, especially one who devises court masques.[62] The manipulation of words and appearances is intrinsic to all art, and in a profound sense to all human life. Men and women are so constituted that they cannot gratify even their most basic material needs without artifice, a point made, for example, in the jocular "hymn" which opens *Pleasure Reconciled to Virtue*:

> Room, room, make room for the bouncing belly,
> First father of sauce, and deviser of jelly,
> Prime master of arts, and the giver of wit,
> That found out the excellent engine, the spit,
> The plow, and the flail, the mill, and the hopper
> The hutch, and the bolter, the furnace, and copper,
> The oven, the bavin, the mawkin, the peel,
> The hearth, and the range, the dog, and the wheel.[63]

Whereas animals eat what nature provides, men are driven to invent a culinary technology, so that their bellies' demands become a fecund source of cultural innovation. This compulsion to embellish and transform our surroundings, in which appetite merges with imagination and inventiveness, is at once our species' glory and its greatest curse. It is ultimately responsible for everything that separates civilized life from savagery, but it also underlies the extraordinary human capacity for chicanery, perversion, and self-delusion.

In Jonson's universe the ability to use and create culture is therefore profoundly linked to the ability to exploit and deceive. Great villains display qualities of intelligence, energy, and resourcefulness essentially similar to those that distinguish great artists and creative statesmen. And so in spite of his moral concerns, Jonson often conveys genuine admiration for the talents of successful charlatans. This ambivalence comes through most vividly in plays like *Volpone* and *Sejanus*, whose villains play with such mastery on the characteristic aspirations of their societies. Volpone embodies the acquisitive, materialistic spirit of

Venice, just as Sejanus epitomizes the ambition and consummate treachery of imperial Rome. Each is a brilliant actor, exploiting his victims with almost superhuman skill, and each has a magnificent gift for rhetoric, which emphasizes the vitality and resourcefulness that for a time allow him to mold his own destiny.[64] We consequently become enthralled by their intrigues, almost in spite of ourselves.[65]

There remains, however, a disquieting undercurrent in the language and the action of both plays, suggesting a hidden deformity beneath the rich surface. A good example is the famous speech in which Volpone tries to seduce Celia with a catalog of the riches he will shower upon her:

> See, here, a rope of pearl, and each more orient
> Than that the brave Egyptian queen caroused;
> Dissolve and drink'em. See, a carbuncle
> May put out both the eyes of our St. Mark
> . . . .
> A gem but worth a private patrimony
> Is nothing; we will eat at such a meal.
> The heads of parrots, tongues of
> nightingales,
> The brains of peacocks, and of estriches
> Shall be our food. . . . [66]

Superficially the passage reinforces the sense of opulence that clings to Volpone's world, but the moment we examine the imagery it becomes repulsive. The thought of dining on parrots' heads and ostriches' brains will not appeal to people who keep their wits about them, while the reference to putting out the eyes of Mark suggests that moral violence of Volpone's deceptions. The pursuit of wealth and the glories it brings has annihilated any sense of the true needs of healthy individuals. This rhetorical effect mirrors the larger movement of the play, as Volpone's preoccupation with manipulating his surroundings and gratifying his appetites deprives him of deeper human qualities.[67]

It is typical of Jonson that these sinister meanings appear only to readers or spectators who think about Volpone's speech instead of getting caught up in its superficial brilliance. For Jonson, language is opaque and deceptive to those who merely see its surface. It is revealing for those who can look through it, to discern the attitudes and qualities of mind a speaker unwittingly reveals even in the act of trying to conceal his true intentions.

Within the relatively short compass of his poems, Jonson could not provide comparably developed portraits of deception and delusion, but these also frequently turn upon the behavior of men and women hopelessly entangled in their own pretensions:

> Don Surly, to aspire the glorious name
>   Of a great man, and to be thought the same,
> Makes serious use of all great trade he knows.
>   He speaks to men with a Rhinocerotes nose,
> Which he thinks great; and so reads verses, too:
>   And, that is done, as he saw great men do.
> H'has tympanies of business, in his face,
>   And, can forget men's names, with a great grace.
> He will both argue, and discourse in oaths,
>   Both which are great. And laugh at ill made clothes;
> That's greater yet: to cry up his own neat.[68]

The point here is not simply that Don Surly is a fraud, but that in his obsession with external marks of status he has emptied himself of substance. Instead of proceeding from self-knowledge, his behavior is patchwork of artificial gestures, creating a transparent facade around a spiritual void.[69]

For Jonson and his readers this vision gained added significance through reference to a courtly milieu dominated by conspicuous consumption, intense competition, intrigue, and ostentation. Volpone's Venice and Sejanus's Rome represented prominent features of Jacobean London; Surly's antics may have reflected those of a real lord. Castiglione and his numerous followers, in England as on the continent, had defined the ideal courtier as an individual who fashions his personality to suit his environment and his patron's pleasure. Jonson knew how destructive such an aspiration could be. His poems and plays convey a fundamental critique of a kind of adaptability and manipulative egotism intrinsic to court life.

How then does one live in such a society without being corrupted by it? Jonson nowhere provides an entirely straightforward answer. His writings are remarkably reticent about the nature of virtue, perhaps because he regarded it as a quality that defies description.[70] If vice is all show and no substance, virtue is just the opposite, an intangible inward possession that words and appearances can never capture.[71] One can nonetheless infer much about Jonson's concept of virtue by examining his poems of praise.[72]

As one might expect, those poems sometimes suggest that virtue grows out of a capacity to reject luxury and artifice in favor of more natural and wholesome values:

> How blest art thou, canst love the country, Wroth,
>   Whether by choice, or fate, or both;
> And though so near the city, and the court,
>   Art tane with neither's vice, nor sport:
> That at great times, art no ambitious guest
>   Of sheriff's dinner, or Mayor's feast.
> Nor com'st to view the better cloth of state;
>   The richer hangings, or crown plate. . . . [73]

Instead of assimilating himself to his surroundings, in order to manipulate and exploit them, the good man relies on an inner nobility that always remains somewhat detached from the world. He will either withdraw physically from corruption, as Wroth does, or maintain an aloof integrity in its midst:

> . . . Thou, whose noblesse keeps one stature still,
>   And one true posture, though besieg'd with ill
> Of what ambition, faction, pride can raise;
>   Whose life, ev'n they, that envy it, must praise;
> That art so reverenced, as thy coming in,
>   But in the view, doth interrupt their sin. . . . [74]

In these lines to the third Earl of Pembroke, as in much of Jonson's laudatory verse, righteousness possesses a monumental grandeur and permanence which secures it against the onslaughts of evil.[75]

This imagery owes more than a little to the Platonic conviction that Truth is eternal and constant, whereas passions and sense perceptions are in constant flux. In Jonson's work the weak and the vicious constantly get sucked into a world of swirling instability, whereas the strong and upright appear to have anchored themselves in a permanent moral order, existing independently of particular circumstances. Yet for the most part Jonson did not portray moral goodness as if it proceeded entirely from an inner rational faculty which only needed to be freed from the world's corruption to emerge victorious. He was too fully aware of the complexity of the relationships between people and their social milieus to believe in the possibility of complete self-sufficiency. Men have no choice but to become engaged in their surroundings, if only because solitude is no adequate defense against corruption.[76]

The capacity to lead a good life therefore depends on self-discipline, but perhaps even more on the power to discriminate between real good and apparent good. This is never easy, partly because vice so often masquerades as virtue but also because in this world good and evil are thoroughly intertwined. To distinguish between them requires a wisdom that can come only through years of accumulated effort. The good man must fashion his character in much the way a poet develops his style, by studying his surroundings and seeking out models worthy of emulation:

> Roe (and my joy to name) th'art now to go
>   Countries, and climes, manners, and men to know,
> T'extract and choose the best of all these known,
>   And these to turn to blood, and make thine own. [77]

Again Jonson uses a digestive metaphor to suggest how external materials are absorbed into the substance of an individual's character, providing him with the strength and agility needed to meet the world's challenges.

Central to this process is the imitation of good men, who stand as patterns of virtue for others to admire or, to change the metaphor, "stars and planets of the age wherein they live," placed by God so others may navigate by their example. This was an old idea, embodied in works as diverse as Plutarch's *Lives*, the romances of chivalry, and hagiographical treatises. It nonetheless remained a vital one, which Jonson took seriously. He felt compelled to apologize in print for writing laudatory verses to a courtier (perhaps the Earl of Salisbury) who did not deserve his commendation. [78]

The concept of imitation was also closely bound up with the important ideal of true friendship. Legendary heroes and great men can be emulated only from afar, but friends may be studied at close range:

> . . . So must we do,
> First weigh a friend, then touch, and try him too:
> For there are many slips, and Counterfeits.
> . . . .
> Turn him, and see his Threads: look if he be
> Friend to himself, that would be friend to thee,
> for that is first required, A man be his own.
> But he that's too much that, is friend to none. [79]

The capacity to select the right friends and profit by them is vital to moral development, for no individual is capable of attaining an entirely accurate perception of his own strengths and weaknesses. Only when we see our actions reflected in the praise and criticism of an intimate yet frank and honest companion does true self-knowledge become possible.[80]

This conviction recurs throughout the literature of the Stuart court, though rarely with as much conviction as in Jonson's works.[81] It looks curiously like a courtly counterpart to the puritan concept of the community of saints. In both cases a determination to hold at bay the world's corruption inspired efforts to build tiny societies of high-minded people capable of reinforcing one another's virtues and creating islands of righteousness in a sea of perversity. The sense of being spiritually superior to the world was by no means confined to those who ultimately fought against the Crown.

There were, however, significant differences between the puritan concept of sainthood and the ideals we have been tracing. Like nearly all serious and thoughtful men in this period, Jonson was a sincere Christian whose deep and unpretentious piety colored his entire outlook. In comparison to many of his English contemporaries, however, he seems to have possessed a remarkably calm and lucid faith. Only a handful of his poems show much trace of the agonized spiritual struggle that so often marks the religious verse of Donne or Herbert, to say nothing of puritan diaries and sermons. Jonson did not habitually regard the world as a vale of tears nor, apparently, did he share deeply in the overwhelming fear of divine anger so characteristic of the theology of the period, among Arminians no less than Calvinists. And he did not view human nature as irremediably corrupt. On the contrary, throughout his work runs the conviction that people can lead upright and dignified lives if they will only learn to develop their native intelligence and spiritual vigor. Goodness, for him, was not the fruit of an unmerited gift of grace so much as something individuals achieve by fostering inner resources of mind and imagination.

These convictions often come through most vividly when Jonson chose not to preach about moral principles. His few love poems, for example, portray him as a man who can feel sexual desire and jealousy without losing his composure or his capacity to view his passions with amused detachment. They exemplify the qualities of intelligence, self-control, and self-scrutiny which Jonson so often stressed in his overtly moralistic verse. Similarly his epistolary "Inviting a Friend to Supper" describes a supremely civilized social gathering, in which temperate enjoyment of good food is enhanced by shared intellectual values:

I'll tell you of more, and lie, so you will come
Of partridge, pheasant, woodcock, of which some
May yet be there; and godwit, if we can:
Knat, rail, and ruff too. How so ere, my man
Shall read a piece of Virgil, Tacitus,
Livy, or of some better book to us,
Of which we'll speak our minds, amidst our meat;
And I'll profess no verses to repeat.[82]

Everything from the warm tone of these lines to the last personal detail conveys the Jonsonian ideal of friendship. The poem is classical insofar as it is modeled after several poems by Martial and morally didactic because of the unspoken contrast between this meal and gargantuan court banquets.[83] Yet both the learning and the moral attitudes remain unobtrusive. Ethics has become an "art of living well, and happily" in the true classical tradition.

This urbanely tolerant side of Jonson and of the Latin authors he imitated ultimately proved more influential within the court than his satire. In Charles's reign, court poets seldom wrote as impassioned moralists, but their portrayal of court society as the home of elegant, self-controlled aristocrats was nevertheless profoundly indebted to Jonson and the ideals he had absorbed from classical literature.[84]

COUNTRY VIRTUE

The quintessential expression of this classical concept of aristocratic society was a vision of country life that took shape in the reign of James and left an indelible impression upon the cavalier imagination.[85] This image differs from the more ambivalent view of the countryside taken by Sidney and Spenser, but it developed logically from the basic assumptions of the Tribe of Ben.[86] If virtue and happiness come from conformity to nature and contempt for luxury and social pressures, then the good life will flourish in a simple agricultural society more easily than in the competitive and fashion-conscious city. Horace thought the ideal setting for a virtuous man was an estate large enough to afford sustenance and leisure but modest enough to give no opening for luxury and ambition: something bigger than the farm of a constable but smaller than the lands of a justice of the peace, as Abraham Cowley anglicized the concept.[87]

The cavalier image of the countryside existed in embryo in the sixteenth century. Tudor poets often contrasted the purity of an archaic, rustic life with the pressures and temptations of the court. Elizabethan satirists used the manners of rustic gentry as a foil for the vices of the city.[88] Nashe defended peasant festivals against the puritans, anticipating by nearly half a century the cavalier cult of wassail bowls and maypoles.[89] From around 1610 Jonson and a few others enriched this imagery by reviving the vision of rural life embedded in the Georgics of Virgil and Horace's odes to his Sabine farm. The tradition then passed, through Carew, Herrick, and Lovelace, to such figures as Cowley and Izaak Walton.

In Stuart England, as in Imperial Rome, this literature bore an aroma of the older, pastoral tradition. However, the Stuart poets succeeded in breaking away from pastoral formulas to sketch a view of rural happiness as it might occur in the seventeenth century. Some of their imagery came straight out of Roman poetry, but they also added original, English motifs, such as descriptions of country hospitality:

> The rout of rural folk come thronging in,
> (Their rudeness then is thought no sin)
> Thy noblest spouse affords them welcome grace;
> And the great Heroes, of her race,
> Sit mixed with loss of state, or reverence.
> Freedom doth with degree dispense
> The jolly wassail walks the often round,
> And in their cups, their cares are drowned.[90]

Pastoralism was always an elegant but transparent pose. No one could have taken Sidney at face value when he appeared at court dressed as a shepherd knight. The allusions to Latin verse of the Juvenalian satirists also tended to be contrived. Joseph Hall, for example, once conjured up a vision of the Golden Age, with its timber dwellings and leather garments, that his contemporaries could scarcely have regarded as a viable alternative to the luxuries of Elizabethan London.[91] On the other hand, Jonson and those who followed his lead subtly idealized a way of life that all aristocrats knew intimately. Where the older poets had recited Greek myths, those at the Stuart court described the living folklore of fairies and May festivals. In place of conventional accounts of the rugged habits of a remote and legendary Golden Age, they wrote descriptions of the solid, old dwellings and unpolished manners that still existed away from London. In short, they conveyed their concept of the good life through vignettes and rituals which might be absorbed almost without conscious effort.

This idyllic vision of the countryside nevertheless remained far more artificial than its creators liked to suppose. The court's poets claimed to look back to a traditional society threatened by the commercial expansion, sophisticated manners, and factious politics of the seventeenth century. But the way of life they described bore little resemblance to the rough-and-tumble world of provincial England in Tudor and medieval times, in which a country gentleman had to face the vexing tasks of collecting rents, negotiating leases, placating mighty neighbors, and coping with the curse of litigation. He lived in an intensely competitive world, in which his relations with tenants and other gentlemen made a critical difference to his prestige and his economic survival. The great estates of the nobility served as the foundation for affinities of retainers and clients, which enabled peers to influence local government and gave them a presumptive right to participate in national affairs.

Elizabethan culture reflected these habits in various ways. The cavalcades and jousts of the court evoked the ethos of a society in which land carried with it the obligation to serve and to fight for the sake of the monarch. The prodigy houses, with their turrets, their expanses of glass, and their great courts, conveyed a sense of limitless wealth and immense households; the amorous language of the sonnet and the rituals of court pageants expressed a personal dependence on the queen which all great landowners took for granted.

By contrast, the Stuart court valued a country estate because it allowed a man to opt out of this sprawling nexus of bonds and obligations:

> Sweet country life, to such unknown
> Whose lives are others, not their own!
> But serving courts and cities be
> Less happy, less enjoying thee.[92]

As Cowley recognized, this attitude was closely allied to the impulse which led gentlemen, after about 1600, to regard the taking of livery as degrading. The new ideal was an economic self-sufficiency which, if combined with moderate desires and ambitions, would enable a man to control his own destiny and decide for himself where virtue lay. The court remained suspect because there clientage, conspicuous consumption, and political competition were a way of life.[93]

These attitudes survived the interregnum to pass into the mainstream of English political thought. By the reign of Queen Anne the juxtaposition of urban vice to rural virtue had become an automatic reflex among many English gentlemen, as had the assumption that the political factions and commercial affairs of London were morally debilitating.[94] It would be wrong to attribute these Augustan attitudes solely to the posthumous influence of Jonson and the cavalier poets, but it is just as misleading to ignore, as most accounts do, the substantial contributions of early Stuart court literature to the ideological heritage of men like Swift and Bolingbroke. Jonson and his colleagues first assimilated to an English environment the classical concepts of rural life that underlay the Augustan country tradition. They revived the ancient equation of virtue with independence—in psychological, social, and economic terms—thereby preparing the ground for later political writers. The early Stuart court poets also enunciated a distrust of organized politics, a conviction that country gentry should rule over an obedient tenantry while the king shouldered the burdens of national affairs, which Tories still took for granted half a century later. The country Tories were not simply the heirs of Shaftesbury and the old country Whigs, as many modern accounts argue. They could also draw upon a royalist tradition stretching back, through country opponents of Cromwell, to the entourage of their royal martyr, King Charles I.

CLASSICAL TRENDS IN ARCHITECTURE AND ART

So far we have examined the influence of classical culture upon the court almost entirely in terms of literature. Yet classicizing tendencies also appeared in the fine arts, leading to an interest in ancient sculpture and, more important, to the revolutionary architecture of Inigo Jones. At least in Jones's case these developments reflected the same determination to understand and assimilate ancient cultural values that forms so prominent a feature of Jonson's work, and a broadly similar orientation to the moral issues raised by court life.

Long before Jones began his career, the basic units of classical architecture—columns, pediments, architraves, and so forth—had become commonplace in English aristocratic buildings, but until the seventeenth century they had almost invariably been used with little attention to general principles of design. Classical ornaments were routinely employed in buildings that were anything but classical in their proportions and style. This approach continued down to the mid-1610s in prodigy houses like Hatfield House and Audley End. In that decade, however, Jones and a few other court architects[95] began to evolve genuinely classical styles. Fortunately, enough of Jones's elevations and masque designs survive from this early period to enable us to glimpse the experimentation that preceded the emergence of his mature style. The fallen city of chivalry from *Prince Henry's Barriers,* for instance, shows him trying with only partial success to picture an ancient cityscape (Plate 1).[96] Despite its Arthurian theme, this scene consists of assorted Roman monuments which Jones had probably seen during a visit to Italy a few years before, including part of the Coliseum, an obelisk, and the Arch of Titus. However, the haphazard arrangement of the monuments only compounds the incongruity of providing a Roman setting for feats of chivalry. Although he could accurately copy entire Roman buildings, Jones still could not redeploy them in a wholly convincing way.[97]

A comparable awkwardness appears in some of the early architectural designs. Jones carefully worked out the relationship between columns, doors, windows, and other features of his facades according to correct classical rules, but the results often tended to look contrived. For some time he had difficulty establishing a satisfactory relationship between the classical ornaments he chose to employ and the underlying structure of the buildings they adorned.

He overcame this problem by undertaking an exacting study of all the sources he could find that might increase his knowledge of ancient architecture, including actual ruins, elevations of Roman buildings published by Palladio and other Italians, and Vitruvius's Roman treatise. "Antipagmenti are the ties around the mutules," he noted in the margin next to Vitruvius's obscure description of a minor feature of the Tuscan order. "This Barbaro [the editor of Jones's edition] nor none of them understood and make the beams with plain and so did I in Covent Garden, but now I understand it thus."[98] No less than Jonson he examined his ancient models in minute detail, to attain a profound and authentic understanding of the classical style he wished to recreate. In a sense he performed this labor not only for himself but also for future generations of English architects, adapting ancient practice with such conviction that later figures imitated him.

The rapport between the work of Jones and that of Jonson goes deeper than this, however. In his poems Jonson sketched a critique of contemporary buildings:

1. Inigo Jones. The Fallen House of Chivalry from *Prince Henry's Barriers*. Devonshire Collection, Chatsworth. Reproduced by permission of the Trustees of the Chatsworth Settlement. Photograph: Courtauld Insititute of Art, London.

Thou art not, Penshurst, built to envious show
Of touch or marble, nor canst boast a row
Of polished pillars, or a roof of gold;
Thou hast no lantern, whereof tales are told.
Or stair or courts; but stands't an ancient pile.[99]

Surviving prodigy houses like Audley End and Hatfield reveal what he had in mind. Their imposing arrays of bay windows, turrets, and receding ranges represent just the sort of ostentation Jonson always regarded as a sign of decadence. He wanted buildings to conform to the same code of discipline, restraint, and natural order as poetry and social manners, and therefore he rejected artful modern styles in favor of unpretentious medieval architecture.

As a Renaissance architect, Jones could not agree unreservedly with this position, but in the 1610s he did gradually evolve a simpler and more subdued style. His earliest elevations contain soaring towers and gigantic scrolled pediments as idiosyncratic as the features of any prodigy house. Indeed, if we can judge from some anonymous designs that are probably his, Jones normally increased the complexity of a traditional Jacobean structure when he added a new wing or entrance to it. After his return from Italy he learned to integrate his work more convincingly and began to display some of the concern for harmonic proportions characteristic of his mature style. Yet he retained a penchant for scrolled pediments reminiscent of the taste for elaborate roof lines of the Jacobean style.[100] Only in the late 1610s did he develop a simpler and purer classicism, "solid, proportionable, according to the rules, masculine and unaffected," as he described it. In successive designs for the Whitehall Banqueting House he pared away all extraneous elements to arrive at a building of rectangular outline, rusticated masonry, and subtle articulation (Plate 2 and Plate 3). Jonson once defined a terse poem as one from which nothing could be taken away without detracting from the meaning. Jones's mature work reflects the same attitude. Spare, disciplined, understated yet elegant, it embodies a new concept of the kind of grandeur appropriate to men of great rank, entirely congruent with the classical outlook we have been tracing.

Can we detect comparable trends in painting? The answer seems to be yes, though the evolution here is more difficult to interpret. As the name implies, the Elizabethan and Jacobean costume portrait required a fancy suit of clothes. As late as the 1620s William Larkin was turning

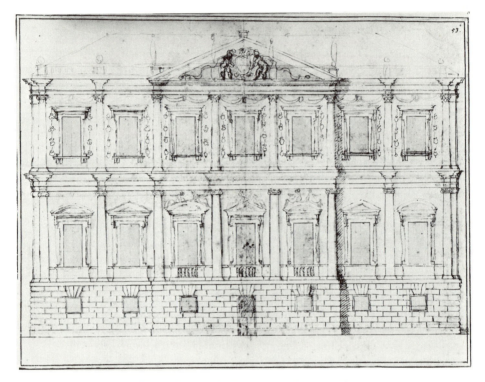

2. Inigo Jones. The Whitehall Banqueting House. Elevation for the penultimate design of the facade. Devonshire Collection, Chatsworth. Reproduced by permission of the Trustees of the Chatsworth Settlement.

3. Inigo Jones. The Whitehall Banqueting House. Royal Commission on the Historical Monuments of England.

out works whose chief appeal lay in their bright colors and careful de-
piction of jewels, oriental carpets, lace, and embroidery. We have seen
that Jonson and others objected strenuously to this emphasis on purely
external symbols of wealth and standing. More important, from the
late 1610s some courtiers refused to wear bright colors and quantities of
brocade, compensating for the loss of visual splendor by a certain gravity of demeanor. This was the Spanish fashion. At Madrid the court
wore only black, and grandees behaved with a haughtiness notorious
throughout Europe. As respect for Spain increased within the English
court, so did the influence of somber clothing and formal behavior.[101]
The Earl of Arundel embodied this concept of nobility as well as anyone in England. His first biographer noted:

> He was of a stately presence and gait, so that any man that saw him though
> in never so ordinary a habit would not but conclude him to be a great per-
> son, his garb and fashion drawing more observation than did the rich ap-
> parel of others, so that it was a common saying of the late Earl of Carlisle,
> here comes Arundel in his plain stuff and trunk hose, and his beard in his
> teeth that looks more like a nobleman than any of us.[102]

Painters had to find a way of conveying this somber dignity. Some of
Mytens's early English works reveal his efforts to do so (see Plate 4).
The garish costumes of Gower and Larkin give way to suits of one or
two colors. Subjects sometimes pose next to pillars or flowing curtains
to enhance the sense of height, and faces are more realistic and alive
than in earlier English work. The effect is often marred, however, by
a morose quality that may have passed at the time for stateliness and
dignity. Moreover, the change was never complete. Buckingham, in
particular, continued to dress opulently. In his portraits he sometimes looks like an ivory-faced doll stuffed inside huge concoctions of
diamond-studded fabric.

The contrast between the somber plainness of Arundel and the
flashy grandeur of Buckingham reflected an underlying disparity in cultural values. Down to the 1620s, many English courtiers retained an
Elizabethan taste for flamboyant opulence and assertive egotism. They
loved massive, colorful displays of wealth in painting and architecture
no less than in clothing, entertainments, and banquets. Yet in the
course of James's reign a reaction began to emerge against the arti-
ficiality and extravagance that too often resulted. Each in their own
way, Jonson, Arundel, and Inigo Jones rejected the ornateness of earlier

4. Daniel Mytens. *Thomas Howard, Earl of Arundel.* The National Gallery, London. (Hangs in Arundel Castle, Sussex, England.)

court styles and sought to define more sober, dignified, and natural forms of aristocratic culture. As long as James ruled, these opposing tendencies existed side by side, without being effectively reconciled. Only in the next reign did the great Flemish portraitist Van Dyck, along with poets like Carew and Waller, succeed in striking a balance between the demand for disciplined restraint and a lingering taste for gaiety, color, and richness.[103]

CONCLUSION: CLASSICAL CULTURE AND THE QUEST FOR MORAL ORDER

The classical forms of literature and art we have been examining helped to convey a distinctive attitude toward court life. The culture of the early Roman Empire appealed to poets and artists because it seemed to embody not only elegant stylistic principles but also a moral outlook suited to their milieu. The discipline and restraint of the Latin traditions that most influenced the court—evident in everything from the simplicity of Jones's architecture to the ethical creed of Jonson's favorite Roman poets—injected a sense of order and dignity into a society too prone to extravagance and licentiousness. It is significant that both Jones and Jonson interpreted Roman culture in ways that reinforced this emphasis. There were Latin poets who wrote in a very ornate style, and as mannerist architects had shown, classical forms could be used in buildings as fanciful and ostentatious as any prodigy house. The classical styles emerging in the Stuart period were a product of careful selection from among several alternative models that had come down from the ancient world.

To put it differently, literary and architectural classicism amounted, on one level, to an effort at recovering elements of a Latin aristocratic culture markedly different from that which James's court had inherited from Elizabeth's court. The new classical forms were symptoms of a more fundamental readjustment in habits, attitudes, and aspirations, caused partly by a reaction against older forms of conspicuous consumption and partly by disgust with the ostentation and apparent corruption of some courtiers. This alteration did not occur suddenly and was not complete even at James's death. In the long run, however, the neo-medieval styles and values of Elizabethan court culture steadily declined, while the trends we have examined in this chapter gained importance.

For a number of reasons, this transition tended to widen the cultural distance between the court and most of England. Elizabethan court culture had formed a bond between the queen's entourage and the nation in a way that the newer styles developing in James's reign did not. Although the Elizabethans could produce works as arcane as anything created at the Stuart court, most of the traditions associated with the Elizabethan cult could communicate, at least on some level, to a broad audience. The austere elegance of the Banqueting House, like the meticulous craftsmanship of Jonson's verse, appealed chiefly to small groups of intellectuals, most of whom resided for at least part of the year in London. The best art and literature of the court no longer served as a vehicle for ideas and attitudes that tended to unify the nation.

At the same time, classical influences on court culture often reinforced an aloof and authoritarian view of politics. This may at first seem to be a paradoxical conclusion, since modern scholars have generally associated classical and neo-classical influences with the rise of republican ideologies.[104] Not all ancient writers were republicans, however. From Plato onward many classical philosophers and historians had expressed deep misgivings about the factiousness and demagoguery that often arise in republics, while praising the rule of wise and virtuous monarchs. These antirepublican strains were particularly pronounced after Augustus restored peace to the empire. It was, naturally enough, this early imperial era to which the court most often turned for inspiration.

Behind the court's distrust of free and open forms of government lay a deeply ingrained fear of mankind's violent and anarchic instincts and a corresponding preoccupation with the need for social discipline. "The vulgar are commonly ill-natured, and always grudging against their governors," Jonson wrote, "which makes, that a Prince hath more business with them, than ever Hercules had with the Bull. . . . There was not that variety of beasts in the Ark as there is of beastly natures in the multitude."[105] In the political arena as in the individual psyche, vice is not simply a penchant for wrongdoing. It is a terribly destructive force, forever threatening to overturn all values and rupture all bonds between men. A statesman must face, on a truly epic scale, tasks essentially similar to those confronting all people who seek to lead virtuous lives. He must

. . . have studied the arts of life;
To compose men, and manners, stint the strife

> Of murmuring subjects; make the Nations know
> What worlds of blessings to good kings they owe:
> And mightiest monarchs feel what large increase
> Of sweets, and safeties, they possess by Peace.[106]

For in public as in private life, peace and happiness depend upon strenuous efforts to control the baser human elements.

These attitudes were not new in the early seventeenth century, nor were they confined to the court. The English had long had a deep fear of popular disorder and aristocratic faction, and the church had always maintained that fallen man could not be trusted to govern himself. The strands of classical influence we have traced did not lead to the formation of a new royalist ideology, but strengthened and enriched a very old pattern of thought which had long buttressed the Crown's authority. They did contribute, however, to the arguments through which the court later justified Charles's personal rule.

NOTES

1. John Donne, *Selected Prose*, ed. Evelyn Simpson (Oxford: Oxford University Press, 1967), p. 134.

2. John Suckling, *Works in Prose and Verse*, ed. L. A. Beaurline (Oxford: Oxford University Press, 1971), p. 70.

3. Logan Pearsall Smith, *Life and Letters of Sir Henry Wotton* (Oxford: Oxford University Press, 1912), vol. 2, p. 1; George Wither, *Britain's Remembrancer*, quoted in Perez Zagorin, *The Court and the Country* (New York: Atheneum, 1971), p. 44. For discussions of this anticourt tradition, see C. Uhlig, *Hofkritik im England des Mittlealters und der Renaissance* (Berlin: De Gruyter, 1973); and Sydney Anglo, "The Courtier: The Renaissance and Changing Ideals," in *The Courts of Europe: Politics, Patronage, and Royalty, 1400–1800*, ed. A. G. Dickens (London: Thames and Hudson, 1977), pp. 33–52.

4. Lawrence Stone, *Causes of the English Revolution*, (London: Routledge; N.Y. Harper and Row, 1972), p. 86.

5. Richard F. Hardin, *Michael Drayton and the Passing of Elizabethan England* (Lawrence: University of Kansas Press, 1973); Margot Heinemann, *Puritanism and Theatre* (Cambridge: Cambridge University Press, 1980). For deprecating views of literature associated with the Stuart court, see Alfred Harbage, *Shakespeare and the Rival Tradition* (London: Macmillan, 1952); and John Danby, *Poets on Fortune's Hill* (London: Faber and Faber, 1952), pp. 152–183. Recent works have been more restrained, but overtones of the same disapproving attitude are evident in many, including Margot Heinemann, *Puritanism and Theater*; Zagorin, *The Court and the Country*; and P. W. Thomas, "Two English Cultures: Court and Country Under Charles I," in *The Origins of the Civil War*, ed. Conrad Russell (London: Macmillan, 1973).

6. Nicholas Breton, *The Court and the Country*, p. 179. This and similar statements were ignored by Zagorin, who borrowed Breton's title for his own book without discussing it in detail. The attitudes Breton portrays do not support the assertion that "all these

[moral and cultural] intimations and meanings of 'Country' were closely interwoven in its application as the name of the Opposition" (Zagorin, "The Court and the Country: A Note on Political Terminology in the Seventeenth Century," *English Historical Review* 77 [1962]: 309). The political connotations of the court-country dichotomy were far more complex and ambiguous than Zagorin and other historians have allowed.

7. Notably *The Gypsies Metamorphosed*, which portrays courtiers as pickpockets. See Dale Randall, *Jonson's Gypsies Unmasked* (Durham, N.C.: Duke University Press, 1975); Jonathan Goldberg, *James I and the Politics of Literature* (Baltimore: Johns Hopkins University Press, 1983), pp. 128–130. Some of the Caroline masques, esp. *Love's Triumph Through Callipolis*, satirize court sexual morals.

8. For a sensible discussion, see Derek Hirst, "Court, Country, and Politics Before 1629," in *Faction and Parliament*, ed. Kevin Sharpe (Oxford: Oxford University Press, 1979), pp. 105–138.

9. John Stow, *Survey of London* (1633 ed.), p. 699. For an example of this type of criticism of London, see *Stuart Royal Proclamations* (ed. James F. Larkin and Paul L. Hughes, vol. 1 (Oxford: Oxford University Press, 1973), p. 21.

10. Joyce Appleby, *Economic Thought and Ideology in Seventeenth-Century England* (Princeton: Princeton University Press, 1978), esp. chaps. 1–3, is the best modern discussion.

11. Cf. Bacon's comment (*The Works of Francis Bacon*, ed. James Spedding et al. [London, 1858–1874], vol. 13, p. 23): "But instead of crying up all things which are either brought from beyond sea or wrought here by the hands of strangers, let us advance the native commodities of our own country."

12. *Works of Ben Jonson*, ed. C. H. Herford and Percy and Evelyn Simpson, 11 vols. (Oxford: Oxford University Press, 1925–1953), vol. 8, p. 593 (hereafter cited as H&S). Cf. Bacon's comment: "The arts which flourish in times while virtue is in growth are military; and while virtue is in state, are liberal, and while virtue is in declination, are voluptuary; so I doubt that this age of the world is somewhat upon the descent of the wheel" (*Works*, vol. 3, pp. 378–379).

13. H&S, vol. 5, pp. 452–453.

14. On this subject generally, see Frank Whigham, *Ambition and Privilege* (Berkeley and Los Angeles: University of California Press, 1984).

15. Bacon, "Of Great Place," in *Works*, vol. 6, p. 398.

16. Cf. Salisbury's complaint: "Give heed to one that hath sorrowed in the bright lustre of a Court. . . . Tis a great task [there] to prove one's honesty and yet not spoil one's fortune. . . . I am pushed from the shore of comfort and know not where the winds and waves of a Court will bear me. I know it bringeth little comfort on earth, and he is, I reckon, no wise man that looketh this way to heaven" (quoted in Wallace Notestein, *The Stuart House of Commons, 1604–1610* [New Haven: Yale University Press, 1971] p. 38).

17. Lines 897–906. Cf. Sir James Harington's lament: "I have spent my time, my fortune, and almost my honesty, to buy false hope, false friends, and shallow praise; and be it remembered, that he who casteth up this reckoning of a courtly minion, will set his sum like a fool at the end for not being a knave at the beginning" (quoted in Louis Le Cocq, *Satire en Angleterre de 1580 à 1603* [Montréal, Paris, Brussels: Didier, 1969], p. 69).

18. *Camden Society Publications*, 4th ser., vol. 12, p. 11.

19. Smith, *Wotton*, vol. 2, p. 21.

20. B. L., Stowe MSS 285, fol. 13.

21. H&S, vol. 11, p. 375. The views being expressed were a cliché; examples could easily be multiplied.

22. This sort of infighting was more or less a normal state of affairs in European

courts. Compared with the lethal struggles under Henry VIII, Edward, and Mary, Jacobean court politics seem relatively docile. However, it is unlikely that this provided much consolation to men caught in the middle of the Jacobean factional battles.

23. This was already true under Elizabeth. See esp. Wallace MacCaffrey "Place and Patronage in Elizabethan Politics," in *Elizabethan Politics and Society: Essays Presented to Sir John Neale*, ed. S. T. Bindoff et al. (London: Athlone Press for University of London, 1961), pp. 98–108, 122, 125. No one has determined how much worse things became in James's reign, but it is clear that far more people were chasing a supply of offices which had remained stable. One reason for the "inflation of honors" and the growing burden of monopolies after 1603 was that new titles and patents were easier to create than new offices, so that a ruler besieged by suitors was under extraordinary pressure to grant them. Even with these concessions, the Crown never came close to satisfying the landed elite's immense appetite for court rewards.

24. Quoted in LeCocq, *Satire en Angleterre*, pp. 74, 75.

25. *Poems of John Donne*, ed. Herbert Grierson (Oxford: Oxford University Press, 1912), vol. 1, p. 163. For a modern account see Richard Cust, "News and Politics in Seventeenth Century England," *Past and Present* 112 (1986): 60–90.

26. Sydney Anglo, "The Courtier: The Renaissance and Changing Ideals," in *The Courts of Europe: Politics, Patronage, and Royalty, 1400–1800*, ed. A. G. Dickens (London: Thames and Hudson; New York: McGraw-Hill, 1977), pp. 33–53, provides a good brief discussion.

27. It is difficult to say how far this reflects a change in social attitudes and how far it is simply a measure of the growing literacy and sophistication of the period. It is suggestive, however, that the fashion for anticourt satires developed about a generation earlier than the boom in newsletters and parliamentary diaries of the 1620s. There does seem to have been a real increase in concern about the court ca. 1590–1610. For a recent case study see F. J. Levy, "Francis Bacon and the Style of Politics," *English Literary Renaissance* 16 (1986): 101–122.

28. F. J. Levy, *Tudor Historical Thought* (San Marino: Huntington Library, 1967), esp. chap. 7; Alvin Kernan, *The Cankered Muse* (Princeton: Princeton University Press, 1959); and LeCocq, *Satire en Angleterre*.

29. Philip Finkelpearl, *John Marston of the Middle Temple* (Cambridge, Mass.: Harvard University Press, 1969), pp. 87–92, discusses the environment in which many of the satires were written. Joseph Hall was the most important satirist who did not belong to one of the Inns.

30. For a survey of the political histories, see J. W. Lever, *The Tragedy of State* (London: Methuen, 1974). Jonson commented in the epistle dedicatory to *Volpone* about the tendency of some members of his audience to discover seditious meanings in plays: "Application is now grown a trade with many, and there are [those] that profess to have a key for the deciphering of everything; but let wise and noble persons take heed how they be too credulous, or give leave to these invading interpreters to be overfamiliar with their fames, who cunningly, and often, utter their own virulent malice under other men's simplest meanings." (H&S, vol. 5, pp. 18, 19). Shortly after Essex's rebellion, Greville destroyed two of his tragedies for fear they might be construed in this way and get him into trouble for libels and covert political meanings which he never intended.

31. Quoted in John Nichols, *Progresses of James I* (London, 1828), vol. 1, p. 500.

32. William Camden, *Remains Concerning Britain* (London, 1674), p. 264.

33. Criticism of foreign rulers was also dangerous, since their ambassador might complain to the king. What mattered was whether the allusions in a play seemed sufficiently pointed to offend a powerful individual. For interesting recent discussions of censorship and its effect on English Renaissance literature, see Annabel Patterson, *Censorship and*

Interpretation: The Conditions of Writing and Reading in Early Modern England (Madison: University of Wisconsin Press, 1984), and Philip J. Finkelpearl, "The Comedian's Liberty: Censorship of the Jacobean Stage Reconsidered," *English Literary Renaissance* 16 (1986): 123–138.

34. Randall, *Jonson's Gypsies*, makes a strong case for the argument that Jonson intended the masque to be subversive. This seems plausible, since so far as we know Jonson was never patronized by Buckingham but did have friendly relations with courtiers like Arundel and Pembroke, who disliked the duke. Even if Randall is correct, we should probably see the masque not as an attack on the court as an institution but as an assault on an unpopular favorite by a poet expressing views widespread within the court itself.

35. This is the greatest methodological difficulty arising out of the interesting recent work of scholars like Patterson and Butler, who attempt to rediscover the hidden political dimensions of early seventeenth-century drama. They are certainly correct to insist that early Stuart literature often did have a veiled political significance and not infrequently contained criticism of the royal court. Patterson is also correct in arguing that the censorship imposed on writers the need to convey their messages in indirect ways and that readers understood this fact and became adept at finding hidden meanings. The problem is that it is generally impossible to determine whether the hidden meanings discovered by a modern critic were intended by the author or recognizable to a seventeenth-century audience. There is consequently no way of controlling the imaginative fecundity of a critic intent on showing that dramatists were expressing the political ideas he would like to attribute to them. Butler, especially, seems to give inadequate attention to this problem.

36. Discreetly veiled because direct criticism might offend the prince and encourage envious detractors. For Castiglione, one of the uses of dissimulation was to guide the prince without letting him know he was being controlled.

37. I disagree here with Philip Edwards, *Threshold of a Nation* (Cambridge: Cambridge University Press, 1979), chap. 6. Edwards holds James and his court in utter contempt (e.g. pp. 149–150), and so argues that Jonson's masques and laudatory verse were hollow flattery, whereas his satiric attacks on the court must have reflected Jonson's real views. There is no good reason to suppose that Jonson shared Edward's evaluation of James, which is far more simplistic and unequivocal than that of most contemporaries. Jonson undeniably portrayed power and authority in radically divergent ways, depending on the sort of work he was writing, but this does not prove that he was inconsistent and frequently insincere. The contrast between the idealism of the masques and the jaundiced view of courtiers and politicians conveyed by the tragedies and satires stems from basic philosophical assumptions. Like most seventeenth century thinkers, Jonson regarded government as both a providential source of justice and an exercise of power by fallen men in a depraved world. By its nature political power is morally ambiguous: it fulfills divine ideals, yet to a greater or lesser extent it is always corrupted. A court poet must convey this insight to his readers, and one way of doing so is by alternating satiric and idealistic images of court life.

38. Among Jacobean poets, Michael Drayton especially illustrates how nostalgia for Elizabethan and medieval culture could fuse with attacks on the vices of James's court. He continued to write epics into the 1620s, long after they had gone out of fashion, inserting into them thinly veiled satires of the king and his associates, counterpointed by calls for a heroic prince to appear and revive the old English virtues. See Hardin, *Drayton*, for a discussion.

39. J. M. Shuttleworth, ed., *The Autobiography of Lord Herbert of Cherbury* (London: Oxford University Press, 1976), pp. 53–60.

40. H&S, vol. 8, pp. 205, 206.

41. Linda Levy Peck, *Northampton: Patronage and Policy at the Court of James I* (London: Allen and Unwin, 1982), chap. 8, and "Problems of Jacobean Administration: Was Henry Howard, Earl of Northampton, a Reformer?" *Historical Journal* 19 (1976): 831–858; Menna Prestwich, *Cranfield: Politics and Patronage Under the Stuarts* (Oxford: Oxford University Press, 1966), chap. 5. The real reason for Cranfield's fall was political, but he nonetheless suffered public humiliation and disgrace.

42. A good brief discussion is provided in Mervyn James, *English Politics and the Concept of Honour, 1485–1642* (Past and Present Supplement, no. 3, Oxford: Oxford University Press, 1978), pp. 72–96.

43. *Dramatic Works of Shakerley Marmion* (Edinburgh and London, 1875), p. 120.

44. This discussion is indebted to Richard Peterson, *Imitation and Praise in the Poems of Ben Jonson* (New Haven: Yale University Press, 1981). See, in addition, H. A. Mason, *Humanism and Poetry in the Early Tudor Period* (London: Routledge, 1959); Ira Clark, "Ben Jonson's Imitation," *Criticism* 20 (1978): 107–120; and Katherine E. Maus, *Ben Jonson and the Roman Frame of Mind* (Princeton: Princeton University Press, 1984). A superb discussion of the subject in a European context is Thomas Greene, *New Light in Troy* (New Haven: Yale University Press, 1983).

45. H&S, vol. 8, p. 638.

46. On Jonson's use of the classics, see esp. Peterson, *Imitation and Praise*, the final chapter in Thomas Greene, *New Light in Troy*, and George Parfitt, *Ben Jonson: Public Poet and Private Man* (New York: Barnes and Noble, 1976), chap. 6. It should be noted that classicism in this sense does not preclude an interest in native traditions or in romance. Especially in his late works, Jonson sometimes imitated Elizabethan and medieval forms, such as the pastoral and the morality play. See Anne Barton, *Ben Jonson: Dramatist* (Cambridge: Cambridge University Press, 1984), esp. chaps. 14–16.

47. H&S, vol. 4, p. 43.

48. For an extended discussion of the way Jonson's work implicitly demands a vigorous and critical response from its audience, see Richard Dutton, *Ben Jonson* (Cambridge: Cambridge University Press, 1983), esp. chaps. 2 and 3.

49. Cf. Bacon's comment in *The Advancement of Learning* (*Works*, vol. 3, p. 318): "If the invention of the ship was thought so noble, which carrieth riches and commodities from place to place, and consociateth the most remote regions in participation of their fruits, how much more are letters to be magnified, which as ships pass over the vast seas of time, and make ages so distant to participate of the wisdom, illuminations and inventions, the one of the other." Jonson shared this view of literature as the basis for a community that reaches beyond the present, to achieve an almost Burkean sense of rootedness in the past.

50. See K. McEuen, *Classical Influence upon the Tribe of Ben* (New York: Octagon, 1968), esp. chap. 1.

51. The playful side of Jonson and the range of his art are stressed in Alexander Legatt, *Ben Jonson: His Vision and His Art* (London and New York: Methuen, 1981).

52. Thus Horace, in Jonson's translation of the *Ars Poetica* (H&S, vol. 8, p. 352), proclaimed:

> Orpheus, a priest, and speaker for the Gods
> First frighted men, that wildly liv'd at odds
> From slaughters, and foul life; and for the same
> Was Tigers said and Lions Fierce, to tame.
> Amphion, too, that built the Theban towers,
> Was said to move the stones, by his Lute Powers,
> And lead them with soft songs, where that he would.
> This was the wisdom, that they had of old,

Things sacred, from profane to separate;
The public from the private; to abate
Wild raging lusts; prescribe the marriage good;
Build Towns, and carve the laws in leaves of wood.
Cf. Jonson's own comments in *Discoveries* (H&S, vol. 8, p. 636) and Camden's comments in *Remains*, p. 406. Citations could be multiplied.

53. H&S, vol. 8, pp. 159, 160.

54. This sense of deep affinity between his own work and that of historical and legal scholars provides a vital clue to Jonson's outlook. Having been educated by the great antiquarian Camden, Jonson always saw himself as the colleague of men like Selden and Sir Robert Cotton, both of whom were his close friends. His literary imitation of the classics is in some ways similar in spirit to the sort of legal antiquarianism shown, for example, in Selden's contributions to the debates over the Petition of Right in the Parliament of 1628 (*Commons Debates, 1628*, ed. Robert C. Johnson et al., 4 vols. [New Haven: Yale University Press, 1977–1978]). Selden and his colleagues attempted to preserve the common law by applying appropriate precedents from the past to the situation of 1628. In their own minds they were not engaged in a pedantic quest for arcane bits of legal knowledge, but were attempting to revivify the political wisdom embedded in the common law by using the correct precedents to point out a solution to the political crisis in which they found themselves. In much the same way, Jonson tried to use the insights and models of poetic expression found in classical literature to enhance his portrayal of his own society and to convey the qualities of mind and spirit needed to live properly within it.

55. H&S, vol. 4, p. 293. The description was applied to Virgil, but it could fit Horace or Martial equally well. The classical satirists claimed to write "*sermones*" or conversations and therefore cultivated an unpretentious, "plain" style modeled after the speech of upper-class society. For the influence of this style on Jonson, see Wesley Trimpi, *Ben Jonson's Poems: A Study in the Plain Style* (Stanford, Calif.: Stanford University Press, 1962). See, however, Peterson's reservations, *Imitation and Praise*, pp. 234, 235.

56. H&S, vol. 4, p. 269.

57. Although it takes a different approach from this chapter, Maus's *Jonson and the Roman Frame of Mind* is the most rigorous scholarly discussion of Jonson's relationship to the Roman classics.

58. H&S, vol. 8, p. 564.

59. Ibid., p. 588. "But her [the soul's] Reason," Jonson went on, "is a weapon with two edges, and cuts through." Thus, if the reason is dull or inactive the soul remains entangled. See Legatt, *Jonson*, chap. 1 for a discussion of the artificial worlds which Jonson's characters create for themselves.

60. H&S, vol. 8, p. 607.

61. On this point, see esp. Legatt, *Jonson*, pp. 23–24.

62. For two recent studies of Jonson's ambivalence concerning his theatrical art, see Jonas Barish, "Ben Jonson and the Loathed Stage," in *A Celebration of Ben Jonson*, ed. William Blissett et al. (Toronto: University of Toronto Press, 1973); and John Gordon Sweeney III, *Jonson and the Psychology of Public Theater* (Princeton: Princeton University Press, 1985). One need not agree entirely with Sweeney's psychoanalytic interpretation to recognize that for Jonson the moral value of the theater was deeply problematical.

63. *Complete Masques*, ed. Stephen Orgel (New Haven: Yale University Press, 1969), pp. 263, 264.

64. Cf. Mosca's speech in act 3, scene 1 (H&S, vol. 5, pp. 66, 67):
But your fine, elegant rascal, that can rise
And stoop, almost together, like an arrow;
Shoot through the air as nimbly as a star;

Turn short as doth a swallow; and be here,
And there, and here, and yonder, all at once;
Present to any humor, all occasion;
And change a visor swifter than a thought
This is the creature had the art born with him;
Toils not to learn it, but doth practice it
Out of most excellent nature: and such sparks
Are the true parasites.

65. On this point, see Jonas Barish, *The Antitheatrical Prejudice* (Berkeley and Los Angeles: University of California Press, 1981), p. 146: "They [Jonson's villains] are armed against our disapproval with a formidable weapon: the inventiveness of their talent, the gusto with which they exercise it. They command their own changes; they dictate their own motions; they keep the turning world turning; and even as we recognize the subversive nature of their actions we find ourselves drawn to them in admiring fascination." As a number of critics have commented, all this has the effect of making us vicarious accomplices to the crimes we witness on the stage. We cannot condemn a character like Volpone without condemning part of ourselves, a fact which demands a more complex and thoughtful response than smug moral disapproval. For two different discussions, see Dutton, *Jonson*, esp. chap. 2, and Sweeney, *Jonson and the Psychology of Public Theater.*

66. H&S, vol. 5, p. 83.

67. Cf. the similar ambiguity in one of Mosca's speeches to Voltore (ibid., p. 34):
. . . And gentle sir,
When you do come to swin in golden lard,
Up to the arms in honey, that your chin
Is borne up stiff with fatness of the flood . . .
What is really being described here (though Voltore does not know it) is the cloying, suffocating quality of Volpone's gold. For more extensive discussions, see the introductory essays by Alvin Kernan and Jonas Barish in the Yale editions of both plays; John J. Enck, *Jonson and the Comic Truth* (Madison: University of Wisconsin Press, 1966), chap. 5; Dutton, *Jonson*, chap. 2; and Barton, *Jonson: Dramatist*, chap. 4.

68. H&S, vol. 8, p. 35.

69. As Leggatt puts it (*Jonson*, p. 13), "What Jonson fears is the disguising that leads to loss of self."

70. See Stanley Fish, "Authors-Readers: Jonson's Community of the Same," *Representations* 7 (1984): 26–58, for the view that Jonson's laudatory verse is governed by a strategy of never saying anything at all about the people it praises or the qualities that render them praiseworthy, beyond the tautological assertion that they are who they are and every perceptive onlooker will realize what this means. See also Harris Frieberg, "Ben Jonson's Poetry: Pastoral, Georgic, Epigram," *English Literary Renaissance* 4 (1974): 111–136.

71. For a suggestive discussion, see Thomas Greene, "Ben Jonson and the Centered Self," *Studies in British Literature* 10 (1970): 352–398.

72. The best account is Peterson, *Imitation and Praise.*

73. H&S, vol. 8, p. 96.

74. Ibid., p. 66.

75. Cf. Peterson, *Imitation and Praise*, chap. 2.

76. Legatt (*Jonson*, p. 128) comments: "For him [Jonson] the retreat [from the world] can never be final; there is always something for the retired man to do. . . . Even the poems that appear to advocate retreat alternate that advice with fierce attacks on the world. In Jonson, when virtue retreats it is not to a monastic cell but to a fortified tower

with plenty of ammunition." One of the obvious points of *Epicoene* is that Morose's at-tempts to keep out the world and its folly by imposing a reign of silence in his house only makes him the more ludicrous and the more vulnerable to chicanery.

77. H&S, vol. 8, p. 80.

78. Ibid., p. 48. The juxtaposition of this poem to one praising Salisbury is sug-gestive though not conclusive.

79. Ibid., p. 216.

80. Cf. Bacon's comment (*Works*, vol. 6, p. 441): "For there is no such flatterer as is a man's self; and there is no such remedy against flattery of a man's self as the liberty of a friend."

81. We find it, e.g., in a letter to Sir Francis Cottington from Sir Thomas Went-worth (Knowler, vol. 1, p. 163): "I . . . govern myself as little by opinion as most men do, yet I could be content . . . sometimes to hear from a faithful wise friend what judg-ments others have of me; for so I may come to see my Errors, which I should be sure to amend." Earl Miner, *The Cavalier Mode* (Princeton: Princeton University Press, 1971), chap. 6, discusses the theme of friendship in early- and mid-seventeenth-century poetry.

82. H&S, vol. 8, p. 65.

83. For a fuller discussion of Jonson's use of classical source materials in this poem, see Greene, *New Light in Troy*, pp. 281–288.

84. For a further discussion, see Earl Miner, *Cavalier Mode*, esp. chap. 2, and below, Chapter 8.

85. See Maren Sophie Røstvig, *The Happy Man* (Oslo: Norwegian University Press, 1954). Røstvig tends to underestimate the degree to which Jacobean poets had already begun to assimilate the *beatus ille* tradition from Horace and Virgil. For a recent inter-pretation, see James Turner, *The Politics of Landscape* (Cambridge, Mass.: Harvard Uni-versity Press, 1979).

86. For Sidney and Spenser, see Bartlett Giametti, *The Earthly Paradise and the Re-naissance Epic* (Princeton: Princeton University Press, 1966), chap. 5.

87. Abraham Cowley, *Essays*, ed. A. B. Gough (Oxford: Oxford University Press, 1915), p. 21.

88. LeCocq, *Satire en Angleterre*, pp. 62, 63.

89. L. G. Salinger, "The Elizabethan Literary Renaissance," in Boris Ford, ed., *The Pelican Guide to English Literature*, vol. 2: *The Age of Shakespeare* (Harmondsworth: Penguin, 1955), p. 76.

90. Jonson, "Robert Wroth," H&S, vol. 8, p. 98. Roman poetry described hospi-tality between friends and that given by patrons to their clients, but there was no Latin equivalent to the English tradition of giving hospitality to tenants and poorer neighbors.

91. Joseph Hall, *Collected Poems*, ed. A. Davenport (Liverpool: University of Liver-pool Press, 1941), pp. 33–35.

92. Robert Herrick, "The Country Life to the Honoured Mr. Endymion Porter," in *Poems*, ed. L. C. Martin (Oxford: Oxford University Press, 1965), p. 229.

93. For a discussion of the social changes to which the last two paragraphs have re-ferred, see Lawrence Stone, *Crisis of the Aristocracy* (Oxford: Oxford University Press, 1965), esp. chaps. 5 and 10.

94. Pocock, *The Machiavellian Moment, Florentine Political Thought and the Atlantic Republican Tradition* (Princeton: Princeton University Press, 1975), chaps. 12–14; Isaac Kramnick, *Bolingbroke and His Circle: The Politics of Nostalgia in the Age of Walpole* (Cam-bridge, Mass.: Harvard University Press, 1968).

95. The term ceases to be anachronistic at just about this time.

96. The following discussion is based in part on a lecture by Stephen Orgel.

97. The awkwardness of this design contrasts with the intelligence of many of Jones's borrowings from Renaissance sources. See John Peacock, "Inigo Jones's Stage Architecture and Its Sources," *Art Bulletin* 64 (1982): 195–216.

98. Gordon Toplis, "Inigo Jones: A Study of Neo-platonic Aspects of His Thought and Work" (M.A. thesis, Liverpool, 1967), p. 192.

99. "To Penshurst," H&S, vol. 8, p. 93.

100. John Harris, "Inigo Jones and the Courtier Style," *Architectural Review* 144 (1973): 17–24, discusses the early evolution of Jones's style.

101. Thus Bacon wrote to George Villiers (the future Duke of Buckingham) in 1616: Let vanity in apparel, and which is more vain, that of fashions, be avoided. I have heard that in Spain (a grave nation, whom in this I wish we might imitate) they do allow the players and courtesans the vanity of rich and costly clothes, but to sober men and women they permit it not" (*Works*, vol. 13, p. 23). The advice was lost on its recipient, but the attitude is significant.

102. BL, Harl. MSS 6272, fol. 170.

103. Below, Chapter 6.

104. E.g., Pocock, *Machiavellian Moment*, chap. 10.

105. H&S, vol. 8, p. 593.

106. Ibid., p. 261.

5 THE DISCOVERY OF EUROPEAN ART: COLLECTING AND PATRONAGE

The classical influences we have been tracing were one major stimulus to the development of early Stuart court culture. Another, of at least equal importance, was a growing admiration for continental painting and sculpture, which the English court first fully discovered in this period.[1] At the beginning of James's reign England had assimilated less of the artistic culture of the Renaissance than virtually any kingdom in western Europe.[2] By the 1630s the situation was completely transformed: Van Dyck was among the two or three most fashionable portraitists in all Europe, and London's art collections could rival those of any continental city.

This transformation was foreshadowed in the 1590s and early 1600s by the painting of Peter Oliver and Marcus Gheeraerts and the interest in continental styles taken by a few peers and leading courtiers. But it began in earnest only in the 1610s, among a handful of royal and aristocratic patrons who laid the foundations for the artistic brilliance of Charles's court. In examining court art, we will therefore be dealing with trends rooted in a much narrower and more elevated social milieu than were the literary fashions traced in previous chapters. Jonson was a product of the city as much as the court who, for all his originality, built upon well-established, native traditions. By contrast, Jones's mature style had no discernible roots in Elizabethan architecture, while Van Dyck, Orazio Gentileschi, and most of Charles's other artists were trained abroad.[3] They were essentially practitioners of foreign traditions transplanted into England by the efforts of a small but extraordinarily wealthy and prominent group.

THE GREAT ARISTOCRATIC COLLECTIONS

That group, in turn, consisted mostly of younger men whose cosmopolitan aesthetic tastes were largely a by-product of the regime's policy of détente with Spain and her satellites. The Anglo-Spanish peace not only created a climate more favorable to sympathetic contact with foreign cultures than had prevailed during the religious wars of the previous reign. It also opened Flanders, Spain, and Italy to relatively large numbers of English aristocratic tourists.[4] Before 1603 few of the queen's subjects braved the risks posed by the Spanish and Roman inquisitions to travel to Mediterranean countries, and those who did had more serious goals than attaining a knowledge of Renaissance art. In the seventeenth century, however, several developments encouraged leisurely foreign travel by English lords and wealthy gentry. The momentary cessation of warfare helped, but so did a more flexible attitude on the part of the Vatican, which began to welcome visits to Italy by wealthy English heretics in the hope that it might convert them, or at least soften their hostility toward Catholicism. English peers and gentlemen could therefore venture south of the Alps without fear of persecution and mingle openly with the aristocracies of Venice, Florence, and Rome itself.[5] Relatively few actually did so, but this minority included a number of future courtiers, such as Sir Kenelm Digby and the Earl of Arundel.[6]

In addition to facilitating travel abroad, the Jacobean peace allowed England to reestablish embassies in Brussels, Madrid, Venice, and Florence after a hiatus of nearly four decades.[7] Several royal servants spent years in these embassies, and, as one might expect, a few developed into knowledgeable connoisseurs of Renaissance art. Wotton returned from more than a decade of service in Venice to write the first book on architecture produced by an Englishman since 1553.[8] Sir Dudley Carleton, who represented James in Brussels and Venice, amassed a collection of ancient statues sufficiently distinguished to exchange, in 1620, for a large number of pictures from the personal collection of Rubens.

By that date, a number of much greater collections had been as-sembled in England. A few of these were started much earlier. Leicester is known to have acquired several Italian paintings as early as the 1580s, while the Earl of Shrewsbury and Queen Anne were both col-lecting in the first years of James's reign.[9] Only after 1610, however, did a small coterie of great courtiers begin to purchase foreign art on a grand scale. The earliest leader of this group was Prince Henry, who procured Venetian masterpieces, assembled a fine collection of ancient medallions, appointed Inigo Jones as his Surveyor, and recruited for-eign artists to his service, including the Dutch painter Mierevelt, the Florentine engineer Constantinio de Servi, and the French landscape architect Saloman de Caus.[10] Several members of Henry's entourage carried on his work after his premature death. The third Earl of Pem-broke bought paintings attributed to Veronese, Titian, and several other Italian masters. But the most important collector was the Earl of Arundel, who sent agents all over Europe to look for art treasures and bought on such a scale that Rubens once called him "one of the four evangelists and a supporter of our art."[11] Arundel made the acquaint-ance of Van Dyck, Rubens, and Honthorst before any of them came to England, and for a time he employed the Dutch painter Daniel Mytens in his household. He excavated ruins in Rome, sent an agent to the Ottoman Empire to hunt for Greek antiquities, and assembled En-gland's first collection of ancient statues, now in the Ashmolean Mu-seum of Oxford. By the 1620s his galleries rivaled the finest on the Continent; by the Civil War he owned 799 paintings, including 40 Holbeins, 13 Brueghels, 16 Dürers, and at least a dozen attributed to Tintoretto, Veronese, Giorgione, Raphael, and Corregio.[12]

Arundel also retained Inigo Jones as an expert adviser and archi-tect. In 1614 they traveled together through Italy, touring ancient ruins and purchasing art. Two years later we find them examining a consign-ment of paintings from Italy. In 1618 Jones acted as an intermediary between Sir Dudley Carleton, who bought paintings in Flanders, and both Arundel and Pembroke, who repurchased them in England. About the same time he also designed a new gallery for Arundel's Lon-don palace to house the earl's collection.[13]

By the time Buckingham rose to prominence in the late 1610s, art collecting had become fashionable. Not to be outdone, he retained his own architect and art expert, Balthazar Gerbier, and began to assemble another great collection. For the next five years Gerbier went scurrying around Europe, sending back enthusiastic reports of the treasures his patron should acquire:

> I have met with a most beautiful Tintoretto, of a Danae, a naked figure . . . that flint as cold as ice might fall in love with. . . . But my lord, after your excellency shall have made a large collection, I beg you to attack Monsieur de Montmorency, for he has the most beautiful statues that can be spoken of . . . two slaves by Michelangelo. . . . He is so liberal that he will not refuse them.[14]

Buckingham's most spectacular coup as a collector came in 1625, when he visited Rubens's house in Antwerp and bought virtually every piece of art it contained.

THE COLLECTING AND PATRONAGE OF CHARLES I

Born in 1600, Charles grew up as the fashion for European art developed, and he became an avid convert from his early years. He inherited Henry's collection, added to it, and during his trip to Madrid saw perhaps the finest group of Renaissance masterpieces in Europe. Upon returning to England, he worked energetically to build up the court's artistic resources—taking an active interest in a new tapestry factory employing Flemish weavers that James had established in the London suburb of Mortlake, buying Italian paintings, befriending Daniel Mytens and Inigo Jones, and commissioning works from Rubens and other leading continental artists.[15]

After his accession Charles patronized the arts on a scale only the Crown could afford. He sent agents to Europe to purchase masterpieces and recruit talented artists. Mytens returned to the Netherlands to master the latest styles of his homeland; Buckingham recruited Orazio Gentileschi from the household of the Queen Mother of France. Several courtiers went to Italy, including Charles's trusted companion Endymion Porter, the composer and amateur artist Nicholas Lanier, and two of Gentileschi's sons. Working with a merchant named Daniel Nys, they kept an eye on the art market. In 1628 Nys succeeded in procuring the collection of the Duke of Mantua, one of the greatest in all Italy, for £15,939.[16] The next year, on a visit to London, Rubens wrote in amazement that he had never seen so many great paintings in one place as in the galleries of the king and the court nobility.[17]

By this date Gentileschi, Mytens, and Inigo Jones were also producing work that was at least competent by the standards of Italy or Flanders. But the court still lacked an artist of international repute, a deficiency Charles wanted to overcome. He made overtures to Guercino and Rubens and for a year patronized the Dutch artists Gerrit von Honthorst and Cornelius Broom, apparently as a trial.[18] Finally, in 1633, Van Dyck agreed to join the English royal household.[19] His arrival capped two decades of steadily increasing sophistication and modernity in English court art, completing the revolution Henry and his circle had begun.

THE KING'S ARTISTIC ADVISERS

Although the king's achievement as a patron is clear enough, the methods he used to finance and direct the development of court art have never received systematic study. The royal collection's size and the brilliance of Van Dyck, Jones, and other court artists have conjured up, in the minds of some scholars, images of a massive and systematically organized program of cultural innovation. Some have asserted, on the basis of fragmentary evidence, that Charles's investment in culture contributed materially to the financial difficulties of the Crown and therefore to the outbreak of civil war.[20] This view is almost entirely wrong. To a remarkable extent, Caroline royal patronage depended on informal, ad hoc procedures and forms of shoestring financing.

Charles succeeded so well as a collector and patron because he relied on the advice and assistance of a sophisticated entourage. His pronounced aesthetic taste placed a premium on artistic expertise within the court. In the company of men who conversed knowledgeably on the topic, his normally cold and aloof manner often gave way to warm enthusiasm. The Tuscan envoy Salvetti once found himself cornered by a monarch eager to learn the latest gossip about Florentine artists, while a Venetian ambassador recorded how, in the midst of a conversation about Italian politics, Charles

> interrupted me and changed the subject to pleasant and general topics, hunting, pictures and the like, in which he takes the greatest delight. I

responded and he detained me for a full hour, treating me with much friendliness and more confidence than is usual with him.[21]

Throughout his reign, the king surrounded himself with companions who could satisfy his passion for talk about art. All the great aristocratic collectors sooner or later won his favor, including even Arundel, who had the temerity to cross Buckingham in the 1620s and suffered a spell of imprisonment at the king's command. Among the royal privy chamber servants, Endymion Porter and Sir Kenelm Digby both enjoyed reputations as connoisseurs of painting. Charles also liked the company of artists, befriending Mytens, Jones, and Gentileschi.[22] Rubens received many long audiences during his trip to London; Van Dyck had to contend with royal visits to his studio.[23]

The enthusiasm binding together this little coterie of patrons and professional artists comes through vividly in Panzani's description of a scene following the arrival of several paintings sent by the Vatican:

> As soon as the King was told by the Queen that she had received the pictures he rushed to see them, calling to him Jones, . . . the Earl of Holland and the Earl of Pembroke. The very moment Jones saw the pictures he greatly approved of them and in order to be able to study them better threw off his coat, put on his eyeglasses, took a candle and, together with the King, began to examine them very closely, admiring them very much. . . . They let the Earl of Arundel know the paintings had arrived in court and he came immediately to see them.[24]

The next day, Charles playfully put Jones's expertise to the test, removing the labels from the pictures to see how many Inigo could identify by "the artist's hand." Panzani found Jones bragging about his success at this game in the queen's apartments.

By conversing with the members of his entourage and with a few Italian ambassadors, Charles could have learned about virtually all the significant artistic traditions of the late Renaissance and early Baroque. Arundel established friendships with several Venetian noblemen, some of whom probably remembered Tintoretto, Titian, Veronese, and Palladio. Jones met the Italian architect Scamozzi and toured the Venetian *terra ferma* taking notes on Palladian villas.[25] Gentileschi had been a close friend and artistic disciple of Caravaggio.[26] Van Dyck grew up in Antwerp, the chief center of Flemish art, working for a time in Rubens's studio. Endymion Porter and Sir Francis Cottington had strong links to the Spanish court; Mytens knew many Dutch artists, perhaps including Rembrandt, whose work was, in any case, represented in Charles's collection. In the late 1630s papal envoys kept the king abreast of developments in Rome, then the most important center of Italian Baroque art. Artistic currents from all over Europe converged at the English court.

The experts clustered around Charles assisted his collecting and patronage in several ways. They advised him on what to purchase and helped to assess the value of works he procured. Jones seems to have stayed at the royal elbow in the 1620s as Charles assembled his collection.[27] A few years later Gentileschi knew enough about the king's taste to advise the papacy about what gifts to send to England.[28] Whenever possible the king relied on trusted personal servants to buy art for him abroad or to negotiate with foreign artists. The purchase of the Mantua collection was the most important, but it was by no means the only example of this method. As he considered moving to England, Van Dyck received visits from Balthazar Gerbier, Endymion Porter, and finally the Earl of Arundel.[29] In 1627 Sir Kenelm Digby went on a privateering expedition to the Mediterranean and returned with a Greek frieze for the king. Several years later Sir Francis Cottington purchased samples of Spanish court art while on an embassy to Madrid.[30] The queen's favorite, Walter Montagu, went to Rome in the mid-1630s and procured casts of ancient statues worth over £200. The work of building the royal collection was conducted mostly by an informal team whose members knew Charles's taste from personal experience.[31]

ADMINISTRATION AND FINANCING OF CULTURAL ACTIVITIES

Charles also relied on a few trusted companions to supervise cultural activities within his household. For all the dramatic stylistic innovations taking place during his reign, he made no significant changes in administrative procedures and never established regular methods of paying for cultural experiments. Whenever possible he employed old household departments and their budgets; when he could not fit his patronage into an inherited institutional and financial structure, he improvised new arrangements. The only source of centralized control holding the whole ramshackle structure together was his own personal initiative and that of his cultural advisers.

Music One area where Charles converted an ancient department of the royal household into an agent of cultural change was court music.[32] He inherited an establishment of nearly eighty musicians, grouped into a number of orchestras and ensembles known collectively as the King's Music.[33] Deriving essentially from the reign of Henry VIII, this organization had an annual budget which increased from £1,333 in 1603 to about £1,600 during James's reign and just under £1,900 in the late 1630s. Under Elizabeth and James the Crown retained some of the finest composers England has ever produced, including Byrd and Dowland. By the 1610s, however, Elizabethan styles had come to sound old-fashioned, at least to people familiar with the Italian experiments which led, about this time, to the first operas and the earliest Baroque compositions.[34] When the Venetian Busino witnessed a masque in 1618 he praised everything but the music, which seemed to him unworthy of comparison with the "elegant and harmonious" compositions of his native land.[35]

By that date several English composers had begun experimenting with Italian forms. The most ambitious, Nicholas Lanier, attempted in 1617 to compose an entire masque in a recitative style ostensibly based on Italian models.[36] When the post of Master of the King's Music fell vacant in 1625, Charles appointed Lanier to it. Lanier then recruited young men schooled in Italian styles to replace older musicians as they died off.[37] By the early 1630s the court even boasted a student of Monteverdi.

The results of this attempt to drag English composition into the seventeenth century proved to be mixed. At its best, as in the instrumental compositions of William Lawes, Caroline court music is an original synthesis of native and Italian styles reminiscent of the great traditions of Elizabeth's reign yet enlivened by devices picked up from Baroque and operatic composers. Too often, however, the efforts to assimilate Italian techniques resulted in derivative and uninspired work, now remembered only by specialists in musicology. Not even the best of Charles's composers achieved the stature of Byrd or Monteverdi, but they did initiate experiments that led to the first English opera in the 1650s and ultimately to Purcell. In the short run they produced accompaniments to masques and other court functions that were, at least superficially, as up-to-date as the court's art.

As Lanier did his work, Henrietta Maria created a second orchestra.

From her independent household revenues she carved out £2,000 a year—slightly more than the budget of the King's Music—to pay French musicians and Englishmen able to play or compose in French styles. She also granted a pension to the chief musician of her brother's court in Paris, presumably for supplying her with information and song-books. The two leading schools of early seventeenth-century composition, those of Italy and France, were each therefore represented by an orchestra and a staff of composers at the English court. Yet only the queen had built from the ground up. Her new and well-financed musical establishment contrasts with the patchwork arrangements employed by her husband.[38]

Architecture Charles's method of achieving fundamental cultural changes through traditional methods and sources of money appears with equal clarity in his approach to architecture. Since the Middle Ages the royal household had included an Office of Works, consisting of masons, carpenters, and other artisans who constructed and maintained the king's buildings.[39] In 1615 Inigo Jones became the Surveyor, or head of this organization, the first man possessing a knowledge of Renaissance architectural theory to do so. He quickly set about teaching the department's artisans to work in a mature classical style, a task of immense importance because in England master masons and carpenters still designed most buildings. Jones's underlings took private commissions all over London and in the provinces, spreading his innovations. Two of them—the Works' master mason, Nicholas Stone, and the Surveyor's assistant, John Webb—became architects in their own right.[40]

James had expanded the Works' budget from £4,000 a year to a peak of over £20,000, and this inflated figure did not include the construction of new buildings, such as the Whitehall Banqueting House, which cost an additional £15,000.[41] Under Charles, however, expenditures shrank back to about £10,000 a year, still more than double what the parsimonious Elizabeth had provided for the upkeep of her residences, but given the increase in prices and the age of most royal palaces probably not an unreasonable sum.[42] A large portion of this money went for routine repairs no monarch could have avoided without abandoning many of the Crown's aging Tudor palaces. But Jones also engaged in some modernization and renovation. The Works accounts record payments for a painting depicting Saturn devouring his children, murals of the sack of Troy, statues for the new Cockpit in Court Theater, and the queen's chapels, along with assorted pillars, pilasters, and carved putti for the interior decor of royal palaces.

The motives behind this work are easy to guess. The early seventeenth century was a great age of palace-building. Louis XIII added extensively to the Louvre, Philip IV erected the Buon Retiro, and the papal court put up villas and townhouses all over Rome and the surrounding countryside. Charles wanted to outdo all his foreign rivals, so he commissioned a design for a palace larger and more imposing than any then in existence. It was far too grandiose a project for the Stuarts to build. It looks as though the king, unable to fulfill his architectural dream, set about remodeling the interiors of his old-fashioned residences room by room. The fact that he did so mainly in wood and stucco, for about half the cost of James's architectural maintenance, speaks eloquently of the financial constraints upon royal patronage.

Charles did manage to erect a few relatively small buildings, notably the Queen's House at Greenwich, the Cockpit in Court Theater, and chapels for his wife at St. James and Somerset House.[43] Each was financed separately, with money from the exchequer, the queen's coffers, the duchy of Lancaster, and any other sources the king could find, at costs ranging from £4,000 for the Somerset Chapel to about £7,500 for the Queen's House.[44] Setting aside the Mantuan collection, these structures were the most expensive forms of cultural patronage in which the king engaged, yet all were far more modest than some residences erected by English aristocrats in James's reign, such as Hatfield House and Audley End, to say nothing of the gargantuan building projects of continental princes.[45] The Buon Retiro cost Philip IV an estimated £600,000, more than Charles spent on *all* forms of cultural patronage during his entire reign.[46]

Quite apart from work on their own palaces, many early seventeenth-century rulers helped finance and direct ambitious projects of civic architecture. Henry IV of France erected the Place Royale and other large residential quarters, while a series of popes rebuilt Rome as a monument to the Catholic faith and their own glory. Again, the Stuarts could not afford to imitate these European rivals, but they did manage to achieve something in this area through indirect methods.

In the 1610s the Crown established a commission charged with overseeing all construction in the capital and enforcing royal proclamations against buildings erected on new foundations. Jones and the Earl

of Arundel were both members. The chief purpose, initially, was to restrain London's runaway growth, especially the creation of more of the
suburban slums which had sprouted up all around the old city.[47] But particularly in Charles's reign the commission promoted some ambitious
projects. It tried to exclude the poor from the vicinity of Whitehall and
attempted to force all the goldsmiths in London to open shops on a
single street—measures intended to regulate the capital's commercial
and residential growth.[48] The commission also used its power to approve or reject designs for all new London buildings, in order to impose
some measure of uniformity.

In addition, the Crown gained control of two large projects of civic
architecture. The first was the renovation of old St. Paul's Cathedral, a
Romanesque and Gothic structure which had fallen into such disrepair
that it threatened to collapse. Work began under James, bogged down
for lack of funds, and finally reached completion in the 1630s after the
Crown launched a nationwide campaign. London merchants, country
gentry, and the nation's clergy were all pressured into donating, with
Charles himself contributing £4,000 to build a giant Corinthian portico before the cathedral's main entrance, topped by brass statues of
himself and his father. Charles also threw his own weight and that of
the Privy Council behind the fund-raising. "Wherever there was found
slackness in raising and collecting money in this behalf," Rushworth
later wrote, "persons of wealth or authority were to be quickened by
letters monitory sent from the Council table."[49] The king's emotional
commitment to the project comes through in a vindictive letter he
wrote in 1635 to the cathedral dean and chapter concerning a local
tenant who refused to contribute:

> It is a thing of unsufferable example that a tenant which gains so much by
> the Church should be so ungrateful as not to contribute anything. . . .
> These are therefore to . . . require you . . . not to suffer . . . Mrs. More
> . . . to renew the said lease. . . . And that you register this our letters as a
> memorial of that unthankfulness of hers in the Register Book where you
> usually record other business.[50]

Laud and a board of commissioners supervised the renovation, but
Charles himself was the driving force behind it.

The second of Jones's major London projects was Covent Garden.
The famous "piazza" was originally the centerpiece of a much larger development, stretching from St. Martin's Lane in the west to Drury Lane

in the east and northward to Long Acre, built under the auspices of the ground landlord, the Puritan Earl of Bedford. However, because the site fell within the area in which building on new foundations was prohibited, Bedford had to obtain a special license, which the Crown granted in 1629. It has long been known that in return Bedford agreed to build the piazza according to plans approved by the Crown and that he employed Jones as an architect.[51] A previously undiscovered document indicates that royal interference was even more extensive. In 1634 Bedford was sued in the Star Chamber for creating a nuisance to London and Westminster by building Covent Garden.[52] A draft of the earl's testimony in this case survives and indicates that Charles personally intervened to alter the original Covent Garden plans:

> Before the building was upon this license [erected] the plot of it was showed to his Majesty's view and his Majesty was also graciously pleased to view also the plans in his own person, attended by diverse lords commissioners for buildings, whereupon *he so altered the plot of the buildings that were to be erected* that the Earl was by that alteration (in regard of the plot, the piazza & co. which by that alteration he was to build) put to £6000 more charges . . . by giving of larger time to his tenants and abatements in their rents which necessarily followed *by reason of their being held to build according to his Majesty's alterations.* . . . The Earl himself built none [i.e., no houses] save *three piazza houses all of which are built . . . fully according to his Majesty's alterations of the plot.*[53]

The information is tantalizingly vague, but it leaves no doubt that extensive last-minute changes were made and that the main responsibility lay not with Jones but with the king.

Nor did the Crown's interference end with the final approval of Bedford's plans. For the remainder of the 1630s the Privy Council repeatedly intervened in the affairs of Covent Garden, overseeing the construction of sewers, the provision of drinking water, and the paving of streets and closing down all but two of the area's taverns and alehouses.[54] The elegant new suburb with its uniformly built brick houses, suitable for "gentlemen and persons of quality," was very much a monument to Charles's tastes, even though he paid not a penny toward its construction.

Masques and Paintings Music and architecture were the two spheres of culture most extensively patronized by Tudor and medieval kings, who created specialized household departments to regulate both. Other

forms of royal cultural patronage had never been extensive enough before the seventeenth century to require bureaucratic supervision or
regular sources of funding. When a Tudor monarch wanted to procure a
new portrait, he might draw upon any source of ready cash to pay for it.
If he wished to retain an artist permanently, he would simply grant the
individual a pension. The rapid development of the masque under the
Stuarts, and Charles's passion for art, for the first time created a situation in which more orderly procedures might have been desirable. Yet
the Stuarts did nothing to meet this need. Administrative and financial
arrangements present a picture of almost total disorganization.

The masques nominally fell under the supervision of an Office of
Revels, established to supervise the more rudimentary dramatic spectacles of the Tudor period. James granted Ben Jonson a second reversion
to the post of Master of Revels, but he did not live long enough to inherit the office. The Revels remained under the control of a relative of
the Earl of Pembroke named Henry Herbert, who had no appreciable
skills as a poet or artist. He and his staff were therefore confined to the
burdensome task of making arrangements for masque audiences, while
Inigo Jones worked with a series of poets and musicians on the actual
productions.

The procedures followed in devising masques cannot be reconstructed with any certainty and were probably never well defined.[55] In
Charles's reign, Jones usually seems to have been in charge, though
sometimes he shared the responsibility with a poet and probably with
the monarchs themselves. In the mid-1630s Jones asked Salvetti to procure for him a book illustrating stage sets for Florentine *intermezzi*, the
Italian equivalent of the masque. Salvetti wrote to the Duke of Tuscany
that he was certain Charles also wanted to see this volume.[56] It seems
likely that the king and his architect set down together with it to plan
masque designs.

The masques' cost, which appears to have averaged out to slightly
more than £1,400 for each, was frequently covered by warrants autho-
rizing direct payment from the Exchequer.[57] Sometimes the royal wardrobe helped pay for the costumes, and the scene painting was frequently
though not always financed out of the Works account. The Chamber, the Exchequer, and the queen's household also occasionally
contributed.[58]

An even greater absence of formal organization prevailed among
the court's artists. Charles attached painters and sculptors to the house-

hold in any way that seemed momentarily convenient. At the outset of the reign, Daniel Mytens held the title Painter to the King. When Van Dyck arrived in England, this post was simply duplicated to accommodate him; until Mytens returned to the Netherlands, Charles had two official painters.[59] Gentileschi, on the other hand, was at first Buckingham's painter rather than the Charles's.[60] Only after the duke's death did Charles grant him a pension of £100 a year, made retroactive "from the time of his first coming into this kingdom . . . in . . . 1626."[61] When Hollar arrived in 1636, he was appointed drawing master in the recently organized household of the royal children.[62]

Once an artist joined the king's household he did not always enjoy an adequate or regular salary. In principle, every royal servant received an annual pension, sufficient for his maintenance at a level appropriate to his rank. Van Dyck for example, was entitled to £200 a year, the income of a lesser gentleman. Unfortunately the royal treasuries never had enough ready cash to pay all the pensions Charles granted, so artists were left competing against other household servants and aristocratic suitors the king chose to gratify for whatever funds came in. Since payments often fell years in arrears, painters and sculptors had to support themselves by selling their work. The Crown paid them separately for each piece it commissioned but, as we have seen, most of their patronage usually came from ordinary courtiers and gentry visiting London.

Thanks to the semi-annual declared accounts of the Exchequer, we can form a reasonably precise estimate of the amount of money the king actually spent on his artists.[63] These itemize all works of art purchased by the Crown, even in the case of those costing only a few pounds.[64] The accounts have disappeared for three terms out of the thirty between 1625 and 1640, and a few items may have slipped through the audits unrecorded, but there is no reason to suppose that Charles spent substantially more on art than these documents reveal. In all, between 1625 and 1640, the Exchequer laid out £17,541 for tapestries, £7,830 for new paintings (of which £3,000 went for the Whitehall Banqueting House ceiling), and £2,520 for statues. In seven years Van Dyck received somewhat less than £2,000, plus whatever he managed to collect of his pension. There is no way of calculating how much he earned from private commissions, but at his usual price of about £30–£50 a portrait the sum would certainly have exceeded by a substantial margin the patronage of the king.

CONCLUSION: THE COST AND CHARACTER OF ROYAL PATRONAGE

In the early Stuart period the Crown never devoted more than a tiny fraction of its resources to cultural patronage. Even if the full budget of the Office of Works is included, the annual expenditure probably averaged out to less than £30,000 a year under Charles, and perhaps slightly more under James, compared to a household budget that reached £250,000 and total revenues eventually approaching £1,000,000. Charles could achieve so much partly because the expense of artistic and literary patronage remained relatively modest and partly because others contributed indirectly to the support of his court's cultural life.

This did not prevent at least one parliamentary writer from complaining about money wasted "on old rotten pictures and broken nosed marbles."[65] Precisely because they were a relatively novel and highly visible form of conspicuous consumption, court paintings and masques may have appeared more important, as examples of the court's extravagance, than their actual cost warranted.[66] And if we measure some of Charles's expenditures by any standards other than those of a Baroque court, they do appear extravagant. The £1,400 spent on each masque formed a comparatively small item in the household budget equal, for example, to only twice the annual cost of feeding the king's hounds. However, it also exceeded the total annual income of some barons and the yearly wages of more than a hundred laborers. The purchase of the Mantua collection aggravated an already serious financial crisis; by 1642 the royal collection represented an appreciable investment.[67]

Even the expense of the king's art needs to be placed in perspective, however. If Charles spent more than previous English monarchs on paintings, he spent less on other forms of culture, such as the great outdoor pageants that traditionally accompanied events like coronations and royal weddings. James had disbursed over £36,000 on his coronation and over £4,000 on fireworks and river pageants alone at the wedding of Princess Elizabeth. Total expenditures for this last event came to about £100,000, more than double the combined cost of the Banqueting House and the Mantuan collection.[68] Scholars have too often taken an excessively narrow view of the cost of Caroline patronage, commenting on the extravagance of Charles's innovative tastes without noticing the economies netted by his abandonment of older forms. The result is a highly misleading impression that he spent far more even than James on cultural display. In fact, the Crown's total expenditures on all forms of culture, including building and pageantry, declined after 1625.

There is, in short, no justification for the highly colored language modern historians have sometimes used in describing the expense of Caroline patronage. Charles's support for the fine arts and literature did not significantly increase the burden of government on the English taxpayer. Even a casual glance through the accounts of the Exchequer will reveal many more wasteful and expensive luxuries than the king's art. Despite professed intentions to cut back on the number of parasites hanging around Whitehall and to reduce waste in government, Charles proved no more successful than his father at resisting the requests of his retinue for money or reducing the venality and inefficiency that had crept into nearly all areas of court life since the 1590s.[69] So long as this root problem remained unsolved, no amount of frugality with respect to culture would have significantly relieved the Crown's finances.

With its lax administration and limited costs, the patronage of Charles I also differs sharply from that of later absolutist kings, notably Louis XIV. Versailles supported and controlled art and literature through a rationally organized system of patronage and censorship run through court academies and backed by immense resources.[70] French classicism was an officially sponsored cultural philosophy, imposed from above through the artistic and literary bureaucracies organized by Richelieu, Mazarin, and Colbert. By contrast, Caroline court culture grew out of the activities of a handful of artists, poets, and musicians, supported by a small group of patrons whose most prominent members happened to be the king and queen.

Indeed, perhaps the most striking finding to emerge from our survey is the extent of Charles's personal role in shaping court culture. Because of the informal methods he used, we cannot be certain just how active he was. We can never know what instructions he may have given Van Dyck while watching him paint, or how fully he and Inigo Jones discussed the latter's masque designs and architectural plans. All the evidence, however, points to a close partnership between the king and his artists and artistic advisers. Charles appears to have personally selected many of the paintings in the royal collection. He recruited Van Dyck, apparently after failing to attract Guercino and rejecting Honthorst and Broom. And he was evidently the animating force behind the renovation of St. Paul's Cathedral and the creation of the Covent Garden piazza. In short, wherever enough information survives to permit a judgment, the king emerges as a patron with pronounced tastes and strong convictions very much in control of the innovations taking place under his auspices. In his reign royal cultural patronage was not an extension of a bureaucratically organized absolutist state so much as a direct expression of the monarch's personality.

On the other hand, we also need to recognize that even in the 1630s much of the court's patronage was directed by figures other than Charles: Henrietta Maria, the Earl of Arundel, the Duke of Buckingham, and numerous lesser courtiers. These figures differed from each other in some of their preferences, a fact that helped diversify court culture. Arundel had a special love for Holbein and Dürer. Buckingham was even more addicted to Rubens than most Caroline collectors, whereas Charles seems to have favored Titian. Henrietta Maria preferred French styles, while Cottington and others had a taste for Spanish fashions. Yet all these connoisseurs shared a cosmopolitan outlook and a love for art, music, and the theater. Consequently, the culture taking shape under their collective auspices had a certain coherence and consistency, without ever becoming entirely uniform.

In some ways the relative informality of English court patronage proved to be a handicap. There were no Caroline academies to spread the innovations of Jones, Van Dyck, and the king's musicians or to construct an official cultural philosophy. In other respects, however, the absence of tight, centralized controls proved advantageous. Artists, poets, and musicians were not only spared the stultifying effects of official canons of taste but also were able to find patrons other than the government, a fact of critical importance when the court collapsed in the Civil War.

NOTES

1. Henry VIII's patronage of Holbein and the interest in continental art taken by a few mid-Tudor and Elizabethan patrons did not have a deep or lasting impact.

2. Eric Mercer, *English Art, 1553–1625* (Oxford: Oxford University Press, 1962), pp. 155–158; Roy Strong, *The English Icon* (London: Routledge; New Haven: Yale University Press, 1969), pp. 13–20; Mark Girouard, *Robert Smythson and the Architecture of the Elizabethan Era,* 2d ed. (New Haven and London: Yale University Press, 1983), p. 18. Although this was already beginning to change, it was only in the Stuart period that true appreciation for continental aesthetic culture ceased to be an exceptional attribute. See Lucy Gent, *Picture and Poetry* (Leamington Spa: James Hall, 1982), for a fine discussion.

3. So, for that matter, was Oliver, the most accomplished artist working in England before the late 1610s (Roy Strong, *The English Renaissance Miniature* [New York and London: Thames and Hudson, 1983]). In *Theater of the World* (Chicago: University of Chicago Press, 1969), Frances Yates traces Jones's roots in the artisan culture of Elizabethan London. It does seem likely that if we knew more about Jones's early life and the environment in which he matured we would become aware of strong native elements in his work. On the other hand, his mature architectural style is undeniably the product of classical and Italian influences.

4. On this topic generally, see John Walter Stoye, *English Travellers Abroad* (London: Cape, 1952).

5. Ibid., p. 112; Lawrence Stone, *The Crisis of the Aristocracy* (Oxford: Oxford University Press, 1965), p. 696.

6. Stone, *Crisis of the Aristocracy*, pp. 692–702. For an interesting case study of the developments discussed in this and the next several paragraphs, see D. J. Howarth, "Lord Arundel as a Patron and Collector, 1604–1640" (Ph.D. thesis, Cambridge University, 1979), now published as *Lord Arundel and his Circle* (New Haven: Yale University Press, 1985).

7. See Stoye, *English Travellers*, pp. 133–174, for an extended discussion of the Italian embassies and their significance as training grounds for courtiers and civil servants.

8. *The Elements of Architecture* (London, 1624).

9. For Shrewsbury, see Howarth, "Lord Arundel," pp. 5–6.

10. H. M. Colvin, D. R. Ransome, and John Summerson, *History of the King's Works*, vol. 3 (London: Her Majesty's Stationery Office, 1975), pp. 121–127, gives an account of Jones's early career and surveyorship under the prince. For an example of Henry's attempts to recruit a foreign artist, see the letters of Sir Dudley Carleton to Adam Newton in BL, Harl. MSS 7002, fol. 70, 107v, and 108.

11. Maria F. S. Hervey, *The Life, Correspondence, and Collections of Thomas Howard, Earl of Arundel* (Cambridge: Cambridge University Press, 1921), p. 176, n. 2; Howarth, *Lord Arundel*.

12. Stone, *Crisis of the Aristocracy*, p. 719.

13. Sir John Summerson, *Inigo Jones* (Harmondsworth: Penguin, 1966), pp. 35–37, 44; Edward Sherburne to Sir Dudley Carleton, April 9, 1616: "I have attended my Lord of Arundel to Mr. Secretary his house, where his Lordship with Mr. Inigo Jones has fully viewed the pictures" (SP 14/86/132); *The King's Arcadia: Inigo Jones and the Stuart Court*, ed. John Harris et al. (London: Arts Council of Great Britain, 1973), pp. 100–102.

14. Philip Gibbs, *The Romance of George Villiers, First Duke of Buckingham* (New York: Methuen, 1908), p. 284. See, also, I. G. Philip, "Balthazar Gerbier and the Duke of Buckingham's Pictures," Burlington Magazine 99 (1957), pp. 155–156.

15. Per Palme, *The Triumph of Peace* (Stockholm: Almquist and Wiksell, 1956), p. 26. In July 1624 Mytens was granted a pension of £50 a year and denization "by direction of the Prince's highness" (PRO, SO 3/8).

16. PRO, SO 3/9, July 1631. The sum was borrowed from Burlamachi and appears to have been repaid in three installments in November 1629, January 1631, and July 1631 (ibid.). Stone, *Crisis of the Aristocracy*, p. 719, states that the total cost was £18,000 without citing a source.

17. Rubens to Pierre Dupuy, August 8, 1629, in *The Letters of Peter Paul Rubens*, trans. and ed. Ruth Magurn (Cambridge, Mass.: Harvard University Press, 1955), p. 320.

18. A warrant was issued to the Exchequer in November 1628 to pay Honthorst and Broom £500 "for work done by them for His Majesty and for sundry pictures" (PRO, SO 3/9). For Honthorst, see Palme, *Triumph of Peace*, p. 264.

19. His pension of £200 a year was granted in May (PRO, SO 3/9).

20. See, e.g., Girouard, *Robert Smythson*, p. 4: "The Stuarts . . . built on a considerable scale and planned more extravagantly than they built. They patronized artists of the first reputation—Rubens, Bernini, Van Dyck—and in Inigo Jones found the first Englishman who had a true understanding of Renaissance architecture. This encouragement of the arts brought England into the mainstream of European culture. But it was highly unpopular with a large and vocal section of the country. . . . It was one of the elements that greatly increased Crown expenditure; the consequent efforts to raise money led to the new and unpopular taxes, or the recourse to disgruntled and belligerent Parliaments, that ultimately resulted in the Civil War."

21. Dispatch of January 27, 1634, BL, Add. MSS 27962G, p. 171; Dispatch of August 11, 1636, CSPVen., vol. 24, p. 45.

22. The Tuscan ambassador commented on the amount of time Charles spent with Gentileschi after the latter's arrival in England in a dispatch of December 4, 1626, in *Eleventh Report of the Royal Commission on Historical Manuscripts* (London, 1887), Appendix 4, part 1, p. 97.

23. Below, pp. 129–130.

24. Dispatch of January 30, 1635/36, PRO, 31/9/17, p. 30. For a discussion, see Rudolph Wittkower, "Inigo Jones: Puritanissimo Fiero," *Burlington Magazine* 90 (1948): 50, 51. I have followed Wittkower's translation.

25. Summerson, *Inigo Jones*, p. 36.

26. G. Ward Bissel, "The Baroque Painter Orazio Gentileschi: His Career in Italy" (Ph.D. thesis, University of Michigan, 1966), chap. 1.

27. In August 1628, Jones, Nicholas Lanier, and William George, clerk of the wardrobe, were ordered to make an inventory of the king's paintings, which may indicate that they were supervising Charles's acquisitions (PRO, SO 3/9).

28. Panzani dispatch of July 11, 1635, PRO, 31/9/17.

29. The circumstances surrounding Van Dyck's removal are briefly discussed in Christopher Brown, *Van Dyck* (London: Phaidon, 1982), pp. 137–40.

30. CSPVen., vol. 21, p. 549; SP 16/289/70. The importance of such personal knowledge is indicated in a letter from Arundel to his Italian agent in 1636: "You do very well to be careful of getting something of Titian for his Majesty . . . but for buying things for the King without order . . . I should not advise it, for His Majesty knows best what he hath gusto in, and I know well that in the other way [i.e., purchasing without instructions] one may both stay long for his money, from them that should pay it, and be esteemed officious instead of serviceable." (Quoted in Hervey, *Arundel*, p. 393.)

31. For an especially detailed and well-documented discussion of an example of such cooperation, which reached me too late to be taken into account in this book, see Paul Shakeshaft, "'To much bewiched with thoes intysing things': the letters of James, third Marquis of Hamilton and Basil, Viscount Feilding, concerning collecting in Venice, 1635–1639," *Burlington Magazine* 128 (1986), pp. 114–132.

32. Although strictly speaking it is not a form of artistic culture, music developed at the Caroline court in ways closely paralleling changes in the fine arts. It is therefore convenient to discuss musical patronage here.

33. Walter Woodfill, *Musicians in English Society* (Princeton: Princeton University Press, 1953), chap. 8. The Chamber accounts (PRO, AO 1/342) give an itemized yearly budget, on which the following discussion is mostly based.

34. For a brief discussion of these styles and their impact in England, see Willa M. Evans, *Henry Lawes: Musician and Friend of Poets* (New York: Modern Language Association of America; Oxford: Oxford University Press, 1941).

35. Stephen Orgel and Roy Strong, *Inigo Jones: The Theater of the Stuart Court*, 2

vols. (London: Sotheby Parke Bernet; Berkeley and Los Angeles: University of California Press, 1973), vol. 1, p. 283.

36. Ibid., p. 271. Notice the comment before the first lines: "(Spake in song, *stilo recitativo*)."

37. These appointments can be followed through Signet Office Docket Books. Thus Stephen Nau was appointed as a composer in November 1628; Henry Lawes, another composer, was granted a pension as a lutenist in August 1632; and his brother William, perhaps the greatest Caroline composer, won a pension in June 1635 (PRO, SO 3/9).

38. This description is based chiefly on the accounts of the queen's household in PRO, Sc 6, Ch I/1695–1699.

39. The most thorough account is H. M. Colvin et al., *History of the King's Works,* vol. 3 (London: Her Majesty's Stationery Office, 1975).

40. Palme, *Triumph of Peace,* pp. 48–50; Colvin et al., *King's Works* (vol. 3), chap. 7. As we have seen, the 1620s and 1630s were a period of active building in London, especially in the area north of the Strand, near Jones's own house and the main center of operations for the Office of Works. Some of the builders were courtiers, including Endymion Porter; others were carpenters and bricklayers residing in districts being built up. (A draft of Porter's building lease for the northwest corner of the Covent Garden piazza survives at Alnwick Castle MSS, Y/III/2/3, envelope 5. For a local carpenter constructing houses in Covent Garden, see YIII/2/5, envelope 9.) Two members of the Works staff, Thomas Bagley and George Neale, bequeathed houses or tenements in their wills; of these the former also left a legacy of £3 "to my very good friend Inigo Jones" (PRO, PROB 11/165/30 and Westminster Public Library Register Camden, fol. 224). All this is very suggestive, though not conclusive. There were many opportunities for Jones to influence building practices, even apart from his powers as a commissioner for buildings (below). How far he actually did so is probably an unanswerable question.

40. PRO, E 351/3391.

42. For a discussion, see Colvin et al., *King's Works* (vol. 3).

43. Summerson, *Inigo Jones,* pp. 75–81.

44. Colvin et al., *History of the King's Works,* vol. 4 (London: Her Majesty's Stationery Office, 1982), p. 119.

45. See Lawrence Stone, *Family and Fortune* (Oxford: Oxford University Press, 1973) chap. 2, for Hatfield House, which cost nearly £40,000.

46. For a discussion, see Jonathan Brown and J. H. Elliot, *A Palace for a King* (New Haven and London: Yale University Press, 1981), p. 102. I have converted Spanish currency into pounds at the seventeenth-century exchange rate and rounded off the result, since the costs given by the authors are only approximate.

47. For a discussion, see Palme, *Triumph of Peace,* pp. 47–48.

48. SP 16/250/51 and 378/65.

49. John Rushworth, *Historical Collections* (London, 1680), vol. 2, p. 90.

50. SP 16/281/34.

51. It has never been entirely clear whether Jones designed the whole piazza or only St. Paul's.

52. He was let off after paying an additional £2,000 to the Crown in return for a confirmation of his original license, which closed several loopholes in the original grant. For the number of houses already built, see SP 16/402/75.

53. Alnwick Castle MSS, YIII/2/4, envelope 10, paper entitled "The Charges of the Information which Mr. Attorney hath Delivered to the Earl of Bedford" (italics added). The Alnwick YIII MSS consist of the papers of Bedford's solicitor, John Scawen, who left his former employer and entered Northumberland's service in 1639, taking a large num-

ber of papers relating to Covent Garden with him. In addition to the items mentioned, these include a number of leases and information relating to Bedford's relations with his Covent Garden tenants.

54. The evidence for this supervision is contained in the Privy Council registers, e.g., PRO, PC 2/43/199, 396, and 633 and 44/69, 121 and 549.

55. For a discussion, see Orgel and Strong, *Inigo Jones*, vol. 1, p. 52.

56. BL, Add. MSS 27962G, p. 72.

57. £1,400 is the figure most often given in warrants for masque payments recorded in the Signet Office Docket Books. Since one occasionally finds additional warrants for further payments, this figure should probably be regarded as a minimum. For example, in December 1634 the Signet Office issued three separate warrants to pay Michael Oldisworth £1,400 "to be employed towards the charge of a Masque to be presented at Whitehall at Twelfthtide next," to pay George Kirke £150 for the king's masquing apparel, and to pay Oldisworth £1,400 toward the expense of the queen's Shrovetide masque. Thus we have a total of £2,950 for two masques. The most likely explanation for these entries is that £1,400 was considered the basic cost of a masque but that additional money was sometimes provided on an ad hoc basis to pay for items like Charles's masquing costume. It is possible that the estimated cost will have to be revised upward after a thorough study of all possible sources of masque payments, including Chamber, Wardrobe, and Works accounts and debts to tradesmen that were not immediately liquidated. It seems highly unlikely that many masques cost much more than £1,400, however.

58. These departments were usually reimbursed, though sometimes only after a period of years. Thus the Master of the Great Wardrobe was allowed £2,456 in May 1636 for a (lost) masque performed by Henrietta Maria in the 1625/1626 season (PRO, SO 3/11). Orgel and Strong, *Inigo Jones*, provide whatever documentation the authors could find on these points before the text of each masque. Additional information can be extracted from the Signet Office Docket Books, the audited accounts of the Exchequer, and the accounts of the departments involved, all in the PRO.

59. For a discussion, see Ellis Waterhouse, *Painting in Britain, 1530–1790* (Harmondsworth: Pelican, 1964) pp. 35–46.

60. In fact, he set up his studio in a "great upper room" of York House itself (PRO, E 78/5973).

61. PRO, SO 3/9, January 1629/30. About the same time, Charles also assumed the obligation of paying Gerbier the pension of £200 that Buckingham had granted him, and confirmed Buckingham's grant to Gerbier of a house adjacent to York House. It looks as if the king was assuming the artistic patronage obligations of the murdered favorite.

62. *Dictionary of National Biography* s.u. Hollar, Wenceslaus; F. C. Springell, *Connoisseur and Diplomat: the Earl of Arundel's Embassy to Germany in 1636* (London: Maggs, 1963), p. 150. On Hollar's career generally, see Katherine S. Van Erde, *Wenceslaus Hollar: Delineator of His Time* (Charlottesville: University of Virginia Press for the Folger Shakespeare Library, 1970).

63. PRO E, 405/280–285.

64. For example, in Michelmas term of 1635 Peter Oliver received £100 for "pictures made or to be made." The accounts show that the Crown usually paid in lump sums for several works, often completed over the course of a few years. Usually it was late in its payments.

65. Probably Sir Balthazar Gerbier (of all people) in *The None-Such Charles His Character* (1651), p. 85. If this anonymous pamphlet is in fact by Gerbier, to whom it is often attributed, his sincerity is highly questionable, since he had earlier served as one of Buckingham's purchasing agents. He may have been motivated chiefly by envy of Inigo Jones

and others who had more success in helping Charles purchase his "old rotten pictures." Gerbier (or whoever wrote the work) evidently thought the line would be well received, however, and this may indicate some public resentment of the king's art.   .

66. Charles Carlton, *Charles I: The Personal Monarch* (London: Routledge, 1983), p. 145, asserts: "In spite of—or perhaps because of—the king's exquisite tastes, careful management, unequalled judgement and diligent pursuit and patronage of excellence, his collection upset many." This seems plausible, but Carlton provides no evidence apart from Gerbier's slur.

67. Ibid., pp. 144, 145 points out that when sold in the early 1650s the collection brought nearly £50,000. Many of Charles's paintings were gifts, however, while others had probably appreciated in value on the continent, where much of the royal collection was purchased.

68. BL, Add. MSS 58833, fol. 17v. I wish to thank Conrad Russell for calling this document to my attention.

69. Robert Ashton, "Deficit Finance in the Reign of James I," *Economic History Review* (1957); Frederick Dietz, *English Public Finances* 2d ed. (New York: Barnes and Noble, 1964), esp. chap. 6. The audited accounts reveal that the cost of royal pensions actually increased above Jacobean levels in the 1630s.

70. For a recent discussion, see Ranghild Hatton, "Louis XIV," in *The Courts of Europe,* ed. A. G. Dickens (London: Thames and Hudson, 1977), pp. 233–262.

6 THE DISCOVERY OF EUROPEAN ART: AESTHETICS AND IDEAS

We have so far examined the artistic changes occurring at the Stuart court through a nuts-and-bolts study of administration and patronage. But those changes ultimately involved far more than the assembling of great collections and the recruitment and supervision of foreign artists. Court art and architecture were not just decorative embellishments; they also served to project the aura of prestige, power, and sanctity which clung to the king and his entourage. Caroline works often accomplished this purpose in profoundly different ways from those of Elizabeth's reign. The contrast between a Van Dyck portrait and one by Gower or Peake, for example, cannot be described purely in stylistic terms, for it reflects a change not only in techniques of painting but also in ideas about how a great aristocrat should look and how an artist should express his grandeur. Similarly, the orderly arrangement and well-proportioned facades of the Covent Garden development expressed not only a taste for classical architecture but also a new ideal of planned urban development. Social, political, and religious values were not simply part of the historical context of court art. They were often intrinsic to what men like Van Dyck and Inigo Jones sought to achieve, and to what Charles I and his companions saw when they looked at a painting, a masque set, or a building.

Reconstructing the social and intellectual dimensions of court art is by no means an easy task, however. Because art demands an intuitive response, appealing to our emotions through the senses, it inevitably calls into play very basic and largely unconscious habits of thought and imagination, produced by our own cultural upbringing. The danger of anachronistic interpretation therefore becomes especially acute in dealing with visual media. The comparative reticence of early Stuart courtiers about their response to art further compounds the problem. Nothing exists for this period comparable to the voluminous notebooks in which Horace Walpole recorded his reactions to hundreds of paintings and buildings in the eighteenth century, or the systematic treatises and art histories of the Italian Renaissance.[1] To avoid a completely impressionistic interpretation, however, we must attempt to reconstruct the basic modes of thought and feeling that shaped the responses of early Stuart patrons to visual culture.

THE ARTIST AS CRAFTSMAN

Since the Romantic movement, works of art have been valued chiefly as expressions of individual creative genius. We look upon a painting or statue as something that reflects the mind of the artist: his thoughts, emotions, fantasies, and unique way of seeing the world. The Elizabethans generally took a much more prosaic view. For them the artist remained what he had nearly always been in the Middle Ages—a skilled craftsman, turning out luxury objects for the rich.[2] People esteemed the fine arts chiefly for their decorative functions and capacity to express specific social ideals. For example, most statues adorned tombs, from which they peered out over the churches where communities gathered to worship, as visible reminders of the illustrious forebears of leading local families.[3] Similarly, people bought portraits— virtually the only type of painting in which Elizabethans took an interest—partly to add splashes of color to the long galleries of country houses, but primarily to commemorate themselves, their relatives, friends, ancestors, and patrons.[4]

The artist's main task was to contribute to the lavish displays of wealth and grandeur that were inseparable from the lives of the great. The Elizabethans loved bright colors, glittering light, and intricate two-dimensional patterns, predilections they gratified in many different ways, frequently at tremendous expense.[5] They dressed in costumes of kaleidoscopic opulence, fashioned from embroidered cloth, studded with pearls or jewels, topped by elaborate lace collars. The queen's wardrobe was reputed to have brought £60,000 when auctioned off after her death, the cost of a fairly large palace.[6] Each major event in the court's life—from its progresses to its holiday pageantry—was conducted with an eye to flamboyant spectacle.

All the arts reflected this sensibility. Statues were nearly always painted, sometimes quite garishly, and were often set in enclosures ornamented with slabs of colored marble, coats of arms, and emblematic devices. Great houses often featured soaring towers and expanses of glass, to provide illumination within and the sparkle of reflected sunlight without.[7] But it was above all Elizabethan painters who responded to the taste for complexity, color, and ostentation. A glance at a portrait like Gower's of the Countess of Leicester (Plate 5), with its flat, lifeless face and painstaking attention to jewels, embroidery, and lace, reveals the qualities patrons most valued. This work was at once an emblem of status, since only a very wealthy lady could afford such clothes, and an object conforming to the same passion for unrestrained decorative effects that governed the work of embroiderers, goldsmiths, and armorers. Even Hilliard probably owed his prominence chiefly to the jewel-like qualities of his miniatures, which satisfied on a diminutive scale the same concept of beauty. As he once wrote, his credit "excelleth all others . . . in giving luster to pearl and precious stone, and worketh metals and gold and silver . . . being fittest for the decking of princes' books or to put in jewels or gold."[8]

This taste for color and ostentation derived from some old and deeply rooted traditions. It stemmed in part from the liturgical practices of the medieval church, with its stained-glass windows, golden chalices, elaborate processions, and rich vestments. This scenic apparatus became deeply controversial after the Reformation, but the partial success of Protestant attacks on religious art and ceremony appears, in the short run, to have reinforced the taste for secular pageantry, almost as if in compensation. The Tudors deliberately promoted court ceremonies that might help fill the void left by the declining magnificence of the English church after the breach with Rome. The Elizabethan love of visual splendor also had important temporal sources. Since the Middle Ages the sight of lofty castles, liveried retainers, fluttering banners, and beautifully emblazoned coats of arms had expressed the power of the realm's great families. Elizabethan fashions in this kind of pomp differed from those of the thirteenth and fourteenth centuries, but the under-

5. George Gower (attr.) *Lettice Knollys, Countess of Leicester*. Reproduced by permission of the Marquess of Bath, Longleat House, Warminster, Wiltshire, England. Photograph: Courtauld Institute of Art, London.

lying attitude remained essentially the same: the greater an individual's status, the more impressive his house, his clothing, and his retinue should be. By capturing the gorgeous trappings of rank, painters were in effect conveying how Elizabethans sought to visualize what it meant to be a peer or a monarch.

A particularly good illustration of this point, showing how both secular and religious elements could fuse in the grand, ceremonious spectacles Elizabethans loved, is a painting of the queen in a procession attributed to Robert Peake and executed around 1600 (Plate 6).[9] Like most of her portraitists, Peake converted Elizabeth into an iconic symbol. All references to her personality have evaporated, so that her rank is conveyed almost entirely through iconographic symbols and the procession's rich appearance. The sun shines brightly over the entire scene, clearly illuminating the colors worn by the queen's entourage, the fine details of her own costume, and the aristocratic houses in the background, toward which she and her train are heading. The sumptuously dressed men who surround her, bearing up the canopy and serving as human ornaments to her journey, include some of the realm's greatest figures. This attending crowd seems to jostle and bustle around her: limbs are in motion, faces are animated, and here and there the courtiers turn to talk to one another. But the queen sits motionless and silent, her features reduced to a schematic mask set off by the jewels of her crown and robes, the decorated canopy over her head, and the magnificent lace collar, which surrounds her face like an aureole of light. It is probably no accident that she looks like the statue of some Roman Catholic saint being carried in a great Counter-Reformation procession. Peake shows us the half-deified royal figure, referred to by some panegyrists as history's second greatest virgin, to whom the common people could transfer the awe and reverence once accorded the Mother of God.

This approach to visual culture would probably have inhibited appreciation for Renaissance art even if Elizabeth's courtiers had been able to examine more works by continental masters of the first rank. Men who coveted the visual feasts that Gower and Peake provided might well have regarded the painting of Raphael and Titian as dull. English patrons and artists certainly chose at times to reject Renaissance models lying ready to hand, in order to develop more ornate and fanciful styles. Hilliard knew many naturalistic portraits by Flemish mannerists, but these had little effect on his work.[10] He was strongly

6. Robert Peake. *A Procession by Queen Elizabeth, ca. 1600.* Mr. Simon Winfield Digby.

influenced by the French school of Clouet, but this did not prevent him from developing a style completely alien to Renaissance concepts of form and spatial realism.[11] Lord Burghley owned architectural treatises containing elevations far more up-to-date, by continental standards, than those he employed for Theobolds and Burghley House.[12] The qualities of harmony, proportion, and realism intrinsic to high Renaissance art simply did not appeal strongly to most English patrons, who had their own distinctive sense of visual beauty.

Yet it was not only the existence of original native traditions that inhibited understanding of Renaissance aesthetic values. The problem lay deeper, in the unwillingness of all but a few Elizabethan aristocrats to regard painting, sculpture, and architecture as subjects worth serious intellectual attention. The Tudor elite did not much concern itself with skills regarded as purely manual in nature. The role of a gentleman was to enjoy the labor of others, not to inquire too curiously into how artisans earned their wages. Social prejudice therefore inhibited interest in the fine arts. The contrast between the roles of poetry and painting in the Elizabethan court illustrates this clearly. Literary craftsmanship appeared to be a natural extension of the linguistic and rhetorical training normally given to young gentlemen. Consequently, the queen herself had no inhibitions about writing verse, and many courtiers could knowledgeably discuss fairly technical literary problems. On the other hand, few members of the royal entourage appear to have studied systematically the techniques of painting, and none, so far as we know, ever tried to paint.[13]

These limitations did not prevent Elizabethan patrons from instructing portraitists and artisan builders as to the kind of work they wanted. On the contrary, the queen and her courtiers often interfered in planning even minor details of their portraits and residences. With few exceptions, however, they did so in very unsystematic ways. A nobleman building a house, for example, often suggested features he wanted incorporated and the general layout of the plan, but he rarely attempted to draw up detailed elevations.[14] Normally a great house still remained a matter for improvisation, to be decorated with whatever fanciful devices a patron might conceive and to be erected by a team of masons and carpenters without formal architectural training.

THE PHILOSOPHY OF ARTIFICIAL WORKS

Already in Elizabeth's reign, however, influences were at work helping to prepare the ground for a more appreciative attitude toward the fine arts. Despite prevailing prejudices, a few prominent courtiers and a handful of country gentlemen did take an interest in Renaissance painting and architecture.[15] More important, the last few decades of the sixteenth century witnessed an unprecedented boom in aristocratic building.[16] Opulent country houses went up all over England as peers and gentlemen strove to outdo their neighbors and rivals. From the 1580s most of the larger houses included long galleries decorated with small collections of portraits, so that painters enjoyed more patronage than ever before. Forms of culture ostensibly unworthy of sustained intellectual attention by gentlemen in fact consumed enormous amounts of time, energy, and money.

In light of these conditions, it is scarcely surprising that by the last decade of the century we begin to encounter signs of a livelier interest in the principles of painting and architecture. A man named Matthew Haydocke translated the treatise on art of the Italian mannerist Lomazzo in the late 1580s. In 1598 this book went through a second edition, complete with a new preface calling upon both patrons and artists to study "the excellency of ancient works" of painting and sculpture and summoning the gentry to begin collecting "monuments of sundry masters, both German and Italian."[17] About the same date, Gheeraerts developed a more naturalistic and psychologically expressive style of portraiture, evidently with the encouragement of the Earl of Essex, Sir Henry Lee, and other leading figures at court.[18] Architectural theory had also come into fashion among some London wits. "By Phoebus here's a neat, fine street," a character in *The Poetaster* proclaims, in an attempt to show off. "I protest to thee, I am enamored of this street, 'tis so polite and terse. . . . I study architecture too; if ever I should build I'd have a house of that perspective."[19] Although Jones's earliest buildings and the first large English collections still lay more than a decade in the future, people in and around the court had already begun to discuss art in a more systematic and thoughtful way. This trend must have fostered curiosity about the paintings and buildings courtiers encountered in Flanders and Italy as they began touring the continent.

It would be a mistake to suppose that Englishmen began to study manuals of art and architecture chiefly to educate their aesthetic taste.

What seems to have intrigued them most was simply the idea that manual skills might profitably form the subject of systematic, philosophical thought. Until well into the Stuart period, artistic interests nearly always appeared as one facet of a much broader concern with technological problems and scientific experiments.

Continental art theorists probably helped encourage this eclectic attitude by presenting painting and architecture as universal disciplines, drawing upon and illuminating every area of human knowledge.[20] By observing the behavior of nature, they argued, the artist learned not only to understand nature's powers but also to imitate them through his work. He thereby acquired a knowledge more useful than that of academic philosophers, culminating in technical skills rather than abstract theories and leading to the production of objects that would delight both the mind and the senses. In achieving this goal, he employed all the liberal arts, from music and mathematics which taught the nature of harmony, to history and moral philosophy, which helped him depict human character and emotion.

The English quickly absorbed the scientific and practical elements of this philosophy while relegating aesthetic concerns to a secondary position. They were interested in techniques rather than concepts of beauty, and consequently made no attempt to distinguish between the fine arts and other forms of craftsmanship, or varieties of scientific investigation requiring manual operations. One of the earliest and most enthusiastic pioneers of this species of thought was Elizabeth's court astrologer, John Dee. Decades before Inigo Jones designed his first building, Dee tried to interest his countrymen in the study of Vitruvian architecture. He did so, however, primarily because he regarded Vitruvius as the exponent of a lost science dealing with the methods of manual labor. According to Dee, architecture is a discipline grounded in mathematics, exercising a

> principality . . . above all other arts . . . to be master over all that make any works: whereupon he [the architect] is neither smith nor builder, but the head, the provost, the director and judge of all artificers. . . . He only searcheth out the causes and reasons of all artificial things.[21]

So defined, Vitruvian classicism is less an affair of columns, pediments, and proportions than the study of all technological sciences. It comprises subdisciplines like "thaumaturgike," the "art mathematical which giveth order to make strange works . . . to be greatly wondered at. By sundry means this wonder work is wrought . . . by weights . . . by strings strained, or springs, therewith imitating . . . lively motions."[22] To promote this kind of knowledge, Dee tried to provide instruction in geometry to English artisans. "How many a common artificer is there in these realms," he wrote in the preface to a translation of Euclid, "who with his own skill and experience . . . will be able by these good helps and informations to . . . devise new works, strange engines and instruments for progress in the commonwealth?"[23]

Architecture thus became a science dedicated to the discovery of methods for manipulating the natural world, comprising the knowledge of the inventor, the engineer, and even the magician, since in Dee's view mathematics held the key not only to technology but to demonology and astrology as well. A man who knew the right formulas might artificially control the spiritual forces that govern the universe.[24] Through this kind of "science," Dee hoped to bring about the imperial dream of a reborn Golden Age in which all the forces of the cosmos would serve human needs and support the benevolent rule of England's royal Astrea.

No one has determined how much influence this occult philosophy had over the intellectual climate of Elizabeth's court.[25] It is clear, however, that in the early seventeenth century several figures close to the court were experimenting with pursuits similar to the less occult of Dee's "Vitruvian" sciences. The "wizard earl" of Northumberland set up a laboratory in the Tower of London, where he had been sent for his alleged role in the Powder Plot, and there pursued experiments with his fellow prisoner, Sir Walter Raleigh. Raleigh, in turn, wrote warmly of "a kind of magic" comprising "the whole philosophy of nature . . . which bringeth to light the inmost virtues and draweth them out of nature's hidden bosom to human use."[26] Sir Francis Bacon, in *The New Organon*, contrasted the sluggish process of the intellectual disciplines, standing "almost at a stay, without receiving any augmentation worthy the human race," with the "mechanical arts, which having in them some breath of life are continually growing and becoming more perfect."[27] At the heart of his famous empirical philosophy lay a determination to devise new manual skills: "for the end which this science of mine proposes is the invention not of arguments but of arts . . . to command nature in action."[28]

Bacon's essay "Of Building" shows how this pragmatic and inventive mode of thought carried over into the study of architecture in the modern sense. This piece contains a wealth of useful information for the builder of a country house. He should avoid places hemmed in by hills, where the air stagnates; he must restrict the use of glass, or his house will heat up in the summer; the kitchen must not be too near the stairway, or its odors will permeate the building. Bacon dismisses aesthetic concerns, however, with this deprecating comment: "Houses are built to live in and not to look on, therefore let use be preferred before uniformity, except where both may be had."[29] He had absorbed the practical observations of Vitruvius and the Renaissance architectural manuals, while rejecting the core of stylistic principles.

This approach to the manual arts probably appealed to English courtiers largely because it ran parallel to the old humanist conviction that a gentleman's education should prepare him to serve the commonwealth. In stressing the technological and scientific uses of art, men like Dee and Bacon were in effect arguing that it formed part of the necessary equipment of a ruling elite. The concept of an architecture as "the master over all that make any works" was calculated to appeal to men who felt that manual labor was beneath them but that commanding others was a natural function of their rank.

PRINCE HENRY AND THE VIRTUOSOS

To a remarkable extent this orientation survived into the 1610s, despite the new phase of systematic collecting and enlightened patronage that began in that decade. A taste for Renaissance painting and classical architecture developed organically out of the fascination for technological and quasi-scientific pursuits characteristic of figures like Dee and Bacon.

Prince Henry was fascinated by ingenious machines in which art fused with mechanical gadgetry and scientific speculation. Inigo Jones, Constantinio de Servi, and Saloman de Caus all excelled at designing these contraptions, whereas none had as yet emerged as a classical architect of any stature.[30] The atmosphere surrounding these "masters of artificial works" comes through in some of Jonson's comic portraits of Jones. In the masque *Neptune's Triumph*, Jones appears as a cook boasting about his trade:

A master cook! Why he is a man of men
For a professor. He designs, he draws,

He paints, he carves, he builds, he fortifies,
Makes citadels of curious fowl and fish

. . . .

H'has nature in a pot . . .
He is an architect, an engineer [inginer]
A soldier, a physician, a philosopher,
A general mathematician![31]

Even more revealing is a book by de Caus entitled *Les raisons des forces mouvantes*, detailing the discussions of natural philosophy and mechanical inventions with which he entertained the prince.[32] Some 400 folio pages long and lavishly illustrated, it is the most voluminous surviving document of the relations between an early Stuart patron and one of his artists. It provides a revealing glimpse of the interests prevalent within Henry's household.

De Caus set out to explain how men could harness the basic natural sources of movement. He began with a neo-Aristotelian theory of physics that involved an analysis of the dynamic properties of the four elements of earth, air, fire, and water. He writes that if air is compressed it will seek to expand with explosive force, and that water will rise violently if heated by fire. These observations lead to the formulation of axioms about the elemental forces producing motion in nature. Using these basic principles, de Caus went on to construct physical theorems, similar in form to the geometric proofs of Euclid, concerning the construction of machines. At first he confined himself to simple devices, involving pumps, gears, pulleys, springs, and weights—Dee's science of thauamaturgike. Then he began to combine these in ever more complex mechanisms. There resulted a wonderland of marvelous contrivances: a water pump for extinguishing fires; moving statues of wood nymphs playing on organs powered by waterwheels, operating on the same principle as a modern music box; a fountain that harnesses the elemental fire of the sun by focusing its rays through lenses upon containers of water (Plate 7). Magic, said Raleigh, is "the connection of natural agents . . . wrought by a wise man to the bringing forth of such effects as are wonderful to those that know not their causes."[33] It would be difficult to find a better illustration than de Caus's book.

The fashion for antiquarianism reinforced interest in the manual arts from another direction. In their efforts to reconstruct the past of a nation that had produced few historians, most of them unreliable, the antiquarians fell back on evidence provided by inscriptions, coins,

7. Saloman de Caus. A solar powered fountain from *Les raisons des forces mouvantes.* The Folger Shakespeare Library, Washington, D.C.

ruins, and other physical remains. Camden, especially, had shown how much a researcher could learn by traveling through the kingdom, examining the sites of ancient roads and cities, and talking to plowmen about objects uncovered in their fields. By the Stuart period, courtiers had become familiar with the idea that the objects created by a society can often reveal as much about its way of life as written records, so when they went abroad on grand tours they took an interest in monuments, statues, and other curious or impressive works that might illuminate the cultural history of the places they visited. Some purchased "antiquities" to take back to England as souvenirs and conversation pieces.

This orientation is reflected clearly in the chapter on "antiquities" that Henry Peacham, a former tutor in Arundel's household, added to the 1634 edition of his influential manual of upper-class breeding, *The Complete Gentleman*. Peacham astutely recognized that Roman artifacts sometimes provided information about iconographical traditions, imperial proclamations, and assorted historical facts that cannot be found in conventional literary sources. "Would you see a pattern of the *Rogus* or funeral pile, burnt at the canonization of the Roman emperors?" he asked his readers. "Would you see the true and undoubted models of their temples, altars, deities, columns, gates, . . . bridges, sacrifices, vessels . . . and a thousand things more? Repair to old coins and you shall find them." And with all this knowledge went "the content a man has to see and handle the very same things which were in use so many years ago."[34] Peacham wanted to bring antiquity to life by seizing upon even commonplace details that might lend substance to his mental picture of the Greco-Roman world. The collections of ancient statues and inscriptions by Arundel and other courtiers probably stemmed from this kind of historical curiosity as much as from aesthetic motives.

In the decade following Henry's death, a new concept of aristocratic breeding developed, encompassing the assorted interests we have just traced. The stress upon languages, history, and political analysis characteristic of Tudor humanism gradually broadened to take in a hodgepodge of additional pursuits. "A gentleman should talk like a gentleman," the essayist William Cornwallis wrote, early in the century, "which is like a wise man. If thy guests be weary of thy parlor, carry them into thy gallery . . . if thou meetest a fellow that would fain show he is a mathematician . . . be content to talk with him of circles and quadrangles."[35]

Peacham's book codified the new ideal of the "virtuoso," or gentlemanly amateur of all the arts and sciences. Its title page foreshadowed the work's main theme through two figures, labeled "Nobilitas" and "Scientia." Nobilitas is surrounded by drums, pikes, banners, and guns, to suggest the accomplishments of the soldier, while Scientia is accompanied by a compass, a globe, a painter's palette, and three books labeled Plutarch, Thucydides, and Tacitus. This iconography reflects the conventional Renaissance concept of the perfect courtier as a man who combines military prowess with a knowledge of all subjects necessary to the statesman. The frontispiece interprets this last category to include geography, navigation, painting, and classical history, and most of the book is devoted to a discussion of these civilian disciplines. According to Peacham, the "compleat gentleman" engages in experiments, devises inventions, learns to identify the gods and heroes depicted on ancient medallions, and assembles "rarities" of all kinds, taking special delight in those that amaze onlookers, such as striking paintings, freaks of nature, and ingenious machines. Ostensibly he does all this to serve the commonwealth, but in fact most of his pursuits simply distinguish him as a man of learning and intelligence. Art and science had come to be valued for their own intrinsic appeal, quite apart from any practical function.

Throughout the early Stuart period, wherever we find a marked concern with the fine arts we also encounter this eclectic pattern of interests. Arundel was described as "a great friend . . . to all new inventions."[36] Along with his gallery full of Rubenses, Buckingham assembled England's first major collection of exotic stuffed animals.[37] But no one exemplified the new type better than Charles himself, who invented scientific instruments, spoke knowledgeably about theology, music, philosophy, antiquarianism, and mathematics, and displayed a truly universal range of interests.[38] "He was skilled in things of Antiquity," his first biographer, William Perrinchief, recalled in the 1650s:

> [He] could judge of medals whether they had the number of years they pretended unto; His libraries and cabinets were full of those things on which the length of time had put the value of rarities. . . . He could judge of fortifications. . . . He had excellent skill in the building of guns [and] . . . ships. . . . He understood and was pleased with the making of clocks and watches . . . he delighted to talk to all kinds of artists, and he did sometime say, He thought he could get his living . . . by any trade he knew of, except the making of hangings [tapestries]: although of these he understood much and greatly delighted in them.[39]

Here is Peacham's collector of antiquities and Dee's master of artificial works, personified upon the throne.

ART AND NATURAL PHILOSOPHY

The Stuart habit of associating the fine arts with mechanics, experimental science, and assorted other pursuits is not congenial to most modern scholars. With few exceptions, art historians have ignored the eclectic interests of the court's patrons and of figures like Inigo Jones, preferring to treat the development of painting and architecture in isolation. When mentioned at all, the virtuoso is usually dismissed as a dilettante, excessively preoccupied with useless mechanical toys and freaks of nature, lacking the discipline to pursue any significant course of studies for more than a short time.[40] However, the achievements of Charles and the Earl of Arundel as patrons, and the quality of Jones's architecture, should make us wonder if this deprecating attitude is not wide of the mark. Perhaps in some way now difficult to understand, scientific curiosity and aesthetic values were twin aspects of a deeper intellectual impulse, working itself out according to a logic since lost to Western culture. It may help us get to the bottom of this problem if we view it from the other end, in terms of the approach early Stuart courtiers took to natural philosophy.

By the end of the period we have just covered, Europe stood on the brink of the scientific revolution.[41] Galileo was already an old man as Charles and Buckingham began collecting art in the 1620s; Kepler had published his work on the laws of planetary motion; Descartes would soon begin investigating the laws of optics. The outlines of a new physics and a more rigorous empirical methodology had begun to emerge. Yet older Aristotelian, Platonic, and Hermetic philosophies inherited from antiquity and the Renaissance were not yet thoroughly discredited and continued to influence even scientists of the first rank. Investigators across Europe were trying in the 1610s and 1620s to grope their way toward a scientific method and a body of fundamental principles that might command universal assent from educated and unbiased men. Yet they had not arrived at this goal, so that a good deal of creative and unrestrained speculation continued to flourish.

The English court certainly contained figures who were interested in scientific issues and aware of recent discoveries. Wotton sent Salisbury a report of Galileo's work with the telescope as early as 1610. In

1623 Hervey dedicated his seminal book on the circulation of the blood in animals to Prince Charles, who a few years later appointed him a royal chaplain.[42] In the late 1630s Sir Kenelm Digby was in touch with Mersenne's important scientific circle in Paris.

Few people around Charles I, however, appear to have had a deep understanding of the more technical mathematical and scientific ideas that were already becoming essential in astronomy and physics. Arithmetic, geometry, and Pythagorean concepts of harmony certainly attracted attention. Charles himself seems to have invented a primitive slide rule, and Inigo Jones always insisted on the importance of mathematics to architects like himself. But one looks in vain for a figure at the English court capable of devising sophisticated and original mathematical solutions to significant scientific problems.

English courtiers instead tended to formulate hypotheses in terms of traditional ancient and Renaissance philosophies. A good example is Sir Kenelm Digby, a bedchamber servant of the king whom Peacham singled out as the most complete gentleman of the age. Digby was an avid experimenter, convinced that theory must be grounded in empirical observation. He once wrote:

> I think there is nothing truer than that the maxims of the natural sciences . . . are nothing else but constant and unvarying rules gathered out of the heedful and accurate observing of the tracks and motions of such agents as by their excellent and perfect composure do proceed at all times . . . in a perfect and unerring way.[43]

The postulates he set out to prove, however, often derived from the Neoplatonic metaphysics he had learned as a youth, or theological speculations that absorbed him as an adult, rather than from any body of theory we would consider scientific. Thus after the death of his wife he became absorbed in experiments to determine whether he could regenerate plants from their burned and pulverized remains. He wanted to lend scientific credence to the doctrine of the resurrection of the body, so as to reassure himself that in the afterlife he would enjoy again the sexual pleasures of marriage.[44]

This seems mere quackery until we realize that Digby approached the universe not as a great mechanism working according to scientific laws of motion, but as a hierarchy of forms leading up to a divine source man can learn to perceive only through his senses. Experiments might therefore illuminate problems in theology, or even form the basis for religious meditation. All philosophy must "be reduced to practice," he once wrote to a friend, "which consists entirely in knowing and enlarging and elevating one's soul to the point at which it attains the capacity to catch fire."[45] Digby here managed to combine experimental methods with the kind of spiritual exercises popularized by the Counter-Reformation. Although no one else in England quite matched the exuberance of his quest for empirical evidence of metaphysical beliefs, he typifies the eclectic approach to natural philosophy common at the Stuart court.

The result was a natural philosophy that was often *more* empirical than the physics of Galileo or Descartes. Lacking the encumbrance of a rigorous system of theoretical principles to guide their interpretation of the evidence and suggest significant problems, English experimenters sought to prove their hypotheses in obvious, tangible ways. From common-sense observations they proceeded directly to attempts at producing strange or useful effects, which demonstrated their understanding of and mastery over natural forces. The machines of de Caus, the experiments of Digby, and Bacon's famous discussion of the empirical method all derived from this fundamental orientation.

The same habits of thought shaped responses to Renaissance and Baroque art. Courtiers valued paintings largely for the masterful ways in which artists produced lifelike images through the manipulation of colored pigment on flat surfaces. No less than one of de Caus's machines, a work by Rubens or Titian was viewed as a masterful technical achievement, delighting beholders by its capacity to reproduce the visible features of the natural world.

Consequently, as they began collecting, court patrons also sought to understand the principles underlying the painter's skills. Throughout the 1610s they showed a particular concern with the science of perspective, which had barely influenced English art before this period.[46] Holbein had understood and employed perspective techniques—though rarely in obvious ways—but most of his Elizabethan and Jacobean successors did not. From Hilliard to Gheeraerts, they generally disguised their deficiency by painting sitters in shallow spaces or against solid backgrounds. About the time Prince Henry began buying Venetian paintings, however, signs of a budding interest in perspective began to appear. In 1611 an English translation of Serlio's discussion of perspective drawing was printed with a dedication to the prince.[47] A few years later Peacham followed with an original book on the topic.[48] About the same time, Jones produced his first extant experiment in perspective drawing, the sketch for The Fallen House of Chivalry in *Prince Henry's Barriers* (Plate 1), and Robert Peake painted portraits of Henry and Queen Anne showing deep landscape backgrounds. Both Jones and Peake still had much to learn about this kind of art, but it looks as though the court's most advanced patrons had commissioned experiments in the sort of spatial realism exhibited by Italian paintings just then arriving in England. A few years later Mytens's first known English portraits, of the Earl of Arundel (Plate 4) and Countess of Arundel, display the same preoccupation. In each of these a gallery containing the earl's art collection opens like a tunnel behind the sitter in a virtuoso demonstration of perspective skill.[49]

The court's connoisseurs of art also developed an interest in the techniques of depicting light, shadow, and animation. De Caus wrote another volume, dedicated to Henry, on the science of lights and mirrors. By way of introduction, he wrote:

> I have discussed in this book certain methods for arranging shadows properly on solid bodies. This is a very necessary part of perspective for painters, because in painting nothing can be well represented if the shadows are not made properly. In addition I have demonstrated the manner in which solid bodies appear in mirrors, a subject little treated before this.[50]

De Caus jumbled together explanations of artistic techniques with discussions of the nature of light and shadow and instructions on playing tricks with mirrors, in a fashion typical of this period. Fifteen years later Henry Wotton was still preoccupied with illusionistic effects in his panegyric of the royal collection:

> Here would the spectator swear the limbs and muscles of Tintoretto to move; there the birds of Bassano to chirp, the ox to bellow and the sheep to bleat. . . . Neither do the Belgians want their praise, who if they paint landscapes, all kinds of vegetables seem in their verdure, the flowers do smile, the hills are raised.[51]

We seem to be back in the gardens of de Caus, with their spring-driven nymphs and toy birds warbling away with artificial whistles.

However much this preoccupation with artistic methods and trompe-l'oeil effects may differ from the concerns of modern art lovers, it would have provided an excellent starting point for Stuart patrons seeking to understand continental styles radically unlike anything that native artists produced. Those patrons had to learn, at the most basic level, how Renaissance and Baroque masters depicted the world. In particular, they had to learn to appreciate the painterly techniques of Venetian and Baroque artists. The Elizabethan miniaturists and costume portraitists excelled at depicting the exact appearance of costumes bathed in bright, even light. Every fragment of some miniatures—indeed, sometimes almost every tiny brush stroke—reproduces the outlines of real physical objects. Consequently one can take the lace collar on a one-inch portrait and blow it up to six or seven times its original size without destroying the impression of precision. On the other hand, the evocative effects so evident in Venetian and Flemish Baroque art had almost no counterpart in Elizabethan painting. The English had to learn that pictorial realism did not consist simply in the meticulous reproduction of sharply illuminated objects, but might involve attempts to suggest three-dimensional space, motion, surface textures, and gradations in lighting.[52]

Patrons like the Earl of Arundel and Charles I developed into discerning connoisseurs of European painting because, when they entered their galleries, they were not idle spectators passively contemplating artistic beauty. They wanted to understand how paintings were made and therefore inquired minutely into the process of artistic creation. That is why they enjoyed the company of professionals like Jones and Gentileschi, who could explain all the professional secrets. If we can believe Perrinchief, the king eventually acquired such mastery that when visiting his artists' studios he sometimes grabbed a brush to "supply the defects of art in the workman, and suddenly draw those lines, give those airs and lights, which experience had not taught the painter."[53] For Charles the act of examining a good painting must have been an intellectual adventure leading to discoveries about visual phenomena and manual skills, awakening a sense that he had penetrated some of the mysterious secrets of the cosmos.

A man who examined in this way hundreds of paintings by the greatest masters of the sixteenth and early seventeenth centuries would come away with an understanding of far more than the technical side of the late Renaissance and early Baroque art. Outside the work of a few mannerists, painterly, illusionistic effects were almost never an end in themselves. The brilliant highlights and dark shadows of Caravaggio, the glowing colors of Titian, and the vibrant animation of Rubens's work served larger, dramatic, religious, and philosophical ends. Painting was an "imitation of nature," but nature was also a shadow or mask of God, conveying profound messages to those who understood her language. By artificially mimicking natural phenomena, an artist might therefore communicate through what Wotton once called "the tongueless eloquence of lights and shadows and silent poesy of lines."[55] The modern distinction between poetic feeling and scientific analysis had no place in the mentality of early Stuart courtiers. Unless we grasp this point, we will misunderstand not only their concepts of art but also their ideas about history, religion, and government.

THE ARTIST AS MORALIST

So far we have examined aesthetic values in relation to ideas about the physical world and man's place within that world. Yet painting and sculpture are also mirrors held up to human nature, capable of evoking moods, suggesting character traits, and conveying psychological insights. Elizabethan and early Stuart patrons recognized this and took a keen interest in the ways art captured the thoughts, feelings, and "humors" of people. This strain of ideas represents something of a humanistic counterpart to the scientific and technological concerns traced so far.

PAINTING AS A MIRROR OF THE SOUL

The Renaissance artist regarded himself as a discerning student of mankind, adept at reading the spiritual makeup of individuals through their expressions and gestures. He approached this task in the same empirical and analytical spirit that he employed to explore the physical universe. "The greatest part [of portraiture]," Hilliard wrote, in a passage based on Lomazzo, "is the grace in countenance, by which affections appear, which can neither be used nor well judged of but by the wiser sort . . . whereof it behoveth that [a painter] be in heart wise."[55] To achieve this skill required diligent observation:

> The curious drawer [must] watch, and as it [were] catch these lovely graces, witty smilings and these stolen glances which suddenly like lightning pass and another countenance taketh place. . . . So hard a matter he hath in hand . . . noting how in smiling . . . the eye changeth and narroweth, holding the sight just between the lids as a center, how the mouth a little extendeth . . . the cheeks raise themselves to the eyewards, the nostrils

play and are more open, the veins in the temple appear more and color by
degrees increaseth, . . . the eyebrows make straight arches, and the forehead casteth itself into a plain as it were for peace and love to walk upon.[56]

This looks like a remarkably naturalistic doctrine for a man who normally painted figures of less than three or four inches and whose influence led to an iconic style even in large portraits. It is a mark of
Hilliard's ability that, despite the limitations imposed by the miniature
form and the milieu in which he worked, his portraits often do convey
the kind of insight he described. However, almost none of his contemporaries could have fulfilled his precepts except in very perfunctory ways.

Hilliard did not press his argument beyond a discussion of portraits,
but on the continent a painter's ability to convey psychological qualities often served larger, didactic purposes. Through a historical or allegorical subject, the artist might show virtuous and vicious characters in
action, impressing upon his audience the moral significance of an anecdote or parable. Wrote Sir Philip Sidney, paraphrasing the conventional continental view:

> Painters . . . the more excelleth who having no law but wit bestow that in
> colors . . . which is fittest for the eye to see, as the constant, though la-
> menting look of Lucretia, when she punished in herself another's fault:
> wherein he painted not Lucretia whom he never saw, but painteth the out-
> ward beauty of such a virtue.[57]

Again the artist became an imitator of nature who recreates the essential forms of vice and virtue for the pleasure and instruction of his
audience.

In Italy these concepts had developed largely as an attempt to prove
that painting deserved as much prestige as history, moral philosophy,
poetry, and other intellectual disciplines. In England, however, they
rapidly became the basis for *literary* theory as, for example, in Sidney's
definition of poetic creativity: "The poet . . . lifted up with the vigor of
his own inventions, doth grow in effect into another nature, in making
things either better than nature bringeth forth or quite anew forms such
as never were in nature."[58] Sidney couched this argument in visual
terms, as applicable to the fine arts as to literature: "Poesy is . . . an art
of imitation . . . that is to say, a representing, counterfeiting or figuring
forth . . . with this end, to teach and delight."[59]

Whether or not such discussions derived from Italian theorists of the visual arts, they provided the basis for an assimilation of the functions of artists and poets. In the seventeenth century the bond grew stronger, thanks to the influence of Horace and his famous dictum, *ut pictura poesis.* "Whosoever loves not picture," Jonson wrote, "is injurious to Truth and all the wisdom of poetry. Picture is the invention of heaven; the most ancient and most atuned to nature."[60] Literature itself operates through images:

> The conceits of the mind are pictures of things and the tongue is the interpreter of those pictures. The order of God's creatures in themselves is not only admirable and glorious but eloquent; then he who could apprehend the consequence of things in their truth, and utter his mind as truly, were the best writer.[61]

Painting, no less than poetry, is rooted in ethics:

> From moral philosophy [art] took the soul, the expression of the senses, perturbations, manners, when they would paint an angry person, a proud, an inconstant, an ambitious, a base, a magnanimous, a just, a merciful, a compassionate. . . . Socrates taught Parrhasius and Clito (two noble statuaries) first to express manners by their looks in imagery.[62]

Despite his famous quarrel with Inigo Jones over the relative merits of pictures and poetry, Jonson did admire the expressive power of good painting.[63]

More important, poetry often relied in practice upon visual images borrowed from painting and court spectacle. Yates has shown that the *Faerie Queen* drew many of its scenes from the panoply of court tournaments. Jonson and his followers frequently conveyed moral ideas through visual imagery: vice would appear in a "rhinocerotes" nose or pretentious suit; virtue in the solid lines of an old house, the throng of happy country folk in its hall, and the dignified bearing of its owner.[64] The literary experiments of the period could therefore, in principle, have served to inspire painters. Something like this happened in Italy: the pastoral genre helped generate landscape painting, satires contributed to the rise of caricature, and the vivid imagery of Roman sermons encouraged Caravaggio in his pursuit of a more naturalistic religious art.[65]

Can we detect signs of a comparable rapport between poetry and painting in England? The answer seems to be yes, but only up to a point.[66] The portraits of the late Elizabethan and early Jacobean period

fall naturally into several categories, corresponding to ideas of aristocratic character also found in court literature. Some belong to the
world of the court joust and the neo-chivalric epic. They not only show
figures in armor, often in front of battle scenes, but also display the
bright colors and symbolic emblems that appeared in court pageants
and in the cavalcades preceding military expeditions. Other paintings
show statesmen in dark clothes, with serious demeanors expressing
high-minded devotion to the queen and the cause of true religion.
They embody a very different, civilian concept of aristocratic virtue,
deriving from humanist and Protestant traditions.[67] In the 1590s a series of portraits appeared depicting the fashionable mood of melancholy.[68] In them figures lounge on the ground, gazing out from under
big, droopy hats, against backgrounds of trees and wild plants to show
they have retreated from society.

On the other hand, English painters never developed anything like
the technical proficiency needed to generate an artistic renaissance
comparable to that taking place in drama and poetry. From the 1590s
some of them did succeed in creating more lifelike portraits, which
dimly reflect the psychological interests so evident in late Elizabethan
and Jacobean literature. Yet, with few exceptions, artists relied on stereotyped poses and obvious props: armor for heroism, dark clothes and
limpid bodies for melancholy; a Bible or skull for piety. Even Gheeraerts excels as a psychological portraitist chiefly by comparison with
predecessors like Gower and contemporaries like Peake. Though his
paintings show some animation and often convey a sense of personality,
his range was far more limited than that of European contemporaries
like Caravaggio and Rubens. The subtlety and profundity of Donne,
Jonson, and Shakespeare had no real parallel in the visual arts.

THE MASQUES AND THE ARTISTIC LANGUAGE OF INIGO JONES

James's court did produce a hybrid genre peculiarly suited to linking poetry and moral philosophy to art. The masques of Ben Jonson and Inigo
Jones were didactic spectacles, integrated along poetic lines but appealing to all the senses. The comic anti-masques represented caricatured
vices, while the masquers embodied virtues. Glittering costumes, mechanical contrivances, and elegant music rounded out the effects,
making each masque a "real banquet of the sense" and a compendium
of all the rarities a virtuoso could desire.[69] In *Time Vindicated*, anti-
masquers representing eyes and ears put it this way:

Eyes: This will be better;
I spy it coming, peace. All the impostures,
The prodigies, diseases, and distempers,
The knaveries of the time, we shall see now.

Ears: And hear the passages and several humors
Of men as they are swayed by their affections,
Some grumbling, and some mutinying, some scoffing
Some pleased, some pining, at all these we laughing.[70]

The essence of the form lay in an attempt to make moral qualities audible or visible through stylized imitation of behavior.

So long as Jonson dominated the masques he kept visual effects subordinate to poetic librettos. Verse provided the "soul" of each performance, whereas stage scenes, dances, and music furnished a "ravishing" body. Even so, Jones's sets must have contributed substantially to the court's artistic education. Often modeled upon French or Florentine entertainments, painted after 1610 according to the rules of perspective, and employing mythological symbols culled from Renaissance dictionaries, they were visually far more sophisticated than Elizabethan court entertainments.

In the 1620s the scenery of the masques began to eclipse Jonson's poetry, and Jones emerged as the dominant partner. Masques became intricate visual statements in which every detail of costume and scenery conveyed a symbolic truth. As Jonson fulminated:

. . . O Shows! Shows! Mighty Shows!
The Eloquence of Masques! What need of prose
Or verse or sense t'express Immortal you?
You are the spectacles of State! Tis true
Court Hiero-gly-phicks! & All arts afford
In the mere perspective of an Inch board!
You ask no more than certain politique eyes!
Eyes that can pierce into the mysteries
Of many colors! read them! and reveal
Mythology there, painted on slit deal!
O to make boards speak! There is a task!
Painting and Carpentry are the Soul of a Masque![71]

What had begun as an attempt to flesh out poetry with visual and musical effects ended as a form of artistic discourse in which verse played a subordinate role.

Jones's masque designs thus appear to have grown out of an attempt

to use visual images in almost exactly the way that Jonson used poetry—as an eloquent form of moral discourse, revealing the essential
nature of vices and virtues. It is possible to delve more deeply into this
subject, for Jones has left a number of scraps of evidence concerning his
views about the didactic significance of art. Some of these sources were
first discovered some thirty years ago by D. J. Gordon, who noticed that
the proscenium arches for the two masques of 1631, *Tempe Restored* and
Albion's Triumph, provided allegorical statements about the assumptions
underlying Jones's work. Both arches replied to satires Jonson had written against Jones after their collaborations ended in a violent quarrel,
and both defended the primacy of visual imagery over poetry through
closely parallel symbols. Two figures dominated the arch to *Tempe Restored* representing Invention and Knowledge. Below these Jones placed
groups of children, some with ugly masks before their faces, others with
darts. Beneath the children were two satyrs, one representing envy
under a mask of friendship, the other representing "curious ignorance."
The satyrs and children represented Jonson's satire and his unsuccessful
attempts to frighten Jones; Invention and Knowledge stood for Jones's
own work. The proscenium arch to *Albion's Triumph* symbolized Jones's
position through analogous figures, Theorica and Practica. As Gordon
noted, these had long stood for the functions of the architect, who
combines a theoretical knowledge of mathematics with a practical
understanding of building. In fact, Jones copied the scene from the title
page of Scammozi's *L'idea della archittetura universale*. He clearly regarded his work, on the masques no less than on buildings, as a conjunction of theory and practice. What did this concept mean to him?

Gordon assumed that Theorica and Practica could have nothing to
do with the themes of the masque that followed and must therefore refer only to the design of court spectacles. One largely untapped body of
evidence suggests that this was not so. By good fortune forty-seven
books owned by Inigo Jones have come down to us, of which twenty-
one contain marginal comments.[72] Consisting not only of architectural
treatises, but also of histories and philosophical works, they reflect his
broad reading and reveal the relatively uncommon passages he considered worthy of notation. Many of the marginal comments suggest that
the relationship of theory to practice was fundamental to Jones's concept not only of art but also of history, ethics, and politics. When taken
in conjunction with the masques, they point to a remarkably coherent
outlook, which represents a logical extension of the attitudes we have
been tracing.

Two passages marked in Jones's volumes state explicitly that all rational activities depend upon two distinct types of thought, which are analogous to those represented in the proscenium arches. Aristotle had written in the *Ethics:* "There are, then, in the intellectual power two principles, speculative or scientific and . . . practical or discursive."[73] Jones underlined these words and summarized the passage. Second, Jones wrote the following textual summary in the margin in his copy of a work by the Italian philosopher Piccolomini: "What reason or the rational power is / the rational power divided into two parts that is into two Intellects. Speculative and practick / The first stays in the truth found, the second accommodates the truth to human operations."[74]

These ideas should be understood in relation to the Platonic conviction that knowledge is transcendent, immutable, and ultimately inexpressible. "We say then," reads Jones's copy of the *Republic* in a marked passage, "that they who see many beautiful things, but not beauty itself . . . and many just things, but not justice, and similarly with other things have opinions but not knowledge."[75] Truth must therefore be obtained through contemplation and insight, rather than through observation and action. The passages cited in the previous paragraph have in effect complemented this idea with its converse: if theoretical truth is never encountered directly in the world, then the mind must learn to work on two levels, to see both the immutable perfection of pure forms and the relationship of those forms to terrestrial concerns. One part of reason must "stay in the truth found," as Piccolomini put it, while the other descends to earth to apply the truth.

The division of reason into two faculties also affected Jones's ethical thought. He shared Jonson's conviction that moral conduct derived from rational control of the senses, as several marked passages in his books show. But he believed in two moral faculties rather than one: "Prudence perfects the appetite to the good and intellectual virtue perfects the intellect to the truth" reads a marked passage in his copy of the *Ethics.*[76] Other passages marked by Jones in this work and others show that he equated Prudence with moral discipline. It fights against passion, orders the affections, and keeps reason from being overwhelmed by base desires.[77] Intellectual virtue, by contrast, consists of insight into the abstract nature of moral truth, which must guide Prudence toward the proper ethical goals. "The will doth will that which the intellect showeth it either true good or apparent" reads another marked comment in the *Ethics.*[78] Morality depends upon an ability to respond to the sights, sounds, and demands of this world in accordance with insights into a higher reality behind it. Consequently, ethical conduct is closely related to art, since both involve a rational ordering of senses and appetites. As still another marginal translation in the *Ethics* puts it, "Moral virtue is an elective habit / election is a deliberative appetite."[79] In this paradoxical phrase, "deliberative appetite," lies the crux of the matter: the virtuous man has so refined his desires that he has, in a manner, taught them to reason.

This mode of thought manifests itself in several places in the masque designs, but perhaps never so strikingly as in a passage from the book on Stonehenge which John Webb compiled from Jones's notes in 1655. In the course of its discussion of Roman Britain, this book remarks of the ancients: "History affords only *Contemplation*, whereby their great Actions are made conceivable to reasoning: but the ruins of their buildings *Demonstration*, which obvious to sense, are even yet as so many eye-witnesses to their admired achievements."[80] The actions of the Romans are not a philosophical idea, but the thought underlying this passage grows directly out of the concepts we have just examined. Again the characteristic distinction between contemplative and terrestrial or sensual knowledge is at work, here as an argument that architecture speaks more eloquently of the past than historical knowledge. The entire book on Stonehenge elaborates on this conviction. Jones thought that the Romans erected Stonehenge so its ordered proportions would civilize the barbarous ancient Britons. The building of Covent Garden, the renovation of St. Paul's, and the planned construction of a new royal palace for Charles I reflected the same view: these projects were intended to function, simultaneously, as civilizing influences on Jones's contemporaries and as monuments to posterity of the "admired achievements" of Charles I.

All this suggests that Jones regarded the political functions of his work in a manner very reminiscent of the approach to natural philosophy of the virtuoso. De Caus used his insight into the dynamic properties of natural forces to design useful engines. In much the same way, Jones's *knowledge* of moral and political philosophy would lead to the *invention* of works capable of instilling civility. The principles represented before the proscenium arch of *Tempe Restored* express in a very precise way the methodology of an artist seeking to serve the state. It is clear too that for Jones a work need not have an overt message to possess social value. Artistic beauty will by itself instill salutary attitudes. To understand this notion, we must probe further. Why did he believe that a well-proportioned building could serve political purposes?

The answer lies in his interest in Platonic and Pythagorean theories of musical harmony, which appears in every facet of his work. He always designed his buildings on the basis of musical proportions; eight different harmonic ratios were built into the facade of St. Paul's alone.[81] The masque designs, Jones's marginalia, and even the satires written against him by Jonson betray the same concern:

> *Vitruvius.* O Captain Smith! or hammer armed Vulcan! with your three sledges and your anvil you are our music. . . . Plant yourselves there and beat time at our anvil. Time and measure are the father and mother of music, you know, and your Colonel Vitruvius knows a little.
>
> . . . .
>
> Well done, my musical, arithmetical, geometrical gamesters! or rather my true mathematical boys! it is carried in number, weight and measure, as if the airs were all harmony, and the figures a well-timed proportion.[82]

This fascination with music stemmed from two related considerations. First, harmony provided just the kind of link between theoretical truth and concrete experience Jones needed. According to a neo-Pythagorean tradition fashionable in the sixteenth century, certain simple mathematical ratios constitute the basic, rational structure of the cosmos and consequently hold the key to all the sciences. On the other hand, numbers also possess a sensible quality, since we may see quantitative relationships and hear musical harmony. Harmonic proportions are therefore vehicles through which abstract truths become immanent in the material world. As a marginal note in his copy of Plutarch's *Moral Works* put it, "Sense and Intellect united be considered the part of music."[83] The second facet of Jones's musical theory developed logically from these ideas. As a sensually apprehensible expression of Truth, harmony may serve as a pedagogical device capable of imposing rational order upon appetites and habits of conduct. Thus, in the margin of his Vitruvius, Jones noted: "Music is divided into two parts / Theoric / Practic which helps manners by poetry."[84] The *locus classicus* for these ideas is Plato's discussion in *The Republic* of the pedagogical functions of dance and music. In Jones's copy this passage is copiously annotated:

> The end of music [is] love of the beautiful.
>
> So we are no musicians if we perceive not the image of temperance, liberality, etc. and likewise the contraries.
>
> If by this [music] we perceive the virtues and vices, we also perceive the

Images and despise this neither in little nor in great things but respect the art of meditation.[85]

THE RELATIONSHIP OF THE ARTS TO POLITICS

The principles we have just traced were more than a rationalization of Jones's position in his quarrel with Jonson over the relative merits of poetic and visual imagery. They also indicate how Jones wanted people to experience his stage sets. In every masque he literally tried to embody political ideas in painted scenery and in the roles he created for the monarchs and their entourage. He represented the chaos threatening England by discordant music, scenes of natural disorder or ruined cities, and strangely dressed figures impersonating vices Charles wished to restrain. The blessings of royal government appeared as classical cityscapes, gardens, and peaceful landscapes, in front of which the monarchs danced to harmonious music as personifications of Heavenly Beauty or Heroic Virtue.[86] The climax to each performance came when the masquers moved out into the audience to begin the revels, thereby merging the allegorical world of their spectacle with the real world of the court. By heightening the excitement of the court's Christmas festivities and drawing upon all the resources of art, poetry, and music, Jones hoped to translate the doctrines of divine right kingship into a seductive aesthetic experience capable of persuading the senses and emotions as well as the mind.[87]

There is a danger, however, in pushing this argument too far and converting the masques into a kind of Platonic dream world where Charles could retreat from the intractable problem of government. "Viewed from outside the Banqueting House," Stephen Orgel has argued,

> the masque could be seen to provide the monarchy with an impenetrable insulation against the attitudes of the governed. Year after year designer and poet recreated an ideal commonwealth, all its forces under rational control, its people uniquely happy and endlessly grateful. . . . After a decade of ideals, a disenfranchised Parliament at last declared its authority by virtue of the realities of power, and the absolute rule of the Stuart monarchy was revealed as a royal charade, a theatrical illusion.[88]

The evidence presented in this chapter suggests a different conclusion. For Jones and other enthusiasts of the fine arts at the early Stuart court, the artist was not simply a creator of ideal images, capable of inspiring contemplation of otherworldly truths. More important, he was also a man who sought to apply philosophical insights to practical tasks. The marginal notes we have just investigated reflect an outlook that had less in common with Neoplatonic idealism than with the inventive philosophy of Jones's English contemporary, Bacon:

> These be the two parts of natural philosophy, the inquisition of causes and production of effects; speculative and operative; natural science and natural prudence.
> This . . . will indeed dignify and exalt knowledge, if contemplation and action may be more nearly and straightly conjoined and united together than they have been.[89]

This does not mean that Jones was a Baconian, only that a common impulse lay behind the work of both men, namely the desire to use theoretical knowledge as a guide to the progressive development of arts, through which men could improve life in this world.[90] We should therefore expect Jones to regard the ideals expressed in the masques not as substitutes for political activity but as guides to statesmanship.

If we turn to one more marked passage from Jones's library and compare it with views expressed by a few other Caroline courtiers, we can begin to see how the partnership of theoretical and practical intellects might have functioned in politics. "As doctors cannot help the sick if they do not know the causes of maladies," Polybius had written in the course of his discussion of political theory:

> so those who treat history are useless if they do not know the nature [*raison*] of places, times, causes and occasions. Nothing is more necessary or desirable than to know the causes of all things that happen, because this will provide the opportunity to provide great projects and to easily avoid [misfortune].[91]

Jones wrote "*bonne comparison*" beside the passage. In common with many other ancient and Renaissance theorists, Polybius believed that history recorded a few basic, recurring disorders of human society which the acute observer can learn to diagnose and perhaps to cure. By studying historical causality, a man can therefore learn to manipulate political life in much the way that Bacon, de Caus, and Raleigh sought to manipulate the natural world.

The Earl of Newcastle regarded history in this light. Shortly after

becoming tutor to Prince Charles in the late 1630s, he wrote to his
royal ward:

> What you read I would have it . . . the best chosen histories, that so you
> might compare the dead with the living, for the same humors is now that
> was then, there is no alteration but in the names, and though you meet
> with a Caesar for Emperor of the whole world yet he may have the same
> passions in him. And you are not to compare fortunes so much as humors,
> wit and judgement, and thus you shall see by their excellency and errors
> both of kings and subjects.[92]

One encounters the same view in Bacon's works:

> The poets and writers of history are the best doctors in this knowledge [of
> human affairs]; when we may find painted forth with great life, how
> affections are kindled and incited, and how pacified and restrained . . .
> how they work, how they vary . . . how they are enwrapped, one within
> another . . . how to set affection against affection, and to master one by
> another, even as we use to hunt beast with beast.[93]

Just as the end of natural philosophy is command over the physical universe, so the proper goal of history is an art or technology of government: "For whoever has a thorough insight into the nature of man may
shape his fortune almost as he will, and is born for empire."[94] In the
same vein, Jonson wrote: "In being able to counsel others, a man must
be furnished with a universal store in himself, to the knowledge of all
nature. . . . There are the seats of all Argument and Invention. But
especially, you must be cunning in the nature of man."[95] It is worth
noting that argument and invention were terms normally employed to
describe the design of masque sets. The statesman here resembles the
artist, not because he works through symbolic images but because he
employs an essentially similar analytical and manipulative method. He
too is an artificer, molding the raw materials of social life into a har-
monically ordered political structure.

The ideas of political order conveyed through the masques stand in
roughly the same relationship to the world view of the late Renaissance
as do the theories of Montesquieu or Adam Smith to the universe
of Newton. Enlightenment philosophes constructed political theories
from concepts of scientific law and mechanical equilibrium. Jonson,
Jones, and their contemporaries thought instead in terms of humors—
conceived as psychological manifestations of the four Aristotelian ele-

ments of earth, air, fire, and water—or they invoked Neoplatonic concepts of harmonic order and natural hierarchy. Yet no less than the political and economic theorists of the eighteenth century, they sought a rational understanding of social life rooted in universal principles capable of guiding political action.

We had best postpone detailed discussion of the political attitudes that emerged from this outlook until we come to the subject of ideas about royal government in Chapter 9. The critical point for now is that the attempt to express political philosophy through art did not lead to an etherealized view of national affairs. On the contrary, the court's aesthetic culture lent support to an ambitious effort to transcend the limits that historical tradition had imposed upon the state and to establish government on the foundation of rational principles.

CONCLUSION: THE NEW VISUAL CULTURE AND IMAGES OF AUTHORITY

Behind the evolution of both art and literature within the Jacobean court lay a determination to develop a fresh typology of vice and virtue, more flexible, naturalistic, and compelling than that inherited from the Tudor and medieval past. Jones imitated French and Italian artists for essentially the same reason that Jonson and other poets turned to Latin satirists. Each sought a model for more accurate observations of the minds and manners of men, as revealed through facial expressions, gestures, and deeds, or through social artifacts such as buildings and clothing. Each believed that by doing so he could help reform his contemporaries.

Yet ethical principles find expression in words more easily than in pictures. Jones and his colleagues confronted the double challenge of developing a flexible visual language while educating their audience to draw moral values out of aesthetic experiences. We can watch Jones struggling to do so and appreciate the difficulties involved in some of the masque sketches. For all his desire to appeal directly to the senses, he often fell back on heavy-handed symbolism. If the queen appeared as celestial beauty, her dress glistened with stars. Fame, Prudence, Peace, and other attributes of Stuart rule came straight out of iconographical dictionaries. The mimicry of the anti-masques and the marriage of light, painting, and music Jones created may have charmed the senses, but to understand the masque required a familiarity with the stock symbols of mannerism. And although he copied from Italian and classical sources, the habits underlying Jones's designs often did not differ much from those upon which Tudor allegorical conceits rested.

Especially in the later masques, Jones sometimes escaped from this dependence on stock symbols to communicate directly through the expressiveness of his art. A melancholy lover from *Love's Triumph Through Callipolis* (1632) provides a good example (see Plate 8). We know that Jones collected drawings and engravings, including some caricatures. Here we see the result, a sketch that captures the ridiculousness of a prevalent court vice without recourse to words or symbols. So too the atmosphere conveyed by some of Jones's landscapes far transcends anything an Elizabethan artist could have produced. Thus the backdrop to the pastoral drama *Artenice* (Plate 9) evokes a feeling of rustic simplicity far more effectively than the play itself. In the maturity of these drawings, as in the majesty of the Banqueting House and the vivacity of Van Dyck's portraits, the visual arts at last achieved something like parity with court literature.

As a result the court's better artists came to employ an array of extraordinarily subtle and sophisticated techniques to convey ideas about the social and political order. This led to revolutionary changes in the kinds of visual culture the royal household employed to express the king's majesty. By way of illustration we may compare Peake's canvas of Elizabeth on her progress (Plate 6) to Van Dyck's famous *Charles I à la Ciasse,* now in the Louvre (Plate 10). These two paintings, completed barely a generation apart, represent radically different ways of depicting the dignity of the royal office. Van Dyck was a far more accomplished and realistic artist than Peake, so that in the former's canvas we confront a subtly idealized image of Charles's actual appearance rather than a flat, iconic mask. Outward symbols of wealth and power remain, for example, in the elegance of the king's costume, the sword and cane, both emblems of the right to command, and the fact that Charles wears a hat while the attendants stand uncovered. Hat honor, as the Quakers later called it, was an important expression of deference employed in every context from casual social encounters to formal diplomatic receptions. The significance of the king's headgear would have struck contemporaries immediately.

These props are much less obvious, however, than the jewels, lace, embroidery, and canopy in Peake's work, and the imagery of royal authority is constructed according to an essentially different logic. In sev-

8. Inigo Jones. A Melancholy Despairing Lover from *Love's Triumph Through Callipolis*. Devonshire Collection, Chatsworth. Reproduced by permission of the Trustees of the Chatsworth Settlement. Photograph: Courtauld Institute of Art, London.

9. Inigo Jones. Proscenium and Standing Scene from Honorat de Bueil, *Artenice,* performed by Henrietta Maria and her ladies, February, 1626. Devonshire Collection, Chatsworth. Reproduced by permission of Trustees of the Chatsworth Settlement. Photograph: Courtauld Institute of Art, London.

10. Anthony Van Dyck. *Charles I à la Ciasse*. Cliché des Musées Nationaux, Paris. (Hangs in the Louvre Museum, Paris.)

eral ways the painting expresses a central motif of Caroline cultural propaganda: that the king, through the vigor of his mind, imposes order upon his environment. First there is the horse, a traditional image of raw animal power that must be brought under control by a skilled rider. Van Dyck emphasizes the symbolism by using filtered, dappled light to pick out the powerful muscles, the restless hoof, the tousled mane, and the alert expression of the man holding the reins, who obviously respects the beast's explosive spirit. There is probably also another dimension of symbolic meaning: since Plato the image of a man directing a great horse had been a common metaphor for the fashion in which reason controls passion within a virtuous soul. It was often said of Charles that he could rule his kingdom because he had first learned to subdue his own lusts: Van Dyck may have intended to allude to this claim.

The human figures in the painting, on the other hand, are suffused in an air of serenity created by the soft, golden light, the cool shadows of the forest, and their own calm and somewhat meditative expressions. A second attendant seems lost in contemplation as he gazes at a distant landscape. We are close to the mood of Marvell's mystical reveries about dark, green woods. The juxtaposition of this tranquil young man to the impulsive beast behind him further emphasizes the distinction between man's rational nature and the turbulent, sensuous passions we share with animals. And this contrast, in turn, would have called to mind a number of fundamental ideas we have encountered throughout this study concerning the critical importance of reason and intellectual discipline in human affairs.

Charles himself, however, is not lost in contemplation or shrouded in the forest's shadows. He stands in front of his attendants, in a clearing where the sun more sharply illuminates his features and accentuates the contrast between his red, white, and black costume and the more subdued brown, green, and yellowish hues of the rest of the scene. He looks more substantial than the other figures and so dominates their little world. And unlike his companions, whose attention is fixed on objects in the painting, he looks directly out at us, his glance reinforced by the elbow that sticks out jauntily at a right angle to the plane of the picture, his head held with an air of confidence, his eyes piercing and his expression faintly quizzical, as if he were deciding whether to include us in his group of companions. In a typically Baroque manner his image invades and controls our space, conveying the aura of vitality which sets kings apart from ordinary mortals, giving them a natural power to command. That vitality, in turn, suggests the union between intellectual insight and practical power upon which effective government must rest. The king mediates between the otherworldliness of his companions and the raw, physical strength represented by the horse in a way that symbolizes a philosphical concept of monarchy.

Van Dyck drew upon an impressive range of advanced stylistic techniques to construct this image. The masterful use of light and contrasts in texture derives from Titian, Caravaggio, Rubens, and other early Baroque masters; the forest scene has a long tradition of landscape art behind it; the equestrian imagery could be traced back, again through Titian and other Renaissance and Baroque painters, to classical antiquity.

The very sophistication of this painting, however, would have rendered its message inaccessible to all but a handful of connoisseurs, most of whom belonged to the king's entourage. If Van Dyck's image can appeal intuitively to any sensitive modern viewer, it is because Renaissance and Baroque visual culture have become part of our heritage. In Charles's reign few Englishmen outside the court ever saw a painting even vaguely similar, in appearance or compositional techniques, to this one. Nothing in their background had conditioned them to respond to its extraordinarily subtle and intricate symbolism. The contrast between Peake's canvas and Van Dyck's reflects two very different visual cultures, one rooted in forms of public spectacle that had long been part of English society, the other deriving from foreign traditions of painting, assimilated by a small group of connoisseurs. Even more clearly than the classical poetry of Jonson, the Baroque sophistication of court art reflects the ways styles developing around Whitehall broadened the cultural gulf separating the court from most of the nation.

NOTES

1. Lucy Gent, *Picture and Poetry* (Leamington Spa: James Hall, 1982), does an excellent job of examining descriptions of art in contemporary drama and poetry for clues as to how contemporaries thought about visual culture. Unfortunately the material does not exist to permit us to test the relevance of her findings to the attitudes of leading patrons or artists.

2. Eric Mercer, *English Art, 1553–1625* (Oxford: Oxford University Press, 1962), pp. 152–154.

3. Ibid., chap. 6.

4. Mercer, *English Art*, p. 152. The miniature represents a special category of intimate, personal portraiture, intended to be carried around in a locket or kept in a private drawer (ibid., pp. 195–196).

5. Mark Girouard, *Robert Smythson and the Architecture of the Elizabethan Era*, 2d ed. (New Haven and London: Yale University Press, 1983), pp. 18–21.

6. Conrad Russell, *The Crisis of Parliaments* (London: Oxford University Press, 1971), p. 260.

7. Girouard, *Robert Smythson*, pp. 32–34.

8. Nicholas Hilliard, "A Treatise on the Art of Limning," ed. P. Norman, *Walpole Society* 1 (1913), 16. Hilliard was himself a goldsmith who probably made jewelry. The best and most recent account of his career is in Roy Strong, *The English Renaissance Miniature* (London: Thames and Hudson, 1983), chap. 5.

9. For a discussion, see Roy Strong, *The Cult of Elizabeth* (London: Thames and Hudson, 1977), pp. 17–55.

10. Indeed, he seems deliberately to have reacted against them. Mid-Tudor artists tended to employ deep shadows to bring out facial relief; Hilliard always painted his sitters in bright, even light.

11. Strong, *English Renaissance Miniature*, pp. 76–81.

12. Sir John Summerson, *Architecture in Britain* (Harmondsworth: Penguin, 1953), chap. 3, esp. p. 56; Lawrence Stone, *Crisis of the Aristocracy* (Oxford: Oxford University Press, 1965), p. 710.

13. John Buxton, *Elizabethan Taste* (London: Macmillan, 1963), pp. 91–132, has challenged this view, which can certainly be overstated. Thomas Elyot had urged gentlemen to study painting during the reign of Henry VIII, and Hilliard was himself a gentleman. Nevertheless, it remains true that, *by and large*, painting did not enjoy a very high status until well into the seventeenth century. For a discussion, see Mercer, *English Art*, pp. 150–151. Even in the seventeenth century, Jonson ridiculed Jones's pretensions by implying he was really nothing but a craftsman. See, e.g., *A Tale of a Tub*, in *Works of Ben Jonson*, ed. C. H. Herford and Percy and Evelyn Simpson, 11 vols. (Oxford: Oxford University Press, 1925–1953), vol. 3, p. 63; (hereafter cited as H&S):

> Indeed, there is a woundy luck in names, sirs,
> And a vain mystery, an'a man new where
> to vind it. My godsire's name, I'll tell you,
> Was In-and-In Shittle, and a weaver he was
>
> . . . .
> And he nam'd me In-and-In Medlay; which serves
> A joiners' craft . . .
> . . . But I am truly
> *Architectonicus professor*, rather.

Poets also had to defend their calling, especially before the age of Sidney, but verse became a respectable avocation some decades before painting.

14. Girouard, *Robert Smythson*, pp. 8–14.

15. Stone, *Crisis of the Aristocracy*, p. 714; Frances Yates, *Theater of the World* (Chicago: University of Chicago Press, 1969), chap. 2, n.p.

16. Summerson, *Architecture*, chaps. 2, 4, and 5.

17. *A Tracte containing the artes of curious painting* (Oxford, 1598), epistle to the reader.

18. Roy Strong, *The English Icon* (London: Routledge; New Haven: Yale University Press, 1969), pp. 22–24.

19. Jonson, H&S, vol. 4, pp. 234–235.

20. Erwin Panofsky, "Artists, Scientist, Genius: Notes on the Renaissance Dammerung," in *The Renaissance: Six Essays* (New York: Harper Torchbooks, 1962), pp. 121–182.

21. Preface to *The Elements of Geometrie of the Most Auncient Philosopher Euclide of Megra,* trans. H. Billinsley (London, 1570), n.p.

22. Ibid.

23. Ibid.

24. Peter J. French, *John Dee: The World of an Elizabethan Magus* (London: Routledge, 1972), chap. 5. For discussions of the magical traditions that may have influenced Dee, see also Yates, *Theater,* and Nicholas H. Clulee, "At the Crossroads of Magic and Science: John Dee's Archemastrie," in *Occult and Scientific Mentalities in the Renaissance,* ed. Brian Vickers (Cambridge: Cambridge University Press, 1984), pp. 73–94.

25. Despite the extensive writings of Frances Yates on the topic. See *French Academies of the Sixteenth Century* (London: Warburg Institute, 1947), esp. chap. 1; *Giordano Bruno and the Hermetic Tradition* (Chicago: University of Chicago Press, 1964), chap. 15, *Astrea* (London: Routledge, 1975), pp. 88–111; and *The Occult Philosophy in the Elizabethan Age* (London: Routledge, 1979).

26. *History of the World* (London, 1651), p. 172.

27. *The New Organum and Other Writings,* ed. F. H. Anderson (Indianapolis and New York: Bobbs-Merrill, 1960), p. 8.

28. Ibid., p. 19.

29. *The Works of Francis Bacon,* ed. James Spedding et al. (London, 1858–1874), vol. 6, p. 481.

30. Jones's career as an architect had barely begun at this time, although if Stone is right he had aready helped in the design of Hatfield House (*Family and Fortune* (Oxford: Oxford University Press, 1973), pp. 79–81). John Harris, "Inigo Jones and the Courtier Style," *Architectural Review* 144 (1973): 17–24, sheds considerable light on Jones's early evolution as an architect and suggests that the classical style we know developed only toward the late 1610s.

31. *Complete Masques,* pp. 411, 412.

32. Published in Paris in 1613.

33. Raleigh, *History of the World,* p. 173.

34. Henry Peacham, *The Complete Gentleman* (London, 1634), p. 123.

35. William Cornwallis, *Essayes,* ed. Don Cameron Allen (Baltimore: Johns Hopkins University Press, 1946), pp. 36, 37.

36. David Lloyd, *Memoires* (London, 1668), p. 288.

37. Walter Houghton, "The English Virtuoso in the Seventeenth Century," *Journal of the History of Ideas* 3 (1942): 69.

38. SP, 16/407/86; William Lilly, *On the Life and Death of King Charles* (1774; 1st ed., 1655), p. 177.

39. Richard Perrinchief, *The Royal Martyr* (London, 1676), p. 253. Whether Charles really understood all these disciplines is an open question, but he clearly liked to dabble in such pursuits.

40. The classical statement of this view is Houghton, "English Virtuoso," e.g., p. 205. Despite my criticism of Houghton, his work remains essential for this subject.

41. See E. J. Dijksterheus, *The Mechanization of the World Picture,* trans. C. Dikshoorn (Oxford: Oxford University Press, 1961), esp. pt. 4.

42. William Harvey, *On the Motion of the Heart and Blood in Animals,* trans. A. Bowie (Chicago: Gateway, 1962). The original Latin edition was dedicated to Charles.

43. Sir Kenelm Digby to Sir Tobie Matthew, September 15, 1641, BL, Add. MSS 41846.

44. New York Public Library MSS, 39M39 (photographic reproduction of a letter book in a private collection).

45. Sir Kenelm Digby to P. Hilaire, January 8, 1637, BL, Add. MSS 41846, fol. 2.

Compare his statement in the same letter fols. 6, 7): "Now, to know God in this valley of ignorance and the obscurity we have no other means than to read the story [histoire] of his grandeur and excellence in the book of his creatures. . . . It is by this stairway that we must rise to have some communication with Him." He goes on to write that one must begin by studying the material world but that when a soul discovers that this will not satisfy "her infinite appetite" she will be filled with "disturbance and anxiety" and will "take flight" until "at last, filled with admiration and amazement she will find herself engulfed in the abyss of light that surrounds the Creator."

46. For an interesting discussion, see Roy Strong, "Some Early Portraits at Arundel Castle, *Connoisseur* 197 (1978): 201, 202; and Strong, *English Renaissance Miniature*, p. 110.

47. *The first Books of Architecture, made by Sebastian Serly* (London, 1611).

48. *Graphice, or the Most Auncient and Excellent Art of Drawing and Limming* (London, 1612).

49. Marred, however, by the uncertain placement of the sitters in space.

50. *La perspective avec la raison des ombres et miroirs* (London, 1612), dedication "Au Serenissime Prince Henry."

51. A *Panegyric to King Charles* in *Reliquiae Wottonianae* (London, 1651), p. 155.

52. Strong has recently shown that Hilliard employed a relatively free technique, almost reminiscent of impressionism (*English Renaissance Miniature*, p. 53). But Strong goes on to discuss the way in which Hilliard delineated every tiny detail of his sitters. Even Hilliard had a more linear style and a more limited range of painterly techniques than Venetian and Baroque artists, in particular. Cf. Lucy Gent's conclusion (*Picture and Poetry* [Leamington Spa: James Hall, 1982], p. 17): "The concept of painting which . . . prevailed in England until the 1570s and for many men lingered long after was, I would argue, the medieval one of line and colour." Her excellent analysis of the slow development of the concept of "shadowing" in English painting supplements my argument.

53. Perrinchief, *Royal Martyr*, p. 253.

54. *Reliquiae Wottonianae*, p. 155.

55. Hilliard, "Treatise on Limning," p. 23.

56. Quoted by J. Pope Hennessy, "Nicholas Hilliard and Mannerist Art Theory," *Journal of the Warburg and Courtauld Institutes* 6 (1943): 99.

57. "Apology for Poesy," in *Selected Poetry and Prose of Sidney*, ed. David Kalestone (New York: Signet, 1970), p. 224.

58. Ibid., p. 221.

59. Ibid., p. 223. This parallel has also been noticed by Norman K. Farmer, *Poets and the Visual Arts in Renaissance England* (Austin: University of Texas Press, 1984), esp. pp. 9–11. In a valuable opening chapter, Farmer also shows that Sidney had an unusually sophisticated appreciation for continental art and art theory.

60. H&S, vol. 8, p. 610.

61. Ibid., p. 628.

62. Ibid., p. 611.

63. Admired but also distrusted. Jonson's chief complaint against painting is that it can never fully express the intellectual truths that are the proper subject of poetry. Thus while stressing the parallels between the fine arts and poetry, he also insisted on the greater range and accuracy of the latter: "Poetry, and Picture, are arts of a like nature; and both are busy about imitation . . . for they both invent, fain and devise many things, and accommodate all they invent to the use, and service of nature. Yet of the two the pen is more noble than the pencil. For that can speak to the Understanding; the other, but to the sense" (H&S, vol. 8, p. 635). Other comments by Jonson suggest that even this contrast needs to be qualified. Painting can express flashes of insight—for example, into the

"senses, perturbations and manners" of those it depicts—but it cannot connect these insights into a coherent moral discourse. Thus pictures can stimulate the understanding, but by themselves they cannot fully satisfy it. Jonson's use of pictorial imagery is congruent with this attitude. His plays and poems are full of images and vignettes that foreshadow or underline intellectual meanings which emerge completely only through words or dramatic action. For a somewhat different view, see Farmer, *Poets and the Visual Arts*, pp. 26–30.

64. Ibid., passim, provides a discussion of the use of pictorial techniques by (among others) Sidney, Donne, Jonson, Carew, Lovelace, Waller, and Herrick.

65. E. H. Gombrich, "The Renaissance Theory of Art and the Rise of Landscape," in *Norm and Form* (London: Phaidon, 1966), pp. 107–121; and Walter Friedlander, *Caravaggio Studies* (Princeton: Princeton University Press, 1955), esp. chap. 6.

66. For another discussion of this topic, see Gent, *Picture and Poetry*.

67. See, e.g., de Critz's portrait of Sir Francis Walsingham (repr. in Strong, *English Icon*, p. 263). Painted ca. 1585, this makes a striking contrast to the nearly contemporary portraits by Gower and the costume portraitists. De Critz could paint elaborate costumes as well; the puritan, Walsingham perhaps demanded a simpler style.

68. Strong, *English Icon*, pp. 21–25.

69. Ben Jonson, "Love's Welcome to Bolsover" (H&S, vol. 7, p. 808):
If love be called a lifting of the sense
To knowledge of that pure intelligence
Wherein the soul hath rest and residence
When were the senses in such order placed?
The Sight, the Hearing, Smelling, Touching, Taste,
All at one banquet
. . . And hence,
At every real banquet of the sense,
Welcome, true welcome, fill the compliments.

70. *Complete Masques*, p. 392.

71. "An Expostulation with Inigo Jones," H&S, vol. 8, pp. 403, 404.

72. Now housed in the Worcester College Library in Oxford, except for Jones's copy of Vitruvius, which is in the possession of the Duke of Devonshire. For a listing, see *The King's Arcadia: Inigo Jones and the Stuart Court*, ed. John Harris (London: Arts Council of Great Britain, 1973), pp. 217, 218. All page references in the notes below are to the volumes formerly in Jones's possession. I have translated all quotations from the texts.

73. Jones's copy of Aristotle's *Ethics* (see above, note 72), *L'ethicà d'Aristotile*, trans. Bernardo Segni (Venice, 1551), p. 173.

74. Jones's copy of Piccolomini's work, Alessandro Piccolomini, *Della institution morale* (Venice, 1575), p. 366.

75. Jones's copy of Plato's *Republic*, *La republica di Platone*, trans. Pamphilo Fiorimbene (Venice, 1554), p. 224.

76. Jones's copy of Aristotle's *Ethics*, p. 185.

77. See, e.g., the passage marked by Jones on p. 85 in Plutarch's *Opuscoli Morali*, *Opuscoli Morali di Plutarco Cheronese*, trans. Marc'Antonio Gandino (Venice, 1614). "The office, then, of prudence is, according to nature, to restrain and control the disordered effects and motives that are born in the soul."

78. Jones's copy of Aristotle's *Ethics*, p. 84.

79. Ibid., p. 175.

80. John Webb and Inigo Jones, *The Most Notable Antiquity of Great Britain Vulgarly Called Stonehenge . . . Restored* (London, 1655), p. 108.

81. Gordon Toplis, "Inigo Jones: A Study of Neo-platonic Aspects of His Thought and Work" (M.A. thesis, Liverpool, 1967), p. 244.

82. H&S, vol. 7, p. 108.

83. Jones's copy of Plutarch's *Moral Works*, p. 234.

84. Jones's copy of Vitruvius (see above, note 73), p. 46.

85. Toplis, "Inigo Jones," pp. 122–123.

86. Cf. Roy Strong, *Splendor at Court* (Boston: Houghton Mifflin, 1973), p. 220.

87. On this, see esp. Stephen Orgel and Roy Strong, *Inigo Jones: The Theater of the Stuart Court*, 2 vols. (London: Sotheby Parke Bernet; Berkeley and Los Angeles: University of California Press, 1973), vol. 1, p. 52.

88. Stephen Orgel, *The Illusion of Power* (Berkeley and Los Angeles: University of California Press, 1975), p. 88.

89. Bacon, *Works*, vol. 3, pp. 351, 294.

90. I do not want to imply that Jones was not influenced by Platonic and Neoplatonic thought, only that we need to use such terms with extreme care. It is possible to read into some of Plato's works the same kind of movement between theoretical and practical modes of thought we have been tracing in Jones's marginalia. Misunderstandings arise when Jones and his masque designs are interpreted as an outgrowth of Platonic theories of symbolic imagery, developed by Renaissance thinkers interested in the use of emblems and mythological paintings to represent religious and philosophical ideas. Jones was undoubtedly familiar with this body of theory, but he was not limited by it. His library contained not only various manuals of art and architecture produced during the sixteenth century, but also works by Plato himself, Aristotle, Herodotus, Thucydides, Polybius, and Plutarch. We have no reason to believe that he habitually thought in terms of the ideas and vocabulary of the Neoplatonic theory of emblematic symbolism as developed by the Florentine Academy and its followers.

91. Jones's copy of *Les Cinq premiers livres des Histoires de Polybe Megalopolitein*, trans. Louis Maigret (Lyons, 1558), p. 77.

92. BL, Marl. MSS 6988, fol. 111.

93. Bacon, *Works*, vol. 3, p. 438.

94. Ibid., vol. 6, p. 757.

95. H&S, vol. 8, p. 565.

7 CHARLES I AND THE CONSOLIDATION OF A COURT CULTURE

The reign of James I witnessed a series of fundamental innovations in the art, literature, and music of the royal court, but even in the early 1620s these experiments had not entirely supplanted the court culture of the late sixteenth century. Prodigy house architecture, neo-chivalric pageantry, and verse and costume portraiture in the tradition of Hilliard survived side by side with newer forms, creating a cultural mosaic of bewildering diversity.

About the time of Charles's accession a more cohesive and unified court culture began to emerge. The restless experimentation of Jacobean poets, playwrights, musicians, and art patrons gave way to efforts at refining forms that had already developed by the early 1620s. Jones continued to work in the mature classical style he had first perfected in the Whitehall Banqueting House. Gentileschi and Van Dyck settled in England, bringing to fruition the cosmopolitan artistic culture that had begun to develop in the time of Prince Henry. Court poets like Carew, Suckling, and Lovelace assimilated the styles of Jonson and Donne, while Shirley, Brome, and Davenant built upon the satiric tradition of the private theaters.[1] Taste also became more uniform as the newer, classical and Baroque values finally supplanted older Elizabethan fashions. A transitional period was succeeded by a time of consolidation and synthesis.

Two things chiefly account for this. First, after 1625 the extensive patronage and pronounced tastes of the royal couple and a few other great courtiers lent greater unity to the entire culture of fashionable London. Although Charles and his immediate entourage never paid most of the costs of the capital's cultural amenities, they did provide a crucial source of leadership. Even in the 1630s the theatrical companies retained considerable independence, and not all poets looked to the court for patronage. Nevertheless, the Caroline court was much more of an arbiter of taste than its Jacobean predecessor.[2]

Second, a much younger group of patrons, artists, poets, and musicians emerged in the 1620s and 1630s, accustomed since adolescence to the stylistic techniques and cultural values developing during the early seventeenth century. Having grown up as James reestablished England's ties with Spain and Italy, knowing the art of Titian and Rubens, the drama of Shakespeare and Jonson, and the poetry of Jonson and Donne, they felt at home in the sophisticated atmosphere of the Stuart capital as neither their elders nor their provincial contemporaries could.

The significance of this generational change has been obscured by the convention of distinguishing sharply between the Elizabethan and Jacobean periods while treating the reigns of the first two Stuarts more or less as a unit.[3] Yet in many ways 1625 was a more decisive cultural watershed than 1603. True, the years around the turn of the century witnessed more radical experiments in poetry and drama than the 1620s, but to a remarkable extent these were the work of men born in the 1560s and early 1570s, who had already reached maturity before Elizabeth's death.[4] Bacon, Shakespeare, and Marlowe were less than a decade older than Jonson, Donne, and even Inigo Jones, who was already twenty-eight at James's accession. It takes some effort to realize that George Chapman, who competed with Jonson as a dramatist for the Jacobean private playhouses and lived until 1631, was older than Marlowe and almost contemporary with Sir Philip Sidney.

Charles came to the throne just as this older generation was disappearing. Shakespeare died in 1616, to be followed two years later by Raleigh and Francis Beaumont, and before 1632 by Bacon, Fletcher, Webster, Donne, Campion, and Drayton. Jonson lived on until 1637, and Jones lived into the 1650s, but they now found themselves surrounded by colleagues and patrons twenty or thirty years their junior. At the time of his accession Charles was twenty-five, Buckingham was thirty-two, and Henrietta Maria was only sixteen. With few exceptions they recruited talents as young as themselves. Herrick and Carew were born in the early 1590s; Van Dyck, Waller, Davenant, and Suckling were born in the first decade of the seventeenth century. Lovelace was born in 1618. These younger patrons, poets, and artists assimilated the experiments of the previous few decades, along with important French, Spanish, Flemish, and Italian influences, to create an original court culture of considerable brilliance.

THE INFLUENCE OF EUROPEAN CULTURES

One of the most important influences shaping the ambience of Charles's court was the large number of social, political, and cultural bonds connecting Whitehall to its counterparts across the Channel. By 1625 more than twenty years had passed since James made peace with Spanish Europe. The young men who went abroad on grand tours or in the train of Jacobean embassies had since risen to positions of leadership, so that except for a few older figures, like Archbishop Laud, nearly all the court's leaders had visited the continent, and many had spent years or even decades there. Endymion Porter, one of the king's closest companions, grew up in the household of the Count-Duke of Olivares.[5] Sir Kenelm Digby, who belonged to Charles's retinue of privy chamber servants, traveled during his youth through Italy, Spain, and France, mastering languages and dabbling in philosophy.[6] Among those who rose to the Privy Council in the late 1620s, Sir Francis Cottington had lived for more than a decade with the English embassy at Madrid, while the Earls of Holland and Carlisle both had substantial diplomatic experience. Arundel, who spoke fluent Italian, had toured the continent repeatedly.[7]

Meanwhile the grand tour had continued to grow in popularity among court families. In a single year Secretary Windebanke sent one son to Rome, one to Florence, and one to Madrid, so that each could master the language and customs of a different Mediterranean court.[8] Ambassadors stationed in England naturally tried to facilitate these journeys in the hope of winning influential friends, so that young English courtiers often received lavish entertainment from foreign heads of state. Even staunch Protestants availed themselves of this hospitality. Thus in May 1640, immediately after the dissolution of the Short Parliament raised the political temperature in London to feverish levels, the papal envoy passed on to Barberini the thanks of the Earls of

Holland and Pembroke for courtesies extended to their younger relatives.[9] Both earls soon joined Parliament's rebellion, and both patronized puritan clergy, but this did not prevent them from welcoming civil relations with a Roman cardinal.

It was not only by traveling abroad, however, that English courtiers came into contact with foreign cultures. Every embassy in the English capital was a tiny enclave of a continental, court society. Since diplomacy formed part of the daily routine for many high-ranking ministers, contact with French, Spanish, and Italian lords was often frequent and intimate. Windebanke and Cottington, in particular, seem to have formed warm friendships with several ambassadors. The foreign diplomats, in turn, provided up-to-date information about their homelands and often procured luxurious gifts for English acquaintances. Salvetti obtained annual shipments of Tuscan wine for Lord Treasurer Weston and other royal officials. The Earl of Holland acquired a gardener and exotic plants from a French ambassador, while Sir Francis Windebanke had his efforts to spare English Catholics from the penal laws repaid with paintings by Correggio and Albani, sent by Cardinal Barberini himself.[10]

The household of Henrietta Maria provided an especially close link to the court of France. Panzani once described French as "almost a second vulgar tongue" at the court, an assertion borne out by the glacial pace at which the queen learned her subjects' language. Charles was delighted when his wife acted in *The Shepherd's Paradise* in 1632, because doing so gave her much-needed practice in pronunciation.[11] Even in the 1640s she conducted her correspondence with the Earl of Newcastle in French, and her few English letters betray her uncertainties about English diction, pronunciation, and spelling.[12] With her Capuchin monks, her foreign musicians, and her fondness for French pastoral drama, Henrietta Maria created a little pocket of Parisian court culture in the heart of Westminster. "The relation of our Carnival . . . will please the Queen," her favorite, Walter Montagu, reported from the French capital in 1637, "because there was only one comedy at the Cardinal's. I assure myself that yours was much better."[13] Here we have a queen of England trying to outdo the chief minister of Louis XIII in producing a kind of drama fashionable at the Louvre.

ART COLLECTING AND OTHER CULTURAL DIVERSIONS

The most visible manifestation of this fascination for European culture was the court's art collections. Collecting was part of a lifestyle that had developed in the city-states of Italy and then spread to Spain, the Low Countries, and parts of Germany before reaching England. The distinguished galleries and refined taste of the royal entourage symbolized its participation in an international aristocratic culture. No one appreciated this fact better than Rubens, who traveled throughout the continent during his career without finding a more congenial environment than that which he encountered in London in 1629. He wrote:

> This island . . . seems to me to be a spectacle worthy of the interest of every gentleman . . . not only for the splendor of the outward culture, which seems to be extreme, as of a people rich and happy in the lap of peace, but also for the incredible quality of excellent pictures, statues and ancient inscriptions which are to be found in this court. . . . I confess I have never seen anything in the world more rare.[14]

Enjoyment of art and other cultural diversions formed part of the fabric of English court life. Panzani went to a feast at Arundel House in the mid-1630s and spent the evening conversing in Italian with the earl's wife as he watched performances of rural dances and comic entertainments. Arundel then produced a collection of drawings by Michelangelo for his guests to examine.[15] The next year another papal representative, George Con, dined with the monarchs at Somerset House, along the Strand. Afterward the party moved to Arundel's adjoining residence to tour the galleries:

> His majesty said he would narrate to me a miracle of the Earl, which was that he had sent a picture by Holbein to the Grand Duke. I replied that the Earl could perform twenty similar miracles, because he had in one room more than thirty pieces by that same painter. The Earl hereupon vehemently denied having this power while I besought him to remember the doctrine of free will. He protested that he was most ready to support that doctrine in everything except the giving away of pictures.[16]

On less formal occasions courtiers sometimes amused themselves by watching artists work. Con attended two meals *al fresco* at "the casinos where they work the marbles," along with Arundel, his son Maltravers, Prince Rupert, and Secretary Windebanke.[17] Van Dyck's studio in

Blackfriars attracted a stream of illustrious visitors. According to the Genoese art historian Bellori, who got his information from Sir Kenelm Digby, it

> was frequented by the highest nobles, for example the King, who came daily to see him and took delight in watching him paint and lingering with him. . . . Van Dyck kept servants, carriages, horses, and musicians and buffoons and with these diversions he entertained all the greatest persons, gentlemen and ladies, who went daily to his house.[18]

Contemporary evidence bears out this account. One of Shirley's comedies alludes to an artist:

> Not an Englishman I warrant you,
> One that can please the Ladies every way,
> You shall not set with him all day for shadows,
> He has regalios, and can present you with
> Sudrets of fourteen pence a pound, Canary
> Prunellas, Venice glasses, Parmesan
> Sugars, Bologna, sausages all from Antwerp;
> He will make apodridas most incomparably.[19]

The lines could refer only to Van Dyck. The Earl of Newcastle wrote to the artist: "Next the blessings of your company and sweetness of conversation, the greatest happiness were to be all over but one eye, so it . . . were ever fixed upon that which we must call yours."[20] An Exchequer warrant records payments for a landing stage for boats built at Van Dyck's house, to enable the king to visit him more conveniently.[21] The residence of a painter a generation removed from a family of Antwerp silk merchants had become one of the centers around which court society revolved. It would be difficult to imagine more forceful testimony to the prestige that artistic skill had attained.

THE ROLE OF LITERATURE: VERSE, SATIRE, AND THE STAGE

If the court's aesthetic culture had been imported from Italy, Spain, and Flanders, its literary tastes derived essentially from indigenous traditions. There was consequently more continuity with the Elizabethan and early Jacobean periods in this sphere. However, the new reign did bring a subtle but important change in the social role of literature. Few Jacobean poets ever felt entirely secure within the court. The professionals, especially Jonson, had to fight for acceptance by a society in which literary talent and scholarly attainments still did not automatically confer gentility. Most of the gentlemen amateurs, including Donne, dismissed their verse as a youthful avocation, fearing it would seem too frivolous for a royal servant.

In Charles's reign, by contrast, poets were often swept up into court society. Both Charles and Henrietta Maria liked their company and sometimes promoted them to posts of honor. Thomas Carew won a place within Charles's retinue of personal servants; Waller, Davenant, and several lesser poets enjoyed secure positions within the queen's entourage. Sir John Suckling gained entry to the court largely on the strength of his reputation as a wit. Long before this period, men associated with the court had written verse—Wyatt, Sidney, and Raleigh come to mind. But without exception these earlier figures either held or aspired to hold positions of real political power; they were politicians by trade and poets by avocation. In the Caroline period this ceased to be true. Men who wrote stylish verse were welcome in court society even when, as was usually the case, they had no real political role to fulfill.[22]

Quite apart from the more serious writers patronized by the Crown, the court was full of gentleman amateurs who turned out odd poems without ever aspiring to rival the professionals. By his own admission Suckling belongs in this category, but so do numerous other courtiers with less appreciable talents. We will never know how many of these existed, since few probably took care to preserve their work, but we do catch occasional glimpses of their efforts. Endymion Porter modestly denied his reputation as a wit by admitting he could write verse only with difficulty.[23] In the late 1630s the Earl of Holland wrote love poems to the Countess of Carlisle, "the silliest things I ever saw," as another noblewoman described them.[24] The chief motive, in this case, was undoubtedly political: although a woman of over forty, the duchess was a close friend of Holland's patron, the queen, whereas his relations with Her Majesty had lately deteriorated. Amorous verse had always been a convenient vehicle for pleas to a powerful lady, but not since the 1590s had there been so many powerful ladies at court. This helps explain the great popularity of courtly love poems in the 1630s.

Courtiers who did not feel up to the challenge of writing verse sometimes attempted to tease and embarrass one another by composing satiric prose character portraits. Thomas Wentworth wrote characters

of rivals he disliked, which he sent to Laud and Windebanke; the Earl
of Holland reputedly kept an entire book of them. In 1635 a newsletter
writer reported: "There is an excellent song which privately passes
about, of all the Lords and Ladies in town." Only one specimen seems
to have survived: the character of the Countess of Carlisle which Tobie
Matthew had the audacity to print. Its finely wrought style suggests
what court wit-combats must have been like:

> She is in disposition inclined to be choleric, which she suppresses; not, per-
> haps, in a consideration of the persons who occasion it, but upon a belief
> that it is unhandsome towards herself; which yet . . . doth so kindle and
> fire her wit, as that in very few words, it says something so extracted, as it
> hath a sharpness . . . to disrelish, if not kill, the proudest hopes which you
> can have of her value of you.[25]

A few days after this piece appeared someone threw an anonymous
"Character of a Lady" through Sir Tobie's window, "a very witty one,
far exceeding any of his. . . . Most think it written of my Lady Carlisle. . . . King, Queen, all have seen it." Viscount Conway, "a great
gatherer of these things," promised to send a copy to Wentworth in
Ireland.[26]

At least as important as poetry and prose satire in providing the
court elite with a cherished diversion was the stage.[27] The importance
attached to plays by men and women of fashion in the 1630s comes
through vividly in a letter written by a certain Ann Mericke to a friend
at court. After gossiping about the latest trends in feminine dress and
the behavior of court gallants, it concludes:

> I could wish myself with you . . . to see the *Alchemist* which I hear this
> term is revived and the new play a friend of mine sent to Sir John Suckling
> and Tom Carew (the best wits of the time) to correct. But for want of these
> gentle recreations I must content myself here with the study of Shakespeare
> and the *History of Women*, all my country library.[28]

Women had attended playhouses for thirty years and more before Mrs.
Mericke composed these lines. Nevertheless, it is difficult to imagine a
letter of quite this tone written much before the 1630s. The development of the London season had created a new type: the lady of fashion
pining away in the country, amusing herself with books while she
dreamed of rejoining the capital's glamorous whirl.

In taking such an admiring attitude toward the theater, Mrs. Mericke simply followed the lead of her social superiors, from the royal couple on down. Elizabeth and James had invited players to perform at court, but Charles was the first monarch to build a theater attached to Whitehall itself, to facilitate the twenty or thirty performances he commanded each year.[29] The royal family and court aristocrats not only watched plays but also participated actively in their production. The queen loved to act. Walter Montagu wrote a pastoral drama to please her, which she immediately decided to perform. Thomas Killigrew, a gentleman of the king's privy chamber and scion of an old court family, wrote a play for a London company; the Earl of Newcastle, while head of Prince Charles's household in the late 1630s, co-authored three humors comedies, ostensibly in the style of Ben Jonson.[30] Even the king provided plot outlines to James Shirley.[31] If he did not stoop to become a royal playwright, he could not entirely resist trying his hand at this court diversion.

Every Christmas season the court's enthusiasm for the stage climaxed in a round of performances capped by the royal masques. Year after year all but the most pressing items of business lapsed for weeks as the royal entourage indulged its love of the stage. "Their Majesties being occupied with the festivities of Christmas, business is not spoken of in court or city," Salvetti lamented in January 1627, a time of acute diplomatic and financial crisis.[32] The masque rehearsals consumed surprising amounts of royal time and energy. In February 1635 Salvetti reported that the queen and her ladies passed the Christmas season by dancing publicly twice a week and practicing a masque daily. Two years later Charles and his train were rehearsing every day.[33]

VALUES, IDEALS, AND MODES OF THOUGHT AND FEELING

Cultural works also helped to define the social values and ideals of the royal entourage. Even at a distance of three centuries Caroline art and literature manages to convey a seductive vision of an elegant aristocratic society with a character unmistakably different from that of the Tudor period. They do this partly by descriptive means, as with the portraits of Van Dyck, which capture so well the surface brilliance of court life. But it is also a matter of more subtle qualities of tone and style: the polished conversational diction of court poetry, the well-assimilated

classical features of both literature and architecture, the sense of refinement and discipline evident in paintings, poems, and buildings alike.

But we cannot take this impression as an entirely accurate reflection
of social realities. Courtiers can rarely have looked as distinguished in
the flesh as they do in Van Dyck's portraits, and they would not often
have spoken with the grace and wit of a good cavalier poem. The court
was far less refined and less uniform in its values and lifestyles than the
cultural documents, by themselves, might suggest. One would never
guess, for example, that the delicate man with long golden curls in Van
Dyck's portrait of the Earl of Holland invested in Caribbean piracy and
patronized the Puritan radical John Everard. Cultural works presented a
stylized and sometimes distorted image of reality, shaped by artistic and
literary traditions and the personalities of their creators as much as by
the tone of court society.

Those images, however, are significant pieces of historical evidence, conveying more effectively than anything else the standards to
which many courtiers aspired and the ways in which they liked to see
themselves. Taken in conjunction with evidence gleaned from other
sources, art and literature can shed invaluable light on the court's outlook in the 1630s.

FREEDOM, SENSUALITY, AND DECORUM

We have already noticed how frequently cultural developments within
the Jacobean court reflected the uncertainties of a period when old values were breaking down and new ones had not yet fully emerged to take
their place. In a number of ways Caroline court culture suggests a resolution of these conflicts. Not only is it more uniform in tone than that
of the early seventeenth century, it also conveys a remarkable capacity
to enjoy sensual pleasures while preserving an air of propriety and discipline. In the 1630s a new equilibrium emerged between the licentious
impulses and strenuous morality that had so often clashed during
James's reign.

That equilibrium appears, for example, in the subtle tension between passion and discipline that enlivens much of the court's best
poetry. Carew, Suckling, Waller, and Lovelace frequently convey a tremendous zest for the fleeting joys of love and youth, but they normally
wrote with an unerring sense of decorum. Consequently they convey a
comforting assurance that we can enjoy life to the fullest without relin-

quishing the composure and self-control that make civility possible. The very cadences of their language usually carry an air of good breeding, even when expressing thoughts that might have inspired rudeness:

No tears, Celia, now shall win
My resolved heart to return;
I have searched thy soul within,
And find nought but pride and scorn;
I have learned thy arts, and now
Can disdain as much as thou.[34]

The tone is so calm and even that the underlying determination to insult and injure does not seem particularly ill-mannered. Many Jacobean poets liked to imitate the rhythm and syntax of angry or passionate speech. Their Caroline successors normally preferred to understate strong feeling by expressing it in relatively balanced, smooth lines, evoking a feeling of civilized restraint.

This equilibrium of passion and reason, freedom and restraint, shaped the whole tone of the court, not just its literature. Whitehall in the 1630s was a place of gallantry and sophistication in which some people led dissolute lives, but it was not racked by the scandals that had so marred the surface of James's reign. The licentious elements of court life were kept within bounds by a ruling couple who tried to distinguish between innocent pleasures and unbecoming vices.

It took some time for this moderation to triumph. Like his older brother, Charles reacted strongly against the excesses of his father's court and vigorously set about cleaning house once he took the throne. He delivered moral aphorisms to young men who came to pay their homage, fined courtiers for swearing, and reportedly blushed whenever anyone uttered obscenities in his presence. He tried to turn his marriage into a model of virtuous love, though a series of feuds with his temperamental young wife momentarily frustrated him. For a while the court's tone became almost somber. "If you saw how little gallantry there is at court," the Countess of Carlisle complained in 1627, "you would believe that it were no great adventure to come thither after having the small pox, for it is most desolate and I have no great desire to return."[35]

From the outset, however, the conduct of other court leaders moderated the impact of Charles's prudery. Buckingham behaved as extravagantly as ever, while the Earls of Holland and Carlisle also perpetuated the pleasure-loving ways of the previous reign. But the most important influence in restoring a touch of gaiety to court society was that of Henrietta Maria. Charles admired and imitated the court of Spain, famed throughout Europe for its gravity and ceremoniousness. His wife came from a French court equally well known for its relative informality, its colorful fashions, and its gallantry.[36] In 1626 her French attendants had already earned English disapproval for dancing and cavorting too freely in her presence. The next year Charles sent them home, primarily for political and diplomatic reasons but also to remove their influence upon his wife. The young queen found herself surrounded by servants picked by Buckingham, whom she regarded as a mortal enemy.

Before long she managed to turn the tables on the duke. Among her new attendants was the countess of Carlisle, the wife of one of James's Scots and the court's most famous beauty. It did not take long for this vivacious and worldly-wise lady to cast her spell over Henrietta Maria. In May 1627 the French ambassador, Bassompierre, commented upon

> the favor the countess of Carlisle has with the Queen, who has already taken her three times to have supper with her, along with the countesses of Exeter, Oxford and Bouchier, without inviting the Duchess of Buckingham . . . at which Buckingham was not a little offended. These parties took place in extreme privacy, rarely used in England and caused a great stir, since the Queen rarely associates with subjects in small supper gatherings.[37]

The meetings were not only small and private, but lively enough to offend English prejudices concerning conduct becoming royalty. In a revealing passage Bassompierre noted: "The King once found himself in these little festivities . . . but behaved with a gravity which spoiled the conversation, because his humor is not inclined to this sort of debauche."[38]

After Buckingham's death in 1629, Charles fell deeply in love with his wife, who consequently gained considerable influence. A faction soon gathered around her, consisting, in Panzani's words, of "lively young men [who] . . . delight the Queen very much, who as a young woman loves to gossip and hear lively stories and witticisms."[39] This feminine influence soon altered the ambience of the court, affecting even the conduct of politics. Weston agonized over his inability to handle Henrietta Maria tactfully. Panzani summed up the qualities desirable in an ambassador to England as "youth and all the cavalier virtues." In particular, he must cultivate the queen, "who delights in perfume, beautiful clothes, in seeing life carried well and in lively discourse. He must also seek to win the ladies of the court, since here many negotiations are conducted through women."[40] The papacy was in a special position, since its only real connections with England were through Henrietta Maria's household, but other states also found they could not ignore women while doing business at Whitehall.[41]

Despite the gaiety, both monarchs frowned on promiscuity and crude sexual improprieties. In the court's masques and panegyrics Henrietta Maria always appears as a chaste Queen of Beauty whose soft influence refines masculine passion, purging the court of immorality and the kingdom of discord:

> Thy sacred Love shows us the path
> Of Modesty and constant faith
> Which makes the rude male satisfied
> With one fair female by his side;
> Doth either sex to each unite,
> And forms love's pure Hermaphrodite.[42]

Artificial as these tributes were, they reflected an underlying royal attitude.

The most radical manifestation of the effort to purify the sexual morality of Whitehall was the cult of "Platonic" love that flourished around the queen. In the pastoral dramas and a few of the poems written for her, sexual passion becomes a purely spiritual bond between a man and a woman, purged of all physical connotations:

> True love . . . is a Spirit extracted out of the whole mass of virtue; and two hearts, so equal in it as they are measured by one another, are the vessels where it [is] refined, heated, naturally by each others' eyes, and joined by pipes as subtle as our thoughts.[43]

We need not take these claims too seriously; the court produced more anti-Platonic poems than statements of Platonic love. The cult of disembodied love never appears to have won many converts and was certainly far less influential than some modern scholars have supposed.[44] Platonic-love doctrines probably served mainly as a topic for fashionable debates in mixed company. Their most important practical function was to blunt the strong misogynist prejudices of the age by justifying the social and political favor the queen and other ladies bestowed upon their male servants. As such they were the Caroline equivalent to the Elizabethan cult of virginity, a device for masking political intrigue with harmless flirtation.[45]

Quite apart from these considerations, the court developed a much more open and uninhibited attitude toward erotic passion than was common in the early seventeenth century, when moralists generally condemned strong sexual desire even if it did not lead to illicit acts. Puritans talked of the lawful pleasures of wedlock, but they did not normally justify ardent passion between man and wife: marriage should cool the fires of lust, not stoke them.[46] But ever since the Middle Ages erotic play had been part of a courtly lifestyle. Charles's servants had no intention of abandoning this tradition.

Sensitivity to moral conventions remained strong enough to encourage attempts to disguise the carnal element in courtly love. The Platonic technique of purifying lust by lending it an ethereal, disembodied quality helped do this. The Caroline poets were masters at dissociating erotic feeling from illicit acts. When they chose they could write almost pornographic verse, as in Carew's "The Rapture," which enjoyed an enormous popularity.[47] More often, however, they managed to evoke the physical side of love while at the same time distancing themselves from prurient behavior. Sometimes, by choosing light and airy images, they described a woman in very erotic ways without compromising her purity:

> Go thou gentle whispering wind
> Bear this sigh, and if thou find
> Where my cruel fair doth rest
> Cast it in her snowy breast;
> So, inflamed by my desire
> It may set her heart afire.[48]

Although the imagery is suggestive, the sexual innuendo remains under control, partly by Carew's equivocation (It *may* set her heart on fire") but mainly because he chose such an insubstantial vehicle for his lust. The wind may

> Boldly light upon her lip,
> There suck odors, and thence skip

To her bosom, lastly fall
Down and wander over all.

But it is only a wind carrying a harmless daydream, whose fulfillment remains very much in doubt. A lady may therefore read of its whispering antics without feeling compromised.

In other contexts Platonic ideas of disembodied love could enrich and justify a romance that might still end in physical fulfillment. Carew wrote to an absent mistress:

Then though our bodies are dis-joined
As things that are to place confined;
Yet let our boundless spirits meet,
And in love's sphere each other greet;
There let us work a mystic wreath,
Unknown unto the world beneath;
There let our clasped loves sweetly twin;
There let our secret thoughts unseen
Like nets be weaved, and intertwined.[49]

Lifted from their context, these lines perfectly express the "Platonical" view of love. But Carew does not want to remain forever enjoying this airy passion. Instead, the spiritual union preserves love during a temporary separation:

. . . seated in those heavenly bowers,
We'll cheat the lag, and lingering hours,
Making our bitter absence sweet,
Till souls, and bodies both, may meet.[50]

Finally, the capacity to write of erotic passion as an airy, spiritual quality often contributed immeasurably to the poetic resonance of the cavaliers' greatest love lyrics, as in the famous closing verses of Herrick's "Corinna's Going A-Maying":

Come, let us go, while we are in our prime,
And take the harmless folly of the time
    We shall grow old apace and die
        Before we know our liberty.
        Our life is short, and our days run
        As fast away as does the sun;
And as a vapor, or a drop of rain,

Once lost, can ne'er be found again:
   So when or you or I are made
   A fable, song or fleeting shade,
   All love, all liking, all delight
   Lies drowned with us in endless night.
Then while time serves, and we are but decaying,
Come, my Corinna, come, let's go a-maying.[51]

This is a frank celebration of sexual play, tinged with thoughts of death and more than a hint of putrefaction. But the language is so tactful and the imagery is so delicate that it seems neither bawdy nor especially morbid. There is just enough qualification in the phrase "harmless folly of the time" to hold in check the overtones of seduction. The evanescent quality of vapors, mists, and fleeting shades purifies the references to decay, just as the gaiety of the occasion and slightly lilting, colloquial quality of the final couplet balance the thought of eternal oblivion. We are left with a delicate evocation of the beauty and impermanence of youthful love, purged of guilt and remorse. And since these lines appeared in print just when a Puritan commonwealth set about suppressing May dances as occasions of lust, they also made a political statement. Passion is not in itself evil, and the thought of death does not lead immediately to fear of hell. Men and women may enjoy the festive, playful side of life without feeling they have betrayed a God who created the warmth of spring and intense emotions of the young, as well as the chill of winter and the world-weariness of old age. A state that fears the harmless follies of its people will set itself against a whole dimension of human nature, erecting a tyranny more oppressive than anything the king ever contemplated.

FORMALITY, CEREMONY, AND AESTHETIC SENSIBILITY

The approach taken by Charles's entourage to rules of etiquette followed a similar evolution, becoming gradually less rigid as the reign progressed. Few things detracted more from James's prestige than his inability to force others to treat him with appropriate dignity. Suitors pressed in upon him, entering his presence by back stairs and driving him to distraction with their importunate requests. "I would you had first my doublet and then my hose," he once shouted in exasperation, "and maybe when I were stark naked you would leave me alone."[52] Charles quickly put a stop to these practices. "The King observes a rule of great decorum," the Venetian ambassador observed less than a month after his accession. "The nobles do not enter his apartments in confusion, as heretofore, but each rank has its appointed place. . . . The king has also drawn up rules for himself, dividing the day from his very early rising, for prayers, exercises, business, eating and sleeping."[53] Privy chamber servants received new instructions forbidding them to wear any but approved colors and to slouch in the royal presence or lean against the supports of the canopy over the throne, and regulating everything down to who might watch as the king removed his boots. "The English are excessively punctillious," the Venetian ambassador complained as these measures went into effect, "and stand upon their King's honor more, perhaps, than any other nation in the world."[54]

Charles always preserved this formal dignity on state occasions, but he soon learned to lay aside the more stringent rules in private. "He would have those about him converse rather with himself than with His Majesty," Perrinchief wrote, "and with them would mingle discourses as one of the people."[55] Unlike his contemporary Philip IV of Spain, he never became a "prisoner of ceremony."[56]

The king's desire to retreat from the formality of his office should be seen in relation to similar changes taking place, from a much earlier date, in the habits of the English aristocracy. For some time, life within the greater country houses had been moving away from the hall and the great chamber, with their throngs of servants and attendants, into more intimate parlors and withdrawing rooms.[57] People sought to escape from the encumbering ceremonies of rank and the pressure of being always the center of attraction, into the privacy of small gatherings. Thus Thomas Wentworth liked to "retire into an inner room and sit two or three hours taking tobacco and telling stories with great pleasantness and freedom . . . laying aside all state . . . which in public he would require."[58] The movement of peers and gentry into the city, away from their tenants and dependents and into a society which prized good conversation, reinforced this trend.

But it was one thing for a man like Wentworth, who had recently emerged from the broad ranks of the gentry, to behave in this way, and quite another for a peer of ancient lineage or a king to do so. Not everyone approved of the movement toward greater freedom of manners. The Earl of Arundel, in particular, always maintained the greatest formality. "He was a person of great civility," his biographer, Edward Walker, wrote, yet with that restriction as that it forbade any to be bold or saucy with him, though with those whom he affected, which were lovers of State, Nobility and Curious Arts he was very free and conversable, but they being but few, the stream of the times being otherwise, he had not many confidants.[59]

It is not surprising that he complained that "the great affability in the King and the French garb of the court would bring Majesty into contempt." Selden drew a similar conclusion. "In Queen Elizabeth's time, Gravity and State were kept up. In King James's time things were pretty well. But in King Charles's time there has been nothing but Trenchmore, and the Cushion-Dance, omnium gatherum, tolly-polly, hoite come toite."[60]

To appreciate the complaints against the decline in "gravity and state" of Caroline conservatives, we need to recognize how much more important ceremonies were in the seventeenth century than in our own society. Ceremonies differentiated between individuals, marking the hierarchical gradations of a social order based on the principle of inequality. They kept inferiors from becoming too familiar with those above them, creating an aura of respect and authority which the elite carefully maintained, with the whip and the pillory if necessary. "What preserves you kings more than ceremony," the Earl of Newcastle wrote in the late 1630s to his royal ward, the Prince of Wales:

> the cloth of estates, the distance people are with you, great officers, heralds, trumpets, martials men making room, disorders to be labored by their staff of office. . . . I know these master the people sufficiently, aye even the wisest, though he know it and [be] not accustomed to it, shall shake off his wisdom and shake for fear of it, for this is the mist [that] is cast before us and masters the Commonwealth.[61]

Yet as Newcastle knew, public processions of "officers, heralds, trumpets [and] martials men" had become increasingly less common under the Stuarts. Elizabeth had frequently staged great court rituals before her people, James did so only rarely, and Charles virtually never.[62] The nobility also generally cut back on public ceremony. The great aristocratic funerals and cavalcades of liveried retainers riding behind court noblemen, which had been a familiar sight in the sixteenth century, were rarities by the 1630s.

As this decline took place the evocative power of elaborate ceremonies was also subtly undermined by the impact of the Reformation.

Many court rituals incorporated liturgical elements, to transfer religious emotions into the secular sphere. Thus during his coronation Charles prostrated himself in front of the main altar of Westminster Abbey, paying homage to the Almighty, before the officiating bishop first placed the crown on his head. However, the ritualism of the old church was one of the main targets of Protestant polemics. The reformers repudiated the Mass, but many also set out ruthlessly to strip away the aura that clung to the scenic paraphernalia of Catholicism.[63] Before the Civil War this ridicule was almost never directed against secular rituals, but in the long run these rituals were also affected. Puritans especially sometimes took a hardheaded, matter-of-fact attitude toward elaborate ceremonies in secular as well as religious life. Cromwell once dismissed the mace of Parliament by saying contemptuously, "Take away these baubles." The attitude reflected by that statement was inimical to the effect that court ritual was supposed to create. The early seventeenth century was therefore a period in which both religious and secular trends were undercutting traditional ceremonial forms.

This does not mean that ceremonies had lost their central place in court culture. We have already seen how in visual culture a taste for flamboyant display gave place to more intimate and subtle effects. A parallel change occurred in the court's approach to ceremony. Great public rituals and formal rules of behavior gradually declined, but a delicate ritualism pervades Caroline court culture.

Every reader of the cavalier poets knows of their love for the traditional rituals of English life: May dances, weddings, church ales, Christmas feasts, and the like. Already apparent in the 1630s, this taste blossomed in the 1650s in conscious defiance of puritan efforts to stamp out pagan and papist ceremonies. Under the Protectorate the mere act of watching countryfolk dancing about a maypole, or celebrating Christmas in the traditional manner, symbolized defiance of Cromwell's government.

Not only did the court and cavalier poets write appreciatively of folk rituals, they also continually invented original ceremonies. In their hands almost any idea or emotion might take on a ritualistic form. Recent studies have shown how central this mode of thought is to Herrick's work, but it is by no means peculiar to him.[64] It occurs in the poems of Donne and some other Jacobeans, as well as in the verse of most Caroline court poets. Thus, Carew once turned the act of taking a ribbon from his mistress into a deliberate parody of the Catholic cult of saints:

> This silken wreath, which circles in mine arm,
> Is but an Emblem of that mystic charm,
> Wherewith the magic of your beauties binds
> My captive soul. . . .
>
> To that my prayers and sacrifice, to this
> I only pay a superstitious kiss,
> This but the Idol, that's the Deity,
> Religion there is due; Here ceremony.[65]

In this instance the ritualism is overt. In Waller's famous song, "Go, Lovely Rose," it is far less obtrusive, yet it contributes no less to the poet's meaning:

> Go lovely Rose,
> Tell her that wastes her time and me,
>   That now she knows
> When I resemble her to thee
>   How sweet and fair she seems to be.
>
>   Tell her that's young
> And shuns to have her graces spied
>   That hadst thou sprung
> In deserts where no men abide,
>   Thou must have uncommended died.[66]

The commonplace lover's ritual of sending a flower to a mistress becomes the vehicle for an extraordinarily delicate emotional message.

The same method of loading ordinary acts with ritualistic significance also shaped political verse. Carew converted the act of welcoming the king to dinner at an aristocratic house into a pagan religious ceremony:

> Sir,
> Ere you pass this threshold stay,
> And give your creature leave to pay,
> Those pious rites which unto you,
> As to our household gods are due.
>   Instead of sacrifice, each breast
>   Is like a flaming Altar, dressed
>   With zealous fires, which from pure hearts
>   Love mixed with loyalty imparts.[67]

Here the ceremonies are mostly invisible, since they take place within the breasts of those who have turned out to greet the king, but they are nonetheless essential to the event.

Behind this love of ceremony lay a fascination for the ways in which apparently casual gestures and fleeting sensations might convey psychological and spiritual values. Renaissance culture often expressed ideas emblematically, and the Elizabethans experimented endlessly with intricate symbolic metaphors and pictures. Charles's generation inherited this tradition, but learned to use emblematic forms in more flexible and subtle ways.[68] Waller's song can serve again for illustration: although the rose had long figured as a symbol of transient beauty, the image had rarely been handled with such precision. The originality of the poem lies not in its central metaphor but in its nuances: the tone of futility conveyed by "Tell her that wastes her time and me," which reinforces the references to decay and death; the ambivalent admiration of "how sweet and fair she *seems* to be." These shades of meaning will be understood intuitively more than intellectually, as they reinforce and qualify the poem's main image to create a miniature psychological portrait of an impatient lover beginning to weary of his coy young mistress.

THE COURTIER'S IMAGE

Perhaps the most effective single vehicle for the idealized image of court life we have been tracing was the portraiture of Van Dyck. In his work, for the first time in English painting, the court elite is consistently depicted not as a class of warriors, nor even as an aristocracy of service, but as a caste set apart by its intellectual distinction, spiritual refinement, and instinctive elegance.

We have already noticed how difficult it was for court painters active around 1620 to reconcile the pomp and color of the costume portrait with the gravity favored by such figures as Arundel. With his virtuosity in the handling of light, color, and movement and his sensitivity to mood, Van Dyck moved beyond this impasse. In his portraits poses become more relaxed than in the work of Mytens. Swirling cloaks and undulating curtains create rhythmic movements, silks glisten and jewelry sparkles in the light. Van Dyck enhances these effects by painting his sitters from below, so that they look unusually tall and cast condescending looks down upon us.[69] These techniques recreate the richness of the costume portrait without reviving its ostentation. In

Caroline portraiture even black suits look opulent, while brightly colored ones are rarely garish. Instead of flat, impersonal catalogs of bodily ornaments, we confront vivacious men and women who seem to fit effortlessly into a world of wealth and elegance.

Van Dyck's main contribution was the air of spiritual distinction he gave his subjects. Today he has a reputation for idealizing both the appearance and the demeanor of the aristocracy, in some respects justifiably. He consistently elongated fingers, sharpened features, and made bodies appear more slender than in life, so that in his paintings even the chubbiest figures seem graceful. A comment by Sophia of Bohemia after her first meeting with Henrietta Maria reveals how deceptive these tricks could be: "Van Dyck's portraits had so accustomed me to thinking that all English women are beautiful that I was amazed to find a small creature, with skinny arms and teeth like defense works sticking out of her mouth." [70]

In the context of English portraiture, however, Van Dyck stood apart for his realism, as contemporaries noted. Waller and the Earl of Newcastle both commented on his vivacious images, which seemed to capture the spirit of their absent friends. [71] Others found the effect disconcerting. "The best faces are seldom satisfied with Van Dyck," Sir Kenelm Digby once wrote,

> whereas not the very worst ever complained of Hoskins [the miniaturist]. His art that boardeth in little confineth him to fewer imitations than the other's free pencil, which can boldly reach to all that the eye sees. . . . And this peradventure is why Cavaliers . . . are ever more apt to have their mistress picture in limning [miniature] than in a large draught with oil colors. [72]

Van Dyck's better English portraits capture a great range of moods, ranging from the intensity of the two images of Strafford to the pensive melancholy of the Earl of Warwick, the tranquillity of Lord Wharton, and the coy charm of several ladies. But beneath nearly all of them lies a common emotional denominator which sets them apart, not only from the works of other artists but also from many of his own, earlier works. This tone consists chiefly in an atmosphere of poise, reserve, and psychic balance. Figures never swagger or seem to exert themselves. Their composure and reserve remain even when they dress in armor or pose in front of battles. No one could suppose from the dreamy appearance of Prince Rupert (on the right) in the double portrait of the princes Palatine (Plate 11) that he would soon rank among

11. Anthony Van Dyck. *Double Portrait of the Palatine Princes Charles Louis and Rupert.* Cliché des Musées Nationaux, Paris. (Hangs in the Louvre Museum, Paris.)

the great cavalry officers of Europe. The robust energy of Rubens, whose compositional methods deeply influenced Van Dyck, is refined into controlled movement, flowing through landscapes, costumes, and curtains but held in check by poses and facial expressions. The nervous energy evident in some of the artist's Flemish portraits has vanished; the haughtiness of his Genoese paintings has mellowed into an air of quiet confidence. What comes through above all is a sense of civility enlivened by wit and grace.

These qualities have since become normative for the English elite, but at the time they marked a real attitudinal change. Whether he assumed the role of a warrior, a country lord, or a politician, an early modern nobleman was supposed to possess a commanding presence. Titian imparted a formidable power to his images of Venetian doges; Mor and Holbein captured the swaggering toughness of the Tudor elite. Rubens lent an aura of almost superhuman energy to his aristocratic portraits. Van Dyck's break with these traditions appears at a glance if we place his portrait of the Earl of Northumberland as Lord Admiral (Plate 12) next to Rubens's painting commemorating Buckingham's elevation to the same office (Plate 13). The latter is all action: the Duke rides a galloping horse as angelic figures swirl around him and the fleet assembles in the background. By contrast, Northumberland rests easily against a gigantic anchor, looking confidently out at us while two ships do battle behind him. Buckingham participates in the action; Northumberland seems to dominate it from a discreet distance without losing his composure.

In short, nobility ceases to mean physical prowess and haughty gravity, but consists instead of intellectual cultivation and physical grace. Much the same change occurs as we move from the world of Spenser and Raleigh into that of Waller, Suckling, and Lovelace. The conversational diction and assured tone of the Caroline poets corresponds perfectly to the poise Van Dyck conveys. Poems and portraits capture the same air of lively wit, the same feeling for the outward brilliance of court life, and from time to time the same tone of melancholy lurking just beneath the surface.

CONCLUSION

The reign of Charles I brought to an end a difficult transitional period in English court life, stretching back into the 1590s when the confi-

12. Anthony van Dyck. *Algernon Percy, 10th Earl of Northumberland.* The Duke of Northumberland. (Hangs in Alnwick Castle, Northumberland, England.)

13. Peter Paul Rubens. *George Villiers, First Duke of Buckingham*. Photograph: Courtauld Institute of Art, London. (Destroyed by a fire in the 1940s.)

dence of the high Elizabethan period began to dissolve. Cultural experiments helped to define a response to this breakdown in morale. The association of men like Jonson and Jones with their court patrons became something of a partnership in the pursuit of a more satisfying and morally valid form of courtly life. Consequently, the emergence of original styles in poetry, architecture, and painting went hand in hand with the evolution of new habits and attitudes. In the Jacobean period this cultural ferment added to the complexity of court life. Old Elizabethan forms coexisted beside the emerging elements of a very different kind of aristocratic culture, often in the activities of a single individual. Arundel excelled at the joust before he began collecting pictures; Jones helped create the last great display of neo-medieval court culture under Prince Henry. The diversity of styles mirrored the uncertainty of an elite which had moved irrevocably away from the world of Elizabeth without adequately defining an alternative culture. By the 1630s the court had moved beyond this transition, creating an urbane and cosmopolitan style of aristocratic life unlike anything the Tudor elite had known.

NOTES

1. For the dramatists, Alfred Harbage, *Cavalier Drama* (New York: Modern Language Society of America; Oxford: Oxford University Press, 1936), is still useful, despite its biases.

2. Which is not to say that it was culturally superior. The point is rather that Jacobean court taste was so heterogeneous, and that Jacobean court patronage was so decentralized, that it was difficult to recognize any distinctive court styles in this period. Jones's architecture is perhaps an exception, but it developed late in the reign and was not much imitated even then.

3. Since writing this paragraph I have come across Richard Helgerson, *Self-Crowned Laureates* (Berkeley and Los Angeles: University of California Press, 1984), which systematically pursues the significance of generational change in literary fashions. His findings are essentially similar to mine, though worked out in much greater detail. The reader is referred to his work for a fuller discussion.

4. There were a few exceptions to this statement. Beaumont (b. 1584) and Fletcher (b. 1579) were younger than this late-Elizabethan generation but older than most of the Caroline court poets. Arundel, Pembroke, and Buckingham were also born in the last quarter of the sixteenth century. In general, however, the creative poets, dramatists, and artists who set the cultural tone of the court were born either between 1560 and 1575 or much later, from 1595 to 1620. This meant that there was a much greater difference in age and outlook than one might have supposed between those who were active until the 1620s and those who emerged in the next few years.

5. Gervase Huxley, *Endymion Porter: The Life of a Courtier, 1587–1649* (London: Chatto and Windus, 1959).

6. V. Gabrielli, *Sir Kenelm Digby: Un inglese itialianato nel seicento* (Rome: Storia e letteratura, 1957).

7. The most extensive discussion is D. J. Howarth, *Lord Arundel and his Circle* (New Haven: Yale University Press, 1985). See also M. F. S. Hervey, *The Life, Correspondence, and Collections of Thomas Howard, Earl of Arundel* (Cambridge: Cambridge University Press, 1921).

8. The sons' letters to their father are preserved amid the State Papers, Domestic (e.g., SP 16/332/34). Cf. Panzani's dispatch of October 23, 1636 (PRO, 31/9/17B): "The Grand Chamberlain thanked me for the favor you showed his sons, and finished by saying he prayed his sons might take the Italian, rather than the French humor."

9. Rosetti dispatch of May 10, 1640, PRO, 31/9/18, p. 190.

10. BM, Add. MSS 27962G, p. 34, and H, p. 33; PRO, 31/3/72, p. 202; Panzani dispatch of July 15/25, 1635, PRO, 31/9/17B.

11. Quentin Bone, *Henrietta Maria: Queen of the Cavaliers* (Urbana: University of Illinois Press, 1972), p. 83.

12. There are several examples of her French letters to Newcastle and her English letters to Prince Charles and others in BL, Harl. MSS 6988.

13. PRO, 31/3/70, p. 169.

14. Rubens to Pierre Dupuy, August 8, 1629, in *The Letters of Peter Paul Rubens*, trans. and ed. Ruth Magurn (Cambridge, Mass.: Harvard University Press, 1955), p. 320.

15. Panzani dispatch of January 16, 1635/36, PRO, 31/9/17B.

16. Quoted in Hervey, *Arundel*, p. 399.

17. Ibid., p. 400.

18. Giovanni Bellori, *Le vite de'pittori, sculteri, ed architetti moderni* (Rome, 1672), p. 278.

19. *The Dramatic Works and Poems of James Shirley*, 2d ed., vol. 3, ed. William Gifford and Alexander Dyce (1833; New York: Russell and Russell, 1966), pp. 45, 46.

20. Richard Goulding, *Catalogue of the Pictures . . . at Welbeck Abbey* (Cambridge: Cambridge University Press, 1936), p. 498.

21. Lionel Cust, *Van Dyck* (London: George Bell and Sons, 1906), p. 89.

22. See Helgerson, *Self-Crowned Laureates*, pp. 189–204. Helgerson exaggerates the political importance attached to poetry by the royal entourage, but he is valuable on changing social attitudes and the effects these had on literary style.

23. Dorothea Townshend, *Life and Letters of Endymion Porter* (London, 1897), p. 133.

24. *Historical Manuscripts Commission DeLisle Dudley Mss.*, vol. 6 (London: Her Majesty's Stationery Office, 1967), p. 94.

25. *Cal.S.P.Dom.*, 1635, p. 384; Tobie Matthews, *A Collection of Letters . . . With a Character of the most Excellent Lady Lucy, Countess of Carleile* (London, 1660). See the comment of Wentworth's correspondent, George Garrard, in his letter of February 7, 1637/38 (W. Knowler, *The Earl of Strafforde's Letters and Despatches* (London, 1739), vol. 2, p. 149): "Sir Tobie Matthew hath written two Characters, one on the Lady Carlill, another of our Queen, of which he is so enamored, that he will have it translated into all languages and sent abroad. . . . It is held a ridiculous piece."

26. Knowler, *Strafforde's Letters*, p. 149.

27. For a detailed discussion, see Ann Jennalie Cook, *The Privileged Playgoers of Shakespeare's London* (Princeton: Princeton University Press, 1981), chap. 4.

28. SP, 16/409/167.

29. Gerald E. Bentley, *The Jacobean and Caroline Stage* (Oxford: Oxford University Press, 1966), vol. 6, pp. 267–275, and vol. 7, pp. 12–15. Cf. Prince Charles's letter to

Newcastle in BL, Harl. MSS 6988, fol. 99: "I thank you for the play. I like it so well that I desire to see it when I come to London."

30. For a discussion, see Harbage, *Cavalier Drama*, pp. 74, 75.

31. Ibid., p. 10.

32. *Eleventh Report of the Royal Commission on Historical Manuscripts* (London, 1887), Report, Appendix 4, part 1, p. 102.

33. Dispatch of February 19, 1635 (i.e., 1634/35?), BL, Add. MSS 27962G, p. 79; CSPVen. vol. 24, p. 594.

34. Thomas Carew, "Disdain Returned," in *Poems*, ed. Rhodes Dunlap (Oxford: Oxford University Press, 1949), p. 18. Helgerson, *Self-Crowned Laureates*, pp. 191–194, again provides a useful discussion.

35. SP, 16/120/48. Cf. the well-known comment by the puritan Lucy Hutchinson on the contrast between the Jacobean and Caroline courts (*Memoirs of the Life of Colonel Hutchinson*, ed. C. H. Firth [New York, 1885], p. 84): "The face of the court was much changed in the change of the King, for King Charles was temperate, chaste and serious, so that the fools, bawds, mimics and catamites of the former court grew out of fashion; and the nobility and courtiers, who did not quite abandon their debaucheries, yet so reverenced the King as to retire into corners to practice them."

36. On Spanish formality, see J. H. Elliot, "Philip IV: Prisoner of Ceremony," in *The Courts of Europe*, ed. A. G. Dickens (London: Thames and Hudson, 1977), pp. 169–190. An example of the reputation of the French court is the lines in Massinger's play, *The Guardian* (*Plays and Poems*, ed. Philip Edwards and Colin Gibson, vol. 4 [Oxford: Oxford University Press, 1976], p. 133):

—And are the Frenchmen, as you say, such gallants?
—Gallant and active, their free breeding knows not
The Spanish and Italian preciseness
Practiced among us; what we call immodest;
With them is styled bold courtship.

37. DuMoulin dispatch of May 2, 1627, PRO, 31/3/65, p. 49.

38. Ibid., p. 49.

39. Dispatch of April 26, 1636, PRO, 31/9/17B, p. 1.

40. Dispatch of June 10, 1635, ibid.

41. For a fuller discussion, see R. M. Smuts, "The Puritan Followers of Henrietta Maria in the 1630s," *English Historical Review* 93 (1978): 26–45. Kevin Sharpe argues, probably correctly, that in the 1630s the court favorites of both monarchs never controlled the government ("Faction at the Early Stuart Court," *History Today* 33 [1983]: 39–46). This did not prevent both foreign diplomats and English ministers from worrying about the possible effects of court influence, however.

42. Carew, "To the Queen," in *Poems*, pp. 90, 91.

43. Walter Montagu, *The Shepherds' Paradise* (London, 1629 [sic., for 1656]), p. 77.

44. Earl Miner, *The Cavalier Mode* (Princeton: Princeton University Press, 1971), chap. 5, is a much more sensible and balanced account than most.

45. This is not to say that erotic themes were not sometimes used to symbolize serious political and social ideas. Love, sexuality, and marriage were frequently employed as metaphors for political relationships in Stuart masques and poems (see, e.g., Stephen Orgel and Roy Strong, *Inigo Jones: The Theater of the Stuart Court*, 2 vols. [London: Sotheby Parke Bernet; Berkeley and Los Angeles, University of California Press, 1973], vol. 1, chap. 4; and D. J. Gordon, "*Hymenai*: Ben Jonson's Masque of Union," in *The Renaissance Imagination*, ed. Stephen Orgel [Berkeley and Los Angeles: University of California Press, 1980]). Kevin Sharpe is working on a book that will explore the political significances of Caroline love poetry in depth. However, one needs to distinguish

these deeper layers of meaning from the immediate erotic significance of much Caroline literature, which was important in its own right. This is another topic that needs to be rescued from the heavy-handed moral judgments of nineteenth- and early-twentieth-century scholars.

46. Lawrence Stone, *The Family, Marriage, and Sex in England* (New York: Harper and Row, 1978), pp. 520–527.

47. Even here, however, the images tend to be evocative rather than explicit (though it does not take much imagination to realize what is going on), and the scene is set in a mythical Golden Age, before sin came into the world. The sexuality of the poem is therefore still under some sort of control.

48. Carew, "A Prayer to the Wind," *Poems*, p. 11.

49. "To My Mistress in Absence," ibid., p. 22.

50. Ibid.

51. "Corinna's Going A-Maying," ibid., p. 69.

52. Quoted in D. H. Willson, *James VI and I* (London: Cape, 1956), p. 195.

53. *CSPVen.* vol. 19, p. 21.

54. Ibid., p. 60.

55. Richard Perrinchief, *Royal Martyr* (London, 1676), p. 237.

56. Elliot, "Philip IV of Spain: Prisoner of Ceremony," pp. 169–189.

57. Mark Girouard, *The English Country House* (New Haven and London: Yale University Press, 1978), pp. 51–56, is an interesting discussion of the impact of changing social habits on architecture from the late Middle Ages on.

58. George Radcliffe, *Letters*, ed. T. Whitaker (London, 1910), p. 433.

59. BL, Harl. MSS 6272, fol. 172.

60. *Table Talk* (London: Quaritch, 1927), pp. 175, 176. Both these complaints refer to behavior within relatively intimate social gatherings around the monarch. Charles was probably at least as formal as Elizabeth in public, and he was considerably more reserved in his speech and personal mannerisms. But there does seem to have been a relaxation in the ceremonial rules governing the deportment of the monarch's immediate attendants. When courtiers like Raleigh flirted with Elizabeth they did so from a kneeling position, which preserved the queen's aura of superiority even when she was at her most relaxed and familiar. Charles's attendants were not subjected to such rigorous requirements. In that sense "gravity and state" were declining.

61. BL, Harl. MSS 6988, fol. 112.

62. He canceled his coronation procession and made only one formal entry into London before 1641, when the Dowager Queen of France arrived in England and convention demanded that she be suitably escorted to her lodgings. There was one great progress in the reign—to Scotland, in 1633—but it was virtually the only example of a great outdoor display of the court's magnificence. It is sometimes wrongly supposed that the coronation entry was canceled because of the plague of 1625. It was postponed because of plague, as James's had been in 1603, but was canceled after the epidemic had passed, in May 1626 (see Greater London Record Office, Remembrancia, 6/86). The royal entry scheduled for Charles's return from Edinburgh in 1633 was also canceled (*CSPVen.*, vol. 23, p. 183).

63. For discussions, see Keith Thomas, *Religion and the Decline of Magic* (London: Weidenfeld and Nicolson, 1971), esp. chap. 3, and David Underdown, *Revel, Riot and Rebellions: Popular Politics and Culture in England, 1603–1660* (Oxford: Oxford University Press, 1985), chap. 3.

64. A. Liegh Deneef, *This Poetic Liturgy: Robert Herrick's Ceremonial Mode* (Durham, N.C.: Duke University Press, 1974).

65. Carew, "Upon a Ribbon," *Poems*, p. 29.

66. Edmund Waller, *Poems* (London, 1645, fac. repr., Manston, 1971), p. 49.

67. Carew, "To the King at His Entrance into Saxham," *Poems*, p. 30.

68. On this point, see Miner, *Cavalier Mode*, pp. 232–235.

69. Leo van Puyvelde, *Flemish Painting: The Age of Rubens and Van Dyck*, trans. Alan Kendall (New York: McGraw-Hill, 1970), p. 99.

70. Quoted by Ellis Waterhouse, *Painting in Britain, 1530–1790* (Harmondsworth: Pelican, 1964), p. 49.

71. Waller, "To Van Dyck," *Poems*, p. 19; Goulding, *Catalogue*, p. 498.

72. BL, Add. MSS 41846. A photocopy of this document exists in the Yale University Medical School Library, New Haven.

Part Three

Court Culture, Religion, and Politics in the 1630s

8 RELIGION

It should now be evident that the relationship between the culture of the early Stuart court and the values underlying the Crown's more controversial policies was almost never simple and straightforward. Charles did not try to render art and literature subservient to the needs of the state in the manner of modern totalitarian regimes and some continental monarchs of the seventeenth century. Indeed, the Crown never enforced ideological purity, even among those who formulated and executed royal policies. The court was not organized as a political party; it issued no manifestos, fought no elections, and did not purge itself of dissenting members. And so the idea that its culture possessed an ideological significance may appear, at first glance, highly questionable.

We have seen, however, that throughout the Stuart period cultural forms expressed political values, creating a stock of ideas, images, and symbols that lay ready to hand for the publicists of the Civil War period. It would be difficult to imagine lines apparently more innocent of controversial intent than those Herrick prefaced to his book of verse, *Hesperides:*

> I sing of *Brooks*, of *Blossoms*, *Birds* and *Bowers:*
> Of *April*, *May*, or *June* and *July-Flowers.*
> I sing of *May-poles*, *Hock-carts*, *Wassails*, *Wakes*,
> Of *Bride-grooms*, *Brides* and of their *Bridal-cakes.*

> I write of *Youth,* of *Love* and have Access
> By these, to sing of cleanly-*Wantonness.*[1]

Published in the year of the king's execution, however, next to a title page sporting a gigantic crown, these lines conveyed a provocative challenge to the new commonwealth. No less than the emblematic symbols of the frontispiece to *Eikon Basilike,* wassails, wakes, and songs of "cleanly-wantonness" had become charged with partisan emotion.

Before the Civil War, cultural symbols had not yet acquired the freight of political meaning they took on in the 1640s and 1650s. In the 1630s, however, one can already discern significant cultural differences which helped prepare the ground for what happened after 1642. The remaining chapters explore how court culture helped shape and articulate religious and political values in ways that affected government policies in the 1630s and contributed to the emergence of a partisan royalism after the personal rule collapsed.[2]

ECCLESIASTICAL CONTROVERSIES AND RELIGIOUS CULTURE

No other set of issues caused as much trouble for the government of Charles I as did controversies over religion. Unprecedented taxes and violations of the common law provoked angry complaints and, in 1628 and 1641, efforts by Parliament to restrain abuses of the prerogative. But it is doubtful that these protests alone could have precipitated a civil war. If the king's acts were often of dubious legality, any attempt to seize control of the state from him was clearly illegal. For fifteen years Charles eluded all attempts to make him live within the limits of the constitution as others understood it, and when the reckoning finally came in the 1640s, the parliamentary leadership faced the awkward dilemma of defending the rule of law by illegal deeds.[3] From the outset Parliament had to contend with the widespread reluctance of conservative gentry, both at Westminster and in the provinces, to accept the consequences of this embarrassing fact.[4]

What gave the parliamentary movement the momentum to move beyond this impasse was the belief that the court was endangering not only English liberty but also Reformed religion.[5] From the attacks on Arminian clergy that helped disrupt the king's relations with his early

Parliaments, to the riotous events surrounding the fall of episcopacy in 1641, ecclesiastical problems aroused a level of passion matched by nothing else. Once war broke out, puritanism lent an ideological stiffening to the parliamentary cause without which armed resistance might never have begun.

The ceremonialism and clericalism of Archbishop Laud and the 'popery' of Henrietta Maria were the most important causes of religious opposition to the court. Yet other irritants also contributed, including the court's habit of watching masques and plays on the sabbath, its friendly relations with Spain, and the presence of royal ministers suspected of Catholic sympathies. Bound up with all these issues, at least after 1626, was resentment of the clergy's support for prerogative government. To some observers the Crown's ecclasiastical policies appeared symptomatic of a deeper and more ominous problem. The court seemed to have repudiated the religious values associated with the Reformation and with England's long struggle against tyrannical foreign powers, in favor of popish ceremonies, libertinism, and arbitrary government.[6]

This image grossly oversimplified the internal politics of Charles's court, which harbored a welter of mutually antipathetic religious factions. Laud argued for the suppression of Catholicism even while he silenced puritans and preached against worldliness, but never succeeded in imposing uniformity, even on the Privy Council. The Earl of Holland kept a puritan chaplain, whereas Cottington, Weston, and Windebanke tottered on the brink of conversion to Rome.[7] In any case, the court's Catholics were usually too divided among themselves—with Jesuit missionaries openly criticizing both the queen and the pope's envoys—to contemplate an alliance with "Arminians." Only after 1637 did a unified Catholic party begin to crystallize around Henrietta Maria and the papal envoy, George Con.[8] Until then, court factions tended to cut across doctrinal lines, making it impossible to interpret Whitehall's politics in terms of alliances based on religious ideology. Even in the 1640s Pym and his allies greatly exaggerated the dangers posed by plotting court papists.[9]

Like many conspiracy theories, however, this one remained convincing because a number of developments lent it some plausibility. Charles did appoint Catholics and crypto-Catholics to positions of power, and even some court Protestants were fascinated by the spiritual values and liturgical practices of the Counter-Reformation. Laud was

not a Roman agent, but he promoted doctrines and ceremonies reminiscent of the Roman church while undermining beliefs which many
Englishmen regarded as essential bulwarks of the Reformation. In any
number of ways the policies and the climate of the court were profoundly uncongenial to men who saw the English church as part of an
international Reformed tradition. The collapse of royal government in
1642 and the emergence of a parliamentary opposition is fully intelli-
gible only against this background.

THE LAUDIAN COUNTER-REFORMATION

The ascendancy of Laud and his followers represented the triumph of
an aggressive, counter-reforming faction that had never previously
dominated the English church.[10] Until the 1620s most bishops shared
with conforming puritans a broadly Calvinist outlook, especially on
topics relating to the process of salvation.[11] Disagreements existed over
ceremonial matters and problems of church government, but even
on these issues many bishops sympathized with puritan scruples and
winked at clergy who quietly dispensed with objectionable rituals.
Archbishop Abbot, who directed the church from 1611 until the
1620s, tried to foster unity among all but the most intransigent Protestants. Under him men who were later stigmatized as puritans held
benefices throughout England and posts in the Chapel Royal.[12] Calvinists also dominated the universities and held many bishoprics, and
so generally felt comfortable within the established church.

Even under Abbot's primateship, tensions and disagreements remained. Some of these stemmed from the frequently bitter confrontations
over ceremonies, clerical vestments, and ecclesiastical government of
the late Elizabethan and early Jacobean periods. In addition, a few Jacobean bishops, notably Neile of Durham and Andrewes of Winchester,
disagreed with the Calvinist consensus and lobbied behind the scenes
for a change in the church's orientation. In the 1620s these dissidents
were sometimes labeled Arminians by their opponents, after the Dutch
theologian Arminius, whose attacks on Perkins and Beza had split the
Dutch church.[13] They retaliated by labeling their opponents puritans,
in an effort to associate them with presbyterian radicals. The outbreak
of the Thirty Years' War and the pursuit of the Spanish match sharpened this antagonism, as most Calvinists rallied to an anti-Spanish policy while their rivals generally supported the king. James accordingly

became increasingly wary of Calvinist clergy and more sympathetic to Neile and Andrewes.[14]

The accession of Charles, who distrusted "puritans" and liked liturgical ceremony, accelerated this change.[15] In 1627 Laud was appointed to the see of London, according to one intimate because the king saw in him a man who would reduce to obedience "the grandees of the puritan faction," who made the city their "retreat and receptacle."[16] By that date he had also supplanted Abbot as the king's chief ecclesiastical adviser. During the next few years the Arminians took over both universities, most bishoprics, and the machinery for licensing books for the press. Calvinists were thrown on the defensive, especially after Laud became primate in 1633. "His grace of Canterbury is a gallant man," Cottington remarked shortly thereafter:

> Amongst other reformations he has forbidden all preaching in private houses. . . . There is also a declaration in print by his Majesty's commandment, in favor of wakes and Maypoles, which is as hardly digested by the puritans, as the putting down of lectures, a thing which the Archbishop endeavors much.[17]

As Laud continued to enforce these measures, while introducing altar rails and crucifixes into parish churches, loyal English Protestants found their convictions being stigmatized as puritan.

The controversy between Arminians and Calvinists centered around the latter's doctrine of double predestination.[18] Behind this dispute, however, lay the broader problem of interpreting the central Protestant concept of justification by faith. For an orthodox Calvinist all men are predestined to salvation or damnation because none can achieve true faith by his own efforts. Sin has so corrupted our nature, hardening our hearts against God, that we can truly understand the Gospels only if God miraculously gives us the power to do so. Once bestowed, the gift of faith is irresistible. God therefore elects those he will save and damns everyone else, regardless of individual merit.

Against this position the Arminians argued that grace works in cooperation with each individual's freely willed efforts to achieve salvation. Faith does not normally come as a sudden and radical transformation of the soul, but grows slowly in a believer struggling to cultivate his religious instincts and overcome his propensity to sin. "Make thine understanding and thy will and thy memory (though but natural faculties) serviceable to God," Donne urged in a court sermon, "for though they be not naturally instruments of grace, yet naturally they are susceptible to grace."[19] To an orthodox Calvinist such arguments seemed all too reminiscent of the Catholic doctrine of salvation through faith and good works.[20]

Laud always claimed neutrality on this particular issue. "I am yet where I was," he wrote to a man who sent him a treatise against predestination in 1630, "that somewhat about these controversies is unmasterable in this life."[21] He forbade the clergy to discuss the issue, deemphasized doctrinal controversies within the universities, and said he only wanted to bury a dispute that caused dissension among Christians. Under the circumstances this stance was disingenuous. The doctrine of predestination was too deeply embedded within the belief-system of many English Protestants for Laud to pull it away without causing upheaval. Taught at the universities, emphasized in catechisms and sermons, it had long shaped discussions of salvation and Christian discipline. However obscure the theological controversy sometimes became, it stemmed from fundamental differences in religious outlook.

RELIGIOUS RATIONALISM AND PAGAN INFLUENCES

There was, moreover, a very real danger from a Calvinist point of view that any deviation from Reformed theology by the clergy would open the floodgates to misunderstandings and heresies among the laity. This problem existed at every level of society, from the village to the court, partly because in many districts remnants of the cult of saints and the encrustation of medieval folk beliefs that had grown around the gospels remained more influential than Reformation theology.[22] England was never uniformly Protestant in any rigorous sense; the godly had not only to defend their faith but to convert many of their fellow countrymen to it. The missionary zeal of puritan clergy—their sense of being at odds with the world and their intolerance for dissent—can be understood only against this background.

In these circumstances Calvinist doctrine offered the immense advantages of clarity, consistency, and uncompromising rigor. It left no doubt that a Christian life must derive from deep, inner faith, rooted in the Gospels and the preaching of God's ministers. Precisely because of its greater flexibility and its openness to beliefs and rituals that could not be grounded in biblical texts, Arminian theology represented a less rigorous position.

In some ways the problem was especially acute at court. Here little danger existed that people might reject Protestant ideas from ignorance or unthinking adherence to medieval traditions. But more than any other segment of English society, the court lay open to the influence of both classical pagan literature and the Baroque spirituality of the Counter-Reformation. To maintain the kind of intense, biblical piety cherished by puritans in this environment required extraordinary tenacity. The logic of Laud's attack on puritanism could be pushed further than he himself desired, undercutting Protestant orthodoxy.

For example, where Laud encouraged the clergy to emphasize morality more than doctrinal disputes in their sermons, some laymen disparaged all theological argument and conceived of religious life primarily in ethical terms. "He was no bigot or puritan," a contemporary wrote about the Earl of Arundel, "and professed more to affect moral virtues than questions and controversies." [23] Especially among people of secular temperament this attitude could too easily reduce Christianity to a religion of externals, devoid of the inward spiritual struggles which puritan diaries convey so vividly. Clergy of all denominations warned against this danger. "Be not deceived my brethren," Joseph Hall admonished the court in 1628.

> It is a sad and austere thing to be a Christian. This is not frolic, jovial, plausible; there is a certain thing called true mortification. . . . Never make account to be a Christian without the hard task of penitence. It will cost you tears, sighs, watchings, self-restraints, self struggling, self denials. [24]

On this point puritans and Laudians agreed wholeheartedly. But the more often the court clergy disparaged puritan zeal, the harder it must have been to insist on the need for such painful effort. [25]

The prestige of classical literature within the court exacerbated the problem. [26] Ancient philosophy seemed to provide a sane and rational approach to religion, adapted to practical moral needs and devoid of the tangled metaphysical problems that plagued Christian history. Moreover, the Greek fathers, whose authority Laud revered, had attempted to harmonize Christianity with Hellenistic philosophy. It is not surprising that many courtiers followed their lead. Thus Henrietta Maria's recusant poet, William Habington, described the character of a "Holy Man" in terms more Stoic than Christian: "In prosperity he gratefully admires the bounty of the almighty giver and useth, not abuseth plenty; but in adversity he remains unshaken, and like some eminent mountain hath his head above the clouds."[27] The confessions of a few courtiers come remarkably close to purely philosophical creeds. "The just and principal consideration," Sir Kenelm Digby wrote about his faith, "I conceive to be that all honor and glory be given to that general and omnipotent Cause of causes, whom all nations adore; wherein we are not likely to err if we look into our hearts."[28] When Digby lost his wife he sought consolation not in prayer and meditation upon scripture, but in the poetry of Horace.[29] Only after a long sojourn in Paris and reconversion to Catholicism did he develop an intensely Christian spiritual life. In the same vein, Suckling once remarked casually, "I know it to be the opinion of many good wits that Christianity has added little to the store of the world's religion."[30]

One finds a similar tendency to mingle Christian and pagan elements in some court hymns. In a piece written for the Chapel Royal, Herrick turned the Christ child into a pantheist God of spring:

> Why does the chilling Winter's morn
> Smile like a field beset with corn?
> Or smell like a Mead new-shorn,
> Thus on a sudden? Come and see
> The cause why things thus fragrant be:
> 'Tis He is born, whose quickening Birth
> Gives life and luster, public mirth
> To Heaven, and the under-Earth.
> We see him come, and know him ours,
> Who with his sunshine and his showers
> Turns all the patient ground to flowers.[31]

William Cartwright's hymn, "On the Nativity," describes the Incarnation as a marriage between heaven and earth, thereby reducing the central mystery of Christianity to one of the most universal pagan myths.[32] The cavalier love of maypoles sprang from the same impulse. Charles and Laud knew as well as any puritan that May dances were vestiges of Celtic paganism. But whereas puritans regarded these festivities as blasphemous, the court saw them as manifestations of a natural religious instinct compatible with Christianity.

Laud himself responded vociferously whenever he sensed a tendency to reduce religion to bland philosophy or pagan myth. Wentworth once made the mistake of sending him a rambling discourse on the vanity of the world, embellished with allusions to art and poetry. The archbishop replied testily: "If you will read the short book of Ecclesiastes you will see a better disposition of these things than in any anagrams of Dr. Donne's or any designs of Van Dyck."[33] Yet Laud had inadvertently placed himself and his church in a vulnerable position. Calvin developed his strenuous arguments about man's depravity precisely to prevent the easy transition from lukewarm Christianity to modern Stoicism dressed up with Christian ornaments. He recognized that once salvation was seen as an educative process, in which men learned to perfect their natural faculty for rational and moral conduct, the way lay open to a thorough adulteration of scriptural traditions with pagan ideas.[34] Only by stressing the supernatural character of redemption could one preserve the primacy of biblical ideas.

The Catholic church had also rejected predestination, but its rigorous sacramental system and well-developed traditions of meditation reduced the risk of unduly compromising central Christian mysteries. Equally important, Rome might combat deviations from orthodoxy through the Inquisition and the Index of Forbidden Books. Despite his ceremonialism, his attempts to encourage oral confession, and his use of the High Commission, Laud did not really possess comparable weapons. The fact that he and most of his colleagues came from humble backgrounds (one contemporary described them as "lordly prelates raised from the dunghill") made it all the more difficult for them to restrain courtiers from freely reinterpreting religious doctrine.

Charles himself always remained both orthodox and pious, but already in the 1630s we can discern signs within the court of an erosion of faith in scriptural teachings that did not seem congruent with the dictates of reason, and of a marked waning of religious enthusiasm. "The King hath been troubled with a bile these five or six days," Viscount Conway wrote in October 1637. "If he should be kept from Church still, I think nobody would go."[35] These trends point unmistakably toward the Deism and religious apathy of many late seventeenth-century aristocrats.

CEREMONIALISM

In the short run such tendencies were less threatening to reformist orthodoxy than the pervasive influence at court of Roman Catholic tastes and attitudes. With respect to this issue, even more clearly than when facing the worldliness of some courtiers, Laud appeared to have sold the pass to God's enemies. By seeking to promote "the Beauty of Holiness" through a revival of liturgical practices inherited from the medieval church, he convinced many opponents that he wanted to smuggle popery back into England by underhanded means.

Court clergy argued quite openly for an eventual reconciliation with Catholicism and emphasized the point by introducing Catholic devotional practices into the Chapel Royal. Panzani reported that Laud "ordered the psalms to be sung in notes according to the Gregorian method used in the Church of Rome, and that the King himself made the first essay," that a chaplain preached in favor of oral confession before the entire court, and that a book published by royal license praised the Virgin Mary.[36] In 1636 he heard sermons denouncing both Calvin and Henry VIII. Lord Herbert of Cherbury, then at work on a history of Henry's reign, sought out the papal envoy to assure him it would contain nothing disparaging to the Roman faith. The court had shifted most of its animosity away from papists and toward puritans.[37]

There was a long Church of England tradition behind this irenic and moderate policy. Since the reign of Henry VIII the English church had claimed to represent a *via media* between the competing faiths of Rome, Wittenberg, and (after Calvin's appearance) Geneva. For two reasons, however, the Laudians posed a greater danger than earlier English ceremonialists had. The liturgical reforms of the 1630s were more determined and provocative than any the realm had seen since the accession of Elizabeth, but in addition the international situation had changed in ways that magnified fears of papist subversion.[38] During the ideological wars of the sixteenth century, irenicism was often a natural ally of the Reformation, since it could justify an alliance between Protestants and Catholic *politiques*. But as England withdrew from the continent's wars and established friendly ties with Spain and various Italian states, irenic ideas seemed to facilitate the intrigues and proselytizing of court Catholics. Across the Channel, bitter disputes between Arminians and Calvinists split the Dutch church, while in France one after another of the leading Protestant nobles followed the example of Henry IV and converted to Rome. It was all too easy to blame these setbacks on Catholic subversion and to fear that England's turn would come next.[39] The suspicion that Laud had secretly accepted the bribe of a cardinal's cap, or that Charles had become the tool of a "Jesuitical" faction, were misguided but not entirely irrational. They stemmed not only from the puritan habit of seeing a conspiring Jesuit behind every

bush, but also from the accurate perception that the government's attitude toward Catholicism had softened at a time when the Reformation
was on the defensive throughout Europe.

The court's tolerance of Catholic theology and fascination with Roman liturgical practices derived partly from its cosmopolitan outlook.
Many courtiers probably encountered more papists than puritans in
their day-to-day lives, under conditions that promoted tolerance and
mutual sympathy. Anyone who wanted the queen's favor or who valued
the friendship of an ambassador from a Catholic kingdom had to treat
"papists" with cordiality and respect. The stereotypes created by generations of conflict could not easily survive in an environment where
people of different religions routinely socialized and intrigued together.
It is scarcely surprising that some courtiers converted to Catholicism
while many others came to believe that only the intransigence of a
few bigots on both sides prevented reconciliation between Rome and
Canterbury.

But the attraction that Catholic forms of worship held for the king
and many of his courtiers also stemmed from more deeply rooted causes.
The pronounced aesthetic sensitivity of the court, its facination with
ritualistic modes of thought and behavior, fostered receptivity to the
splendor of the Roman church and distaste for puritan austerity. Both
the king and Laud believed that visible expressions of piety created an
essential atmosphere of reverence. "If a man by eschewing superstition
grow to be profane, what hath he gotten?" Charles wrote in the margin
of a book.[40] Laud, more causticly, complained that men came into
church with no more respect than "a tinker and his bitch come into an
ale-house."[41] "It is true, the inward worship of the heart is the great
service of God," he wrote,

> and no service is acceptable without it; but the external worship of God in
> his Church is the great witness to the world, that our heart stands right in
> that service of God. Take this away, or bring it into contempt, and what
> light is there left "To shine before men?"[42]

From one point of view "The Beauty of Holiness" was an ecclesiastical
counterpart to the concern for ceremony and aesthetic beauty evident
throughout Caroline court culture.

The archbishop appears to have pursued ritualistic forms of devotion with remarkable energy. If we can believe Prynne—admittedly

a hostile witness—Laud converted the eucharistic rite into a tiny melodrama.

> He . . . came near the bread, which was cut out and laid in a fine napkin, and then he gently lifted up one of the corners of the said napkin, and peeped into it till he saw the bread (like a boy that peeped after a bird-nest in a bush), and presently clapped it down again, and flew back a step or two, and bowed very low three times towards it . . . then laid his hand upon the gilt Cup . . . so soon as he pulled the cup a little nearer to him he let it go, flew back and bowed again three times. . . .[43]

Such behavior scandalized Calvinists.

For all Laud's efforts, however, the Church of England's art and ceremony were no more than pale reflections of the splendors of Rubens's Antwerp or Bernini's Rome, a point that Henrietta Maria and her associates took pains to demonstrate. At every opportunity they dangled exquisite examples of religious art before the king and other court aesthetes, teasing them about Protestant scruples against idolatry. The queen once contrived to gamble away a golden crucifix in a card game with her husband, leaving him in the embarrassing position of deciding whether to keep it. She complained that Barberini's first shipment of paintings contained no religious works. When he sent her a picture of Saint Stephen she jokingly told Panzani she feared the king would steal it, then hung it within the curtains of her bed as an ostentatious gesture of piety.[44] Her chapels contained dozens of religious images, the majority representing the Virgin.[45]

The most spectacular example of the queen's efforts to proselytize through art occurred during the first Mass performed in her chapel at Somerset House in 1636. Determined to impress the Protestant court with the beauty of Catholic worship, she instructed her monks to spare no expense. They pressed into service the sculptor Dieussart, who had just arrived from Rome. He designed a gigantic "machine," suspended above the main altar on pillars, to display the host. "It represented in oval," one of the Capuchins recalled later, "a Paradise of glory, forty feet in height," with a prophet on either side. The scene was raised above seven ranges of clouds "in which were figures of archangels, of cherubim, of seraphim, to the number of two hundred, some adoring the Holy Sacrament, others singing and playing on all sorts of musical instruments, the whole painted according to the rules of perspective."[46] Behind the device Dieussart hid a choir, whose music seemed to emanate from the painted angels. He illuminated the apparatus with four hundred lights and covered it with curtains, so that it could be unveiled dramatically the moment the congregation had filled the chapel. The queen wept with happiness when she first saw Dieussart's work, and Charles spent an hour and a half studying it after the Mass ended.

Behind this enthusiasm for religious art and ritual lay a spirituality with much closer affinities to Baroque Catholicism than to puritanism. Most puritans tried to avoid relying on images, even in their religious meditations. Their accounts of conversion experiences, in sermons and diaries, rarely contain much visual detail. The words of the Bible and sermons, rather than visual imagery, dominated their concept of faith. The Catholic church, by contrast, encouraged believers to develop their powers of visual imagination as an aid to piety.[47] As Walter Montagu put it, in a book defending religious art written after his conversion to Rome, a painting might serve as a way

> of suggesting unto, moving or affecting the mind even in pious and religious affections. For instance, in remembering more feelingly, and so being impassioned more effectually with the Death, Bloodshed and bitter Passion of our savior, when we see that story fully and lively represented unto us in colors . . . by a skillful hand.[48]

The Jesuits, especially, instructed their followers to meditate by visualizing events of Christ's life in minute detail.

In Charles's reign this strain of Counter-Reformation piety began to color the style of worship prevalent within Whitehall. One finds it in court sermons. "See him, Oh all ye beholders," Joseph Hall preached before the king in 1628:

> See him hanging upon the tree of shame, to rescue you from the curse . . . see him stretching out his arms to receive and embrace you; hanging down his head to take view of your misery, opening his precious side to receive you into his bosom . . . pouring out thence water to wash you and blood to redeem you.[49]

As in Catholic societies, these mental images sometimes became focal points for personal, psychic rituals. Thus Donne once suggested that Christians spend Good Friday thinking about death and putrefaction, to prepare for a joyous Easter devoted to thoughts of heavenly bliss.[50]

The Caroline predilection for evocative imagery was nowhere more pronounced than in pious meditations upon death:

. . . Let every passing Bell
Possess my thoughts next comes my doleful knell:
And when night persuades me to my bed,
I'll think I'm going to be buried:
So shall the Blankets that come over me,
Present those Turfs, which must cover me,
And with as firm behavior I will meet
The sheet I sleep in as my Winding sheet.
When sleep shall bathe his body in mine eyes,
I will believe that then my body dies:
And if I chance to wake, and rise thereon,
I'll have in mind my Resurrection.[51]

This bedtime ritual of Robert Herrick typifies a genre of morbid spiritual exercises, devoted to contemplation of the sights and sounds of death. When Sir Kenelm Digby awoke one morning to find his wife had died in the middle of the night, he immediately set about collecting mementos.[52] He clipped her hair, made casts of her feet and hands, and called in Van Dyck to paint the corpse. "When I go into my chamber," he later wrote of this portrait, "I set it by my side, and by the faint light of a candle methinks I see her dead indeed, for that maketh painted colors to look more pale and ghastly than they do by day light."[53] Donne rose from his deathbed to mount a court pulpit for a last sermon on death, his body wrapped in a funeral shroud, his emaciated face staring at his audience as in emblem of mortality. Puritan clergy also admonished their parishioners to think about death, but the sensuality of these meditations was as alien to Puritan piety as altar rails and crucifixes.

THE RELIGION OF MONARCHY

In the 1620s and 1630s the court's Arminian theology and sensual approach to religious mysteries began to color the political theology of loyalist clergy, who treated the king, in a very literal way, as the living image of God on earth. The splendor of his court, the reverence accorded him, and the majesty of his authority all became part of a distinctive spirituality. To appreciate how this happened, we must first examine arguments concerning the divine nature of royal power.

THE THEOLOGY OF DIVINE RIGHT

The Stuarts always claimed that God had provided them with a pre-rogative in the state as absolute and uncontrolled as God's own authority over the universe. James told the Parliament of 1609:

> Kings are justly called Gods for that they exercise a manner of resemblance of Divine power upon earth: if you will consider the attributes of God, you shall see how they agree in the person of a King. God hath power to create or destroy, to make or unmake at his pleasure, and to God are both soul and body due. And the like power have Kings: they make and unmake their subjects, and in all cases, yet are accomptable to none but God only. They have power to exalt low things and abase high things and make of their subjects like men at Chess; A pawn to take a Bishop or a Knight, and to cry up, or down any of their subjects as they do their money.[54]

The Laudian clergy denounced as blasphemous attempts to argue that monarchy derived from purely historical causes.[55] Thus when a lecturer at Cambridge, in the course of his defense of royal government, asserted that kings were originally appointed by their people, he was deprived of his post by royal authority.[56] Even an apology for monarchy was subversive if it did not acknowledge the divine source of royal power.

These claims were far less exceptional in the seventeenth century than they appear today. Theories of divine-right monarchy, articulated by Catholic and Protestant theologians alike, dominated the political thought of Europe. The *Book of Martyrs,* for example, assumed that God appointed kings and that the church could find worldly prosperity only when God chose a devout ruler—so did some of the most vociferous critics of Charles's policies, who echoed divine-right rhetoric in their speeches and writings.[57]

Differences arose when people tried to integrate these ideas within a broader framework of belief. Many Englishmen understood the divine right of kings in terms of eschatological concepts best exemplified in Foxe's *Book of Martyrs.*[58] Men are ruled by kings because God has so willed: monarchs are instruments in the hand of the Lord. Tyrants punish the wicked and chastise sinning peoples, whereas godly rulers reward the righteous and protect the church. All Christians must therefore submit to royal authority. Theologians differed about how far this doctrine of nonresistance extended. A few, such as Knox, developed justifications for rebellion against ungodly princes, but some puritan radicals vehemently denounced such resistance.

> Rebellion against lawful authority: this the Lord punished, yea he extraor-
> dinarily plagued Rebels, making the earth to open and swallow some, and
> fire to devour others; Rebels can look for no good end, see it in Absalom,
> though he had most of Israel to take his part. Let the end of him, *Bichri*,
> and *Zimri* make men take heed of rebellion.[59]

So wrote Richard Bernard, a man who flirted with Separatism, denounced Laudian innovations, and toyed with the sort of millenarian
schemes later espoused by the radicals of the New Model Army. In the
same vein, preachers often warned that God's vengeance would follow
disobedience to God's chosen royal agents.

> I profess . . that my conscience apprehends nothing so likely to provoke
> *Gods* heavier Judgements upon this land, than our willfulness and disobe-
> dience; our obtuseness and contumacy, first against God in heaven; sec-
> ondly against his Deputy on earth.[60]

Although uttered by one of Charles's chaplains, with reference to the
parliamentary intransigence of the 1620s, these words were fully congruent with the Providential concept of history of Foxe and other
puritans.

The eschatological nature of these arguments implicitly qualified
the concept of royal divine right. As instruments of Providence, kings
needed to foster God's purposes or risk punishment, in this world as
well as in the next. As the Old Testament showed, the Almighty could
impose a terrible vengeance on those who failed him.[61] In practice,
Foxeian ideas proved at least as useful to men who opposed Stuart policies as to supporters of the court; we have noticed how easily they were
turned against James at the time of the Spanish match. So long as royal
authority rested upon an eschatological vision of England's destiny, it
was all too easy to object to the conduct of particular kings who appeared to betray their sacred trust.

Consequently, it is not surprising that Caroline theologians generally approached the divine right of kings from an entirely different direction. They not only drew arguments out of scriptural history, but
also argued that an absolute royal prerogative was rooted in the structure of the cosmos. As Laud's chaplain, Peter Heylin put it, "the law of
Monarchy is founded upon the law of nature, not on positive laws."[62]
Just as God rules omnipotently over a hierarchically structured universe, so the king must stand as an absolute monarch atop a hierarchical society.[63]

   This argument was far from original, resting as it did on concepts of natural law that had been commonplace since antiquity.[64] However, the Stuart clergy provided a theological framework within which arguments based on natural hierarchy fit more gracefully than in a Calvinist system. Calvin's willful, violent, and seemingly capricious God had never been easy to reconcile with Hellenic concepts of a benignly ordered universe, eternally preserving its rational structure. Before God's majesty the most exalted beings became so many pawns of divine omnipotence; even the angels of a puritan universe were mere agents of God, raised to glory because they did his work.[65] Moreover, nature has fallen from its pristine state, so that men may never rely entirely upon its laws. As Elizabeth's favorite, Fulke Greville, put it:

> Let each then know by equal estimation,
> That in this frail freehold of flesh and blood,
> Nature itself declines unto privation
> As mixed of real ill and seeming good;
> And when Man's best estate is such a strife
> Can order there be permanent in life?[66]

   If nature consists of a blend of "real ill and seeming good," in which no stable order can exist, then an argument based on natural principles is weakened. Whatever the ultimate source of its authority, the state must in practice partake of the instability and perversity of a fallen world.

> There was a time before the times of story,
> When nature reigned, instead of laws and arts,
> And mortal Gods with men made up the glory
> Of one republic, by united hearts
>   Earth was their common seat, their conversation
>   In saving love, and ours in adoration
> But by decree of fate this Corporation
> Is altered since, and earth's fair globe miscarried,
> Man's craft above the Gods in estimation
> And by it, wisdom's constant standard varied:
>   Whereby the sway of many years is gone
>   Since any godhead ruled an earthly throne.

Because the Laudians depicted God as a much more tranquil deity, who obeyed the laws implanted within the creation, their theology proved better suited to showing that royal power derived from eternal principles.

The loyalist clergy and the laymen who repeated their arguments elaborated the analogy between God's monarchy over the universe and the king's power over society in several ways. They described the king as a vehicle through whom God conferred political benefits on men, much as God conferred natural benefits through natural causes. Laud preached:

> A King is given as a blessing to others . . . when in the riches of God's grace upon him . . . he turns the graces which God hath given him to the benefit of them which are committed to him. For mark the heavens and the earth shall learn. God did not place the sun in the heavens for height, but that it might have power to bless the inferior world, with beams, and light, and warmth and motion. David was thus and thus was Christ and such is every King.[67]

Discord will follow an eclipse of monarchy as surely as darkness follows a solar eclipse, for nature cannot function if its proper order is impaired. The clergy buttressed this argument by asserting that men are naturally inclined to live under kings: "God by his Law written in [human] hearts led [men] To government, to devolve their power in the hand of one, for eschewing injuries, and procuring both public and private good."[68] These ideas, in turn, could readily expand into a justification for royal absolutism, for if it was the natural function of kings to rule, then it was against the law of nature for anyone to compromise their power.[69]

THE KING AS AGENT OF REDEMPTION

These arguments sometimes fused with underlying forms of spirituality to produce a religious cult of the monarch. In court religion the distinction between the sacred and the profane was much less clearly marked than in most forms of puritanism, and the ways in which men came to know God were much more varied. Laudians argued that the soul must be shaped through sensual experiences to prepare it for the imprint of saving grace. They aimed not only to convert people to the message of the Gospels but to instill in them a greater capacity for awe and reverence. In Charles's court the power of the king and the visual splendor surrounding him were treated as essential to this educative process. Royal authority was described as a tangible projection of God's majesty, ordained so that men, who can understand spiritual mysteries only through their senses, may appreciate the glory of their Creator and learn to humble themselves before Him.

Perhaps the most elaborate justification of this attitude is a sermon preached by the royal chaplain, Isaac Bargrave, on the second anniversary of Charles's accession. Bargrave began by describing the fall of Adam as a violation of universal order, stemming from the sin of disobedience. God "made Order the measure of creation [and] placed man among the creatures here as the chief Administrator of order. But alas! disobedience and order could never long dwell together." Adam's transgression has left an indelible imprint on mankind, a profound rebelliousness which is the root of all sin. This was all more-or-less conventional theology, but Bargrave's emphasis upon order and disobedience—as opposed to lost innocence, temptation, pride, or lust—opened the way to a political interpretation of sin and salvation. To cure fallen man, the sermon continued,

> As *God* holding his Scepter in heaven, labors by all the means both of his mercies and judgements, to retract us from that fatal way: so he established Scepters on earth, as a ready means to help to reduce us to the perfection of a man on earth, that so he may better subdue us to his *own* Will in heaven.[70]

Man is not saved by faith alone, as Luther and Calvin had maintained, but by faith conjoined with obedience: "As faith is the chiefest of the *Theological*, so obedience is the chiefest of the moral virtues."[71] And that obedience must be learned through submission to an earthly king. "If any man say I fear God," asserted Matthew Wren, another royal chaplain, "and feareth not the *King*, he is a liar. . . . It is impossible for him that feareth not the King whom he hath seen, to fear God, whom he hath not seen . . . Because the Image of God . . . is upon Kings."[72] It is sacrilege, Wren went on, even to regard the king's majesty as separate from God's.

Sometimes the clergy actually reversed the usual comparison between the king and God by arguing that the Creator should be worshiped as a monarch. Thus Henry King argued for liturgical ceremonies by analogy to the royal court: if the monarch was honored through ritual and pageantry, then why not God?[73] Donne proclaimed, with reference to a scriptural passage, "I would ask no more premeditation at your hands, when you come to speak to God in this place, than if you send to speak with the King: no more fear of God here, than if you went to the King."[74]

It was a logical extension of these ideas that the ritualism and opulence of court life foreshadowed the beauty of heaven. Senhouse preached on the subject of Charles's coronation:

> It hath ever been the guise of godly good men, from the beholding of worldly things to beget heavenly thoughts, to turn the sight of every solemnity into a school of Divinity, and from things they see here downward, to make a prospect upward. . . . From the hearing of music, he is now with God, who is said to have entered upon the meditation of the holy harmony of heaven: And from your Crowning, think of the Crown of life.[75]

Over two decades later Walter Montagu expanded this argument into an essay on the theological significance of court life. Not only did he regard rituals as symbolic of divine mysteries. From the riches of courts men may "make optic glasses . . . through which they do the easlier [sic] take the height of celestial glories: and surely the sight of our minds is much helped by such material instruments, in the speculations of spiritualities." By relishing the honors and wealth of a court we develop "spiritual conceptions and appetites; concluding by these glories (which are but the shadows of those they signify) that the substance itself must needs be above what the eye hath seen, or ear heard."[76]

Court art, poetry, and dramatic spectacles further amplified and reinforced this attitude. The king was routinely represented as a divine figure, to whom even brute beasts paid homage.[77] Thus in Van Dyck's famous Louvre portrait, Le Roi à la Ciasse (Plate 10), the horse bows before the king in a gesture modeled, as Julius Held has shown, after nativity scenes depicting the homage of animals before the infant Jesus.[78] Ben Jonson portrayed Charles as a pantheist God of nature:

> He makes the time for whom 'tis done:
> From whom the warmth, heat, life begun;
> Into whose fostering arms do run
> All that have being from the Sun.
> Such is the font of life, the King,
> The heart that quickens everything,
> And makes the creatures language all one voice,
> In welcome, welcome, welcome to rejoice.[79]

The deference and ceremonial trappings surrounding the king also reinforced the aura of sanctity. Royal servants sometimes contributed to the effect by devising their own extravagant expressions of obeisance. Wentworth paraphrased scripture in writing to the king about the Irish church: "I do humbly beseech your Majesty's quickening Spirit may move upon these Waters, that we may from your Directions receive life, and from your Wisdom borrow light."[80] The effect created by this verbal and ritualistic devotion would then be ascribed to the force of the royal personality. "That Majesty in [the King's] countenance equalleth their place," wrote Struther. "This maketh their very silence to be awful and imperious, it confoundeth sometimes the most resolute Spirits, and putteth posed wits to precipitation."[81]

Palme has shown how the Whitehall Banqueting House emphasized the monarch's divinity during state rituals.[82] It resembles ancient temples and basilicas in structure. On its ceiling one of Ruben's canvases showed James I passing judicial sentence in a scene deliberately modeled after a formula for depicting the Last Judgment.[83] Above the heads of the spectators at royal ceremonies Charles's father had literally become an image of God. The first floor of the Banqueting House was originally more dimly illuminated than at present, but these paintings were bathed in a relatively bright light, symbolic of heaven. During diplomatic ceremonies the royal pavilion stood at the south end of the building, beneath a window similar to those Jones usually placed above the altar when he designed a church.[84] When struck by the sun on a bright morning, this window becomes a dazzling medallion of light in the midst of an otherwise solid wall. The Banqueting House functioned as a temple of royal divinity, expressing the sanctity of the king through an elaborate architectural language.

The masques employed a comparable symbolism. The royal pavilion stood in the middle of the floor beneath a rich canopy, with the court grouped symmetrically around it.[85] The king entered, to the accompaniment of a trumpet fanfare, only after everyone else was seated, and the performance began just after he occupied the elevated chair of state.[86] Masque sets were painted according to the rules of single-point perspective, to be seen from the royal throne: the closer one sat to the monarch, the clearer the masque images became, a way of asserting that the whole masqueing world revolves around the king. Palme has suggested a parallel between these stage sets and Baroque altar paintings, whose illusory space removes the wall of a church to reveal an image symbolizing a religious mystery. In the same way Jones's scenery unfolded behind the masques' proscenium arch, extending the space in which the real court sat into an allegorical masqueing world, exhibiting the philosophical significance of kingship.[87]

Through such spectacles, together with the theology of men like Bargrave, Wren, and Laud himself, the regime attempted to fuse religious piety and reverence for the king into a single pattern of ideas, emotions, and rituals.

DIVERGING RELIGIOUS CULTURES

The concept of divine-right kingship gained an impressive depth and consistency through its association with Laudian theology and court culture. Yet in the process royalist political thought was severed from the broadly Calvinist spirituality which had long been vital to English Protestantism. To make his subjects receptive to his ideas about kingship, Charles had first to convert them to his own theological perspective, for the concepts we have just traced would have been incomprehensible or blasphemous within a Calvinist framework. Laud and the king made a concerted effort to impose their theology upon the realm. They appointed royal chaplains to episcopal sees, silenced puritans, and ordered the clergy to preach the official political doctrines. In a few districts Arminian priests did create pockets of provincial royalism. For the most part, however, the Laudian church failed to uproot attitudes which had grown up over the course of a half-century and more. Even if we interpret the word in its broadest sense, Puritanism was never the religion of the majority of the English people. Those Laud regarded as puritans, however, made up an extraordinarily articulate and influential minority. Too many educated men and women had committed themselves to the Reformed tradition to permit him to succeed without a long and profoundly divisive struggle.

The religious ideas and imagery that grew up around Charles's rule provide one more example of the ways in which the cult of royalty had become more of a courtly phenomenon and less of a national one. We have noticed how the chivalry of Elizabeth's court, with its wide public appeal, gave way to the cosmopolitanism of a narrow group around the throne, and how the public pageantry of the Tudor monarchy declined under the Stuarts. In much the same way the ideas of Foxe were superseded by the unpopular doctrines of the Laudians and the esoteric religious sensibility of men like Walter Montagu.

NOTES

1. Robert Herrick, *Poems*, ed. L. C. Martin (London: Oxford University Press, 1965), p. 5.

2. This is not meant to suggest that the royalism of the 1640s was in any clear and unambiguous sense an outgrowth of the policies of the 1630s. The point is rather that the Cavaliers were stuck with Charles I. Like it or not, royalism in the Civil War meant loyalty to him and at least acquiescence in the religious and political values for which he stood. This was especially true of official publications like *Mercuricus Aulicus*, in which Charles took a direct interest (P. W. Thomas, *Sir John Berkenhead, 1617–1679* [Oxford: Oxford University Press, 1969], chap. 2). Apologists for the cause of Charles I in the 1640s inherited the imagery built up by court poets and painters in the prewar period and made use of it. The subjects under investigation here are therefore of relevance to both periods.

3. A fact that gave royalist propagandists some real tactical advantages. For two recent discussions, see Richard Tuck, "The Ancient Law of Freedom: John Selden and the Civil War," and Robert Ashton, "From Cavalier to Roundhead Tyranny, 1642–1649," both in *Reactions to the Civil War*, ed. J. S. Morrill (London: MacMillan, 1982), pp. 137–162, 185–207.

4. The problem was aggravated by the unwillingness of many gentry to sacrifice the peace of their counties for the national cause. On this point, see esp. J. S. Morrill, *The Revolt of the Provinces* (Cambridge: Cambridge University Press, 1976); Clive Holmes, *The Eastern Association and the Civil War* (Cambridge: Cambridge University Press, 1974), chap. 3; and Allan Everitt, *The Community of Kent and the Great Rebellion* (Leicester: Leicester University Press, 1966). William Hunt's *Puritan Moment* reinforces the point that, at least in Essex, the most determined resistance to the king stemmed from religious ideas more than from constitutionalist ideas. It should be noted, however, that fear of Catholicism and fear of absolutism were often linked.

5. Among recent discussions, see esp. J. S. Morrill, "The Religious Context of the English Civil War," *Transactions of the Royal Historical Society* 34 (1984): 155–178; and "Sir William Brereton and England's Wars of Religion," *Journal of British Studies* 24 (1985): 311–332.

6. For a discussion of the fusion of religious and constitutional fears of the court in the parliaments of the 1620s, see Conrad Russell, *Parliaments and English Politics, 1621–1629* (Oxford: Oxford University Press, 1979), pp. 379–382, 392–417. Caroline Hibbard, *Charles I and the Popish Plot*, (Chapel Hill: University of North Carolina Press, 1983) provides a thorough and important study of the fear of popish courtiers and their conspiracies on the eve of the Civil War. J. T. Cliffe, *The Puritan Gentry* (London: Routledge, 1984), pp. 150–168, explores the range of puritan complaints against the court.

7. The chaplain was John Everard, who in the 1650s published some of the sermons he had preached in Holland's household in a book dedicated to Oliver Cromwell.

8. R. M. Smuts, "Henrietta Maria," *English Historical Review* 93 (1978): 40–45; and Hibbard, *Popish Plot*.

9. For discussions, see esp. Hibbard, *Popish Plot*; and Anthony Fletcher, *Outbreak of the Civil War*. Fear of Catholics and Arminians (whom he regarded as secret Catholics), was a dominant force in Pym's political career from the mid-1620s. See Conrad Russell, "The Parliamentary Career of John Pym," in *The English Commonwealth*, ed. Peter Clark et al. (Leicester: Leicester University Press, 1979), pp. 147–166.

10. As shown by N. R. N. Tyacke, "Arminianism in England in Religion and Politics, 1604 to 1640" (Ph.D. thesis, Oxford University, 1969). Tyacke has provided a sum-

mary in *The Origins of the Civil War*, ed. Conrad Russell (London: MacMillan, 1973), pp. 119–143. The early years of James's reign, during the primacy of Bancroft, should perhaps be regarded as an exception.

11. R. T. Kendall, *Calvin and English Calvinism to 1649* (Oxford: Oxford University Press, 1979), part 1, argues that this consensus was really based on the views of Calvin's disciple, Theodore Beza, and his English follower, William Perkins, rather than on Calvin's own writings. There is no doubt, however, that Perkins's soteriology was perceived by those sympathetic to it as essentially identical to Calvin's. I will therefore use the term "Calvinist" to designate a tradition embracing Beza, Perkins, the formularies of the Dutch Synod of Dort, and the works of others in this tradition.

12. Ivorwny Morgan, *Prince Charles's Puritan Chaplain* (London: Allen and Unwin, 1957). Patrick Collinson, *The Religion of the Protestants* (Oxford: Oxford University Press, 1982), is a superb study of the Jacobean church. It is possible to question how far Abbot's primateship represented the norm; his predecessors, Bancroft and Whitgift, had been hostile to puritanism, although Whitgift was a Calvinist in his soteriology.

13. It is not entirely clear how many of them had actually read Arminius.

14. In this paragraph I have taken into account some of the detailed criticism of Tyacke's arguments contained in Peter White, "The Rise of Arminianism Reconsidered," *Past and Present* 91 (1983): 34–54. I do not think that White has discredited the main thrust of Tyacke's thesis, and some of his own arguments, like the unsupported assertion that a theological consensus was reestablished after 1629, appear dubious. Collinson, *Religion of the Protestants* generally supports Tyacke, as do several of Sir Simonds D'Ewes's comments in his *Autobiography* (London, 1845), e.g., vol. 1, p. 142. D'Ewes had no doubt that "Arminianism" rose between 1620 and 1630 and that it significantly altered the tone of the church. Cliffe, *Puritan Gentry*, pp. 146–157, also tends to support Tyacke.

15. See above, Chapter 2.

16. Peter Heylin, *Cyprianus Anglicus: The History of the Life and Death of William Laud* (London, 1671); p. 165. Most of those Heylin called Puritans would have violently resented the label. His use of the term in this context reflects his partisanship. Russell has shrewdly commented, "If 'puritans' are defined by refusal to conform, then the meaning of puritanism must necessarily change with changes in the attitude of the ecclesiastical authorities. If 'puritanism' is thus politically defined, the ecclesiastical authorities could make and unmake 'puritans' by their own changes of policy" (*Parliaments and English Politics*, p. 28). In that sense Laud made a great many Puritans.

17. Cottington to Wentworth, October 29, 1633, in W. Knowler, *The Earl of Strafforde's Letters and Dispatches* (London, 1739), vol. 1, p. 141.

18. A good brief discussion of the issues involved and their place in an evolving theological tradition is Kendall, *Calvin and English Calvinism*. As he points out, the Arminians had more in common with the "Calvinists" than the latter cared to admit. The differences were nonetheless fundamental.

19. John Donne, *Sermons*, ed. G. R. Potter and E. M. Simpson (Berkeley and Los Angeles: University of California Press, 1953–1962), vol. 9, p. 85.

20. It is true that one can find passages in puritan sermons exhorting believers to prepare their hearts to receive the gift of faith that seem very close to the quoted lines of Donne. In practice the differences between Arminians and Calvinists were often less sharply defined than polemicists cared to admit. Further, as became apparent in the 1640s, some puritan radicals were themselves Arminians. Once the issue of predestination had been raised, however, in the context of a struggle for control of the church, it became the center of an explosive controversy.

21. Laud to Samuel Brooke, December 9, 1630, in SP16/176/46.

22. On this point, see Keith Thomas, *Religion and the Decline of Magic* (London: Weidenfeld and Nicolson, 1971), chaps. 2, 3, and 6; and Keith Wrightson, *English Society, 1580–1680* (London: Hutchinson, 1982), chap. 7.

23. Edward Walker in BL, Harl. MSS 6272, fol. 38. This attitude often drew support from the works of Erasmus and some of his English followers, who had conceived of Christianity as a tolerant and simple faith characterized by a spirit of love and charity. Yet Luther himself had rejected Erasmus's theology, which seemed to harbor dangerous Pelagian tendencies.

24. Joseph Hall, *One of the Sermons Preached at Westminster on the day of the publike Fast* (London, 1628), p. 85.

25. Marc L. Schwarz, "Lay Anglicanism and the Crisis of the Church in the Early Seventeenth Century," *Albion* 14 (1982): 1–19, is an interesting discussion of the sort of rationalist lay piety I am discussing here. As Schwarz points out, this outlook was ultimately no more compatible with Laudian clericalism than with puritan clericalism. However, his use of the term "lay Anglicanism" to designate ideas which many religious English lay Protestants would have emphatically rejected is problematical.

26. For a wide-ranging and interesting discussion of the relationship between Arminianism and a variety of classical and neo-classical traditions, including Epicureanism, see Nicholas Tyacke, "Arminianism and English Culture," in *Britain and the Netherlands,* ed. A. C. Duke and C. A. Tamse, vol. 7 (The Hague: M. Nijhoff, 1981).

27. *Poems,* ed. K. Allot (London, 1948), p. 115.

28. Sir Kenelm Digby, *Loose Fantasies,* ed. Vittorio Gabrielli (Rome: Edizioni di Storia e Letteratura, 1968), p. 99. The quoted passage is attributed in this novel to Theagenes, who represents Digby himself.

29. New York Public Library MSS, 39M39, pp. 76, 77.

30. Sir John Suckling, *Works in Prose and Verse,* ed. L. A. Beaurline (Oxford: Oxford University Press, 1971), p. 171. Cf. George Wither's characterization of court religion in 1627: "Their faith is such/As Reason breeds, and most time, not so much" (*Britain's Remembrancer,* Publications of the Spenser Society 28–29 (Manchester, 1880), p. 394).

31. Herrick, *Poems,* p. 364.

32. William Cartwright, "On the Nativity," in *Comedies, Tragi-Comedies, with Other Poems* (London, 1651), p. 317.

33. Knowler, *Strafforde's Letters,* vol. 2, p. 170.

34. John Calvin, *Institutes of the Christian Religion,* ed. John T. McNeill and Ford Lewis Battles (Philadelphia: Westminster Press, 1960), vol. 1, pp. 258–259: "All ecclesiastical writers have recognized both that the soundness of reason in man is gravely wounded through sin, and that the will of man has been very much enslaved by evil desires. Despite this, many of them have come far too close to the philosophers. . . . [The early church fathers wished to avoid] the jeers of the philosophers with whom they were in conflict. . . . Therefore, they . . . strove to harmonize the doctrine of Scripture half-way with the beliefs of philosophers [about the power of reason and free will]. . . . A little later it will be evident that these opinions . . . are utterly false." Calvin makes it clear that he is opposing not only modern Catholicism but also pagan philosophical ideas that had influenced the church from a very early date. He repudiated statements by such eminent church fathers as Chrysostom and Jerome and admitted that Augustine was the only early theologian (apart from the apostles) who agreed with his own position. He was, in effect, demanding a repudiation of the whole humanist tendency to reconcile the Gospels with the dictates of "natural" moral philosophy.

35. Knowler, *Strafforde's Letters*, vol. 2, p. 125.

36. Panzani, *Memoirs*, p. 136, Panzani dispatches of March 2, March 6/16, March 13/23 and November 11, 1635, PRO 31/9/17B.

37. See, e.g., Panzani's comments in *Memoirs*, p. 134. Herbert's account of the Reformation in his history of Henry VIII's reign reflected the views of many others at court. He openly regarded it as an understandable but unfortunate overreaction to the corruptions of the Roman church. The fundamental division within English Protestantism was between those who regarded the Reformation as a triumph of True Religion against the forces of the Antichrist, and those who saw it as a mixture of reform and sacrilege, which corrected some abuses while creating others.

38. For an account of the liturgical innovations, see Horton Davies, *Worship and Theology in England*, vol. 2 (Princeton: Princeton University Press, 1975), pp. 35–41.

39. So long as the church was under the control of men unequivocally committed to the Reformation, these anxieties remained within limits, although we have seen (above, chapter 2) that they did surface before the 1620s. James's intervention *against* the Dutch Arminians at the Synod of Dort in 1619, and Abbot's impeccable Protestant credentials, helped maintain confidence in the government's religious policies. James's death and Abbot's fall from royal favor radically altered the situation after 1625.

40. Copy of Francis Bacon's *Advancement of Learning* (Oxford, 1640) once belonging to Charles I, in the British Library, p. 307.

41. William Laud, *Works*, ed. William Scott and J. Bliss (Oxford, 1847–1860), vol. 6, p. 57.

42. Ibid., vol. 2, p. xvi.

43. Quoted by Davies, *Worship and Theology*, vol. 2, p. 19.

44. Con dispatch of August 11, 1636, PRO, 31/9/17B.

45. BL Harl. MSS 4898, fol. 643.

46. *The Court and Times of Charles I*, ed. Thomas Birch (London, 1849), vol. 2, p. 311.

47. As is well known. See H. Outram Evenett, *The Spirit of the Counter Reformation* (Cambridge: Cambridge University Press, 1968), p. 48.

48. Walter Montagu, *Miscellanea Spiritualia, or Devout Essays* (London, 1648), pp. 87, 88.

49. Joseph Hall, *A Sermon Preached to His Majesty* (London, 1628), pp. 77, 78.

50. Donne, *Sermons*, vol. 8, p. 174.

51. Herrick, "His Meditation on Death," in *Poems*, p. 392.

52. New York Public Library MSS, 39M39, p. 110.

53. Ibid.

54. *The Political Works of James I*, ed. James McIlwain (Cambridge, Mass.: Harvard University Press, 1918), p. 307.

55. In 1639 this position was officially sanctioned by convocation. See SP16/455/47.

56. Matthew Wren to Laud, December 16, 1627, SP16/86/108.

57. See, e.g., Henry Burton's comment: "My Lord the King is an Angel of God . . . whose vice regent he is" (*An Apology and Appeal*) [London, 1636], p. iii).

58. William Haller, *The Elect Nation: The Meaning and Relevance of Foxe's Book of Martyrs* (New York: Harper and Row, 1963); Paul Christiansen, *Reformers in Babylon* (Toronto: University of Toronto Press, 1978).

59. Bernard, *Bible Battels, or The Sacred Art Military for the Rightly Waging of War According to Holy Writ* (London, 1629), p. 127.

60. Isaac Bargrave, *A Sermon Preached Before King Charles* (London, 1637), p. 36.

61. There was also a Protestant tradition going back to the early sixteenth century,

which looked to the godly people for reform. Christiansen, *Reformers in Babylon,* provides a good discussion of the latent political ambiguities in Foxeian eschatology.

62. Peter Heylin, *A Briefe and Moderate Answer to Henry Burton* (London, 1637), p. 36.

63. In the words of diplomat Sir Thomas Roe, "hereditary and justly possessed Monarchies . . . are of all other [governments] the most simple, and therefore most pure, and like to the divine government" (Roe to Earl of Holland, June 9, 1632, SP16/218/29).

64. Arthur Lovejoy, *The Great Chain of Being* (Cambridge, Mass.: Harvard University Press, 1936); W. H. Greenleaf, *Order, Empiricism, and Politics* (London: Oxford University Press for the University of Hull, 1964).

65. Michael Waltzer, *The Revolution of the Saints* (Cambridge, Mass.: Harvard University Press, 1965), pp. 161–162.

66. Fulke Greville, *Works in Verse and Prose,* ed. A. B. Grosart, 1870; (New York: AMS Press, 1966), vol. 1, p. 5.

67. William Laud, Sermon II, *Works,* vol. 1, p. 36.

68. William Struther, *A Looking Glasse for Princes and People* (Edinburgh, 1632), pp. 7–8.

69. As Wentworth wrote to Secretary Coke (Knowler, *Strafforde's Letters,* vol. 1, p. 245): "my opinion . . . hath ever been, that the honorable and just Redemption of the Subject from Oppression and Wrong, should be the immediate Acts of Sovereignty, indeed the proper Charge and Office of Kings to provide for, without the Interposition of any Parliament, or other Body, betwixt their Light and the eyes of their People, who discerning whence these blessings are communicated, may be justly moved to praise and magnify them for their Goodness and Protection." Although he does not directly invoke religious ideas, Wentworth's words reflect the assumptions we have been tracing.

70. Bargrave, *Sermon,* p. 1 (italics in original).

71. Ibid., p. 6.

72. M. Wren, *A Sermon Preached Before His Majesty* (Cambridge, 1627), p. 25.

73. Henry King, *Two Sermons Preached at Whitehall in Lent* (London, 1627), p. 25.

74. Sermons of April 1629, in Donne, *Sermons,* vol. 9, pp. 59–60.

75. Richard Senhouse, *Foure Sermons Preached at Court* (London, 1627), p. 24.

76. Montagu, *Miscellanea Spiritualia,* pp. 87–88.

77. E.g., a panegyrist named Francesco Cevoli asserted: "So sacred is the Majesty of Princes, that even the most unarmed beasts will defend it, when men will violate it" (*An Occasional Discourse upon an Accident which Befell his Majesty in Hunting*) [London, 1635], p. 7).

78. J. S. Held, "Le Roi à la Ciasse," *Art Bulletin* 40 (1958): 139–149.

79. Ben Jonson, "Love's Welcome to Bolsover," in *Works of Ben Jonson,* ed. C. H. Herford and Percy and Evelyn Simpson, 11 vols. (Oxford: Oxford University Press, 1925–1953), vol. 7, p. 792.

80. Wentworth to Charles I, January 22, 1633, Knowler, vol. 1, p. 183.

81. Struther, *Looking Glasse,* p. 13.

82. Per Palme, *The Triumph of Peace* (Stockholm: Almquist and Wiksell, 1956).

83. Ibid., pp. 242 ff.

84. Ibid., pp. 199 ff.

85. Ibid., pp. 151–152.

86. See the account of a masque performance of 1618 in *Ven. Cal.,* vol. 15, pp. 111–114.

87. Palme, *Triumph of Peace,* pp. 153–155.

9 THE HALCYON REIGN

Side by side with the creed of divine-right monarchy there developed in the 1630s a secular cult of Charles and Henrietta Maria. Its central theme was the peace bestowed by the monarchs upon England, often symbolized by the halcyon, a mythical bird who builds her nest upon the ocean and possesses a magical power to calm the waves. As *Albion's Triumph,* the king's masque of 1631, proclaimed:

> Arms are laid by: early and late
> The traveller goes safe to bed:
> Men eat and drink in massie plate
> And are with dainties daily fed
> Why should this isle above the rest
> Be made (great God) the Halcyon's nest?[1]

In this peaceful reign the arts flourish, manners grow civilized, and the realm fills with innocent revelry, from the dances of the court to the frolicking of country folk around their maypoles. Over it all presides a royal couple who have tamed their own passions, purged the court of ill humors, shouldered the burdens of the realm's affairs, and established a polity based on love:

> . . . The people fix their eyes upon
> The King; admire, love, honor him alone.

In him, as in a glass, their manners view
And frame, and copy what they see *Him* do
That which the murdering Cannon cannot force,
Nor plumed Squadrons of steel-glittering Horse
Love can. . . .[2]

Today this vision seems more than a little ironic. Charles began his reign with wars against France and Spain and, after a disastrous civil conflict, ended it on the scaffold. Whatever blame his enemies and impersonal historical forces may share in these calamities, he certainly brought more strife than tranquility to his kingdom. Yet to many contemporaries his reputation as a gentle, loving sovereign only grew stronger after the events of the 1640s. Parliament's army might denounce the defeated monarch as a man of blood and execute him for crimes against the people, but to his followers he appeared to be a hapless victim of usurpation, destroyed because he was too good for an evil world. From the majestic image of God the Father, holding absolute sway over the commonwealth, he turned into a martyr surrendering his throne and his life with the meekness of God the Son:

He nothing common did, nor mean
Upon that memorable scene,
But with his keener eye
The axe's edge did try;
Nor called the gods with vulgar spite
To vindicate his helpless right;
But bowed his comely head
Down as upon a bed.[3]

The frontispiece of *Eikon Basilike,* the little treatise claiming to give Charles's thoughts during "his solitudes and suffering" which began to circulate on the day of his execution, showed him kneeling in prayer, grasping a crown of thorns, the royal diadem on the ground by his side.

If the king's execution reminded royalists of the crucifixion, the 1630s looked, in retrospect, like a lost paradise destroyed by a great political tragedy symbolically recapitulating man's fall from grace:

Oh thou, that dear and happy isle,
The garden of the world erewhile,
Thou Paradise of the four seas
Which heaven planted us to please,
But to exclude the world did guard

With watery if not flaming sword—
What luckless apple did we taste,
To make us mortal, and thee waste?[4]

This imagery sometimes spread beyond the writings of cavaliers. Perhaps the most remarkable thing about the verses quoted in the last two paragraphs, both by Andrew Marvell, is that they occur in poems dedicated to Oliver Cromwell and Sir Thomas Fairfax. So firmly had Charles become associated with civility and peace that even his enemies occasionally recognized these qualities in him. If we could discover how this iconography developed and what ideas and aspirations it conveyed, we might learn something important about the political culture of the period.

THE CULT OF PEACE AND ITS POLITICAL CONTEXT

The earliest development of the Caroline cult is shrouded in obscurity, because of the disappearance of all the masques performed between 1625 and 1630.[5] We cannot now determine how far the wars led to a break with the peaceful cultural traditions of the previous reign. It is clear, however, that even before the wars ended the theme of peace reasserted itself as the royal cult of the 1630s began to emerge.

In devising the symbology that prevailed for the rest of his reign, Charles could draw upon the services of the greatest allegorical painter of the age. Peter Paul Rubens arrived in London in January 1629 to negotiate a truce between Spain and England and stayed until the following February. In the interim he began two great canvases, the *Allegory of Peace and War* and *A Landscape with Saint George and the Dragon* (Plate 14).[6] The latter anticipates a central motif of the royal cult of the 1630s: the claim that Henrietta Maria has tempered the valor of her husband to establish a reign of peace and harmony. Charles appears as Saint George, just after his famous victory over the dragon, while his wife becomes the princess who inspired his valor. Corpses of the dragon's victims litter the ground as people the saint has rescued look on gratefully. A lamb stands meekly behind Henrietta Maria. In the background unfolds a tranquil English landscape, on which the sun has just broken forth from behind the clouds.

Since George was the patron saint of England and the prototype of

14. Peter Paul Rubens. *A Landscape with St. George and the Dragon*. Her Majesty Queen Elizabeth II.

Spenser's Red Cross Knight, this painting placed Charles squarely within the traditions of English chivalry. Yet the military ethos of that tradition has undergone a symbolic transformation. George's victory over the dragon was commonly regarded—by Laud's chaplain, Peter Heylin, among others—as symbolic of a Christian's victory over Satan. Allegorically, the king has subdued his own passions, and probably the evil humors threatening his realm.[7] The lamb and Lambeth palace, visible in the background, must stand for the church, freed from oppression by Charles's strong arm. The three women who look on from the middle foreground may be the muses, symbols of the king's civilizing influence. The landscape represents the kingdom itself, now released from its devouring monster, who embodies the spirit of war and civic tumult. The royal couple have already become guardians of peace, in an extended sense which encompasses their personal victories over passion, the defense of the church, and their patronage of the civilizing arts.

The masques of the next decade consistently elaborated this message. If James had ruled as a royal Solomon, praised for his wisdom, prudence, and magnanimity, Charles preferred the more romantic role of a royal knight, inspired by the beauty of his wife to purge the realm of vice and discord. In the masques the mutual love of the royal couple becomes a universal influence, capable of reforming men, nature, and even the gods. The mere presence of the king and queen continually brings order out of chaos, quieting storms, transforming wild landscapes into gardens, causing anti-masques of debauched lovers and seditious puritans to vanish from the stage.[8] In the end, however, these achievements are always subsumed within a celebration of England's peace.[9]

In light of all we have learned concerning Charles's direct supervision of his court's culture, it seems highly probable that he helped formulate this imagery.[10] But this does not mean that we can treat the pacific themes of masques and other cultural works as a straightforward expression of the political ideas of the king and his advisers. Charles did not share his father's profound aversion to war and never entirely abandoned the dream of some day wielding military power in Europe. One cannot read through the diplomatic correspondence of the reign without noticing a persistent undercurrent of military ambition within the court. Several powerful figures, notably the Earls of Holland and Northumberland, advocated a French alliance and aggressive measures against the Habsburgs.[11] The queen often supported this faction, which for a brief period in 1635–1636 appeared to be winning the power struggle that followed Weston's death. Lesser courtiers also frequently tended to look favorably on warlike policies. "The gallants of the court are more eager to hear the news of battle than to see a play begin at Blackfriars," Viscount Conway wryly commented in 1635.[12] The portrait of the Caroline court found in most histories, as a place where isolationist and pro-Spanish sentiments had triumphed over any sense of obligation to the cause of international Protestantism, is misleading. It overlooks both the divisions over foreign policy which continued throughout the 1630s and the deeply ambivalent attitudes of Charles himself.

Occasionally the undercurrent of military ambition within the court found expression in cultural works. Thus in 1635 Henrietta Maria took her nephew, the Elector Palatine, to see a revival at the Blackfriars theater of an Elizabethan history play about the sufferings of Germany under a medieval Spanish tyrant.[13] The similarity between the plot of this drama and the plight of the Elector himself would have been obvious.

By and large, it is surprising how infrequently warlike aspirations surfaced in works produced for the monarchs. Only one of the masques, *The Triumph of the Prince d'Amour*, made even a passing allusion to the glories of warfare, and it was written for the Prince Palatine rather than the king. Even this work treated war as inferior to peace, representing Mars by a copper statue, contrasted to a silver effigy of Venus and a golden one of Apollo. The queen's masques never hinted of her advocacy of a French alliance. So pronounced was the emphasis on peace that it sometimes shaped works glorifying military expeditions:

> I saw third Edward stain my flood [the English Channel]
> By Sluce with slaughtered Frenchmen's blood
>   And from Eliza's Fleet
> I saw the vanquished Spaniard fly
> But 'twas a greater mastery
>   No fleet at all to meet
> When they without their ruin or dispute
> Confess thy Reign as sweet as absolute.[14]

So the court poet, Thomas May, celebrated an uneventful expedition by the English fleet, intended to assert Charles's sovereignty over the seas around his kingdom. Even in the midst of civil war Fanshawe encouraged Prince Charles to follow the example of Julius Caesar, who never fought until he had sought peace:

> Grieving as oft as he was forced to kill
> How most religiously he kept his word,
> And conquered more that way than by the sword.
> In whom was all we in a King could crave.[15]

The royal cult was far more unambiguously pacific than royal policies or court sentiment.

The most plausible explanation for this fact is that the Crown needed to justify its withdrawal from continental affairs, not only to the English public but also to foreign governments and to its own servants. The masques and most other forms of court culture were intended for a relatively restricted audience, consisting mainly of courtiers, country peers, prominent gentry, and foreign diplomats. These groups shared an aristocratic code of honor and an interest in international affairs which heightened their awareness of how much England's reputation had suffered from its military reverses and the debilitating financial crisis that accompanied them. In four years of war Charles had added some £600,000 to the debts left by his father, so overburdening the Exchequer that his household often lacked the basic amenities of royal life.[16] In 1630 the situation was so bad that he refused to allow a French countess to visit Henrietta Maria, whom she had traveled to London to see, because he felt ashamed of the tattered furniture in the royal apartments. "Finally the Queen herself desired to see [the Countess]. When she entered the room they shut all the windows to exclude the light and prevent these shortcomings being seen."[17]

"Money is the sinews of war"—a Crown this impoverished became a cipher in European affairs, as the reports of foreign diplomats make clear. "The French ambassador never speaks to me about these particulars except with derision," a Venetian ambassador wrote in the late 1620s concerning English military threats, "as he knows only too well the weakness of the government here."[18] Charles and his ministers knew they had come perilously close to losing the respect of statesmen across Europe. Always painfully sensitive about his reputation among men of rank, he felt these humiliations deeply. They may well have seemed more important to him than domestic political dissension.

The artists and poets responsible for Caroline masques and panegyrics faced a clear challenge. Somehow they had to show that peace is more glorious than war and that a monarch is more virtuous when reveling in the midst of his court than while sweeping all before him on the field of battle. They conveyed such an argument in several ways. Occasionally they portrayed warriors as thugs and barbarians. Thus Davenant's play, *The Platonic Lovers,* castigates two "valiant captains" by commenting:

> If midnight howlings heard in cities sacked
> And fired with the groans of widowed wives
> And slaughtered children's shrieks can pierce the ears
> Of Heaven, the learned think their glorious ghosts
> Will have a dismal welcome after death.
> However, in this world, 'tis good to follow 'em.[19]

In much the same vein, Jonson's *Richmond Entertainment,* presented before Charles during a progress in 1634, included an ancient British captain who urged the king to perform feats of valor. Superficially he resembled the Arthurian knights of *Prince Henry's Barrier,* but his speech ended on a ironic note: "Strike up a warlike sound and you my soldiers think of nothing but fresh booty."[20] Similarly, Davenant included a "mock romanza" in *Britannia Triumphans* (1637), satirizing chivalric romances and serving as a foil to passages glorifying peace.[21]

This disparagement of warlike values was also reflected in other ways. Charles's court produced only two epic poems, both recounting medieval rebellions.[22] Far from glorifying warfare, they treated it as a calamity overcome by the triumph of royal power. On the other hand, pastoralism flourished as never before. Sidney and Spenser had treated pastoral love as a dangerous pleasure that might undercut heroic virtues. The heroes of the *Arcadia* and the *Faerie Queen* had to depart from their pastoral environment to prove their mettle in combat.[23] In Caroline court pastorals, however, the world of shepherds is normally morally superior to that of statesmen and soldiers.[24]

Perhaps the single most effective statement of the theme that innocent pastoral pleasures are superior to military heroism is Thomas Carew's poem, "In Answer to an Elegiacal Letter upon the Death of the King of Sweden from Aurelian Townshend." Carew refuses an invitation to glorify the deeds of the fallen Protestant hero, implying that his death in battle came as a just reward for overweening ambition. Instead, he launches into praises of the happy state of his own country, concluding with the best known tribute to the Caroline peace:

Tournies, Masques, Theaters better become
Our Halcyon days; what though the German Drum
Bellow for freedom and revenge, the noise
Concerns not us, nor should divert our joys;
Nor ought the thunder of their Carabins
Drown the sweet Airs of our tun'd Violins;
Believe me friend, if their prevailing powers
Gain them a calm security like ours,
They'll hang their arms up on the Olive Bough
And dance, and revel then, as we do now.[25]

Closely bound up with these references to innocent merriment is the repeated claim of the masques that Charles has brought the civilizing arts to perfection. In *Luminalia* (1638), for example, the muses decide to take up residence in England after war has chased them from all other countries. In a textual gloss Jones explained that by doing so they have rendered the English models of civility, comparable to the Greeks among ancient peoples.[26] Several masques employed classical cityscapes as emblems of the benefits Charles had bestowed on England; one proudly displayed the Banqueting House. It is significant that the models of civilization always came from the ancient world. Thus in *Salmacida Spolia* Charles appeared seated on a classical throne surrounded—or so Jones claimed—with attendants dressed like those of Augustus.[27] Court architecture reinforced this effect. The Banqueting House is a modified basilica descended from Roman law courts. An unexecuted design for a new Star Chamber and a remodeling of the hall for the House of Lords, both dating from the 1620s, derived from patterns of Roman civic architecture. The great palace designed for Charles would have been impeccably classical—the kind of residence, he must have thought, in which Augustus or Hadrian lived. The England portrayed in works created for the Crown had outgrown her medieval heritage, attaining a cultural brilliance previously enjoyed only by the Greeks and Romans. Neo-medievalism had become largely irrelevant.

THE MONARCH AND HIS KINGDOM: PLATONIC POLITICS?

This imagery of a land happily reveling around fictitious olive trees while enjoying the benefits of a brilliant classical culture is both artificial and somewhat stereotyped. Broadly similar motifs could be found in court entertainments produced throughout Renaissance Europe. In their symbolic language the court's masques and panegyrics nevertheless advanced an ambitious claim. Not only has Charles kept the realm out of war, but his rule has also tamed England's warrior elite, creating a new Golden Age of social harmony and civic virtue. The myth of the halcyon reign stood for much more than neutrality in Europe's conflicts. It also symbolized a vision of the benevolent effects of royal power upon England. We are therefore entitled to ask what light the imagery of the royal cult may shed on the basic assumptions underlying Charles's prerogative government.

In two provocative essays, Stephen Orgel has attempted to answer this question.[28] The masques, he argues, transform politics into a reflection of the king's mind, as if Charles could govern simply by acts of thought, in much the way that a Platonic God rules the cosmos through the force of divine Ideas. These spectacles "provide us with a remarkable insight into the royal point of view, whereby the complexities of contemporary issues were resolved through idealizations and allegories, visions of Platonic realities."[29]

If true, this argument will affect not only our assessment of court culture but also our understanding of the whole political history of Charles's reign. It is, however, open to serious objections on at least two levels. First, Orgel has produced no evidence to show that this Platonic mode of thought affected Charles's actual conduct of government. His analysis rests on an implicit assumption, rooted in whiggish historiography, that the personal rule was an unrealistic attempt to prevent the natural evolution of a more equal partnership between Crown and Parliament. It is certainly true that the Caroline regime, like all early modern governments, sometimes lacked adequate information about provincial affairs and effective means of enforcing its will with local magistrates.[30] But even a brief examination of the government's activities in the 1630s reveals that it sometimes acted more energetically and realistically than Orgel implies, for example, in its enforcement of the Poor Laws after the bad harvest of 1629 and in collecting prerogative taxes.[31] We badly need a systematic study of the years of personal rule, but it is clear that for all the Crown's mistakes and omissions the stereotype of totally isolated and unresponsive regime, living in an atmosphere of unreality, is at best greatly exaggerated.[32]

Second, and more important for our immediate purposes, Orgel's interpretation of the masques is itself open to question. If these entertainments often do appear to show political problems being resolved through the invocation of abstract ideals, this is no more than we should expect. Masques were by nature symbolic allegories that offered little scope for political realism. Their function was to celebrate the monarchs' successes, not to remind them of unresolved difficulties or to explore the mechanisms through which royal policies might be enforced. We therefore need to be wary of taking these entertainments' abstract and generally optimistic imagery entirely at face value as a reflection to the king's full political outlook. [33]

Moreover, we have seen that Inigo Jones, who devised these spectacles, did not believe in the power of Platonic images to transform the world without practical effort and ingenuity. [34] If Orgel is right, then Jones's masques present a view of politics in which "theory" is divorced from "practice" in a manner that appears surprising in light of all we have learned about Jones's mind. When examined carefully, however, the masques actually reveal a more complex political philosophy than Orgel has allowed.

This is especially true of the last of them, *Salmacida Spolia.* Produced shortly before the summoning of the Short Parliament, when the court already suspected that stormier times lay ahead, it deals more explicitly than any previous Stuart entertainment with political dissidence and threatened rebellion. War, allegorized as "Discord, a malicious Fury," is no longer safely restricted to the continent. Filled with envy at England's peace, she has come to stir up civil conflict. Ironically Charles's very successes have made her task easier. His subjects have grown so accustomed to good times that they do not realize how fortunate they are and so fall prey to "malicious spirits" who seek to corrupt them:

> Thou over-lucky, too-much happy isle,
> Grow more desirous of this flattering style!
> For thy long health can never altered be
> But by thy surfeits of felicity.
> And I to Stir the humors that increase
> In thy full body overgrown with peace,
> Will call those Furies hither who incense
> The guilty and disorder innocence.
> Ascend, ascend, you horrid sullen brood
> Of evil spirits, and displace the good!
> The great make only wiser to suspect
> Whom they have wronged, by falsehood or neglect.

The rich, make full of avarice and pride,
Like graves or swallowing seas unsatisfied,
Busy to help the state, when needy grown,
From poor men's fortunes, never from their own.
The poor ambitious make, apt to obey
The false, in hope to rule whom they betray;
And make religion to become their vice,
Needed to disguise ambitious avarice.[35]

She succeeds in raising a storm, probably symbolizing the First Bishop's War and perhaps the English dissidence that crippled Charles's efforts to fight through to victory.

Then suddenly the incantation's of Discord's spirits are "surprised and stopped in their motions by a secret power," the wisdom of King "Philogenes, or Lover of his People," who "will change all their malicious hopes into a sudden calm," represented by a rural scene:

The sky serene, afar of Zephyrus appeared breathing a gentle gale: in the landscape were corn fields and pleasant trees, sustaining vines fraught with grapes, and in some of the furthest parts villages, with all such things as might express a country in peace, rich and fruitful.[36]

From the sky over this scene "Concord" and "the Good Genius of Great Britain" descend, singing of Philogene's patience:

. . . I grieve that, though the best
Of kingly science harbors in his breast,
Yet 'tis his fate to rule in adverse times
When wisdom must awhile give way to crimes

Upon reaching the earth they proceed "to go off in all directions, and incite the people to honest pleasures and recreations, which have ever been peculiar to this nation"—an allusion to the king's Book of Sports, which restrained puritan magistrates from prohibiting traditional rural festivities. Jones next produced a cityscape filled with "select pieces" of classical architecture, to symbolize the court's civilization.[37] The masque thus concludes triumphantly with all the elements of the myth of the halcyon reign: the king who rules through love, the civilizing arts of the classical city, and the idyllic countryside filled with innocent revelry.

At first glance these scenes do appear to resolve political tensions through "idealizations and allegories." If we look more closely, how-ever, it becomes apparent that the masque does not treat politics as a reflection of the king's mind, but rather as a great drama of conflicting passions and interests which Charles must regulate and appease. The realm's disturbances stem from moral corruption, engendered by a "sur-feit" of peace and prosperity, aggravated by demagogic plots. Avarice, indolence, and resentment against discipline have induced Englishmen to pursue their selfish interest at the commonwealth's expense. The rich victimize the poor while the common people, motivated by envy against their superiors, give ear to malcontents who use religion to dis-guise their evil purposes.

Philogenes is said to cure these evils by "the secret power" of his wisdom. If we interpret this as referring to the unaided force of royal ideas, then Orgel's view of the masques is correct. Yet the masque as a whole suggests that Charles is less a Platonic demigod than an indul-gent paternalist enduring the indignities an ungrateful people heap upon him so that he may regain their love and obedience. The "kingly science that harbors in his breast" cannot prevent political "crimes" from occurring; it can only teach him to act with restraint until the forces of discord dissipate:

> If it be kingly patience to outlast
> Those storms the people's giddy fury raise
> Till like fantastic winds themselves they waste,
> The wisdom of that patience is thy praise.[38]

The proscenium arch rounds out this idea by symbolizing qualities con-ventionally associated with effective government, including counsel, eloquence, discipline, knowledge, resolution, and prudence. The imag-ery is certainly vague and abstract, but it does at least hint at the need for political judgment. The king's "secret power" is not a mystical intel-lectual force; it is the mystery of kingcraft, the difficult and obscure art of government which rulers must learn.

This interpretation is strengthened by its strong affinities with the major themes of the great masterpiece of cavalier propaganda, *Eikon Basilike,* which probably derives from Charles's own account of the Civil War.[39] For if the masques do reflect "the king's point of view," then one should expect them to show some similarities with ideas Charles expressed in other contexts. *Eikon Basilike* consistently portrays Charles seeking to reconcile political opponents and calm disorders caused by the factious spirit of the times and the ruthlessness of parliamentary demagogues. In explaining why he did not resolutely oppose the crowds of London that rioted against him in 1641, for example, Charles is made to say:

> Some may interpret it as an effect of pusillanimity in any man for popular terrors to desert his public station. But I think it a hardiness beyond true valor for a wise man to set himself against the breaking in of a sea, which to resist, at present, threatens imminent danger, but to withdraw, gives it space to spend its fury and gains a fitter time to repair the breach.[40]

As in *Salmacida Spolia*, opposition to royal authority is conceived as analogous to a violent meteorological event, overwhelmingly destructive for a time but ultimately transient, provided the king behaves with prudence and moderation.

What both works reveal about the king's mind is Charles's conviction that resistance to his authority derived from the success of demagogues in stirring up intrinsically violent and unstable passions that must in time exhaust themselves. Since passion and ambition are inherent in human life, rebellions must be accepted as part of the natural order. Yet precisely because rebellions stem from selfish and irrational motivations, which tend to destroy any basis for social unity, they cannot last. When faced with the calamities of civil disorder, most people will begin to covet discipline and harmony and so will revert to their allegiance. Those who do not are driven by such a factious spirit that they must inevitably fall out among themselves, thus destroying their power. Time is therefore always on the king's side.

Behind this attitude lay a complex heritage of ideas. On the one hand, the analogy between rebellion and such natural events as storms, floods, and diseases rested upon a philosophical belief that political processes are governed by natural laws fundamentally similar to those which control the physical and biological worlds.[41] Since the state, the human body, and the cosmos are all God's creations, we should expect them to exhibit similar characteristics. Just as God himself must restrain violent natural forces to preserve the order of the cosmos, so the king—as God's counterpart in the state—must protect society from the confusion engendered by human vices. On this level, Stuart political thought did stem from a synthesis of Platonic philosophy and divine-right theology.

The imagery of *Salmacida Spolia* and *Eikon Basilike* also has affinities with the kind of analytical history we encountered earlier in our discussion of Jones's philosophical outlook.[42] Discord's speech effectively summarizes the orthodox Polybian view of the forces that cause flourishing commonwealths to succumb to disunity, namely factionalism, irresponsibility on the part of the rich, envy, and demagoguery. Charles is portrayed as a kind of physician to the commonwealth who perceives the reasons for its diseased state and therefore knows how to produce a cure—in short, as a Polybian statesman who can rule effectively because he understands the "causes of all things that happen" in politics.[43]

We thus confront a synthesis of two patterns of thought which modern scholars have normally regarded as philosophical and ideological opposites. One treats government as a reflection of timeless metaphysical principles which underlie a static, hierarchical structure of authority; the other conceives of politics as a historical process through which men seek to erect stable societies and master their common destinies. Scholars have normally linked the first attitude to a traditional social and cultural order which the Stuarts allegedly sought to preserve. The second is generally associated with the Crown's more advanced opponents. The political "revolution" of the 1640s and 1650s is thereby linked to a parallel intellectual revolution, ushering in the emergence of a more modern, progressive, and scientific outlook.[44]

In fact, what we find in the period is not so much two different species of political thought, each linked to a particular ideological position, as a subtle interplay between empirical and theoretical approaches. Sir Francis Bacon, for example, is often seen as a precursor of the modern empirical approach to politics. In this sphere, as in the natural sciences, it has been claimed, he repudiated the traditional view of nature as a reflection of divine principles of order and treated it instead as "raw matter which, through scientific analysis and control, could be transformed into objects of human need."[45] He was therefore able to envisage a more scientific approach to politics, rooted in an empirical and analytical view of social behavior. Yet Bacon's pronouncements about politics often betray his indebtedness to older patterns of thought very similar to those underlying *Salmacida Spolia* and *Eikon Basilike*:

> Men are full of savage and unreclaimed desires, of profit, of lust, of revenge, which as long as they give ear to precepts [of morality], to laws, to religion sweetly touched with eloquence. . . so long is society and peace maintained; but if these instruments be silent, or sedition and tumult make them not audible, all things dissolve into anarchy and confusion.[46]

This passage does evoke Bacon's efforts to analyze and control the "raw matter" of political life, but one can also imagine it being dramatized on a masque stage, with Religion, Eloquence, and the Law descending from the heavens to subdue Tumult and Sedition. On a deeper level Bacon's words are reminiscent of the Augustinian concept of the state as a bulwark erected against human depravity, and the Platonic habit of seeing the world in terms of a perennial conflict between reason and passion, order and chaos. Traditional concepts of political order have provided a framework within which a more dynamic, empirical analysis could develop.

No other Englishman of the period rivaled Bacon as a political theorist, but several thought about politics in broadly similar ways. Many of the so-called analytic histories of the period were case studies of rebellions, designed to lay bare the basic causes of political instability and to delineate strategies by which rulers might restore order. These works typically showed less concern with constitutional rights than with considerations of political prudence. Leaving aside questions concerning the ultimate nature of authority, they examined how such things as the ambitions of great politicians, the discontent of the common people, and the miscalculations of a ruler might lead to disorder. They did not usually treat political upheavals as contests between rival principles or systems of government. Instead they habitually portrayed laws and institutions threatened by forces tending toward "a dissolution of the frame of government," an absence of any system. Popular rebelliousness and royal despotism were seen as closely related phenomena, since both led to the destruction of orderly procedures by uncontrolled powers. Both therefore tended to destroy the delicate structure of rights, obligations, and marks of distinction which transform an inchoate human mass into a functioning society.[47] Historical clashes between kings and Parliaments were often subsumed within this larger framework and treated as symptoms of a temporary imbalance within the body politic, rather than as a conflict between rival institutions contending for supremacy.

A good example, with marked affinities to the last Stuart masque, is the little treatise on the reign of Henry III published in 1627 by Sir Robert Cotton.[48] Although ostensibly writing about the thirteenth century, Cotton obviously wished to illuminate his own age. In his view, the rebellions against Henry stemmed from causes that must have seemed peculiarly familiar to a Stuart courtier sympathetic to the cause of peace. At the beginning of his reign, England enjoyed a profound tranquillity:

> Few and no others were the distempers then in the State, but such as are incident to all [states], the Commons greedy of liberty, and the Nobility or Rule, and but one violent storm raised by some . . . men . . . misliking those days of sloth, for so they termed Henry's government.[49]

These malcontents began "to show upon the people's discontent . . . to endear and glorify themselves with the senseless multitude, by depraving the King's discretion and government," until the whole realm grew discontented. Henry summoned a Parliament, only to find that the two houses, "that before were ever a medicine to heal up any rupture in the Prince's fortunes, are now grown worse than the malady, since from thence more malignant humours began to reign . . . than well composed tempers." Armed rebellion soon erupted, forcing the king to make war on his subjects. As in *Salmacida Spolia*, however, disorder is ultimately subdued by royal victory over the rebellion and the king's subsequent acts of mercy and magnanimity, by which he quiets the spirit of envy and turbulence that had previously plagued his reign.

There is no reason to suppose that Jones ever read Cotton's book. Nevertheless, he and Cotton portrayed political instability in very similar ways. Both assumed that dissension and opposition to royal authority were normal, especially in times of peace and prosperity. Both feared the plots of demagogues. Each compared the growth of rebellion to the spreading of evil "humors" within a human body, and each prescribed similar cures for this disease of the body politic. *Salmacida Spolia* and *The Reign of Henry III* reflect a common pattern of ideas that is also evident in *Eikon Basilike* and in some of Bacon's political observations.

If we want to understand the ideas underlying Charles's decision to rule without Parliament, this background is far more important than the doctrines of Renaissance Platonism. In the late 1620s the king saw himself as the divinely appointed guardian of order, confronting dangerous sources of discord. He no doubt agreed with Laud's analysis, in a sermon of 1627, which anticipates almost exactly the imagery of the last masque: "When a people have surfeited long on peace and plenty it is hard to please them . . . and every little thing is a burden to them. . . . And in such times malcontents are stirring."[50] Parliament's behavior greatly reinforced these fears. Charles knew full well that the precedents for the attempted impeachment of Buckingham in 1626 were taken primarily from the reigns of kings who were ultimately deposed and murdered. He felt keenly the reversals suffered by his own and the kingdom's honor after the Parliament of 1626 had refused to grant sufficient revenues. He was aware of the parlous state of royal finances and the threat to civic order posed by unpaid and mutinous troops. He recognized that his ministers were being blamed for acts he himself had ordered, that the assaults on "Arminian" clergy were really attacks on his own policies, and that parliamentary complaints of misgovernment were undermining his moral authority. Given the framework of assumptions within which Charles thought about politics, it was not unreasonable to see all this as evidence of a conspiratorial attack on the Crown. The Commons' 1629 assault on his collection of tonnage and poundage—a tax he could not afford to do without—finally convinced him once and for all that the lower house had fallen under the control of "malevolent and ill affected persons," who attempted "to raise such false and scandalous rumors that they might disturb the government, . . . interrupt the course of traffic and trade; discourage . . . merchants, and raise jealousies and suspicions in the hearts of . . . [the] people."[51] In Charles's view the parliamentary leadership was not simply attacking Crown policies; it was undermining government itself. The drastic expedient of prerogative rule was conceived as a defensive measure intended to preserve authority against almost unprecedented attacks.[52]

It remains true that many of Charles's difficulties in the late 1620s stemmed from his own political blunders, his unwillingness to compromise, and his inability to understand the motivations and concerns of men who thought differently from himself. Certain traits in the royal character—in particular, the king's inexperience and political naiveté, his rigid and brittle sense of righteousness, and his willingness to deceive those whom he regarded as invading his prerogatives—contributed materially to his inability to work with Parliament. The point remains, however, that when viewed in terms of seventeenth-century political assumptions Charles's actions appear far less irrational and unjustifiable than when judged by modern standards.

THE CONSTITUTION OF SOCIETY AND CONCEPTS OF HISTORY

If this assessment is correct, we need to ask what light the remaining masques and other works produced earlier in the 1630s, before the personal rule began to collapse, may shed on the basic strategy being pursued by the Crown. Obviously the regime sought to promote obedience and political stability within a framework of prerogative government, but what sort of conditions did it regard as favoring these objectives? And how did it regard the role of cultural reforms in creating a climate more conducive to personal monarchy?

From what has been said so far, we might expect the government to have wanted to impose the court's sophisticated culture upon the entire kingdom as an instrument of political control. Yet this was far from the case. Charles and his entourage shared many of the prejudices of the age against the sophistication of London and Whitehall. Even more than in the previous reign, Caroline court literature created a veritable cult of rustic simplicity. The speech of a "simple husbandman" to the king, which Carew wrote for a royal progress, provides a typical illustration:

> We shall want nothing but good fare,
> To shew you welcome and our care;
> Such rarities as come from far
> From poor men's houses banished are
> Yet we'll have what the season yields
> Out of the neighboring woods and fields
> . . . .
> And having supped we may perchance
> Present you with a country dance.[53]

This cult cannot be taken literally: it did not accurately reflect rural life, and it never led courtiers to abandon London permanently. There can be no doubt, however, about the depth of Charles's conviction that the gentry belonged at their rural seats—dispensing hospitality, upholding order in the provinces, and perpetuating traditional, paternalistic values—rather than in the capital, squandering money and gossiping about politics. Far more energetically than his father, Charles drove the landed elite out of London by issuing proclamations threatening to imprison any gentleman caught there without a good excuse, which he enforced through the Star Chamber. His actions reflect a deeply conservative determination to protect the provinces from contamination by corrupt urban and courtly influences.[54]

On the other hand, the court obviously did not regard all rural traditions as virtuous and all innovation as undesirable; otherwise it would never have patronized its cosmopolitan culture. It wished to strike a proper balance between the refinement of the capital and the rudeness of the country, to encourage advances in the arts without engendering corruption. It conceptualized this balance through a set of myths concerning the remote origins and gradual development of civilization.

The most important of these was the concept of a primitive Golden Age of teeming abundance and civic peace, which figures almost as prominently in Stuart cultural propaganda as in that of Elizabeth's reign.[55] Especially under James I, allusions to this paradise were often explicit, as in the masque *The Golden Age Restored*, in which Astrea descended to the English court to herald the return of her reign. By the 1630s, however, the allusions had usually become more subtle. For example, when in the masque *Chlorida* the monarchs warmed a January night by bringing back the mild wind Zephyrus and ushering in the spring, most courtiers must have recognized that Zephyrus was the wind of the Golden Age and that spring was its season. In place of a specific reference, Jones had created a tissue of oblique allusions to a familiar theme.

Becoming fully attuned to this imagery requires an awareness of the complex nuances acquired by Golden Age mythology during its long history. In the Middle Ages the primitive pagan paradise was often associated with the Garden of Eden, and its return under a just ruler was treated as a reversal of the Fall.[56] Some writers also argued that men only slowly lost Adam's original knowledge of God's laws, so that remote antiquity preserved philosophical insights unknown to later ages. Bacon studied ancient myths as symbolic metaphors, embodying scientific principles familiar to remote antiquity but already forgotten in the time of Plato and Aristotle. In one of his greatest poems, Henry Vaughan wrote of the pristine religious knowledge of the world's youth:

> Sure it was so, Man in those early days
>   Was not all stone and earth;
> He shined a little, and by those weak rays
>   Had some glimpse of his birth.
> He saw heaven o'er his head, and knew from whence
>   He came, condemned hither;
> And as first love draws strongest, so from hence,
>   His mind sure progressed tither.[57]

The Golden Age—and by extension other primitive and rude societies—might therefore symbolize a lost state of innocence.[58]

The seventeenth-century countryside came to share in this atmosphere. "I thought when I first went into the country," wrote Abraham Cowley about his departure from Charles's court, "that without doubt I should have met there with the simplicity of the old poetical golden age."[59] Several country-house poems evoke the Golden Age myth. Thus the hospitality of Saxham reminded Carew of the teeming abundance of the world's first age:

> The season [winter] hardly did afford
> Coarse cates unto thy neighbor's board
> Yet thou hadst dainties as the sky
> Had only been thy volarie;
> Or else the birds, fearing the snow
> Might to another deluge grow:
> The Pheasant, Partridge and the Lark,
> Flew to thy house, as to the Arke
> The willing Ox, of himself came
> Home to slaughter with the Lamb,
> And every beast did hither bring
> Himself to be an offering.[60]

The country house becomes an enclave preserving the lost happiness of man's beginnings amid the fallen, wintery environment in which he now lives.

Rustic and primitive motifs in Caroline court culture did not always refer to the Golden Age, however. The primitive world was often treated as a place of incessant conflict and unrelieved barbarism, rather than of virtue and innocence.[61] In the masque *Coelum Britannicum* an anti-masque of Picts performing a martial dance enters to these lines:

> Behold the rude And old abiders here and in them view
> The point from which your [the monarchs'] full perfections grew
> You naked, wild inhabitants,
> That breathed this air and pressed this flowery Earth
> Come forth from those shades where dwells eternal night
> And see what wonders Time hath brought to light.[62]

These Picts, in turn, seem closely related to the Druids described in Jones's (or Webb's) book on Stonehenge. Life among them was "uncivil . . . full of wars and consequently void of all literature." All buildings resembled those Vitruvius ascribed to the first ages:

> Men lived in woods, caves and forests, but after they had found out the use of fire, and by benefit thereof were invited to enter a certain kind of soci-

ety . . . Some of them began to make for themselves habitations of boughs, some to dig dens in mountains; others, imitating the nests of birds, made themselves houses of loam and twigs . . . to creep into, and shroud themselves in.[63]

In these passages primitive conditions serve as a foil for the brilliant civilizations of Rome and Caroline England. Just what did Jones have in mind in employing this comparison?

The passage from Vitruvius provides a clue. Jones took it from a discussion of the ways in which men rose from their original state, in which they lived like animals, to an appreciation for the benefits of civilized life.[64] Vitruvius claimed that the art of building began in the first human assemblies and grew to perfection as men vied with one another to erect more commodious and beautiful structures. In doing so they enlarged their intellectual abilities while developing manual skills and habits of industry, and so "advanced from the construction of buildings to other arts and sciences."[65] In short, architecture was the mother of civilization, the original science from which all others have developed. Jones would surely have sympathized with this account. He did not discuss man's slow rise from savagery in *Stonehenge Restored* because he believed the Romans dragged the British straight from savagery to high civilization. Yet by quoting a suggestive passage from Tacitus, he did imply that architecture helped tame the Druids:

> Whereas the Britons were rude and dispersed, and thereby prone on all occasions to war; Agricola [their Roman governor], to induce them by pleasure to quietness and rest, exhorted them in private, and helped them in common to build Temples, Houses and places of public resort, commending those that were forward therein and punishing the refractory.[66]

The scene in *Coelum Britannicum* following the dance of the Picts provides further evidence that Jones had such ideas in mind. It consisted of:

> a huge mountain that covered all the scene; the under part wild and craggy and above somewhat more pleasant and flourishing; about the middle part of this mountain were seated the three kingdoms [England, Scotland, and Ireland]. . . . At a distance above these sat a young man in a white embroidered robe . . . holding in his hand a cornucopia . . . representing the genius of the three kingdoms.[67]

This is an emblematic representation of several millennia of British history, from the savagery of the ancient Picts, through the emergence of the three medieval kingdoms and the introduction of agriculture, to the prosperity and unity of the Stuart period. Jones's image encapsulates a progression from disorder to order in both technology and politics.[68]

The remainder of the masque reinforced this message. The masquers, led by Charles himself and attired as ancient British heroes, danced before the mountain to songs about the virtues of royal love. Then the scene changed again, into a garden with a princely villa—an emblem for the cultural achievements of Jones's own age—as the heroes surrendered their arms to Henrietta Maria, whose love had tamed them:

> Yet on the Conquerors neck you tread,
>   And the fierce Victor proves your prey
> What heart is then secure from you
> That can, though vanquished, yet subdue?[69]

Next came the revels, and finally, after the court had danced away the night, a closing display of Jones's ingenuity. Two great, luminous clouds descended from the masque heavens, bearing Religion, Truth, Wisdom, Concord, Government, and Reputation—the attributes of Charles's rule. Then Eternity descended into the Banqueting House to proclaim the gods' intention of converting the king and his attendants into a ring of stars, forever symbolizing the virtues of a perfect reign:

> With wreaths of Stars circled about,
> Guild all the spacious Firmament
> And smiling on the panting Rout
> That labor in the steep ascent,
> With your resistless influence guide
> Of human change th' incertain tide.[70]

Coelum Britannicum defines a vision of history as a gradual ascent from savagery propelled by humanity's quest for a more orderly and rational life. Fruitful fields, princely villas, and harmonious dances are all products of this passion for order, manifested in different social activities. But the pinnacle of British history is the halcyon reign itself: an age of peace and prosperity, in which the arts and sciences flourish under the protection of monarchs who rule by love. These concepts bring up close to the idea we encountered in discussing the aesthetic culture of the court, that the task of a statesman is to construct a harmonious society from the refractory materials of human nature. The masque designs extend this concept into an overarching interpretation of the whole development of British civilization.[71]

Jones's discussion of Stonehenge provides further evidence that he actually did see history in this way. To him the monument stood for a set of myths which look very much like symbols for the ideas we have been encountering. Jones reconstructed what he took to be the original appearance of Stonehenge through the use of a Vitruvian groundplot, originally that of a theater, although he does not tell us so. Instead he presents it as the plan of an ancient temple whose chief traits are its round design and the fact that it is open to the air.[72] He asserts that the Romans associated these features with the god Coelus. As Stephen Orgel has shown, Coelus was the oldest of the pagan gods and therefore a counterpart to the Judeo-Christian Creator.[73] But Jones also equated him with Uranus, the Platonic god of mathematics and hence of harmonic proportions. In addition, Coelus is the deity of heaven, invented because "men . . . by nature soon wanting and by instinct seeking some God . . . deified the best to sense" and worshiped the sky.[74] Vitruvius wrote that men first discovered their capacity for reason by "gazing upon the splendor of the starry firmament."[75] Jones perhaps had this passage in mind: Coelus represents the origins of man's quest for Truth, which lies behind all the civilizing arts.

Finally, and most important, Coelus is also a deified royal hero:

> By historians . . . it's thus delivered . . . he which first reigned over the Atlantides was Coelus, and that he invited men living dispersedly before throughout the fields to convene, and dwell in companies together, exhorting them to build towns, and reducing them from wild and savage [conditions] to the conversation of civil life: Taught them also to sow corn and seeds, and diverse other things belonging to the common use of mankind. . . . The year (before confused) bringing into Order, according to the course of the Sun . . . Whereby many . . . amazed at his future prediction, did verily believe he participated of Divine Nature, and therefore . . . they conferred on him immortal honors and adored him as a God.[76]

It cannot be mere coincidence that Jones entitled the masque of 1634 *Coelum Britannicum*. That entertainment centered around one of the central themes of Caroline political thought: the belief that great, civilizing kings and the governments they create ultimately lie behind all historical progress.

Tragically this progress can too easily plant the seeds of its own destruction, for the more they develop, the more art and reason are subject to corruption. Several masques present caricatures of ancient philosophies portrayed as distortions of Reason. In discussing Stonehenge, Jones refers on several occasions to intellectual and moral decadence. After the Romans had civilized them, the British "proceeded to provocations of vices, to sumptuous galleries, baths and exquisite banquetings," thereby corrupting the gifts bestowed by their conquerors. And the civilization of Rome itself eventually

> began sensibly to wane, and the ambition of the great Captains . . . (some few excepted) tended rather to make parties for obtaining the Purple Robe, than (after the manner of their ancestors) to eternize their names by great and admirable works, or patronizing good Arts, for want whereof they [the Arts] began likewise to decay apace.[77]

The ethical thought of the Stuart court revolved around a sense of opposition between reason and virtue on the one hand and vice, passion, and disorder on the other. The masques apply the same dichotomy to history. Like men, societies may progress through science and discipline, or they may fall into the chaos generated by demagoguery, luxury, and selfishness.

Not only is the reborn Golden Age, when viewed from this perspective, compatible with high civilization, but in a peculiar way civilization is the return of a primordial Paradise, conceived as a state in which man has mastered himself and his environment. If we look again at Carew's poem on Saxham, for example, we may notice that it really praises the agronomy of the place: its domesticated animals, hawking parks, fish ponds, and so forth. The rural estate becomes a man-made paradise which recreates the ease and abundance of a lost, divinely created paradise. In Stuart literature, much the same idea is often conveyed through the image of a garden. "God almighty first planted a Garden," wrote Bacon, "and indeed it is the purest of human pleasures . . . and a man shall ever see that when ages grow to civility and elegance, men come to build stately sooner than to garden finely, as if gardening were the greater perfection."[78] Left implicit is the thought that fine gardening brings us back, full circle, to Eden.

In Marvell's "Upon Appleton House" this symbolism is even clearer. The arrangement of the estate's flowerbeds reflects the military skill of Appleton's owner, Sir Thomas Fairfax, commander of the New Model Army:

> See how the flowers, as at parade
> Under their colors stand displayed;

Each regiment in order grows,
That of the tulip, pink and rose.[79]

The garden becomes an emblem for the social and political discipline
an army represents. Yet the orderly arrangement of the estate also preserves remnants of a primeval paradise lost through original sin:

'Tis not, what once it was, the world,
But a rude heap together hurled;
All negligently overthrown,
Your [Appleton's] lesser world contains the same
But in more decent order tame;
You Heaven's center, Nature's lap,
And Paradise's only map.[80]

Finally, in lines quoted in the beginning of this chapter, the lost paradise is associated with the shattered peace of Charles's halcyon reign.
Marvell included in his poem allusions to all the elements in the symbolic equation we have been deciphering.

CAROLINE PRIMITIVISM

This preoccupation with the primitive roots of civilization found expression not only in symbolic imagery but also in some important
stylistic tendencies. A number of years ago Sir John Summerson noticed that Inigo Jones, alone among the great architects of the period,
was fascinated by the Tuscan order, the most primitive in the classical
repertory. Covent Garden, the most elegant residential neighborhood
in Caroline London, was an essay in the Tuscan mode, which had previously been considered suitable only for barns and stables. Summerson
conjectured that this fact might reflect Jones' Protestant respect for
"primitive" Christianity. But there is no good reason to think that Jones
associated early Christians with primitive societies; after all, Christ was
born in the reign of Augustus.

It seems much more likely that Jones's predilection for Tuscan architecture stemmed from the ideas we have just traced. Not only are the
Covent Garden designs archaic in flavor, they also suggest, by their
massive appearance, the effort and ingenuity required to construct
buildings. This is especially true of the front of the piazza's church with
its dramatically projecting portico resting on large cantilevers and
squat, widely spaced columns. The effect is of a great sheltering porch

supported by pillars and beams whose structural purpose is obvious. Summerson described this facade as a "raw, primitive presentation of the tuscan" and suggested that Jones "envisaged it, perhaps, as . . . closest to natural ideas of construction."[81] This seems to be exactly the point: to view the church with any sensitivity is to perceive the functional requirements from which the elements of classical architecture derive.

The same interpretation applies even more forcefully to certain features of the St. Paul's designs, notably an architrave employing sculpted leaves and animal masks to mimic triglyphs. Summerson writes:

> We have here . . . an attempt by Jones to create out of animal and vegetable motives a kind of proto-Doric, or, if you prefer, a quasi Tuscan, something appropriate to the massive astyler character of his walls—appropriate also, perhaps, to the generally archaic, primitive character of the Norman nave he was enveloping. Such a deliberate quest for the primitive brings us very close to the mood of Covent garden.[82]

It brings us even closer to Vitruvius's account of how men first imitated caves and birds' nests by using logs and branches to construct habitations and so began to master the art of building. The same preoccupation is present in some of Jones's stage sets. Orgel has noticed that a palace in the Jacobean masque *Oberon* rises from a foundation of unhewn rock, through a middle story in the Gothic style, to a Palladian dome.[83] It recapitulates the history of architecture and thus by extension the rise of the civilizing arts.

Many of the most characteristic and appealing features of Jones's buildings appear to have stemmed from his concern to display the "natural" principles underlying architectural forms. For example, he reacted against the fanciful ornamentation of mannerist buildings, criticizing broken pediments because they divorced ornamentation from function. On the other hand, features which emphasize the solidity of a building or bring out its harmonic structure appear throughout his mature work. Thus he liked rusticated masonry, which accentuates the fact that walls are built out of large blocks of stone, and superimposed rows of columns, which articulate the division of a facade into different stories, whose proportions Jones always worked out according to an overall mathematical scheme. The primitivism of Covent Garden is but a radical expression of a stylistic tendency found in more subtle forms throughout his work.

The fascination of court poets with the simple country life is to be understood in similar terms. The countryside stands for a world purged of luxury and court vices, but not of reason and elegance. In retreating to it, courtiers were supposed to take with them their philosophical insight into the order of nature, their verse, and their taste for wine and good food. Similarly the characters in court pastorals always know how to write poetry and philosophize about love. The basic dichotomy underlying these poems is not that of civilization with noble savagery, but that of nature ordered with nature disordered and corrupted.

MYTHOLOGY AND POLITICS

The mythology we have been examining conveyed a view of political life differing in important ways from that advanced by parliamentary propagandists in the 1640s. Pym and his followers stood for the conviction that the laws and liberties of the kingdom derived from immemorial tradition at least as old and as fundamental as the monarchy.[84] They saw Parliament as a Saxon institution, and the common law as the embodiment of a primitive folk wisdom, passed on through juries of English freemen and the judges who codified their pronouncements. A king who violated the law and dispensed with Parliament therefore threatened to dissolve the very foundations of society.

The masques, on the other hand, reflect the Stuart assumption that the political order is the *product* of the king's power. In the beginnings of time, Englishmen did not live under a free constitution. They roamed wild through the forests, preying on each other, until heroic rulers brought them together and taught them the benefits of civilization. Even in historic times the savagery Caesar encountered in Britain and the endemic warfare of the Middle Ages revealed the inability of Britons to live at peace, except under strong kings. May's epics convey this message clearly by dwelling upon the ravages of baronial rebellion and the healing power of the royal prerogative.

> . . . Henry 'stablished in the regal throne
> Jove-like surveys his large dominion,
> To see what parts of state might be decayed,
> What rents so long a civil war had made.
> With physic fit he purges from the State
> Those humors, that did stir and swell so late,
> Digests the reliques, and by Princely arts,
> And policy, corroborates [sic] the parts.[85]

At least a few of Charles's privy councillors regarded the whole tradition of parliamentary government as an unfortunate legacy of medieval disorder. "The Great Charter had an obscure birth from usurpation and was fostered and shown to the world by rebellion," Laud wrote in a private manuscript.[86] Windebanke annotated an unpublished history of Parliament, apparently now lost, with revealing comments:

> Henry I his summons to Parliament it seems was indefinite . . . by making his people swear and do fealty to him, who was a king *de facto* and no *de jure,* that thereby . . . the right heirs of his older brother might be defeated. This general assembly of the Commons [it] is to be wished had been auspicated with a juster and better Action, than the establishing of an usurper's issue.[87]

This was never the view of the entire court, but once they had struck root among the ruling group such attitudes made confrontation far more likely.

Therefore the masques do reflect ideological convictions which played a role in the upheavals of the 1640s. For two reasons, however, we need to beware of oversimplifying the significance of those convictions. First, neither the Crown nor the Commons leadership wanted to provoke confrontation over constitutional principles. Most contemporaries agreed with Thomas Wentworth that "he . . . [who] ravels forth into questions and arguments the right of a king and a people shall never be able to wrap them up again into the comeliness and order he found them."[88] At least in Charles's reign, debates over the limits of the prerogative invariably arose out of disputes over more concrete grievances, like the forced loan of 1627 or the various government measures dismantled by the Long Parliament in 1641. If these practical issues had proven capable of resolution contemporaries would gratefully have left the ultimate problem of the locus of sovereignty as an unresolved mystery of state.

Second, by continental standards Caroline absolutism always remained limited in scope. It did not seek to transform society through a centralized bureaucracy, but only to preserve and refine the existing structure of provincial self-government. Compared to previous English governments, Charles's regime was fairly energetic, making greater demands of county officials and interfering more frequently in their affairs.[89] But compared to the Habsburg autocracy in Castile or the structure Richelieu was constructing in France, these efforts appear modest. Even Ship Money and the government's other extraparliamentary taxes never came close to tapping the nation's full resources, as the much higher exactions of the Civil War and the Interregnum made clear.[90]

The financial and administrative weaknesses of the Crown help account for the relatively limited nature of the government's conduct. Charles did not have the money or the military and bureaucratic resources to impose an efficient dictatorship at the local level. Even without these constraints, however, it seems unlikely that the regime would have systematically remodeled the institutions of local government. For all the visionary qualities of some of the masques, the court always had relatively conservative aims: to protect the realm from external threats, to create a climate of order and stability, to preserve a hierarchical and paternalistic society.[91]

Why then had such resentment of the Crown's policies accumulated by 1640, even among non-puritans? Part of the answer lies in the ingrained provincial conservatism of many gentlemen, who would have resented any moderately energetic government. In addition, however, Charles undoubtedly undercut the legitimacy of his own commands by ruling without Parliament. The personal rule is often portrayed as a temporary triumph for an absolutist dynasty, as in some ways it was. But it is important to remember that it grew out of Charles's failure to enlist parliamentary support. Cooperative Parliaments might have proven invaluable, by clearing the debts of the 1620s, helping the Crown devise and implement its paternalistic social policies, and perhaps legislating long-needed changes in government finances. Without such assistance it became more difficult both to raise money and to enlist energetic cooperation by local magistrates. This, in turn, placed an even larger burden on the Privy Council and the understaffed agencies of the central government, which they proved unable to sustain over the long haul.[92] Whether or not the whole experiment was ultimately bound to collapse, as some historians have claimed, it certainly strained the antiquated machinery of royal government.[93] When a new crisis arose in Scotland in the late 1630s, the whole apparatus of prerogative government collapsed, leaving Charles without a viable political strategy.

The crucial problem is therefore to explain why a working partnership between the Crown and the political nation which Parliament represented proved impossible to sustain. That question must be answered primarily through an analysis of political events beyond the scope of the present study. In several respects, however, a knowledge of the court's cultural history does help to explain why the reign ended in disaster. To begin with, the innovative and cosmopolitan ambience of Whitehall undoubtedly broadened the mental distance between Charles and the vast majority of his subjects. Cultural differences were not insurmountable obstacles to political understanding. Under a more open and flexible monarch they might have made little difference, but Charles I always had difficulty appreciating the outlook of people whose values and interests differed from his own. His cultural outlook compounded the problem created by his shyness, his dislike of public appearances, his self-righteousness and rigidity, and his instinctive suspicion of those who disagreed with him. In religious affairs, especially, cultural developments reinforced fundamental disagreements over theology and liturgical practices, contributing to the most explosive issues of the 1640s.

In addition, however, relations between Charles and parliamentary groups were sometimes complicated by certain cultural assumptions shared by each. The leaders of both the court and Parliament placed a high value on harmony, consensus, and the preservation of a traditional sociopolitical order. Yet both saw these ideals as extraordinarily difficult to maintain in a fallen world where chaos, oppression, and violence were a normal state of affairs. Men of true virtue (or godliness) were always assumed to be a small minority, striving to defend the laws of God and man against the turbulent irrationality of the multitude and the deliberate evil of scheming politicians. These attitudes fostered a view of politics as an arena in which violent passions and selfish interests waged a perpetual struggle, to the detriment of the public interest.

This preconception often led individuals on both sides of any serious issue to place the worst possible construction on the motives and designs of their opponents. In doing so they drew upon an almost inexhaustible stockpile of terrifying anecdotes and archetypal villains culled from the Bible and the histories of antiquity, the Middle Ages, and the modern world. The images of Sejanus, Catiline, and the evil councillors of Richard II and Henry VI; of Münster's Anabaptists and the mobs of the dying Roman Republic; and of the Gunpowder Plot and the St. Bartholomew's Day massacres all lay ready to hand. Even within the Privy Council, among colleagues who had worked together for years, relatively small disagreements sometimes triggered violent accusations.[94] Small wonder that in confrontations between the Crown and Parliament mutual recriminations sometimes escalated until compromise became almost impossible.

The Commons' fear of papist conspirators at court and the court's fear of puritan demagogues plotting to overthrow the state sprang from much the same soil. Neither fear was entirely groundless. There were Catholic intrigues at Whitehall, and the Commons' leaders in the Long Parliament did wish to curb the prerogative in ways Charles regarded as seditious. Yet both fears were greatly exaggerated, and both helped sabotage the quest for a mutually acceptable settlement. In a sense each became a self-fulfilling prophecy. Charles's distrust of the parliamentary leadership helped propel him toward civil war in 1642 and interfered with negotiations after 1646 that might have saved the monarchy. Parliament's effort to rid the kingdom of Arminian and papist courtiers ultimately sent the royal family—minus its Anglican head—into exile in France, where Henrietta Maria and the Jesuit theologians attempted to convert Charles's heirs to Catholicism.

This is not to suggest that the Civil War stemmed simply from culturally induced delusions. Substantive issues, administrative problems, and personal animosities all helped precipitate the conflict. The point is simply that men argued about divisive issues and made the decisions that led to war within a framework of assumptions that inhibited calm discussion and moderate conduct. One historian has blamed the outbreak of civil war on "the imaginative poverty of the age."[95] I believe it is more accurate to speak of a dangerous imaginative fertility. The culture which produced the Roman tragedies of Jonson, the melodramas of Webster and Shirley, and the lush apocalyptic speculation of Brightman and Mede also colored the outlook of both Charles I and John Pym. That culture fostered both visionary hopes and deep fears, which made the explosive situation of the early 1640s even more dangerous than it might otherwise have been.

NOTES

1. Stephen Orgel and Roy Strong, *Inigo Jones: The Theater of the Stuart Court,* 2 vols. (London: Sotheby Parke Bernet; Berkeley and Los Angeles: University of California, vol. 2, p. 457.

2. Richard Fanshawe, "To His Highness . . . in the West . . . 1646," in *Shorter Poems and Translations,* ed. W. Bawcutt (Liverpool: University of Liverpool Press, 1964), p. 71. Although dating from the war years, these verses are based upon a tradition very much in evidence in the masques and court verse of the 1630s, which consistently stress the importance of the monarchs' love for each other and for the realm.

3. Andrew Marvell, "An Horatian Ode upon Cromwell's Return from Ireland," in *Poems and Letters,* ed. H. M. Margoliouth, 2d ed. (Oxford: Oxford University Press, 1952), vol. 1, p. 53.

4. Marvell, "Upon Appleton House to my Lord Fairfax," ibid., p. 72.

5. There were apparently several of these, produced both at Whitehall and at York House. All that remains are a few tantalizing references in contemporary letters and other documents.

6. Ruben's famous Banqueting House ceiling was also commissioned during his visit, though completed only in 1635. I do not discuss this work because it has been treated in several excellent studies, notably Per Palme, *The Triumph of Peace* (Stockholm: Almquist and Wiksell, 1956), pp. 258–267; Oliver Millar, "The Whitehall Ceiling," *Burlington Magazine* 98 (1956); Oliver Millar, *Rubens: The Whitehall Ceiling* (Oxford: Oxford University Press, 1958); D. J. Gordon, "Rubens and the Whitehall Ceiling," in *Renaissance Imagination*, ed. Stephen Orgel (Berkeley and Los Angeles: University of California Press, 1980), pp. 24–50; Julius Held, "Rubens Glynde Sketch and the Installation of the Whitehall Ceiling," *Burlington Magazine* 112 (1970): 274–81; and Roy Strong, *Britannia Triumphans: Inigo Jones, Rubens, and Whitehall Palace* (London: Thames and Hudson, 1980). The ceiling commemorates James's achievements. Its iconography is largely Jacobean in character, although it belongs chronologically to Charles's reign.

7. Peter Heylin, *The History of that Most Famous Saint and soldier . . . George of Cappodocia* (London, 1630), p. 202.

8. The unruly puritan appears among the anti-masques of *The Temple of Love.* Momus in *Coelum Britannicum* also suggests sending an anti-masque of disordered passions to New England, where the unruly humors of the kingdom have already gone. Such topical references are relatively sparse in the masques, but they do occur.

9. By far the best survey is Orgel and Strong, *Inigo Jones.* Roy Strong, *Splendour at Court* (Boston: Houghton Mifflin, 1973), chap. 6 is also useful. To avoid repeating these and other works on the masques, I have not provided a detailed descriptive summary here. See, however, my disagreement with some of Orgel's views (which Strong generally seems to share), below, pp. 254–58.

10. Above, pp. 132–33. He certainly appears to have supervised the iconography of the Banqueting House ceiling even after Rubens returned to Antwerp, since Rubens had to submit preliminary sketches for his approval. Charles may well have helped plan the ceiling paintings from beginning to end.

11. For a discussion, see R. M. Smuts, "Henrietta Maria," *English Historical Review* 93, (1978), pp. 26–45.

12. Knowler, vol. 2, p. 478.

13. Martin Butler, *Theatre and Crisis, 1632–1642* (Cambridge: Cambridge University Press, 1984), p. 33.

14. SP, 16/68/24.

15. Fanshawe, *Shorter Poems*, p. 69.

16. See Frederick Dietz, *English Public Finances*, 2d ed. (New York: Barnes and Noble, 1964), chap. 10 for a discussion.

17. CSPVen, vol. 22, p. 359.

18. A few years later another Venetian envoy commented: "Both the Spaniards and the Dutch abuse to excess his Majesty's patience, and the former with words and the latter with deeds condemn this crown more than is seemly." Reports arrived even from far off Switzerland of the disrespect accorded "any proposals from that pompous and ease loving court of England" (ibid., p. 176, and vol. 23, pp. 245 and 35).

19. *The Dramatic Works of Sir William Davenant*, vol. 2 (Edinburgh and London, 1872), pp. 14, 15. An audience of the 1630s might have taken these lines as an ironic comment on the exploits of volunteers for service in Germany, where atrocities occurred almost daily and about a third of the population eventually died as a result of war. The

political meaning would have been especially clear because the public theaters showed plays in the 1630s glorifying the exploits of the Protestant armies of Sweden and her allies. See Margot Heinemann, *Puritanism and Theater* (Cambridge: Cambridge University Press, 1980), p. 120.

20. Ben Jonson, *The King and Queen's Entertainment at Richmond* (Oxford, 1636), pp. 20, 21.

21. Orgel and Strong, *Inigo Jones*, vol. 2, p. 665.

22. Thomas May, *The Reign of Henry II* (1633) and *The Victorious Reign of Edward III* (1635). The decline of the epic under both the early Stuarts was also due to a change of literary fashion after the age of Spenser, whose achievement may have deterred imitators. It nevertheless seems likely that a more successful royal military policy would have inspired attempts to revive the genre. For an interesting discussion, though one that does not pay much attention to the possible influence of politics upon literary trends, see Richard Helgerson, *Self-Crowned Laureates* (Berkeley and Los Angeles: University of California Press, 1984), pp. 104–105. Butler, *Theatre and Crisis*, is more aware of the complex political background to literature but is so preoccupied with demonstrating that court dramatists sometimes criticized Charles's policies that it largely ignores their more frequent attempts to justify and glorify his actions. It is important to realize that court poets were not obsequious flatterers of the monarch, but there is a danger in overemphasizing their disagreements with the regime and ignoring the fact that the main purpose of masques and panegyrics was to praise. One also needs to guard against confusing criticism of specific policies and abuses (which in many circumstances the king might accept or even approve) with general opposition to prerogative rule.

23. Bartlett Giamatti, *The Earthly Paradise and the Renaissance Epic* (Princeton: Princeton University Press, 1966), chap. 5.

24. Davenant's *Unfortunate Lovers*, e.g., contains the following exchange between the hero and heroine (*Dramatic Works of Sir William Davenant*, vol. 3 [Edinburgh and London, 1873], p. 47):

—A rural residence
Near woods and meads, though it be humble, is
The place where we may love, and be secure.

—Then why did my Father and
Thyself, disquiet all the peaceful world
With hunting after fame? Loaden and crushed
In heavy armour for the chase, toiling
To get us this renown and eminence,
Which since hath ruin'd our content?

25. Thomas Carew, *Poems*, ed. Rhodes Dunlap (Oxford: Oxford University Press, 1949), p. 77. See Michael P. Parker, "Carew's Political Pastoral: Virgilian Pretexts in the 'Answer to Aurelian Townshend,'" in *John Donne Journal* 1 (1982), for an excellent discussion, which does oversimplify the internal politics of the court, however. It is possible to read this poem as an ironic criticism of the Caroline peace, but this does not seem to have been the poet's intention. Carew is certainly aware of the deeply ambiguous nature of the issues he is discussing, but to my ear his celebration of the Caroline peace sounds much more convincing than his double-edged praise of Gustavus Adolphus earlier in the poem. I wish to thank Kevin Sharpe for an interesting discussion on this point.

26. Orgel and Strong, *Inigo Jones*, vol. 2, p. 706.

27. Ibid., p. 733.

28. "Platonic Politics," in ibid., vol. 1, pp. 49–75; and Stephen Orgel, *The Illusion of Power* (Berkeley and Los Angeles: University of California Press, 1973).

29. Orgel and Strong, *Inigo Jones*, vol. 1, p. 51.

30. As several historians have noted. See esp. an important article by Derek Hirst,

"The Privy Council and the Problems of Enforcement in the 1620s," *Journal of British Studies* 18 (1978): 46–66.

31. In some counties the Crown's efforts to control the effects of famine in the early 1630s appear to have brought about a long-term improvement in the efficiency of local government. See esp. Thomas Barnes, *Somerset, 1625–1640* (Cambridge, Mass.: Harvard University Press, 1961); Clive Holmes, *Seventeenth-Century Lincolnshire* (Lincoln: History of Lincoln Committee for the Society for Lincolnshire History and Archaeology, 1980), chap. 8; and Paul Slack, "Books of Orders: The Making of English Social Policy, 1577–1631," *Transactions of the Royal Historical Society* 30 (1980): 1–22. It is possible that Barnes, especially, overestimated the effectiveness of the *Book of Orders*. Hunt, *Puritan Moment*, pp. 247–248, presents a different view, but even this analysis does not really support Orgel's contentions. The short-term success of ship money, forest fines, and knighthood compositions is well known.

32. This point is greatly reinforced by the recent essay of Kevin Sharpe, "The Personal Rule of Charles I," in *Before the Civil War*, ed. Malcolm Tomlinson (London: Macmillan, 1983), pp. 53–78.

33. The symbology of many Elizabethan court jousts is as artificial and abstract as that of the Stuart masques, yet no one has ever accused Elizabeth of practicing "Platonic politics." It is true, as Orgel and others have argued, that there is less evidence of moral tension in *most* Caroline masques than in many of Jonson's Jacobean court entertainments or in Milton's *Comus*, but to suggest that this represents a shift in political outlook is to erect a large argument on dubious foundations.

34. Above, pp. 165–71.

35. Orgel and Strong, *Inigo Jones*, vol. 2, p. 731.

36. Ibid.

37. Ibid., p. 734.

38. Ibid., p. 733. For the proscenium arch, see p. 730.

39. For a discussion of modern scholarship on the authorship of the treatise, see the introduction to the Folger edition of *Eikon Basilike* (Ithaca, N.Y.: Cornell University Press, 1966). The parallels between this work and *Salmacida Spolia* point to an underlying consistency in attitudes to political instability both before and after 1642.

40. Ibid., p. 17.

41. For discussions, see W. H. Greenleaf, *Order, Empiricism, and Politics* (Oxford: Oxford University Press for the University of Hull, 1964); and Corinne Weston and Janelle Greenberg, *Subjects and Sovereigns* (Cambridge: Cambridge University Press, 1981), chaps. 1 and 2. Greenleaf refers to this idea as a "theory of correspondences" between nature and society.

42. Above, pp. 169–70. Along with the edition of Polybius already cited, Jones owned a copy of Guicciardini's *Dell'epitome dell'historia d'Italia*, one of the two most important Renaissance attempts to imitate and extend the Polybian model of historical analysis (the other is Machiavelli's *Discourses*). For two modern discussions of Renaissance historiography dealing with the causes of political instability, see Pocock, *The Machiavellian Moment: Florentine Republican Thought and the Atlantic Tradition* (Princeton: Princeton University Press, 1975), parts 1 and 2; and Quentin Skinner, *The Foundations of Modern Political Thought* (Cambridge: Cambridge University Press, 1978), vol. 1, pp. 153 ff. Twentieth-century scholars often associate this sort of historical writing with republican traditions of "civic humanism." As Skinner points out, this is misleading. It is true that the most mature Renaissance historians, including Guicciardina and Machiavelli, were republicans, but their work was indebted to earlier writers who supported monarchical forms of government.

43. Above, p. 169.

44. See, e.g., Greenleaf, *Order*; Weston and Greenberg, *Subjects and Sovereigns*; Pocock, *The Machiavellian Moment*, esp. chap. 10; and Christopher Hill, *Intellectual Origins of the English Revolution* (Oxford: Oxford University Press, 1965). These books differ considerably in their arguments, but all attempt to forge a link between the emergence of more modern patterns of political thought, on the one hand, and Puritanism, republicanism, or parliamentary propaganda, on the other.

45. Robert Eccleshall, *Order and Reason in Politics* (Oxford: Oxford University Press for the University of Hull, 1978), p. 11. Eccleshall is more aware than most scholars of the complexity of the relationship between traditional and innovative patterns of thought in this period. However, he perpetuates the view that the only intellectual justification given for the policies of Charles I was the theology of divine right.

46. *The Works of Francis Bacon*, ed. James Spedding et al. (London, 1858–1874), vol. 3, p. 302.

47. Cf. Bacon's comment (ibid., vol. 6, p. 703): "It sometimes happens that the king, depraved by the long habit of ruling, turns tyrant and takes all into his own hands; and . . . administers the government by his own arbitrary and absolute authority. Whereat the people aggrieved endeavour on their part to set up some head of their own. This generally begins with the secret solicitation of nobles and great persons, whose connivancy being obtained, an attempt is then made to stir the people. . . . And this condition of affairs is fostered and nourished by the innate depravity and malignant disposition of the common people . . . till the disaffection spreading and gathering strength breaks out at last into open rebellion." Here democracy and despotism are regarded as mutually reinforcing. A belief in the importance of preserving traditional forms and customs was not incompatible with absolutist political thought. From an absolutist's perspective, laws and institutions are at once the product of royal power (since kings were supposed to have created them) and essential tools of government. Royal power was seen as an ordering force within society, shaping and sustaining hierarchical relations between individuals, which in turn strengthen the king's authority. Thus Bodin compared royal power to the keel of a ship, which holds the timbers in place. A king who arbitrarily dispenses with laws, unless in exceptional circumstances, therefore weakens his own power, for the fact that subjects have no right to rebel does not mean that they will not do so if the state becomes oppressive or disordered. See Nannerl Keohane, *Philosophy and the State in France* (Princeton: Princeton University Press, 1980), esp. chap. 2, for a perceptive discussion. The findings of the present work suggest that English thought had much closer affinities with the theories Keohane discusses than is generally recognized.

48. Sir Robert Cotton, *The Reign of Henry III* (London, 1627). For a discussion of the circumstances surrounding the writing and publication of this tract, see Kevin Sharpe, *Sir Robert Cotton* (Oxford: Oxford University Press, 1979), esp. pp. 239, 240. Sharpe's analysis differs from mine in its emphasis, although our two accounts of this work are entirely compatible.

49. Cotton, *Henry III*, p. 104.

50. William Laud, *Works*, ed. William Scott and J. Bliss (Oxford, 1847–1860), vol. 1, p. 45. The peace to which Laud referred was that of James I's reign, and perhaps also the internal peace England enjoyed even during Charles's wars.

51. John Rushworth, *Historical Collections* (London, 1680), vol. 2, p. 666; see also ibid., pp. 1–3. The reference to disruptions of trade alludes to the strike against tonnage and poundage which Parliament encouraged.

52. Cf. Charles's justification of his actions (ibid., p. 661): "It hath so happened, by the disobedient and seditious carriage of those ill-affected persons of the House of Commons, that we, and our Regal Authority . . . hath been so highly contemned, as our

kingly office cannot bear, nor any former age can parallel." There is no reason to think that these words were insincere.

53. Carew, *Poems*, p. 30.

54. Eloquent testimony of the energetic enforcement of this policy is provided by the Bodleian Library (Oxford) Bankes manuscripts which contain extensive lists of gentry violating the proclamations against residing in the capital. These were drawn up by parish officials under the active supervision of the Council, which was obviously intent on amassing the information necessary to prosecute those who defied its will.

55. Above, Chapter 2. Yates pointed out that the "imperial theme" of a revived Golden Age retained its vitality into the Caroline period, but she did not explore the topic systematically. Douglas Brooks-Davies, *The Mercurian Monarch* (Manchester: Manchester University Press, 1984), chap. 2, examines the role of the Hermetic imagery in Stuart court masques.

56. Frances Yates, *Astrea* (London: Thames and Hudson, 1977), p. 4.

57. Henry Vaughan, *Works*, ed. L. C. Martin (Oxford: Oxford University Press, 1914), p. 440.

58. Milton, in *Paradise Lost*, explicitly repudiated this linkage between the classical myth of the golden age and biblical accounts of the Garden of Eden, but not all poets took the same approach.

59. Abraham Cowley, *English Writings*, vol. 1 (Cambridge: Cambridge University Press, 1905), p. 209.

60. Carew, *Poems*, p. 27.

61. This imagery was grounded in a common theme in classical literature: the general pattern of ideas we are about to trace was by no means entirely original. See David Lovejoy and George Boas, *Primitivism and Related Ideas in Antiquity* (Baltimore: Johns Hopkins University Press, 1935), and, for similar themes in Tudor thought, Arthur Ferguson, *Clio Unbound*, (Durham: Duke University Press, 1979), chaps. 10 and 11.

62. Orgel and Strong, *Inigo Jones*, p. 577.

63. *Stonehenge Restored*, pp. 8, 5, and 11, respectively.

64. Vitruvius, *Ten Books on Architecture*, trans. Morris Hicky Morgan (New York: Dover, 1960), book 2, chap. 1, p. 38.

65. Ibid., p. 40.

66. Jones, *Stonehenge Restored*, p. 13.

67. Orgel and Strong, *Inigo Jones*, vol. 2, p. 577.

68. For a similar but more fully developed view, see Jonson's account of medieval and Tudor history in *The Speeches at Prince Henry's Barriers* (*Complete Masques*, ed. Stephen Orgel (New Haven: Yale University Press, 1969), pp. 149, 150). This passage could serve as a commentary on the scene just described.

69. Orgel and Strong, *Inigo Jones*, vol. 2, p. 579.

70. Ibid., p. 580.

71. The same idea occurs in other Caroline sources. Waller, e.g., praised the renovation of St. Paul's Cathedral by making precisely the connections between architecture, harmonic principles, and political order that we might expect to find in Jones's mind (*Poems* [London, 1645; fac. repr., Manston, 1971], p. 16):

> He [Charles] like Amphion makes those quarries leap
> Into fair figures from a confused heap;
> For in his art of regiment is found
> A power like that of harmony in sound
> These antique minstrels sure were Charles-like kings,
> Cities their lutes, and subjects hearts their strings,

Of which with so divine a hand they strook
Consent of motion from the breath they took.

We seem to confront a philosophy in which music, architecture, and government form elements in a single equation. See also Fanshawe's "A Canto on the Progress of Learning" (*Shorter Poems*, pp. 20–21) for a fuller treatment of the same theme.

72. Jones, *Stonehenge Restored*, pp. 56–57.

73. Stephen Orgel, "Inigo Jones on Stonehenge," *Prose* 3 (1974): 109–124.

74. Ibid., p. 105.

75. Vitruvius, p. 38.

76. Jones, *Stonehenge Restored*, p. 107.

77. Ibid., p. 14.

78. Francis Bacon, "Of Gardening," in *Essays* (Garden City, N.Y.: Doubleday, Dolphin ed., n.d.), p. 127.

79. Marvell, *Poems*, p. 72.

80. Ibid., p. 86.

81. Sir John Summerson, *Inigo Jones* (Harmondsworth: Penguin, 1966), p. 89.

82. Ibid., p. 103.

83. Orgel and Strong, *Inigo Jones*, vol. 1, p. 22.

84. J. G. A. Pocock, *The Ancient Constitution and the Feudal Law* (Cambridge, Mass.: Harvard University Press, 1957); and Christopher Hill, "The Norman Yoke," in *Puritanism and Revolution*, 2d ed. (New York: Schocken, 1958).

85. *The Reign of King Henry II, written in seven books* (London, 1633), book 1, n.p.

86. SP16/96/31.

87. SP16/233/51.

88. Quoted by Samuel Rawson, *A History of England Under the Duke of Buckingham and Charles I* (London, 1875), vol. 7, p. 26.

89. The *Book of Orders*, issued in 1629, represented the most ambitious attempt to date to supervise the work of local justices of the peace. See Slack, "Book of Orders," and Barnes, *Somerset*. Michael Hawkins, "The Government: Its Role and Aims," and L. M. Hill, "County Government in Caroline England," in *Origins of the English Civil War*, ed. Conrad Russell (London: Macmillan, 1973), pp. 35–65 and 66–90 are also useful, as is Sharpe, "Personal Rule of Charles I."

90. The Protectorate, which relied on taxes created by the Long Parliament, had roughly two and a half times the revenues of Charles I. See J. S. Morrill, *The Revolt of the Provinces* (Cambridge: Cambridge University Press, 1976), pp. 84, 85, for a discussion of the burden during the war.

91. The efforts of some scholars to see the personal rule as an experiment in absolutism, paralleling the efforts of Richelieu and Olivares and vaguely anticipating the state of Louis XIV, have sometimes obscured these limitations. This perspective is legitimate up to a point, but it can lead to formulations as teleological as any Whig interpretation of the rise of Parliament. Charles could not possibly have foreseen the achievements of the Roi Soleil, and even after 1629 he had to govern through institutions that were fundamentally different from those of France and Spain. There were parallels between English and continental developments, which contemporaries noted with alarm, but there were equally important differences.

92. Hirst, "Privy Council," provides a valuable discussion of this point.

93. For the argument that the personal rule was bound to fail in the long run, see T. K. Rabb, "Revisionism Revised: The Role of Parliament," and Derek Hirst, "Revisionism Revised: The Place of Principle," both in *Past and Present* 92 (1981): 55–78 and 79–99.

94. In 1635 Cottington dropped his opposition to a very expensive wall around Oatlands Park which Charles wanted to build to protect his hunting grounds, despite the objections of most of his Council. Laud's reaction was to accuse Cottington of a treasonous design to alienate the affections of the nation from the Crown by encouraging irresponsible expenditure. See. H. R. Trevor-Roper, *Archbishop Laud* (London: Macmillan, 1940), pp. 219–221, for a discussion.

95. Anthony Fletcher, *The Outbreak of the Civil War*, p. 413, in an otherwise admirable discussion to which the foregoing paragraphs are indebted.

10 EPILOGUE: COURT CULTURE AND THE FORMATION OF A ROYALIST TRADITION

Charles and Henrietta Maria last performed a masque celebrating the blessings of their halcyon reign in January 1640. By then the structure of prerogative government had already begun to crumble, lending a note of urgency to the allegorical triumph of royal love over factious humors acted out before the assembled court. Over the next two years the crisis deepened, until in the summer of 1642 the monarchs left their capital—the queen for the continent, the king to raise an army against the rebellious Parliament. In two civil wars he attempted to impose by force the vision of social harmony he had failed to maintain through politics, before the victorious parliamentary army brought him back to London to die on a scaffold in the main courtyard of Whitehall.

The political turmoil in which Charles's reign ended destroyed the cultural establishment that he and his entourage had constructed. The great royal art collection fell into the hands of Parliament, which auctioned it off to purchasers from all over Europe. The masques ceased forever as the Banqueting House, still decorated by a few of the king's tapestries, became the hall where Cromwell received foreign dignitaries. Mortality and desertion completed the destruction. Van Dyck died even before the outbreak of hostilities; Inigo Jones, Richard Lovelace, and John Suckling did not live long enough to see the Stuarts return to power. Edmund Waller, Thomas May, and Balthazar Gerbier joined the king's enemies. Of the poets and artists who had served the court before the wars, only William Davenant and a few lesser figures managed to resume their posts in 1660. Charles II discovered other talents to serve him, including John Dryden, Peter Lyly, and Christopher Wren, but he showed no more inclination to revive the full cultural program of his father than to repeat the experiment in personal rule. Never again did a monarch and his immediate companions exercise as much influence over English high culture as in the 1630s. In this respect a true restoration never took place; the convening of the Long Parliament marked the end of an era.

What impact did early Stuart court culture have on the political crisis of the 1640s and the legacy of division that crisis left? The question needs to be answered on several levels. Charles's cultural program played a much smaller direct role in precipitating the breakdown of royal government than some scholars have supposed. That program was less expensive than has often been assumed, and its capacity to provoke a hostile response was probably limited, especially away from London. Only a very small minority of the population had ever seen a court masque or a Van Dyck portrait; works never intended for a broad audience presumably had little effect one way or another on public opinion. Some parliamentarians may have been antagonized by what they perceived as the court's wasteful expenditure on masques and paintings, but there is no evidence that this issue was ever more than a minor irritant in the escalating conflict between Charles and the Long Parliament.

In more indirect ways court culture did contribute to the creation of a climate in which the collapse of royal authority was possible. To begin with, even if court masques and paintings did not antagonize many Englishmen, they were not very effective in promoting reverence for the king. The half-century preceding the Civil War saw a marked decline in the effectiveness of the cult of the reigning monarch. Part of the reason was the disappearance of a clear external threat, and part was the reluctance of both James and Charles to satisfy the English appetite for public court ceremonies. Yet changes in the taste and cultural outlook of the royal entourage also played a role. Elizabethan court culture was flamboyant and theatrical, whereas that of the Caroline period was more subdued, reserved, and exclusive. Many Elizabethan court spectacles took place outdoors before large, heterogeneous audiences. Virtually all those of Charles's court occurred within royal or aristocratic palaces and before smaller, carefully selected audiences. More

than any monarch within living memory, Charles was an aloof and distant figure for most of his subjects. This helps explain the widespread
coolness of the English populace toward this cause at the outbreak of
Civil War.[1]

Equally important, a number of Elizabethan cultural traditions survived as vehicles for religious and patriotic aspirations that the Stuarts
failed to satisfy. Foxeian concepts of history, memories of Sidney and
Essex, and romantic concepts of sea warfare all provided an implicit
foil to the conduct of James and Charles, and a model of alternative
policies.

The cosmopolitanism of the royal entourage also contributed to
popular suspicions of the court, especially in London. The English in
general and Londoners in particular were notoriously xenophobic—so
much so that foreign ambassadors sometimes found it prudent to dress
in English clothes to minimize their chances of being harassed in the
city's streets.[2] This hostility was especially marked with respect to
Catholic aristrocrats from the continent, and above all to Spanish
grandees. Courtiers who emulated French, Italian, and Spanish fashions were therefore likely to arouse suspicion, especially in the early
1640s, when London was convulsed with fears of popish plots. The apprentice riots of 1641 and 1642 need to be seen in this context. People
could believe more easily in sinister conspiracies between courtiers and
foreign papists because so many of the former seemed to resemble the
latter in dress, manners, and way of life. Religious fears and nationalis-
tic prejudices fused with class animosities to create an extraordinarily
volatile atmosphere.

After the Civil War broke out, on the other hand, the culture of
the prewar court provided a stock of materials lying ready to hand for
cavalier propagandists.[3] The events of the 1640s lent greater credence
to a number of ideas and images which had already emerged in court
culture before the convening of the Long Parliament. Perhaps the most
obvious example is the court's image of its parliamentary critics as a
group of demagogues, using religious and constitutional rhetoric to
mask seditious plots. Before 1641 few people outside the court appear
to have seen Parliament in this light.[4] After the London apprentice
riots, the emergence of sectarian puritanism in the capital and elsewhere, the Common's attacks on episcopacy, and the other tumultuous
events of 1641 and early 1642, an appreciable segment of the political
nation was converted to the king's view of his opponents. Moreover,

for Charles and his strongest supporters events seemed to confirm their worst suspicions about the envious spirit of the age and the sinister motives of puritans and "popular" leaders.

Similarly the nation's experience of civil war in the 1640s and puritan military government in the 1650s helped lend wider currency to royalist celebrations of Charles's halcyon reign. After 1648 the leaders of Parliament and the army faced the intractable problem of governing England after a bitterly divisive struggle had come close to wrecking both the social order and the political order. With every step the commonwealth's new governors took, they antagonized former neutralists and disillusioned Roundheads, many of whom were soon wishing they could bring the king back. To win supporters the Cavaliers had only to convince people that Charles stood for a less oppressive way of life than the puritan republic, and in this task the cultural legacy of the 1630s proved invaluable. As the godly party tried to impose a moral dictatorship upon the nation, royalists recalled the crown's tolerance for "innocent" pleasures. As people grew tired of the long sermons and interminable disputes of Presbyterian, Independent and sectarian preachers, some began to look back fondly on the old church, with its ornate rituals, orderly hierarchy, and comparatively mild theology. The experience of war on English soil and the burden of very high taxes to support the army undermined militaristic sentiments and fed nostalgia for the "halcyon" years of the 1630s. Above all, the confusion of the 1650s—the military purges, the restless experiments with everchanging constitutional forms, the radical threats posed by Levellers and sectaries—appeared to vindicate the royalist claim that only a king can restrain mankind's innate factiousness. England's first experiment in parliamentary government led to higher taxes, greater social upheavals, and more dictatorial government than the kingdom had ever known. These facts enhanced the attractiveness of the only clearly formulated ideological alternative: the royalist tradition that was anchored in the culture of the prewar court.

Events also gave new credence to claims for the sanctity of the king, though in ways no one could have anticipated before the war. Ordinary Englishmen, who felt little inclination to worship Charles so long as he remained a remote symbol of authority, responded with heartfelt emotion to the sight of a monarch facing execution with exemplary courage and humility. The sobriety of the king's personal life and the emphasis court propaganda had always placed upon his love for his people fitted in perfectly with the saintly image constructed by his followers after 1649. In death Charles did appear to many Englishmen as an image of God on earth, albeit not in quite the same sense advanced by the loyalist clergy of the prewar period.

In turning Charles into a Christ-figure, the Cavaliers also managed to associate the regicides and their puritan allies with the scribes and Pharisees who clamored for the crucifixion. The parallel was drawn in countless sermons preached on the anniversary of the king's death for more than half a century. Down to the triumph of the Walpolean Whigs in the 1710s, this chain of associations remained one of the most powerful ideological weapons in the royalist-Tory arsenal.[5]

In the final analysis, memories of the Stuart martyr formed a peculiarly limited political legacy. To inherit his sanctity the king's heirs had to appear to risk sharing his fate. In times of emergency—during the Exclusion crisis, for example—the Anglican cult of monarchy acquired new life as conservatives began to fear that the events of the 1640s might be repeated. In more normal times, royalist demagogues, such as the "high-flying" Tory clergy of the early eighteenth century, had to engage in farfetched efforts to stir slumbering memories of revolution in order to lend weight to their divine right theology. Ironically, the more secure and powerful an English monarch seemed, the more difficult it became to portray him as a sacred figure.

As important in the long run as these concepts of royal authority was the contribution of the early Stuart court to the cultural outlook of the post-Restoration aristocracy. In the years after Charles II's return to Whitehall a steadily growing section of the political nation adopted a cosmopolitan way of life essentially similar to that which had developed at court in the 1630s. London attracted significantly more peers and gentry in the late seventeenth and eighteenth century than in the years before the Civil War. The theaters reopened, resumed their satire of the foibles of the landed elite, and soon grew more fashionable than ever. Elegant classicist townhouses, stylistically descended from Jones's innovative designs, went up in ever-growing numbers across London's West End. The habit of collecting Italian art and other rarities, together with the scientific pursuits of the early virtuosi, spread well beyond the court, affecting the decor of great country houses and the habits of their owners throughout England.[6] In more subtle ways the urbane wit of early Stuart court poets, together with the concept of aristocratic bearing conveyed by Van Dyck's portraits, left an imprint on the manners of the ruling elite for generations after the Cavaliers went down to defeat.

Bound up with this cultural heritage, the court of Charles I passed on to many Restoration landowners its profound distrust of political activity. We have noticed that the Crown always tried to blame its difficulties on the factious spirit of men who could not remain content in the traditional roles of rustic squires or London citizens, but insisted on meddling in affairs of state that properly concerned only the king and his Council. In many different ways, the cultural values of the court reflected an instinctive distrust of the role political interests had come to play in the lives of some Englishmen. By promoting the multifarious interests of the virtuoso and the Horatian ideal of the quiet country life, the royal entourage created a secularized version of the ancient ideal of the contemplative life for a Protestant society which had rejected the monastic ideal. True, the essential quietism of court culture was often disguised by the lingering influence of humanist ideals of service to the commonwealth. Jonson insisted that poets make valuable counselors for princes; Jones asserted that his buildings and masques reinforced the power of the state; Peacham argued that the virtuoso's experiments would lead to useful inventions. Yet in practice the poets, artists, and intellectuals clustered around Whitehall defined a lifestyle in which innocuous cultural interests absorbed energies that might otherwise be channeled into political or military affairs. As early as the 1630s we can find individuals who are perfectly aware of how useful cultural diversions could be to a government seeking to insulate itself from opposition. "We have had no plays this six months," Thomas Roe complained after a plague closed the theaters in 1630,

> and it makes our statesmen see the good use of them . . . for if our heads had been filled with the loves of Piramus and Thisbe . . . we should never have cared who made peace or war, but on the stage. But now every fool is inquiring what the French do in Italy and what they treat in Germany.[7]

From a Cavalier's perspective the events of the 1640s and 1650s amply vindicated this attitude by proving time and again how destructive the spirit of faction would become the moment rebellion removed the king's controlling hand and gave free play to ambition and popularity. Under the Protectorate, royalist authors developed the ideal of an innocent, passive life spent in the pursuit of harmless pleasures, with greater consistency than their court predecessors. The ideal gentleman, as described by figures like Walton and Cowley, is a man who can happily while away his life walking in dark woods, fishing in remote brooks, conversing with a few good friends, and composing poems without giving any thought to more exalted ambitions:

> If any man be so unlearned as to want entertainment of the little Intervals of Solitude, which frequently occur in almost all conditions . . . it is truly a great shame both to his Parents and to Himself, for a very small portion of any Ingenious Art will stop up all those gaps of our Time, either Music, or Painting, or Designing, or Chemistry, or History . . . or twenty other things will do it usefully and pleasantly; and if he happen to set his affections upon Poetry . . . that will overdo it; no wood will be thick enough to hide him from the importunities of company or business.[8]

The ideal statesman became, in turn, a man who would much prefer to relinquish the burdens of office to return to this happy state.

Scholars have been so concerned about charting the development of traditions of free government that they have underestimated the long-term influence of these essentially antirepublican values. There was much in the theology of puritanism, and in the writings of both Italian and English humanists, to make men suspicious of ambitious politicians and organized factions. Virtually everyone in the century after the Restoration conceived of the ideal commonwealth as one devoid of organized parties and ruled by disinterested patriots. Yet both English humanists and puritans ultimately believed that men are political animals who can serve God and develop their capacity for virtue only through active involvement in communal affairs. Many lords and squires in late Stuart and early Hanoverian England did not. They regarded political activity as at best a necessary evil, justified only by a summons from the Crown or a determination to frustrate the activities of rogues and charlatans seeking to use parliamentary institutions for private ends. From the complexities and lively controversies of Restoration and Augustan politics they longed to escape into a simpler world, in which a virtuous king would preside over a stable, hierarchical society dominated by loyal Anglican landowners prepared to live on their country estates, supported by the labor of a contented, obedient populace. Down to the age of Walpole and beyond, many Tories believed that if only the seditious dissenters, the monied upstarts, and the factious politicians could be controlled, such an idyllic society would come into existence. Even today, one can still catch echoes of this old refrain in political campaigns of both sides of the Atlantic. This lingering distrust of the methods and principles upon which a system of representative government and an open commercial society must depend may have been the most important bequest of the royalist cause to the political culture of future generations.

NOTES

1. For a discussion of the cold reception given Charles by the English population in 1642, see Joyce Lee Malcolm, *Caesar's Due: Loyalty and King Charles, 1642–1646* (London: Royal Historical Society, 1983), chap. 2 and passim. The effect of the decline in court pageantry would have been especially important in and around London. This is also where popular distrust of Charles and support for Parliament was most crucial, especially in the months leading up to the final rupture of relations between king and Parliament.

2. CSPVen, vol. 15, pp. 60, 61: "Foreigners are ill regarded, not to say detested, in London, so sensible people dress in the English fashion, or in that of France, which is adopted by the whole court. . . . The Spaniards alone maintain the prerogative of wearing their own costume, so they are easily recognized and most mortally hated. Some of our party saw a wicked woman in a rage with an individual supposed to belong to the Spanish embassy. She urged the crowd to mob him, by belaboring him and calling him a Spanish rogue. . . . His garments were smeared with . . . stinking mud. . . . Had not the don saved himself in a shop they would assuredly have torn his eyes out."

3. The best study of royalist wartime propaganda is P. W. Thomas, *Sir John Berkenhead, 1617–1679* (Oxford: Oxford University Press, 1969). Malcolm, *Caesar's Due*, chap. 5, is also useful. For royalist poetry in the 1640s and 1650s, see Earl Miner, *The Cavalier Mode* (Princeton: Princeton University Press, 1971).

4. Anthony Fletcher, *Outbreak of the English Civil War* (London, E. Arnold, 1981), chap. 1, gives the best account of the high hopes aroused by the reconvening of Parliament in 1640.

5. Roy Strong, *Charles I on Horseback* (New York: Viking, 1972); Geoffrey Holmes, *Politics in the Reign of Queen Anne* (London: Macmillan, 1967), pp. 97–108; S. P. Kenyon, *Revolution Principles* (Cambridge: Cambridge University Press, 1977), chap. 5.

6. J. H. Plumb, *Sir Robert Walpole: The Making of a Statesman* (Boston: Houghton Mifflin, 1956), chap. 1.

7. Thomas Roe to Elizabeth, Queen of Bohemia, October 29, 1630, SP, 16/174/102.

8. Abraham Cowley, "Of Solitude," in *English Writings* (Cambridge: Cambridge University Press, 1905), p. 133.

SELECT BIBLIOGRAPHY

The bibliography lists the works the author has found most useful in preparing this book or most central to a consideration of its primary themes. It makes no attempt to include all relevant primary and secondary sources. The reader is referred to the notes for additional references.

MANUSCRIPTS

PUBLIC RECORD OFFICE, LONDON

SP14, State Papers Domestic, James I.
SP16. State Papers Domestic, Charles I.
31/3/62−72. Baschet transcripts of dispatches of French ambassadors to England, 1625−41.
31/9/17B. Transcripts of the dispatches of the papal envoy, Gregorio Panzani, 1634−37.
31/9/124. Transcripts of the dispatches of the papal envoy, George Con, 1636−1639.
31/9/18−23. Transcripts of the dispatches of the papal envoy Carlo Rosetti, 1639−1644.
C115/N8/8798−8828. Papers of Sir John Finett, Master of Ceremonies under James I and Charles I. This large heterogeneous collection includes numerous unpublished newsletters from the 1630s.
SO/3/8−12. Signet Office Docket Books, 1624−44, recording grants of offices and pensions by the Crown.

E405/280–289. Declaration books by the clerk of the Pells, giving biannual digests of major categories of receipts and expenditures by the Crown, various terms, 1626–42.

E405/389. Auditors' Declared Account of Receipts and Issues, Easter term, 1627. Replaces a missing account from the previous series.

E351/3257–3271. Office of Works Accounts, 1624–38.

E351/3404. Accounts for Building of Somerset House Chapel.

E351/3391. Accounts for Building of Whitehall Banqueting House.

LR9/20/8. Accounts of Treasurer of Queen's Household, 1632/3.

SC6. Charles, I/1693–99. Accounts of Treasurer of Queen's Houshold, 1625–1635.

AO1/394/61–76. Audit Office, Chamber Accounts, 1623/4–1639/40.

BRITISH LIBRARY

Add MSS. 15970. Letters from the Earl of Arundel to his agent, Sir William Petty, concerning art collections.

Add MSS. 27962. The dispatches of Salvetti, ambassador of the Dukes of Tuscany. Volumes E-I cover the reign of Charles I through 1642.

Add MSS. 34195. Letters of Sir Edward Dering.

Add MSS 38175 and 41846. Letters of Sir Kenelm Digby.

Harl 4049. Diary of Nicholas Stone the younger while in the studio of Bernini. Includes comments on Bernini's bust of the King.

Harl 4898 and 7352. Inventories of art and other furnishings confiscated from the King under the Commonwealth.

Harl 6272. A life of the Earl of Arundel.

Harl 6987. Letters of royal family, latter part of reign of James I.

Harl 6988. Letters of royal family, reign of Charles I.

Harl 7000. Private letters, containing some valuable information about affairs of the reign of Charles I.

Stowe 285. "A Discourse of Court and Courtiers," anonymous treatise, apparently written in the 1630s.

Stowe 976. Includes list of scenic devices for Watt Montagu's *Shepherd's Paradise.*

ALNWICK CASTLE, NORTHUMBERLAND

YIII MSS. The papers of John Scawen, solicitor to the fourth Earl of Bedford until 1639. These mostly concern the development of the Covent Garden estate and include contracts drawn up with local builders, information pertaining to disputes between Bedford and some of his tenants and drafts of the Earl's testimony before Star Chamber in 1634, defending himself against the charge of having created a public nuisance by developing Covent Garden. A complete catalogue is available at the Castle.

WORCESTER COLLEGE LIBRARY, OXFORD

The library of Inigo Jones, containing his marginal notations.

NEW YORK CITY PUBLIC LIBRARY

39M39. Photocopy of a letter book of Sir Kenelm Digby in a private collection.

PRINTED SOURCES

LETTERS AND OTHER DOCUMENTS

Green, Mary A. E. *Letters of Henrietta Maria.* London, 1857.
Historical Manuscripts Commission. *Eleventh Report,* Appendix 4, Part I. London, 1887. Translations of Salvetti's dispatches, 1625–1628.
———. *De Lisle and Dudley Manuscripts.* Vol. 6. London: Her Majesty's Stationery Office, 1966.
———. *Salisbury Manuscripts.* Vol. 12. London: Her Majesty's Stationery Office, 1971.
Knowler, William, ed. *The Earl of Strafforde's Letters and Dispatches.* 2 vols. London, 1739.
Laud, William. *Works.* Ed. William Scott and J. Bliss. 5 vols. Oxford, 1847–60.
McIlwain, Charles H., ed. *The Political Works of James I.* Cambridge, Mass.: Harvard University Press, 1918.
McLure, Norman E. *Letters of John Chamberlain.* 2 vols. Philadelphia: American Philosophical Society, 1939.
Mathew, Tobie. *A Collection of Letters With a Character of the Most Excellent Lady Lucy, Countess of Carleile.* London, 1660.

MEMOIRS, DIARIES, AND AUTOBIOGRAPHIES

Cavendish, Margaret, Duchess of Newcastle. *The Life of William Cavendish, Duke of Newcastle To which is Added the True Relation of my Birth and Life.* Ed. C. H. Firth. 1888; London: Routledge, 1906.
D'Ewes, Simonds. *Autobiography and Correspondence.* Ed. James O. Halliwell, 2 vols. London, 1845.
Hutchinson, Lucy. *Memoirs of the Life of Colonel John Hutchinson.* Ed. C. H. Firth. New York, 1885.
Leveneur, Tanneguy, Comte de Tillieres. *Mémoires inédits—sur la cour de Charles Ier et son marriage avec Henriette de France.* Paris, 1862.
Panzani, Gregorio. *Memoirs Giving an Account of his Agency in England.* Ed. Joseph Berington. Birmingham, 1793.
Roe, Thomas. *The Negotiations of Sir Thomas Roe in his Embassy to the Ottoman Porte.* London, 1740.

Rubens, Sir Peter Paul. *Letters*. Trans. and ed. Ruth S. Magurn. Cambridge, Mass.: Harvard University Press, 1955.

Sainsbury, William N., ed. *Original Papers Illustrative of the Life of Sir Peter Paul Rubens*. London, 1859.

Val, Francois de, Marquis de Fontenay-Mareuil. *Mémoires*. In *Collection complète des mémoires relatifs à l'histoire de France*. Ed. M. Petitor. Paris, 1826.

CONTEMPORARY BIOGRAPHIES AND PANEGYRICS

Cevoli, Fransesco. *An Occasional Discourse upon an Accident which befell his Majesty in Hunting*. London, 1635.

Dauncey, John. *The History of the Thrice Illustrious Princess Henrietta Maria de Bourbon, Queen of England*. London, 1660.

Perrinchief, Henry. *The Royal Martyr*. London, 1676.

Sanderson, William. *A Compleat History of the Life and Raigne of King Charles, from his Cradle to his Grave*. London, 1658.

Warwick, Philip. *Memoires of the Reign of King Charles I*. London, 1701.

Wood, Lambert [pseud.]. *The Life and Raigne of King Charles*. London, 1659.

INVENTORIES OF ART COLLECTIONS

R. Davies. "An Inventory of the Duke of Buckingham's Pictures." *Burlington Magazine* 10 (1907): 376–382.

Miller, Olivar, ed. "Abraham van der Doort's Catalogue of the Collection of Charles I." *Walpole Society* 37 (1960).

———. "The Inventories and Valuations of the King's Goods, 1649–1651." *Walpole Society* 42 (1972).

CONTEMPORARY LITERARY CRITICISM

Digby, Sir Kenelm. *Observations on the 22 Stanza of the 2d Book of the Faerie Queen*. London, 1644.

MASQUES AND ENTERTAINMENTS

J. Nichols, ed. *Progresses of Elizabeth I*. 3 vols. London, 1823.

———, ed. *Progresses of James I*. 4 vols. London, 1828.

Orgel, Stephen, ed. *Ben Jonson: The Complete Masques*. New Haven and London: Yale University Press, 1969.

Orgel, Stephen and Strong, Roy, eds. *Inigo Jones and the Theatre of the Stuart Court*. Berkeley and Los Angeles: University of California Press, 1973. Contains texts of the surviving Caroline court masques together with reproductions of Jones's sketches for sets and costumes and useful additional information.

POETRY, DRAMA, ESSAYS, AND LITERARY REMAINS

Bacon, Sir Francis. *Works.* Ed., J. Spedding, R. L. Ellis and D. D. Heath. 14 vols. London, 1857–1874.

Carew, Thomas. *Poems.* Ed. Rhodes Dunlap. Oxford: Oxford University Press, 1957.

Cartwright, William. *Comedies, Tragi-Comedies, with Other Poems.* London, 1651.

Cavendish, William, Duke of Newcastle. *The Humorous Lovers, a Comedy.* London, 1677.

Cleveland, John. *Poems.* Ed. T. M. Berdan. New Haven: Yale University Press, 1911.

Cowley, Abraham. *English Writings.* Ed. A. R. Walker. 2 vols. Cambridge: Cambridge University Press, 1905–06.

Davenant, Sir William. *The Dramatic Works.* Edinburgh and London, 1872.

———. *Shorter Poems and Songs from the Plays and Masques.* Ed. A. M. Gibbs. Oxford: Oxford University Press, 1972.

Denham, Sir John. *Poetical Works.* Ed. T. H. Bank, Jr. New Haven: Yale University Press, 1928.

Donne, John. *Poetical Works.* Ed. J. C. Grierson. 2 vols. Oxford: Oxford University Press, 1912.

Fanshawe, Richard. *Shorter Poems and Translations.* Ed. N. W. Bawcutt. Liverpool: University of Liverpool Press, 1964.

Habbington, William. *Poems.* Ed. K. Allot. Liverpool: University of Liverpool Press, 1948.

Herrick, Robert. *Poems.* Ed. L. C. Martin. London: Oxford University Press, 1965.

Jonson, Ben. *Works.* Ed. C. H. Hereford and Percy Simpson. 12 vols. Oxford: Oxford University Press, 1925–52.

Lovelace, Richard. *Poems.* Ed. C. H. Wilkinson. Oxford: Oxford University Press, 1930.

Marmion, Shackerley. *Dramatic Works.* Edinburgh, 1875.

———. *A Moral Poem, Intituled the Legend of Cupid and Psyche or Cupid his Mistris.* London, 1637.

Marvell, Andrew. *Poems and Letters.* Ed. H. M. Margolioth. Oxford: Oxford University Press, 1971.

Massinger, Philip. *The Plays.* Ed. W. Gifford. 4 vols. London, 1805.

May, Thomas, *The Tragedy of Antigone, The Theban Princesse.* London, 1631.

———. *The Victorious Reigne of King Edward the Third.* London, 1635.

———. *The Reigne of King Henry the Second, Written in Seaven Bookes.* London, 1633.

———. *The History of the Parliament of England which began November 3 M. DC. XL.* London, 1647.

Middleton, Thomas. *A Game of Chesse.* London, 1624.

Milton, John. *Works.* Ed. F. L. Patterson. 18 vols. New York: Columbia University Press, 1931–1938.

Montagu, Walter. *The Shepherds Paradise*. London, 1626 [for 1656].

Playford, John. *The Treasury of Music*. 1669; rpt. Ridgewood, N.J.: Gregg Press, 1966.

Randolph, Thomas. *Poetical and Dramatic Works*. Ed. C. Hazlitt. London, 1875.

Rutter, Joseph. *The Shepherds Holy-Day A Pastoral Tragi-Comaedie With an Elegie on the Death of . . . the Lady Venetia Digby*. London, 1635.

Shirley, James. *The Dramatic Works and Poems*. London, 1833.

Sidney, Sir Philip. *Selected Poetry and Prose*. Ed. David Kalstone. New York: Signet, 1970.

Spenser, Edmund. *Poetical Works*. Ed. J. C. Smith and E. de Selincourt. London: Oxford University Press, 1916.

Suckling, Sir John. *Works in Prose and Verse*. Oxford: Oxford University Press, 1971.

Townshend, Aurelian. *Poetry and Masques*. Ed. E. K. Chambers. Oxford: Oxford University Press, 1912.

Vaughan, Henry. *Works*. Ed. L. C. Martin. 2d ed., Oxford: Oxford University Press, 1957.

Waller, Edmund. *Poems*. Ed. G. Thorn Drury. London: Routledge, 1904.

SERMONS

Bargrave, Issac. *A Sermon Preached Before King Charles, March 27, 1627*. London, 1627.

Donne, John. *Sermons*. Ed. G. R. Potter and E. M. Simpson. 10 vols. Berkeley and Los Angeles: University of California Press, 1953–62.

Dyke, Jeremiah. *A Sermon Preached at the Public Fast to the Commons House of Parliament, April 5th 1628*. London, 1628.

Farmer, Richard. *A Sermon Preached at Pauls Crosse . . . June, 1629*. London, 1629.

Hall, Joseph. *One of the sermons preacht at Westminster On the day of the publike fast to the Lords of the High Court of Parliament*. London, 1628.

———. *A Sermon Preached to His Majestie on the Sunday before the Fast at Whitehall*. London, 1628.

Holdsworth, Ri[chard]. *The Peoples Happinesse. A Sermon*. Cambridge, 1642.

———. *A Sermon Preached at St. Pauls March 27, 1640*. London, 1640.

Lesly, Henry. *A Sermon Preached Before his Majesty at Wokin*. London, 1627.

Preston, John. *Sermons Preached Before His Majestie and Upon Other Occasions*. Cambridge, 1630.

Senhouse, Richard. *Four Sermons Preached at the Court Upon Several Occasions*. London, 1627.

Struther, William. *A Looking Glass for Princes and People*. Edinburgh, 1632.

Wren, Matthew. *A Sermon Preached Before the Kings Majestie on Sunday the Seventeenth of February Last, at Whitehall*. Cambridge, 1627.